THE

JUNE

PLATT

COOK

BOOK

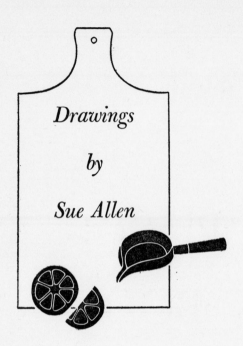

*Drawings*

*by*

*Sue Allen*

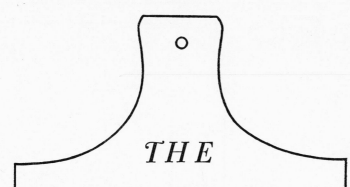

# *THE*
# JUNE PLATT
# COOK BOOK

ALFRED A KNOPF    NEW YORK

*1958*

L. C. Catalog card number: 58–10979

© June Platt, 1958

THIS IS A BORZOI BOOK,
PUBLISHED BY ALFRED A. KNOPF, INC.

Some of these recipes originally appeared elsewhere. Acknowledgment is made to VOGUE, HOUSE & GARDEN, LADIES' HOME JOURNAL, MC CALL'S, and to THE BEST I EVER ATE by June Platt and Sophie Kerr, published by Rinehart & Company.

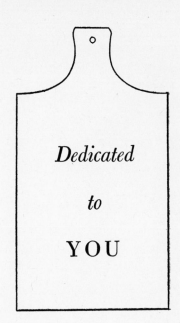

*Dedicated*

*to*

YOU

# Preface

*T*his cook book is fondly dedicated to YOU. With high hopes I have finally brought together a composite of the best recipes from my earlier books plus a collection of new delights. My purpose is to include under one cover bountiful ammunition in the way of classic as well as exciting and new—yet perfectly achievable—recipes for all who, like myself, love to cook, love to eat, and above all love to give parties. My conception of party food does not mean a long-drawn-out menu; the element of surprise is more important—for it is better to bewilder your guests by serving upsidedown cake right side up than to give them virtually the same dishes they might find in a restaurant or prepare at home.

Homemade soup may be slightly out of style, but a party can be built around some of mine (notably Mexican Pozole, Nassau Fish Chowder, and Borsch Natasha). Serve fish as a separate course to prolong the enjoyment of a meal, or try one of my recipes which constitutes a meal by itself. I do not agree with the school that feels a salad can make a meal alone, but I do feel that a good salad adds greatly to the party atmosphere. Sauces play a vital role in cooking, and you will find not only the ones you must know how to make but also many others. Since desserts are my special delight, I am particularly proud of the selections included.

Methods and equipment have changed considerably

*in the past few years; some of the changes I agree with, others I ignore. Purchase the best ingredients—and hope you can afford them—for good olive oil, vinegar, cheese (especially imported Parmesan, grated fresh as you need it), cream, and fresh eggs make all the difference. Skip the new hat and buy yourself some good cooking-utensils and stainless-steel knives. Do not fall for each new gadget on the market, however, but wait until it has been tested and proved indispensable. Seek out a first-class butcher, fishmonger, green grocer—and shop personally. Buy the best cuts! When you cook with wine, brandy, or a liqueur, use the same quality that you would serve at table. Search until you find a pure vanilla extract; and do not overlook the advantages of keeping a vanilla bean in your sugar supply. Shop for only small quantities of dried herbs and spices at a time to insure maximum flavor. Use coarsely ground or cracked pepper. Also, when you serve have hot plates hot and cold plates cold.*

*Timing is the most important factor in the preparation of delicious food. In the recipes the directions are given clearly and concisely, step by step, just as I proceeded myself (often many times before I was sure they were exactly right). I recommend that you read a recipe from start to finish first. Then, after you have assembled the ingredients, follow the directions with patience and confidence, and the results will be rewarding. I am genuinely pleased to have all my favorite recipes here, and I am counting on old friends to invite new friends to party after party and use* The June Platt Cook Book.

# Contents

I     CANAPES AND HORS D'ŒUVRES     1

II     SOUPS AND CHOWDERS     25

III     EGG, CHEESE, AND STARCHY DISHES     49

IV     FISH     75

V     MEAT     121
      BEEF     123
      LAMB     143
      VEAL     157
      PORK     173
      HAM     177
      OTHER MEAT DISHES     182

VI     POULTRY     195
      CHICKEN     197
      TURKEY     228
      DUCK     238
      GOOSE     244
      GUINEA HEN     246
      PHEASANT     249

VII     VEGETABLES     255

VIII     SAUCES FOR MEAT, VEGETABLES, AND FISH     287

IX SALADS AND SALAD DRESSINGS 307

X DESSERTS 323
CREAMS AND CUSTARDS 325
PUDDINGS 345
SOUFFLÉS 355
PASTRY DESSERTS 362
FROZEN DESSERTS 381
DESSERT SAUCES 400
FRUIT DESSERTS 407
CAKES AND CAKE DESSERTS 428
FILLINGS AND FROSTINGS 451
CRÊPES AND PANCAKES 458
COOKIES 465
CANDIES 473

INDEX FOLLOWS PAGE 475

1

# *Canapés &*
# *Hors d'oeuvres*

*W*hen does a canapé cease to be a canapé and become an hors d'œuvre? I'm not sure, and dictionaries give no help at all in answering this question. My dictionary ignores the word hors d'œuvre, and the definition it gives for canapé is dreary, to say the least: "A slice of bread, fried in butter or oil, on which anchovies, mushrooms are served."

We might say that the role of a canapé is to excite the appetite without appeasing it; whereas hors d'œuvres, when served in the plural, may constitute a meal in themselves. The Italian version of hors d'œuvres is known as antipasto, the Scandinavian as smörgåsbord, and the Russian as zakouski. Like canapés, hors d'œuvres may consist of practically anything hot or cold which is delicious and appetizing; but, unlike canapés, they are usually served at table and are considerably more than a morsel. Sometimes only one is served, and yet again a varied collection of them may be offered. I agree with the French, who usually serve them in variety only for lunch.

Good bread and butter are indispensable for both canapés and hors d'œuvres: French, Italian, pumpernickel, oatmeal, or rye are best with hors d'œuvres, while our so-called American white bread is best with canapés—plain, toasted, or prepared as croutons. As for butter, we are blessed with the whipped variety, available almost everywhere. If crackers or potato chips are to be served plain or with a spread, as the simplest forms of canapé, may I suggest that they be heated to insure crispness; I suggest, also, heating salted nuts.

## CURRIED SHRIMP

| | |
|---|---|
| 1 pound boiled shrimp | salt |
| 4 heaping tablespoons mayon- | coarsely ground pepper |
| naise | 8–10 slices white bread, crusts |
| 2 teaspoons imported curry | removed |
| powder | ¼ pound butter |

SERVES 6–8

This curried-shrimp mixture is to be spread on freshly made, warm (not hot), toasted and buttered croutons. It may be spread in the kitchen on small croutons to be served with cocktails before dinner; or it may be served as a first course at the table on larger croutons, but, in this case, double the recipe.

An hour or so before dinner cut 1 pound boiled, shelled, cleaned, and chilled shrimp (page 101) in small pieces. Mix 2 teaspoons imported curry powder with 4 heaping tablespoons mayonnaise; season to taste with a little coarsely ground black pepper and a very little salt. Add the shrimp and mix lightly. Cover tightly and chill until ready to serve.

*[Pre-heat oven to 400°]*

Have ready 8–10 slices white bread, crusts removed, cut in two. Melt ¼ pound butter in small frying-pan and dip both sides of bread lightly in butter and then place on cookie sheet. When ready to serve, place bread in oven and allow to stay until a light golden brown, 6–7 minutes. Cool slightly and serve with the curried shrimp.

## TYPICAL ITALIAN ANTIPASTO

12 thin slices prosciutto
18 paper-thin slices salami
3-4 small, ripe tomatoes, peeled and sliced
24 pickled peppers (hot variety)
8 small pickled beets, sliced
1 head of finochio, pulled apart and washed
2 dozen ripe black olives
2 dozen green olives
3 4-ounce cans red pimientos
½ pound mushrooms, marinated
1 bunch radishes, trimmed and cut
2-3 hard-boiled eggs, quartered
2 7-ounce cans solid pack tuna fish, well drained
1 small tin anchovies
1 head lettuce

Wash and shake dry 1 small head lettuce and spread it over a tremendous platter. Arrange attractively on this bed all or a selection of the ingredients listed. Serve with this whipped sweet butter, fresh Italian bread, salt and pepper, and a cruet of good olive oil and strong red wine vinegar.

## GRILLED SARDINE CANAPES
## WITH HOT PICKLED BLACK-WALNUT SAUCE
*[Pre-heat oven to 500°]*

Canapés:
10 slices white bread, crusts removed
3 4½-ounce cans boneless, skinless sardines
grated rind 2 navel oranges
strained juice 1 lemon
3 tablespoons soft butter
parsley

Sauce:
4 tablespoons juice from pickled black walnuts
2 pickled black walnuts, chopped fine
2 tablespoons capers, chopped fine
2 teaspoons finely chopped shallots
strained juice 1 lemon
1 teaspoon brandy

Toast lightly on both sides 10 slices white bread, crusts removed. Butter them lightly and spread out on cookie sheet. Open 3 small, 4½-ounce, cans boneless, skinless sardines; drain off all the oil. Split the sardines and cover each slice of toast with 3 halves. Sprinkle the strained lemon juice and grated orange rind over all. Broil quickly 2–3 minutes and serve at once on hot platter, garnished with parsley, accompanied by the sauce.

To make the pickled black-walnut sauce, place all ingredients in a small enamel double boiler over boiling water until heated through.

## MADELIN'S SESAME-SEEDED WAFERS
*[Pre-heat oven to 450°]*

24 protein whole-grain wafers    2 tablespoons sesame seeds
2 tablespoons creamed butter

Spread 24 protein whole-grain wafers with 2 tablespoons creamed butter. Place side by side on cookie sheet and sprinkle with 2 tablespoons sesame seeds. Place in oven and bake until lightly browned, 4–5 minutes. Serve hot with cocktails. For variety, substitute caraway or poppy seeds for the sesame seeds.

## CREAM-CHEESE AND CAPER SPREAD

4 tablespoons capers
2 8-ounce packages cream
   cheese
¾ cup heavy cream

4 teaspoons juice from bottle
   of capers
crackers, or potato chips

Mix together until smooth 2 8-ounce packages cream cheese, ¾ cup heavy cream, and 4 teaspoons juice from a bottle of capers. Last of all add 4 tablespoons capers. Chill well. Serve with heated crackers or potato chips.

## RADISHES WITH COQUILLES DE BEURRE

radishes
¼ pound sweet butter

salt

This is a simple, well-known French hors d'œuvre that consists of radishes, crisp and fancifully cut, a bit of sweet butter, and a touch of salt. The butter is served in the shape of shells or curls in a radish dish filled with crushed ice. To make these curls, have ready a bowl of boiling water and a bowl of ice water, a firm bar of the best quality sweet butter, and the butter-curler. Dip the curler for half a minute in the boiling water and then draw it lightly over the butter, pulling the curl into the ice water.

To prepare the radishes, cut the red part away from the white part in such a way as to form red petals around the edge. Cut down into the white part in both directions to make little squares, trim off most of the green stem, and soak the radishes in ice water. Then place them in a radish dish filled with crushed ice.

## DEVILED PECANS
*[Pre-heat oven to 300°]*

2 tablespoons butter
2 tablespoons A-1 sauce
2 cups pecan meats

½ teaspoon salt
⅛ teaspoon cayenne

SERVES 6–8

Melt 2 tablespoons sweet butter in a small iron frying-pan. Stir in 2 tablespoons A-1 sauce. Add 2 cups pecan meats. Sprinkle with ½ teaspoon salt and ⅛ teaspoon cayenne. Stir. Place pan in oven for 15–20 minutes, stirring occasionally with wooden spoon. Drain on paper towel. Serve while still warm.

## CURRIED ALMONDS
*[Pre-heat oven to 300°]*

1 cup shelled almonds
1 tablespoon olive oil

½ teaspoon salt
1 teaspoon curry powder

Place 1 tablespoon olive oil in a small iron pan; add 1 cup shelled almonds; stir. Place pan in oven and roast for 15–20 minutes, stirring occasionally with wooden spoon. Be careful not to burn almonds. Remove from oven; spread out on a paper towel; sprinkle immediately with ½ teaspoon salt mixed with 1 teaspoon good curry powder.

## MARINATED MUSHROOMS

| | |
|---|---|
| 1 pound small fresh mush-<br>　rooms | 1 small bay leaf<br>pinch of thyme |
| ¾ cup good vinegar | parsley |
| ⅓ cup good olive oil | coriander seeds |
| 1 lemon | chervil or fennel |
| 1 clove garlic | salt, ground black pepper |

Wash quickly and dry well 1 pound small, firm mushrooms. Cut off tough part of stems, peel, and drop into an enamel saucepan containing salted water and the juice of 1 lemon. Bring quickly to a boil, cover, and simmer 8 minutes. Drain; let the cold water run over them a second; place in bowl; and strain over them the boiling-hot marinade.

To make the marinade, simmer together for 5 minutes ¾ cup vinegar with ⅓ cup olive oil, 1 crushed clove garlic, a pinch thyme, a small piece of bay leaf, ½ teaspoon coarsely ground black pepper, ½ teaspoon salt, a branch of parsley, and a few coriander seeds.

Cool marinated mushrooms. When cold, place in refrigerator for several hours before serving. Sprinkle lightly with chopped chervil or fennel tops at the last minute.

## RAW MUSHROOMS IN CREAM DRESSING

| | |
|---|---|
| ½ pound fresh mushrooms | grated lemon rind |
| 1 cup heavy cream | salt |
| French or Italian bread | ground black pepper |
| lemon juice | |

Wash quickly, dry, stem, and slice thin ½ pound or more fresh mushrooms, squeezing a little lemon juice over them as you go along. Pour over them 1 cup heavy cream, and season to taste with salt and plenty of freshly ground black pepper, a little more lemon juice, if needed, and a very little grated lemon rind. Serve with crisp French or Italian bread.

## CUCUMBERS IN SOUR CREAM WITH DILL

tender young cucumbers          chopped fresh green dill
sour cream

Peel and slice thin tender young cucumbers. Soak awhile in ice water. Drain well when crisp. Cover with sour cream in which you have mixed a lot of chopped fresh green dill.

To make sliced cucumbers look special, peel and score from end to end with the tines of a fork; then cut in paper-thin slices.

## CUCUMBERS AND TOMATOES
### [On a bed of tomato ice]

6 cucumbers and/or tomatoes          lemons
1 1-pint, 4-ounce can tomato          vinegar
  juice                               Worcestershire sauce
½ pound whipped butter               chopped chervil, or parsley
1 cup French dressing                salt, pepper
French bread

Season to taste with salt and pepper, vinegar, and Worcestershire sauce a can of tomato juice. Empty into ice tray of the refrigerator and freeze until solid. Empty the cubes of frozen tomato juice into a clean ice bag, then pound with wooden mallet until crushed fine. Place in a large glass bowl, and arrange attractively on this bed 6 crisp cucumbers, sliced very thin; or 6 luscious ripe tomatoes, peeled and sliced; or a combination of the two. Garnish with quartered lemons. Sprinkle with chopped chervil or parsley and serve, accompanied by a good tart French dressing, French bread, and whipped butter.

## TOMATOES GUACAMOLE

| | |
|---|---|
| 12 ripe tomatoes | ¼ cup chopped parsley |
| 4 avocados | 1 cup finely cut crisp celery |
| 1 small clove garlic | juice 1 lemon |
| ½ teaspoon cracked pepper | 1 cup French dressing sea- |
| 1 teaspoon (or more) salt | soned with dried tarragon |

Skin 12 ripe tomatoes and store in refrigerator until needed. Later take a thick slice off the round end of each and carefully scoop out all seeds. Replace the removed slice on each as you go along. Cover with wax paper and keep in refrigerator until ready to serve. Before serving fill level full with the avocado mixture. Cover with the removed tomato lids, carefully concealing all the avocado.

To make the avocado filling, place the pulp from 4 ripe avocados in a bowl. Cut in small dice, season with 1 small pressed clove garlic, ½ teaspoon cracked pepper, 1 teaspoon (or more) salt, juice 1 lemon. Mix lightly and fold in 1 cup celery, cut in tiny cubes.

Arrange tomatoes on large oval serving-platter, pour 1 cup well-seasoned French dressing over all, sprinkle copiously with chopped parsley, and serve.

## AVOCADOS A LA TAHITI

| | |
|---|---|
| 3–4 avocados | powdered sugar |
| rum | |

Crossing the ocean alone (tourist), I was invited to have dinner at the captain's table. Avocados were served halved with the usual French dressing. The man on my right from Tahiti assured me that this was all wrong, and told me how to serve them.

Cut in halves ice-cold avocados, remove the pits and brown skin. Pour a little good rum and powdered sugar into the center of each half. Serve.

## SARDINES IN SLICED LEMON

1 7-ounce can boneless, skin-      2 lemons
    less sardines

Open 1 large can boneless and skinless sardines. Extract them carefully one by one and place them side by side on a bed of thinly sliced lemon, from which every bit of yellow and white rind has been cut off. Cover completely with more sliced lemon, and serve.

## CELERY ROOT IN MUSTARD

6 tablespoons heavy cream      ¼ cup olive oil
¾ teaspoon salt               1 large celery root
1 tablespoon vinegar          1 tablespoon parsley or chervil
½ teaspoon coarsely ground    2 teaspoons imported pre-
    black pepper                  pared mustard

Peel 1 large celery root and cut in shoestring pieces. In a bowl place 2 teaspoons imported prepared mustard. Add, drop by drop, stirring constantly with a small wooden spoon, ¼ cup olive oil until mixture is the consistency of mayonnaise; then add 1 table-spoon vinegar, drop by drop, ¾ teaspoon salt, and ½ teaspoon coarsely ground black pepper to taste. Stir in gradually 6 table-spoons heavy cream. Pour over the celery root, toss well, place in serving-dish, and sprinkle with 1 tablespoon chopped parsley or chervil. Serve very cold.

## TUNA FISH IN CHILI SAUCE

1 7-ounce can tuna fish       1–2 lemons
½ cup chili sauce

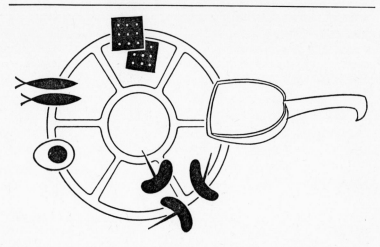

Open 1 7-ounce can tuna fish. Drain off all the oil. Place in dish and pour over it chili sauce. Decorate with quartered lemons, chill well, and serve with French bread and butter.

## HARD-BOILED CURRIED EGGS
## IN MAYONNAISE

eggs

mayonnaise

curry powder

salt

freshly ground pepper

heavy cream

Hard boil 1 egg for each person. Cut in half lengthwise and remove yolks. Rub yolks through a sieve and soften with mayonnaise seasoned to taste with curry powder, salt, and a little pepper. Fill both halves level and reform the eggs; lay in a shallow dish; and cover with mayonnaise that is very slightly thinned with heavy cream. Serve cold.

## BOILED DRIED BEANS AND POTATO SALAD

1 cup dried marrow beans

1 teaspoon salt

1 pound new potatoes

French dressing

chopped parsley or chervil

coarsely ground black pepper

Wash dried marrow beans and put them to soak overnight in cold water. Drain and put them into 1 quart warm water; bring to a boil; reduce the heat; and continue cooking very slowly until well done, but not falling apart. Add 1 teaspoon salt when they are almost done. Cool beans in their own juice.

Meanwhile, cook new potatoes with skins on, drain, and peel while hot. Slice and add to them an equal quantity of the beans, well drained of their juice. Dress with a good tart French dressing, place in small serving-dish, and sprinkle copiously with chopped chervil, or less copiously with chopped parsley. Grind some black pepper over all, and serve.

## HONEYDEW MELON A LA VENISE

| | |
|---|---|
| 1 large honeydew melon | 2 quarts fine crushed ice |
| 2 limes | |

In our crystal-chandeliered, damask-hung, marble-trimmed hotel room on the Grand Canal in Venice, we once ordered melon for breakfast, and this is the way they served it:

A large honeydew melon was cut in several parts, the seeds were carefully removed, and the melon was put together in its original form, the center having been first filled with crushed ice. It was served on a bed of crushed ice on a deep glass serving-platter and was garnished with quartered limes—it looked like a bubbling fountain.

## POLKA-DOT MELONS

| | |
|---|---|
| 1 small ripe honeydew melon | galax leaves or grape leaves |
| 1 large ripe cantaloupe | 3 limes |

These are fun to prepare and look very pretty, but the melons must be sweet. Cut both melons in 6–8 slices each and remove seeds carefully. Using a potato-ball cutter, scoop out of the honeydews 5–6 balls, cutting them evenly in a row down the center.

Now do the same, using the same size cutter with the cantaloupe. Place the cantaloupe balls in the honeydew and the honeydew balls in the cantaloupe. Place the melons on individual service plates, decorated with galax or grape leaves; garnish with quartered limes and serve.

## RIPE FIGS AND PROSCIUTTO

16 ripe figs

1 pound prosciutto, sliced paper thin
2 limes, or lemons, quartered

Wash and chill figs; peel; place in center of serving-platter, and surround with prosciutto. Garnish with quartered lemons, or limes, and serve.

## PINEAPPLE AND WATER-CRESS JUICE

2 cups pineapple juice
2 tablespoons strained lemon juice

1 bunch fresh water cress
2 cups finely cracked ice

SERVES 8

This recipe doesn't belong anywhere in particular in this book, but I happen to like it very much, so here it is. Wash water cress carefully, and remove toughest part of stems. Prepare crushed ice. Place half of each of the above ingredients in an electric-blender. Cover, turn on power, and run until contents are completely blended, about 1 minute. Pour into 4 well-chilled glasses; repeat process, filling 4 more glasses. Serve at once.

## MARINATED GREEN PEPPERS
### [Pre-heat broiler]

8 large, fine green peppers
½ cup olive oil
¼ cup red wine vinegar

½ teaspoon coarsely ground black pepper
1 clove garlic
1 teaspoon salt

Wash 8 large, fine green peppers and dry them. Place on rack under broiler, 6 inches from heating-unit, and broil about 15 minutes, turning the peppers to brown them evenly all over— watch carefully so as not to burn them. Remove from oven and cool for about 10 minutes; then carefully peel off the browned skin. Split and discard stems and seeds. Cut in thin strips. Place in shallow bowl and pour over them the following dressing.

Mix together ½ cup olive oil, ¼ cup red wine vinegar, 1 teaspoon salt, ½ teaspoon coarsely ground pepper. Add 1 clove of garlic peeled and cut in two.

Cover peppers and refrigerate for several hours. Serve with heated French or Italian bread and sweet butter.

## BLINI WITH CAVIAR AND SOUR CREAM

Blini:
¾ cup buckwheat flour
¼ cup white flour
½ package dry yeast
2 tablespoons luke-warm water
1⅜ cup luke-warm milk
½ tablespoon granulated sugar
½ teaspoon salt

1½ tablespoons melted butter
2 eggs
2 extra egg whites
Blini Trimmings:
1 pound (minimum) fresh caviar
½ pound melted butter
2 cups sour cream

Allow 2½ hours for preparation of Blini. Sift ¾ cup buckwheat flour with ¼ cup all-purpose white flour. Measure out into a deep bowl ⅜ cup the combined flours. In separate dish dissolve ½ package dry yeast in 2 tablespoons luke-warm water; add ⅜ cup luke-warm milk. Add mixture gradually to the flour in the bowl, making a smooth batter. Cover with a teacloth and allow to rise in warm place for 2 hours.

Beat 2 eggs. Add ½ tablespoon granulated sugar, ½ teaspoon salt and 1½ tablespoons melted butter. Stir into the yeast mixture, known as the sponge. Add 1 cup luke-warm milk and the remaining ⅝ cup combined flours. Mix well. Beat 2 extra egg whites until stiff and fold into batter. Bake on lightly buttered hot griddle, using about 1 tablespoon batter for each cake. Makes approximately 28 small cakes. Serve immediately with ice-cold caviar, melted butter, and sour cream.

## FRESH CAVIAR WITH TOAST AND TRIMMINGS

1 pound fresh caviar (mini-
    mum)
8 slices hot crisp toast

2 lemons, quartered
4 small onions, chopped fine
4 hard-boiled eggs

Please notice that I say caviar *with* toast. It is quite impossible to spread caviar *on* toast ahead of time and not have the toast limp and tough. The proper way to present caviar is in a glass dish completely surrounded by ice. This must be prepared well ahead of time so that the caviar is ice cold when served. The toast, on the other hand, is brought in crisp and piping hot, lightly buttered or not, as you prefer. The caviar is heaped on the toast by the guest, and, if we are to follow instructions in *Larousse Gastronomique*, the serving-implements should be of crystal or ivory. A tray containing quartered lemons, chopped onion, the chopped whites of hard-boiled eggs, and the powdered yolks, is passed immediately.

## SMOKED SALMON ON TOAST WITH OLIVE OIL AND FRESHLY GROUND BLACK PEPPER

1 pound smoked salmon, cut
    paper thin
10 thin slices white bread
olive oil

peppercorns
2–3 sprigs parsley
2 lemons, quartered

SERVES 6–8

In buying smoked salmon, choose the pale pink variety if possible. Remove crusts from 10 thin slices of white bread. Arrange well-refrigerated smoked salmon on chilled platter and garnish prettily with 2–3 sprigs of parsley and 2 quartered lemons. Toast the bread lightly on both sides and serve at once with the salmon.

Pass a pepper mill and cruet of olive oil. A little olive oil should first be poured over the salmon, followed by a sprinkling of freshly ground black pepper and a few drops of lemon juice.

## SMOKED TROUT WITH HORSE-RADISH CREAM

4 smoked trout
1 cup heavy cream

4 tablespoons pickled horse-
    radish
cracked pepper

Buy 4 smoked trout. Ask the fishmonger to remove the skin and to bone and fillet them. Serve chilled with cracked pepper, horse-radish cream, and thinly sliced, lightly buttered black bread.

To make the horse-radish cream, beat 1 cup heavy cream until stiff and fold in 4 tablespoons drained pickled horse-radish.

## LEEKS VINAIGRETTE

12–16 large fresh leeks
1 cup tart French dressing

1 tablespoon chopped parsley

SERVES 6–8

Remove green part, outer leaves, and root ends from 12–16 large leeks. Split in two or four lengthwise, depending on size. Allow cold water to run through heart of each to remove all traces of sand. Tie in neat bundles. Place in enamel pan that is large enough to hold them comfortably, cover with boiling water, and cook until tender, 20–30 minutes.

Drain and arrange on serving-platter in a neat row, removing strings. Allow to stand a minute or two, and, holding a cloth over them, pour off any remaining water. While still warm, pour 1 cup tart French dressing over all. Chill at least 1 hour. Just before serving, sprinkle with 1 tablespoon chopped parsley.

## 24 HOT MUSHROOM TARTLETS
*[Pre-heat oven to 450°]*

**Pastry:**
1⅓ cups pastry flour
1 teaspoon granulated sugar
½ teaspoon salt
½ cup sweet butter
1 egg

**Filling:**
1 pound fresh mushrooms
2 tablespoons flour
2 tablespoons butter
⅔ cup heavy cream
1½ tablespoons grated imported Parmesan cheese
salt, pepper

These are a great favorite of mine. They are wonderful for a cocktail party or to serve with drinks before dinner.

Make the pastry early in the morning or even the night before. Sift 1⅓ cups pastry flour with 1 level teaspoon granulated sugar and ½ teaspoon salt. Work ½ cup sweet butter into this with the finger tips. Bind together with 1 slightly beaten egg and form into a ball. Place in a bowl, cover tightly with wax paper, and chill in refrigerator.

When ready to bake the tartlets, roll out dough fairly thin, cut out circles with a biscuit-cutter, making them 2½ inches in diameter, enough to line 24 tiny muffin tins. Crimp the edges as well as possible, but don't fuss too much with them. Bake until a delicate brown in a pre-heated hot oven about 12 minutes. When ready to serve, place them back in the oven to just barely warm through and fill them three quarters full with the following hot mushroom mixture.

Wash, dry, cut off tough part of stems, and peel 1 pound fresh mushrooms. Chop them very, very fine. Melt 2 generous tablespoons butter in a pan and add the mushrooms. Cook slowly for 10 minutes without browning until they draw their juice and cook down again. Then add 2 level tablespoons flour, stir a minute or two while cooking; then gradually add about ⅔ cup heavy cream, and cook, stirring all the while, until thick and a smooth consistency. Season to taste with salt and pepper and about 1½ tablespoons of freshly grated Parmesan cheese; continue cooking just long enough to melt the cheese. Fill the little tartlets and serve at once.

NOTE   The same tartlets may be filled with hot baked beans, topped with a dab of chili sauce.

## 24 HOT GNOCCHI TARTLETS

Pastry:
1⅓ cups pastry flour
1 teaspoon granulated sugar
½ teaspoon salt
½ cup butter
1 egg

Filling:
¾ cup grated imported Parmesan cheese
¼ cup butter plus 2 tablespoons
¼ cup cornstarch
¼ cup farina
2 cups milk
2 egg yolks
¼ teaspoon salt

Mix pastry as per instructions given with Hot Mushroom Tartlets (page 17) and line 24 tiny muffin tins. Chill while you prepare gnocchi filling in the following manner.

Grate ¾ cup Parmesan cheese. Melt ¼ cup butter in top of enamel double boiler over low flame, add ¼ cup cornstarch mixed with ¼ cup farina. Stir well with wooden spoon over low flame and gradually add 2 cups hot milk. Continue cooking over low direct heat, stirring furiously until very thick. Now place it over boiling water and continue cooking 3 minutes longer, stirring occasionally. Stir in ½ cup grated Parmesan cheese and ¼ teaspoon salt. Remove from fire and add 2 well-beaten egg yolks. Mix well and pour out immediately into a well-buttered tin, 11" by 7" by 1½", spreading it as evenly as possible. Cool and place in refrigerator, covered with wax paper until ready to fill the tartlets, at which time turn out onto a floured board. Using a tiny 1-inch cutter, stamp out 24 rounds of gnocchi, placing them as you cut them, soft side up, in each unbaked tartlet shell. Now place a tiny dot of butter on each and sprinkle over them the remaining ¼ cup grated cheese.

*Pre-heat oven to 475°.* Place them in pre-heated oven and bake until a beautiful golden brown and well puffed, 15–20 minutes. Serve at once.

These may be prepared for baking several hours ahead of time, but must be eaten as soon as possible after baking, while still warm.

## 24 HOT QUICHE LORRAINE TARTLETS

Pastry:
1⅓ cups pastry flour
1 teaspoon granulated sugar
½ teaspoon salt
¼ pound sweet butter
1 egg

Filling:
½ cup grated imported Swiss cheese
5–6 slices bacon
¾ cup heavy cream
pinch of nutmeg
⅛ teaspoon cayenne
salt, coarsely ground black pepper
2 eggs

Mix pastry according to instructions given with Hot Mushroom Tartlets (page 17), and line 24 tiny muffin tins. Chill while you prepare filling.

Prepare ½ cup grated imported Swiss cheese. Fry slowly until crisp, but not too brown, 5 or 6 slices of good bacon; then break bacon into small pieces. In a bowl beat together 2 whole eggs and ¾ cup heavy cream just enough to mix well. Season egg-and-cream mixture to taste with salt, plenty of coarsely ground black pepper, a pinch of nutmeg, and ⅛ teaspoon cayenne.

When ready to bake the tartlets, put into each a little bacon and about 1 heaping teaspoon grated Swiss cheese; then fill to the top with the egg-and-cream mixture. Bake in *pre-heated 450° oven* for 5 minutes, reduce the heat to 325°, and continue baking about 10 minutes longer, or until tartlets are well puffed and a beautiful golden brown. Remove carefully from the tins and serve at once. It is advisable to leave half of them in the pan while the first half are being passed, keeping the rest to be served later while still nice and hot.


## BUTTERED AND WARMED FRENCH BREAD
### [Pre-heat oven to 475°]

1 16-inch loaf of French bread        aluminum foil
4 tablespoons soft sweet but-
    ter

Slice 1 loaf French bread in 1-inch slices, making 16 pieces, being careful not to cut all the way through, so that loaf will still hold together. Spread slices apart and butter lightly using 4 tablespoons soft sweet butter. Wrap securely in aluminum foil. Place in very hot oven to crisp and heat through, 10–15 minutes. Spread open the foil, place loaf still surrounded by foil in long bread basket, or on platter, and serve piping hot. This may be varied by adding a tablespoon of your favorite chopped fresh herbs to the butter before spreading, or by adding a small quantity of crushed garlic.


## BAKED TOMATO AND ZUCCHINI
### [Pre-heat oven to 400°]

6 small ripe tomatoes               ½ teaspoon dried thyme
2 medium-size zucchini (Ital-       ½ teaspoon dried basil
    ian Squash)                     12 shallots
salt, pepper                        ¼ cup olive oil

Scrub 2 medium-sized zucchini, cut and discard a bit from either end, and boil in salted water for 15 minutes. Peel 6 small ripe tomatoes and slice in ½-inch slices. Cut the zucchini in the same way. Butter a rectangular baking-dish and lay the tomatoes and zucchini in the dish, alternately overlapping each other. Sprinkle well with salt and coarsely ground pepper and crumble over all ½ teaspoon dried thyme and ½ teaspoon basil. Now peel and chop fine 12 little shallots and sprinkle them over the vegetables.

Trickle over all ¼ cup good olive oil. Bake for about 1 hour, or until the vegetables begin to brown and the juice has been well reduced. Serve with crisp Italian or French bread.

## CHICKEN LIVER PATE

1 pound fresh chicken livers
1 large Bermuda onion
½ pound butter
½ teaspoon coarsely ground
    pepper

1 teaspoon salt
¼ cup brandy
1 tablespoon Worcestershire
    sauce
1 tablespoon tarragon vinegar

Peel and chop fine 1 large Bermuda onion. Sauté for 5 minutes in 4 tablespoons butter, stirring constantly with wooden spoon. Add 4 tablespoons butter to the onion; when it has melted add 1 pound fresh chicken livers. Cook until they are no longer pink on the outside, turning them over and over to cook evenly. Sprinkle with 1 teaspoon salt and ½ teaspoon coarsely ground pepper. Heat ¼ cup good brandy and pour over the chicken livers. Ignite, being careful not to burn yourself, and when the flames are out, remove from fire.

Cut the livers in several pieces each and place in electric-blender, being sure to include all the onions and butter in the pan. Run the blender at low speed for a minute or two. Disconnect and scrape down the sides of container. Plug it in again and run at high speed. Now rub the whole through a fine sieve using a wooden spoon. If you do not have a blender, just rub the whole through a coarse sieve first, then rub it through the fine sieve. Discard what will not go through the sieve easily. Cream until very light ¼ pound butter. Add the liver purée, season with about 1 tablespoon Worcestershire and 1 tablespoon of tarragon vinegar, and mix together until perfectly blended. An electric-beater may be used to facilitate the process.

Transfer to small covered container suitable for presentation. Cover the pâté with wax paper before adjusting the lid, as it should not be exposed to the air. Chill until ready to serve on crisp crackers or toasted buttered croutons.

## BILL CHAN'S CHICKEN IN FOIL

3 whole raw chicken breasts
½ teaspoon salt
⅛ teaspoon pepper
½ teaspoon granulated sugar
½ teaspoon sesame oil, or
    light olive oil

1 teaspoon chopped scallions
aluminum foil
1 pint peanut oil (or any
    liquid shortening)
¼ teaspoon powdered ginger
¾ teaspoon soy sauce

Cut white meat of 3 whole raw chicken breasts away from the bones, and slice in domino-size pieces into a bowl. Add ½ teaspoon salt, ⅛ teaspoon pepper, ½ teaspoon sugar, ½ teaspoon sesame-seed oil, 1 teaspoon chopped scallions, ¾ teaspoon soy sauce, and ¼ teaspoon powdered ginger. Stir, to coat evenly with the seasoning.

Cut about 30 pieces of aluminum foil, 5″ by 4″. Place the seasoned bits of raw chicken in center of foil. Fold foil so as to completely seal in the chicken, making neat little packages about 3″ by ¾″. Heat 1 pint peanut oil in a deep heavy aluminum pan until it registers 360° by the fat thermometer. Drop a dozen or so of the little packages into the fat and cook 2 minutes. Remove from the fat with a wire spoon, and repeat the process until all are cooked. The foil retains the heat for a long time, so you need not worry about serving until all are cooked. Serve while the packages still have some warmth, but be careful not to handle until they may be held comfortably. To be opened and eaten with drinks.

## HOT HUNGARIAN GOOSE LIVER (FOIE GRAS) ON TOAST
*[Pre-heat oven to 350°]*

2 7-ounce cans whole French
    goose liver, or
2 8-ounce cans Hungarian
    goose liver

paprika
crisp toast

Open 2 7-ounce cans whole French goose liver, or 2 8-ounce cans Hungarian. Empty the contents carefully onto a flat earthenware or glass baking-dish. Do not remove the fat. Sprinkle copiously with paprika and place in oven just long enough to melt the fat and to heat it through, about 10 minutes. Do not actually cook it, or it will be ruined. Serve with a pile of crisp, freshly made toast, to be spread and eaten with cocktails; or serve as an appetizer or first course at table.

## MARION'S PATE
*[Pre-heat oven to 350°]*

| | |
|---|---|
| 1 pound lean veal | ½ teaspoon ground cloves |
| ½ pound lean ham | ½ teaspoon ground cinnamon |
| ½ pound calf's liver | ½ teaspoon black pepper |
| 1 small Spanish onion | 1 teaspoon salt |
| 1 tablespoon chopped parsley | ½ teaspoon thyme |
| 2 teaspoons imported prepared mustard | grated rind 1 lemon |
| | 1 small clove garlic |
| 1 tablespoon ground ginger | 1 teaspoon plain gelatin |

Marion says to kiss the butcher and ask him to put 1 pound of lean veal, ½ pound of lean ham, and ½ pound of calf's liver through the grinder. Place in big bowl and add 1 peeled and grated Spanish onion, 1 tablespoon chopped parsley, 2 teaspoons prepared mustard, 1 scant tablespoon ground ginger, ½ teaspoon each of ground cloves, cinnamon, and thyme, ½ teaspoon black pepper, 1 teaspoon salt, the grated rind of 1 lemon, and the juice of 1 small garlic clove put through a garlic press. Mix well and place in well-buttered, deep baking-dish, preferably a real pâté dish. Cover with aluminum foil and bake in pre-heated oven for about 1¼ hours.

As it cooks it will form juice; pour this off, but save it carefully. When done, remove from oven. Soak 1 teaspoon plain gelatin in ⅛ cup cold water. Heat the juice to boiling point, add the dissolved gelatin, and stir; pour over the pâté and allow to cool thoroughly. Cover and chill in refrigerator until the jelly has set.

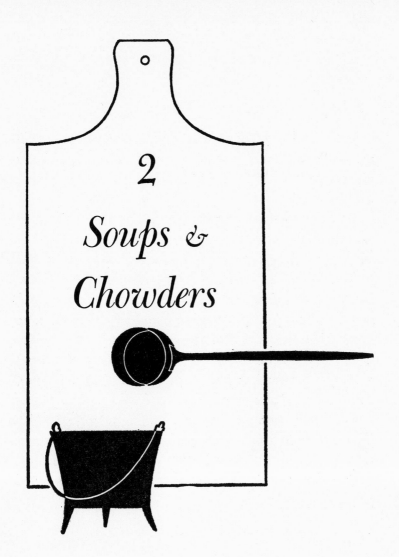

# 2

# Soups &
# Chowders

*Soup* [to quote Grimod de la Reynière] *is to a dinner what an overture is to an opera. It is not only the commencement of the feast, but should give an idea of what is to follow."*

Could anything be more comforting than looking forward to a big plate of hot soup, ladled forth at table from an ample soup tureen, promising, by its very girth, 'seconds for all'? Louis XIV carried his fondness for soup perhaps a bit too far; not being satisfied with one soup he would demand and eat four plates of different soups at one meal. Prosper Montagné, author of Le Grand Livre de la cuisine, wrote: "Soup is indispensable to the harmony of a formal dinner, and never harms the composition of a brief menu." This statement leads me to say that in planning my menus I feel a thick soup, because of its filling factor, should be the overture to a brief menu; whereas a thin or clear soup is the perfect prelude to a lengthy and elaborate meal, provoking the appetite rather than quelling prematurely the pangs of hunger.

## ALBONDIGAS

8 large green sweet peppers
2 large Bermuda onions
6 cans condensed beef consommé
1 teaspoon crushed dried red
  peppers (Italian style)
1 2-pound, 3-ounce can Italian
  peeled tomatoes

2 teaspoons beef extract
1½ pounds twice-ground top
  round of beef
salt, pepper
2 tablespoons chopped parsley
6 tablespoons butter

SERVES 6–8

Wash, split in two, and remove seeds from 8 large green sweet peppers. Cut each half lengthwise in quarters, making 8 pieces of each. Peel 2 large Bermuda onions and cut them in the same way into 8 pieces. Place both vegetables in a deep enamel pan and pour over them 6 cans condensed beef consommé diluted with 3 cans cold water. Add ½ teaspoon crushed dried red peppers (Italian style) and boil gently for ½ hour. The vegetables should be barely cooked through and should still retain their shapes. Add 1 2-pound, 3-ounce can Italian tomatoes (pear-shaped variety) flavored with basil. Dissolve 2 teaspoons beef extract in a spoonful of hot broth from the soup; then stir into the soup. Continue cooking 10 minutes longer.

In the meantime add ½ teaspoon of the same hot crushed dried red peppers as above to 1½ pounds top round of beef which has been put through the grinder twice. Season with a little coarsely ground black pepper, a little salt, and 2 tablespoons chopped parsley. Form into 30 little balls. When almost ready to serve soup, brown these meat balls quickly in 2 tablespoons butter in a large iron frying-pan. When lightly brown on both sides, ladle a spoonful of the hot soup over them and stir lightly to dissolve brown residue in pan, then transfer the meat balls and their clear gravy to a big soup tureen. Add 4 tablespoons butter and pour the vegetables and broth over all. Sprinkle with chopped parsley and serve at once in deep soup plates, accompanied by crisp Italian or French bread.

## ASPARAGUS SOUP

2 large bunches fresh asparagus
3 medium-size old potatoes
4 small white onions
¼ pound of butter

2 cups chicken broth or water
salt, pepper
2 cups heavy cream
1 teaspoon curry powder
2 extra tablespoons butter

SERVES 6–8

Peel or scrape 2 large bunches fresh asparagus; wash thoroughly; cut into thin slivers, using only the tender parts. Peel and dice 3 medium-size old potatoes. Chop fine 4 small onions. Cook the onions slowly in ¼ pound butter, stirring constantly so that they will not brown, about 5 minutes. Add the washed diced potatoes and stir with a wooden spoon; then add about 2 cups boiling water, or better still, chicken broth to cover. Season to taste with salt, and cook gently until the potatoes are well done.

In the meantime cook the asparagus tips in just enough boiling salted water to barely cover them. Be sure and skim them carefully. When done, drain off the water, but save it. Add the asparagus to the potatoes, and rub the whole through a sieve. Place mixture in top of double boiler until ready to heat over boiling water, at which time add the asparagus water and 2 cups heavy cream in which you have mixed 1 teaspoon curry powder. Stir occasionally while heating. Add more salt if necessary and a little coarsely ground black pepper. When scalding hot, pour soup into a hot tureen; add 2 tablespoons butter and stir until melted. Serve at once in hot soup plates. This soup is also good served ice cold, but it may be necessary to thin it with a little cream.

## BAKED IDAHO-POTATO SOUP

4 large Idaho potatoes
4 cans concentrated chicken
   soup
2 cups heavy cream

salt, freshly ground black pepper
2 tablespoons sweet butter
a few chopped chives

SERVES 6–8

I don't know who invented this soup, but it's delicious and so easy to make. Bake in the usual manner 4 large well-scrubbed Idaho potatoes—be sure they are well cooked through. Cut them quickly in half and extract all the mealy potato, letting it fall into an enamel pan. Heat the contents of 4 cans concentrated chicken soup, diluted with ¾ cup water. Mash the potatoes with a large silver serving-fork, or wooden spoon, and add the boiling chicken soup gradually, so as to make the whole as smooth as possible. Then add 2 cups scalded cream. Add salt and freshly ground pepper to taste, and pour into hot soup tureen. Add 2 tablespoons sweet butter. Stir until butter has melted, and serve at once. A few chopped chives sprinkled into each bowl add a nice finishing touch.

## BEEF BROTH (BEEF TEA)

1 pound beef                    2 cups cold water

Put 1 pound fat-free, lean beef, preferably round steak cut in little squares, in a glass fruit jar. Add 2 cups cold water and let it stand for 1 hour. Cover, then place jar on cloth or rack in pan of cold water and heat slowly, until water around the jar registers 140°, or just below the boiling point. Keep it at this temperature on very low flame for 2 hours. Increase the heat slightly and continue cooking a little while longer, until the color of the broth deepens. Remove from fire, strain, and season. When ready to serve, heat in double boiler, because beef tea should never be allowed to boil.

## CATHERINE'S SOUP

| | |
|---|---|
| hearts of 2 heads Boston lettuce | bag of soup herbs |
| 2 bunches water cress | 4 egg yolks |
| 4 tablespoons butter | 2 cups heavy cream |
| 4 cans consommé | salt, pepper |
| | cognac |

SERVES 6–8

Chop fine the hearts of 2 heads Boston lettuce with the leaves of 2 bunches water cress. Cook 5 minutes in 4 tablespoons butter, until leaves and hearts begin to brown. Then add 4 cans consommé and a bag containing ½ teaspoon each of basil, savory, thyme, and marjoram. Simmer for 1 hour, then remove herb bag. When ready to serve, add the yolks of 4 eggs beaten with 2 cups heavy cream, and heat, stirring all the time, but do not let soup boil. Add salt and pepper to taste. At last minute add a little cognac, about ¼ cup, and serve at once.

## BRIAN CONNELLY'S BORSCH

2 yellow onions
2 parsnips
3 carrots
8 sprigs parsley
8 small beets
2 hearts celery
⅛ pound butter
1 head red cabbage
1 heart of finochio (fennel)
½ teaspoon dried marjoram

salt, pepper
2 cans chicken broth (3½ cups)
3 cloves garlic, crushed
1 2-pound can whole peeled tomatoes
3 teaspoons tomato paste
1 pint sour cream
1 pound chippolatas (Italian sausages)

SERVES 6–8

The day before peel and shred very fine on grater 2 yellow onions, 2 parsnips, 3 carrots, 4 small beets, 2 hearts celery. Stew in 4 tablespoons butter on top of stove over very low heat, stirring frequently, for 1 hour; refrigerate.

On the day remove the outer leaves from 1 small firm head red cabbage and shred it fine; add to shredded-vegetable mixture. Scrub 4 more beets and boil until tender; chop them fine and add along with the water in which they were cooked, straining it through cheesecloth. Now add 1 heart fresh finochio (fennel), shredded fine. Season with ½ teaspoon dried marjoram, salt and pepper to taste, and add 3 cloves garlic, crushed; 2 cans clear chicken broth; 1 2-pound can whole peeled tomatoes; and 3 teaspoons tomato paste. Simmer for 4 hours, stirring frequently. Half an hour before serving cook slowly in a frying-pan 1 pound Italian chippolatas (sausages) until thoroughly cooked and well browned. Serve the borsch piping hot in a big soup tureen, accompanied by a plate of the sausage and a bowl of sour cream. Fill heated soup plates with borsch and add sour cream and sausages at the last to each plate. Borsch is a meal in itself, very hearty and very heartening on a cold winter's eve. Buttered pumpernickel goes very well with this.

## CHEDDAR-CHEESE SOUP

| | |
|---|---|
| ½ cup chopped raw carrots | 5 tablespoons butter |
| ½ cup chopped raw celery | 4 tablespoons flour |
| ½ cup chopped raw onion | 4 cups chicken broth |
| ½ cup chopped raw green | 2 cups milk |
| pepper | salt, pepper |
| 3 cups of (lightly packed) | 1 tablespoon chopped parsley |
| grated sharp Cheddar | 2 tablespoons dry sherry |
| cheese | |

SERVES 6–8

For years I had encountered cheese soup here and there without a thrill; then one day we had it at Drover's Inn. It was snowing hard, and we were frozen. I don't remember asking for the recipe, but I fortunately ran across it the other day scribbled on a scrap of paper. I tried it promptly, following the directions carefully, except when it was time to strain out the vegetables. These I decided to leave in. Please try the recipe and see how superb it is, the perfect soup for a very cold night.

Prepare ½ cup each very finely chopped raw carrot, celery, onion, and green pepper. Grate or shred enough sharp Cheddar cheese to make 3 lightly packed cups. Melt 5 tablespoons butter over a low flame in top of 3-quart enamel double boiler. Add the chopped vegetables and cook slowly, without browning, stirring constantly, about 5 minutes. Sprinkle over vegetables 4 level tablespoons flour and stir well for a minute; then add gradually 4 cups hot clear chicken broth. Continue cooking over low flame, stirring constantly, until it comes to a boil and has thickened slightly; then cook at least 5 minutes longer. Add 3 cups grated Cheddar cheese and stir constantly, still over low flame, until the cheese has just melted; then add gradually 2 cups cold milk. Place over boiling water and continue cooking until scalding hot, stirring constantly, about 10 minutes. Season to taste with a little salt and plenty of coarsely ground black pepper; pour into a warmed tureen, sprinkle with chopped parsley, and serve at once.

NOTE   Two tablespoons of good dry sherry may be added. Also, if you wish to be more elegant, the vegetables may be strained out of it at the moment of serving. This soup may be made ahead of time, even the day before, but heat it carefully over boiling water on low flame, stirring constantly, until scalding, but not boiling.

## COLD SENEGALESE SOUP

5 cups clear chicken broth
1 cup finely cut boiled breast
    of chicken
2 teaspoons curry powder
¼ teaspoon cayenne

salt, pepper
4 egg yolks
2 cups heavy cream
2 tablespoons chopped parsley

SERVES 6–8

Place 5 cups strong, clear homemade chicken broth in top of enamel double boiler. Heat to scalding point directly over flame. Beat together 2 cups heavy cream, 4 egg yolks, 2 teaspoons curry powder, and ¼ teaspoon cayenne. Add a little hot broth to this, and stir well, then strain gradually into the hot remaining broth. Place over boiling water and cook, stirring constantly, until thickened, about 5 minutes. Remove and cool. Season to taste with a little salt and pepper and refrigerate until ice cold.

Have ready 1 cup very finely cut white meat of chicken. When ready to serve, add the cold chicken to the cold soup, stir gently, and serve in well-chilled bouillon cups. Garnish with finely chopped parsley.

## CREAM-OF-TAPIOCA VEAL BROTH

| | |
|---|---|
| 2 quarts strong veal broth | 1 cup heavy cream |
| 8 tablespoons minute tapioca | chopped parsley |
| 3 egg yolks | |

SERVES 6–8

Heat 2 quarts strong veal broth (page 46) to boiling point, and then slowly add 8 tablespoons minute tapioca, stirring all the time. Continue boiling until the tapioca is cooked and the broth is thick, about 5 minutes. Put 3 egg yolks in the bottom of a soup tureen. Beat well with fork and add 1 cup heavy cream. Pour gradually onto this the boiling broth while stirring furiously. Continue to stir for a minute; then serve at once, garnish with a little parsley, chopped fine.

## FRESH SORREL SOUP

| | |
|---|---|
| 1 medium-size onion | 2 tablespoons butter |
| 1 pint fresh sorrel leaves, chopped | 2 tablespoons flour |
| 3 large lettuce leaves | 5 cups strong chicken, veal, or beef broth |
| ½ teaspoon dried basil | 4 egg yolks |
| ½ teaspoon of chervil or parsley | 1 cup of sour cream |
| | salt, pepper |

SERVES 6–8

Chop fine 1 medium-sized onion. Wash about 1 pint fresh sorrel leaves, discarding tough stems. Add 3 large lettuce leaves to the sorrel, and chop fine. This should make about 2 cups of greens. Make a little cheesecloth bag containing ½ teaspoon dried basil and ½ teaspoon chervil or parsley.

Melt 2 tablespoons butter in the top of 3-quart enamel double boiler over direct heat, add the chopped onion, and cook a minute or two without browning. Sprinkle with 2 tablespoons flour, stir well, add the chopped greens, and continue stirring a minute or two. Add 5 cups clear, strong chicken, veal, or beef broth and the herb bag. Cook until the greens are tender, about 10 minutes. Remove the herb bag, place soup over boiling water until ready to serve. Remove from fire and stir in gradually 1 cup sour cream which has been beaten together with the yolks of 4 eggs. Season to taste with salt and coarsely ground pepper, and serve at once.

## GAZPACHO

4 tablespoons mixed fresh herbs (parsley, chives, basil, dill, marjoram, or savory)
2 small cloves garlic
6 large ripe juicy tomatoes, or 1 2-pound 3-ounce can Italian pear-shaped peeled tomatoes
2 large green or red peppers
2 lemons

1 cup olive oil
4 cans concentrated clear consommé, or 6 cups of home-made chicken broth
salt, coarsely ground pepper
2 crisp tender cucumbers
1 large Bermuda onion
2 hearts celery
2 cups home-made toasted bread crumbs
2 cups sour cream

SERVES 6–8

No self-respecting cookbook would allow itself to be published without giving a recipe for Gazpacho. The recipe which follows was originally stolen by Sophie Kerr to be included in *The Best I Ever Ate*, published by Rinehart. It is now twice stolen, with Sophie's permission, my permission, and Rinehart's permission.

Prepare 4 tablespoons mixed chopped fresh herbs, depending on what is available, such as parsley, chives, dill, marjoram, or savory, etc. Add 2 small cloves garlic, peeled and put through a garlic press.

Peel 6 large ripe tomatoes. Cut them crosswise in half and remove as many seeds as possible, then chop them roughly and add them to the herbs. If fresh ripe tomatoes are not obtainable, substitute a 1-pound 3-ounce can Italian pear-shaped peeled tomatoes. Wash, stem, quarter, and remove seeds from 2 big sweet red or green peppers. Chop peppers fine and add to the other ingredients. Using a potato-masher, crush the whole together and add gradually the strained juice of 2 lemons and 1 cup good olive oil until the mixture is a paste. Stir in 4 cans concentrated consommé, or 6 cups home-made chicken broth. If you have used fresh tomatoes, thin with 2 cups cold water. Season to taste with salt and coarsely ground pepper. Peel, remove seeds, and chop fine 2 crisp cucumbers and add them to the mixture. Peel and chop fine 1 large Bermuda onion and 2 hearts celery; add.

Is all this worth the trouble? But definitely. All you have to do now is chill the whole for 4 hours before serving. Prepare just before serving 2 cups home-made crisp, toasted bread crumbs, rolled not too fine, to be sprinkled on at table. Don't forget to serve on the side at least 2 cups sour cream as the final touch to this unmatched treat.

## GREEK RICE SOUP

| | |
|---|---|
| 8 cups clear chicken broth | 3 tablespoons strained lemon |
| ½ cup long-grain rice | juice |
| 4 egg yolks | 2 tablespoons butter |
| 8 thin strips lemon peel | salt, coarsely ground black |
| 1 cup heavy cream | pepper |

SERVES 6–8

Heat 8 cups clear chicken broth until boiling in top of 3-quart enamel double boiler over direct heat. Wash ½ cup rice and add it gradually to the boiling broth. Cook until rice is very tender, about 20 minutes. Place over boiling water. Add 8 thin strips lemon peel. Prepare 3 tablespoons strained lemon juice. Beat together in a bowl 4 egg yolks with 1 cup heavy cream.

When ready to serve the soup, add a little of the chicken soup to the egg-and-cream mixture, then add this gradually to the soup, stirring constantly until thickened like custard, about 5 minutes. Stir in gradually 3 tablespoons lemon juice, and season to taste with salt and pepper. Place 2 tablespoons butter in a soup tureen, add the soup, stir until the butter has melted, and serve.

## LILA'S ICED SHRIMP BISQUE

1 pound shrimp
2 crisp young cucumbers
1 medium-size onion
6 cups buttermilk
2 teaspoons fine crystal salt

¼ teaspoon freshly ground
    black pepper
1 scant teaspoon dry mustard
1 teaspoon paprika

SERVES 6–8

Boil 1 pound shrimp in the usual way (page 101), remove shells and black veins, and chop very fine. Peel 2 crisp young cucumbers, remove seeds, and chop very fine. Peel 1 medium-size onion and chop fine. Mix shrimp, cucumber, and onion well, cover, and refrigerate 1–2 hours. When ready to serve, season to taste with 2 teaspoons fine crystal salt, ¼ teaspoon freshly ground pepper, 1 scant teaspoon dry mustard, and 1 teaspoon paprika. Mix well, then pour in 6 cups ice-cold buttermilk, and serve in chilled soup plates.

## LIMA-BEAN AND PEA SOUP

4 cups shelled fresh peas
2 cups shelled fresh lima beans
⅛ teaspoon baking soda
1 teaspoon salt
pepper

½ cup chopped onion, or
    white part of leeks
4 tablespoons butter
4 cups chicken broth
1 cup heavy cream
2 tablespoons butter

SERVES 6–8

This recipe makes about 3 quarts of soup; it may, however, be halved. First put 4 cups shelled fresh peas and 2 cups fresh shelled lima beans into a deep enamel pan. Add ⅛ teaspoon baking soda, 1 teaspoon salt, and 3 cups boiling water. Skim off the foam as it rises to the top and cook about 25 minutes, or until the lima beans are done. The peas will be too soft, but this does not matter. Do not drain.

In the meantime cook ½ cup chopped onion, or the white part of leeks, in 4 tablespoons butter for 2–3 minutes, stirring constantly to avoid browning. Add 4 cups hot clear chicken broth and cook until the broth has reduced to 3 cups. Add this to the peas and beans and put the whole mixture through a fine sieve; or, better still, reduce to a pulp in your electric-blender. Place all this in the top of a 3-quart double boiler over boiling water and stir in gradually 1 cup heavy cream. Season to taste with more salt if necessary and plenty of coarsely ground black pepper. Place 2 tablespoons butter in a hot soup tureen and pour in the scalding-hot-soup. Stir until the butter has melted and serve at once.

NOTE Two 12-ounce boxes frozen peas and one 12-ounce box frozen lima beans may be substituted for the fresh vegetables.

## MEXICAN POZOLE

2 young stewing chickens
3 extra chicken breasts
6 quarts cold water
3 large onions
2 bunches of celery
12 carrots
1 bay leaf
2 teaspoons thyme
½ teaspoon whole pepper-
   corns
sprig of parsley
10 tablespoons butter

8 ripe tomatoes
3 bunches young radishes
1 cup chopped parsley
1 large head Boston lettuce
8 hot pickled peppers
1 large Bermuda onion
4 limes
cayenne
coarsely ground black pepper
crystal salt
2 1-pound, 13-ounce cans
   whole hominy

SERVES 6–8

This is a wonderfully hearty, spicy soup, a meal in itself, suitable for any hungry group at any time—ideal for an after-the-cocktail-party treat. It consists briefly of a delicious chicken soup accompanied by a variety of trimmings, all to be added at the table by each guest to please his or her individual taste. Some of the various ingredients may require a little searching for here and there. For serving-dishes and -utensils, you will need 2 large soup kettles, a tureen, ladle, and extra-large soup plates or bowls.

Once the ingredients have been gathered, the rest is easy. I recommend making corn-meal crisps, which are to be eaten with the soup, the day before or early in the morning of the day (page 40).

Singe, wash, and dry carefully 2 young fowl, and 3 extra breasts, cut up as for fricassee. Place the chicken in a large kettle (preferably enamel) and cover with 6 quarts cold water. Bring to boiling point slowly. In the meantime peel and slice 3 large onions; pull apart and wash carefully 2 bunches of celery; and peel, wash, and quarter 12 carrots. Make a little cheesecloth bag of herbs containing 1 bay leaf, 2 scant teaspoons thyme, ½ teaspoon peppercorns, and a few sprigs of parsley. When the chicken is about to come to a boil, stand by and carefully skim off all the froth as it comes to the surface. Add salt to taste, the herb bag, and all the carrots and onions. Allow to come to boiling point again and repeat skimming process. Be sure that the broth never really boils (which would toughen the chicken), but be certain that it is cooking. In about 2 hours the meat should be tender enough to fall from the bones, but if it isn't, continue cooking until it is.

In the meantime prepare the following ingredients. Peel 8 ripe tomatoes, remove the seeds, then cut them neatly into cubes. Wash and remove the stems and tails from 2 or 3 bunches young radishes. Soak them in ice water, ready to be sliced at the last moment. Prepare 1 cup chopped parsley and shred fine 1 large head Boston lettuce into another bowl, cutting the shreds in not too long pieces. Remove stems and seeds from 6–8 red and green hot pickled peppers, and chop fine; pour over them the vinegar from the jar. Chop fine 1 or 2 large Bermuda onions, and quarter 3 or 4 juicy limes. Have ready a shaker of hot cayenne, one of cracked pepper, and one of crystal salt (or plain salt, if you can't find the crystal variety). Melt some butter and brush the surface of the previously prepared corn-meal crisps and have them spread out on cookie sheets to be heated just before serving.

When the chicken is done, pour off the broth, straining it into another big enamel kettle. As soon as the chicken is cool enough to handle, pull off all the meat from the bones, keeping it in as large pieces as possible, discarding all skin, gristle, fat, and bones. Place the chicken in a separate bowl and cover with enough broth to keep it from drying out. Now sauté the cubed tomatoes about 15 minutes, without browning them, in 8 tablespoons butter. Open 2 1-pound, 13-ounce cans whole hominy, drain off all the juice, rinse in cold water. Add hominy and the tomatoes to the clear chicken broth. Place on fire and bring to boiling point. Add the chicken meat, season to taste with salt and pepper and a little cayenne, and simmer ever so gently until ready to serve, at which time add 2 tablespoons butter.

Now slice the crisp radishes into a little bowl and place them on a big tray along with the bowls of shredded lettuce, chopped parsley, quartered limes, chopped Bermuda onions, chopped hot pickled peppers, and the shakers of cayenne, black pepper, salt.

Heat the buttered corn-meal crisps, watching carefully so

that they do not burn, place them in a basket lined with a napkin, and send all to the table, accompanied by the soup in a beautiful tureen or in its own pot.

The soup should be ladled at the table into extra-large hot soup bowls or plates, including plenty of chicken and hominy with each serving. Then each person adds to the soup any or all of the accompanying trimmings. The corn-meal crisps are to be eaten with the soup, instead of the traditional *tortillas* that would be served in Mexico.

## CORN-MEAL CRISPS
[*Pre-heat oven to 500°*]

| | |
|---|---|
| 1 cup of white water-ground corn meal | 3 teaspoon baking powder |
| | 2 eggs |
| 1 cup of all-purpose flour | 1½ cups milk |
| ½ teaspoon salt | 5 tablespoons melted butter, |
| 1 tablespoon granulated sugar | and more |

Butter copiously 3 large cookie sheets. Sift together into a bowl 1 cup white water-ground corn meal, 1 cup all-purpose flour, ½ teaspoon salt, 1 tablespoon granulated sugar, and 3 teaspoons baking powder. Beat 2 eggs and add 1½ cups milk; add egg-and-milk mixture to dry ingredients and mix until smooth and free from lumps. A few turns of the rotary-beater will help, but don't overbeat. Stir in 5 tablespoons melted butter. Drop batter by tablespoons onto 3 pans, spreading it as thin as possible in large pancake shapes (6 on each pan as far apart as possible). If your oven has 3 racks, so much the better, as ideally these should be cooked immediately. Place pans in pre-heated very hot oven and bake until corn-meal crisps begin to brown at edges, at which time remove from oven, loosen them from the pan with a spatula, and return pans to oven until the cakes are lightly browned all over, or cook for 15–20 minutes in all.

Remove from pan with spatula immediately and serve at once. These may be made ahead of time, but, in this case, it is well to brush them lightly with melted butter and sprinkle a little salt over them before reheating in hot oven. Serve with soup or with cocktails.

## MILK ONION SOUP

| | |
|---|---|
| 4 large onions | salt, pepper |
| ½ pound butter | toasted sliced rolls |
| pinch of sugar | grated imported Parmesan |
| 1½ quarts hot milk | cheese |

SERVES 6–8

Chop fine 4 big yellow onions. Cook slowly in 6 tablespoons butter until lightly browned. Stir frequently, and when very soft add a big pinch of sugar and 1½ cups hot water. Continue cooking slowly ½ hour. Salt lightly and add 1½ quarts hot milk. Cook a minute or two, then add more salt and freshly ground pepper to taste. Pour into a hot soup tureen, in which you have just placed a small lump of butter. Serve at once at table, accompanied by a plate of thin slices of hard roll, which have been lightly toasted on one side, spread while hot with butter and sprinkled with grated imported Parmesan cheese on the other, –and put under a broiler just long enough to brown lightly.

## NASSAU FISH CHOWDER

| | |
|---|---|
| 1 pound fresh halibut | 1 tablespoon mixed whole |
| 3 pounds striped-bass fillets | spices |
| 2 cups fish stock | 1 cup sherry |
| salt, pepper | 2–4 tablespoons of Worces- |
| 4 potatoes | tershire sauce |
| 1 large Bermuda onion | juice 1 lime |
| 1 #3 can tomatoes (4 cups) | ⅛ pound butter |

SERVES 6–8

I had this in Nassau; and the first two weeks at home I made it at least five times.

You will need 1 pound fresh halibut and 3 pounds fillets of striped bass, or other firm white fish, with skin and bones removed from both fish and the meat cut in about 1½-inch squares. Be sure that the fishmonger sends you all the bones, skin, and trimmings. Put these in an enamel pan with about 3 cups cold water and simmer gently until you have about 2 cups strong fish stock.

Now wash the fish, drain well, and put it in a big enamel pan. Sprinkle it with salt and freshly ground pepper. Peel 4 potatoes and dice them in ½-inch pieces. Lay them on the fish. Peel 1 large Bermuda onion, or 6 small white onions, and slice paper thin. Lay the slices on the potatoes. Pour over this 1 large can peeled tomatoes. Then add the 2 cups fish stock and 1 tablespoon mixed whole spices (pickling spices). Bring gently to a simmer, and cook very slowly for 2 hours. Stir occasionally—very gently so as not to break up the fish. Just before serving, add salt to taste, 1 cup sherry, and 2–4 tablespoons Worcestershire sauce and the juice of 1 lime, or, if you prefer, of 1 lemon. At the very last minute add ⅛ pound butter, and when it has melted, serve the chowder in a soup tureen. It will be very hot, but it is meant to be.

## OYSTER STEW

| | |
|---|---|
| 10 tablespoons butter | 2 tablespoons chopped parsley |
| 4 tablespoons flour | 24 shelled oysters and their |
| 2 cups scalded milk | juice |
| 4 small carrots | salt, pepper |
| 2 small white turnips | 2 cups heavy cream |
| 4 small white onions | paprika |
| 4 celery hearts | |

SERVES 6–8

This soup was the specialty of a colored chef on the private railroad car *The Bright Star*, who taught it to a very famous banker, who then taught it to my pretty mother, who taught me how to make it at the age of twelve.

Peel 4 small carrots, 2 small white turnips, and 4 small white onions; and scrape 4 hearts of celery. Wash them all carefully and then cut them up very, very fine. Prepare 2 tablespoons chopped parsley. Melt 4 tablespoons butter in a frying-pan and add the chopped celery, carrots, onions, and turnips. Cook them slowly, stirring constantly, over low heat until they are just beginning to brown lightly, about 20 minutes. Remove pan from fire and set aside. Now make 2 cups of medium-thick cream sauce, using 4 tablespoons butter, 4 tablespoons flour, and 2 cups scalded milk. Add the vegetables and keep warm over hot water. Next put 24 oysters and their juice into an enamel saucepan with 2 tablespoons butter. Salt very lightly and add about ¼ teaspoon coarsely ground pepper. In a separate pan heat 2 cups heavy cream.

When ready to serve, put the oysters on the fire and heat them until they barely curl at the edges. Add the hot cream to the cream-sauce and vegetable mixture. Last of all add the oysters and all of their juice. Sprinkle with 2 tablespoons chopped parsley, pour into warmed soup tureen, and serve at once.

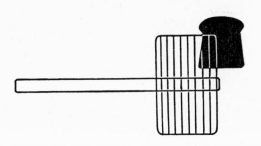

## PEA SOUP WITH WHIPPED CREAM
## AND CROUTONS

4–5 white potatoes
6 white onions
⅛ pound butter
3 pounds fresh peas
small pinch of soda

1 pint light cream
salt, pepper
¾ cup heavy cream
chopped parsley

SERVES 6–8

Peel and cut fine 4–5 white potatoes and 6 white onions. Place ⅛ pound butter in an enamel pan; add the potatoes and onions and 2 cups boiling water; and cook until quite soft. Cook 3 pounds fresh peas separately in 2 cups boiling water, and be careful that they remain green (a small pinch of soda is, of course, the trick). When the peas are tender, pour off the juice, but don't throw it away—you will need it later. Add the peas to the potatoes and put all of this through a fine sieve. Place in a double boiler and keep hot on the back of the stove. When ready to serve, add 1 pint light cream and as much of the juice from the peas as will make the soup of the right consistency; and salt and pepper to taste. Serve piping hot in warmed soup plates with 1 table-spoon of whipped heavy cream, a few tiny croutons, and a pinch chopped parsley.

A variation of this soup is made by serving buttered toasted crumbs instead of the croutons, in which case the crumbs are passed separately in a bowl.

## POTAGE DU CURE

| | |
|---|---|
| 12 ripe tomatoes | white part of 12 leeks |
| 2 bunches celery tops | white part of 2 bunches celery |
| 4 leeks, tops | salt, pepper |
| 5–6 big carrots, shredded | 1 pint light cream |

SERVES 6–8

Cut up 8 ripe tomatoes, cover with cold water, add the well-washed tops of 2 bunches celery and 4 leeks. Boil slowly for 1 hour. In the meantime peel and shred 5–6 big carrots. Wash and cut up fine the white part of 12 leeks, and the white part of 2 bunches celery, from which you have removed as many strings as possible. Peel and dice 4 ripe tomatoes.

When the first tomatoes have cooked 1 hour, put them through a fine sieve, getting as much of the pulp as possible. Add this liquid to the prepared vegetables and boil for 1 hour or so until the vegetables are quite tender. Salt and pepper to taste, and when ready to serve add 1 pint light cream that you have heated in a double boiler.

## ROCKINGHAM LOBSTER STEW

| | |
|---|---|
| 2 pounds freshly boiled lobster meat | 1 cup heavy cream |
| ¼ pound butter | ¼ cup sherry |
| 6 cups milk | paprika |
| | salt, pepper |

SERVES 6–8

Cut 2 pounds freshly boiled lobster meat in small chunks. In 3-quart enamel saucepan, on low flame place ¼ pound butter, stir while it melts, and allow it to simmer until a beautiful golden brown. In the meantime heat 6 cups milk to boiling point. Add the lobster to the browned butter and cook gently about 5 minutes, stirring occasionally. Add the hot milk and bring mixture to boiling point. Season to taste with salt and coarsely ground black pepper and add ¼ cup good sherry. Sprinkle copiously with paprika, and stir in gradually 1 cup heavy cream. Place in heated tureen and serve at once.

## SHRIMP SOUP

| | |
|---|---|
| 2 pounds shrimp | 2 cups heavy cream |
| 2 onions | 1 cup sherry |
| ¼ pound butter | salt, pepper |
| 8 cups milk | |

SERVES 6–8

Boil 2 pounds shrimps (page 101), remove shells, and clean. Then chop shrimps fine. Chop 2 onions fine and cook slowly, without browning, directly over flame in top of large double boiler in ¼ pound butter. Add the shrimps and plenty of freshly ground black pepper, and place over boiling water. Cover and let the shrimps heat through, about 5 minutes; then add 8 cups scalded milk and 2 cups heavy cream, and continue cooking 20 minutes. Just before serving, add about 1 cup sherry, and salt to taste.

## STRONG CLEAR VEAL BROTH

| | |
|---|---|
| 1 large knuckle of veal | 6 peppercorns |
| 2 pounds solid veal, horseshoe cut | 6 carrots |
| | 3 onions |
| 2 tablespoons salt | 1 white turnip |

SERVES 6–8

Put a large knuckle of veal, cut in 3 pieces, in large pot. Add 2 pounds solid veal and pour over both 4 quarts cold water. Let stand for half an hour.

Bring slowly to boiling point; skim carefully; add 2 tablespoons salt, 6 peppercorns, 6 peeled carrots, 3 onions, and 1 peeled white turnip. Simmer gently, partially covered, for 3 hours. Strain and cool. When cold, place in refrigerator until ready to use, at which time remove solidified fat on surface. The solid veal may be cut in medium-size pieces and moistened with sufficient broth to keep it moist until you can think of some way of using it. A little ingenuity could transform it into a curried stew, or palatable hors d'œuvres.

## VICHYSSOISE MEADOWBROOK

| | |
|---|---|
| 6 hearts of leeks | 1 pound white potatoes |
| 2 white onions | salt, pepper |
| ½ pound sweet butter | 1 pint heavy cream |
| 2 quarts chicken consommé | 2 tablespoons finely cut chives |

SERVES 6–8

Ask a hundred people what vichyssoise is made of and ninety-nine of them will say: "Oh, yes, that wonderful soup made of carrots and potatoes and cream"; and most of them will tell you that they have the original recipe for it tucked away somewhere. Well, I don't know who invented it, but I do know that I am positive it should not have carrots, unless possibly you count the one that should have been in the chicken broth in its making.

Cut all the green part off 6 hearts of leeks and split them down the center. Wash thoroughly to remove all the sand. Peel 2 white onions. Chop the leeks and onions very fine. Melt ¼ pound sweet butter in an enamel pan and cook the onions and leeks very, very slowly in the butter, adding a few spoonfuls of water if necessary to keep them from browning. Add 2 quarts chicken consommé and 1 pound white potatoes, which have been peeled and cut up very fine. Add salt and pepper to taste and cook until the potatoes are thoroughly done. Put through a very fine sieve. Add another ¼ pound sweet butter and stir until melted. When ready to serve, add 1 pint heavy cream and heat soup in a double boiler. Never let it boil once the cream has been added.

This soup is equally good served cold, but, in this case, use fewer potatoes, and sprinkle with finely cut chives before serving.

## WATER-CRESS AND POTATO SOUP

| | |
|---|---|
| 3 pounds white potatoes | ¼ pound butter |
| 2 quarts water | 2 egg yolks |
| salt | 1 cup heavy cream |
| 2 bunches water cress | |

SERVES 6–8

Peel and wash 3 pounds white potatoes and cut them up fine. Boil 2 quarts water, add salt and potatoes, and cook until soft. In the meantime wash 2 bunches water cress, carefully cutting off the thick stems. Chop water cress and add to the soft potatoes with ⅛ pound butter. Cook for 10 minutes and put through a sieve. Put the yolks of 2 eggs in the bottom of the soup tureen, beat well with a fork, add 1 cup heavy cream, and pour slowly into this the hot potato and water-cress soup. Season to taste, add ⅛ pound butter, stir, and serve at once.

# 3

# Egg, Cheese, & Starchy Dishes

# GENERAL DIRECTIONS FOR MAKING AN OMELETTE

*T*he three important rules for making a good omelette are: (1) Use a perfectly clean, smooth, not-too-heavy frying-pan with slanting sides. (2) Don't try to make too big an omelette in too small a pan, or, vice versa (10 eggs is the maximum to be cooked in one omelette, which, strictly speaking, is skimpy for 6 people, but this may be stretched by including a filling). (3) Be sure the butter and eggs are of the very best quality.

Break 10 eggs into a bowl, add very little salt and pepper and 3 tablespoons cold water. Beat with large fork just long enough to mix, so that the eggs will run through the prongs of the fork. Heat the frying-pan gradually over low heat and add 2 tablespoons butter, which should sizzle but not brown if the pan is the right temperature. Tilt the pan to spread the butter, then add the eggs all at once. Stir the eggs around well with fork. Allow to cook a bit on the bottom, then lift the edges here and there with a spatula to let the rest of the liquid run under. As soon as you see that there is no more liquid to run under, remove the pan from the fire completely. At this point add a filling if you wish, and place pan back on fire for just a second to set the bottom.

Starting from the handle side of the pan and using a flexible spatula or pancake-turner, roll the omelette up, shoving it along a bit, then reverse and fold the far side over toward the handle. Take a heated serving-platter in the left hand and drop the omelette, bottom side up, onto the platter. Needless to say, serve at once. Sounds easy, but it does take practice. Above all, do not overcook it.

# VARIATIONS

*Fine Herbes*—Fold into eggs before cooking 1 tablespoon each of chopped chives, parsley, and fresh tarragon.

*Ham*—Sauté 1 cup finely diced ham in 2 tablespoons butter for a minute or two until it just begins to brown. Sprinkle with 2 teaspoons flour, stir with a wooden spoon, and add gradually ½ cup heavy cream.

Add filling just before folding omelette.

*Cheese*—Add 1 cup freshly grated imported Parmesan cheese to the eggs before cooking. When almost ready to fold, sprinkle the soft eggs with ½ cup imported Swiss cheese, cut in small dice, and sprinkle lightly with salt and pepper. Allow to cook for about ½ minute, fold, and serve.

*Mushroom*—Slice thin the caps of 1 pound fresh mushrooms. Place stems and peelings in a small pan, cover with cold water, and cook down to ½ cup of essence. Melt 6 tablespoons butter in a large frying-pan. When sizzling hot, add the sliced mushrooms and cook until they have formed their juice, have boiled down, and are about to brown. Sprinkle with 1 tablespoon flour and cook for 1 minute, stirring constantly. Then add gradually the mushroom essence. Blend, then stir in ½ cup heavy cream. Season to taste with salt and coarsely ground pepper and fold into the omelette.

*Sour Cream and Potato*—Sauté ¾ cup peeled, diced boiled potatoes in 1 tablespoon butter until lightly browned, sprinkle with 1 teaspoon chopped parsley, and add ¾ cup sour cream. Fold into omelette.

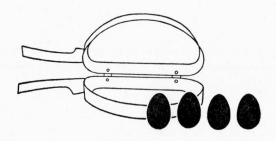

## OMELETTE DU CURE (TUNA FISH OMELETTE)

Omelette:

10 eggs
3 tablespoons cold water
2 tablespoons butter
¼ teaspoon salt
¼ teaspoon pepper

Filling:

1 7-ounce can tuna fish, solid
    pack
2 tablespoons butter
2 tablespoons flour
1½ cups light cream
4 tablespoons freshly grated
    Parmesan cheese
salt, pepper

Sauce:
2 tablespoons cut chives
6 tablespoons butter
juice 1 lemon
grated rind ½ lemon
SERVES 6–8

Brillat-Savarin, in his *Physiology of Taste*, describes how his cousin Madame R., wishing to consult Monsieur *le curé* on some charitable subject, called on the *curé* at five o'clock to find him already at table. Some crayfish soup had just been removed and a salmon trout, an omelette, and a salad were being placed before him. Apparently Madame R. was not invited to partake of the meal, for she later described to Brillat-Savarin how her mouth watered when the *curé* first put his spoon into the omelette and a thick juice ran out, which tickled at the same time her senses of sight and smell.

That night Brillat-Savarin dined with her, and throughout the whole meal she spoke of nothing else but the *curé*'s dinner and, above all, of his omelette.

Later Brillat-Savarin took the trouble to find out just what the omelette consisted of, the recipe for which you may find in his classic work.

One day in France in an *auberge* near Paris, we had an omlette which, although it didn't contain the 2 carp roes that

Savarin's recipe did, was so nearly the same and so delicious that I, too, took the trouble to find out how it was made.

Open 1 7-ounce can tuna fish, pour off the oil, and warm the fish in the top of a double boiler, breaking it up gently with a fork. In a separate pan melt 2 tablespoons butter and stir into it 2 tablespoons flour. Cook a minute or two and add 1½ cups heated light cream. Cook sauce until thick, then remove from the fire, add salt and pepper to taste, and stir in 4 tablespoons freshly grated imported Parmesan cheese. Pour over the fish, mix well, and keep warm over hot water.

In the meantime prepare 2 tablespoons cut chives. Melt 6 tablespoons butter in a little pan and heat until it foams. Skim off the foam. Pour off and keep the clear butter, discarding the milky sediment. (In other words, clarify the butter.) Add to it the grated rind of ½ lemon and the strained juice of 1 lemon. Keep warm over hot water.

Now make a large 10-egg omelette (page 50). Fold in the tuna-fish filling. Turn out on hot platter, pour the butter sauce over all, and sprinkle with cut chives. Serve at once.

## BAKED EGGS IN EGG CUSTARD
*[Pre-heat oven to 375°]*

| | |
|---|---|
| 16 eggs | ½ teaspoon coarsely ground |
| 2 cups heavy cream | pepper |
| salt, pepper | ¼ teaspoon grated nutmeg |
| ¼ teaspoon (or more) cayenne | 12 tablespoons butter |
| | 1½ cups toasted bread crumbs |

SERVES 6–8

Place 1 generous teaspoon butter in each of 8 shirred-egg dishes. Place the dishes on 2 large cookie sheets, approximately 10″ by 14″, preferably ones with sides. Break 8 eggs into a bowl, add 2 cups heavy cream, and beat just long enough to mix well. Season with ¼ teaspoon cayenne, ¼ teaspoon grated nutmeg, ½ teaspoon coarsely ground black pepper, and salt to taste. Heat the dishes in the oven long enough to melt the butter; remove them from the oven and carefully break 1 egg into each. Pour the custard over the eggs, dividing equally. Cover both pans with aluminum foil and place them in oven until the custard sets, 10–12 minutes.

In the meantime melt ¼ pound butter in a frying pan, add 1½ cups toasted bread crumbs, and stir with wooden spoon over low heat until well mixed. When the eggs are done sprinkle the top of each dish copiously with the crumbs and serve at once.

## CHEESE SCRAMBLE WITH BACON

12 eggs                          salt, pepper
¼ pound butter                   1 pound lean bacon
2 cups freshly grated Swiss
  cheese

SERVES 6–8

Break 12 eggs into top of large enamel double boiler (3-quart size) and beat until frothy with rotary beater. Cut into this ¼ pound sweet butter. Toss in 2 cups freshly grated Swiss cheese. Place pan over boiling water and cook, stirring constantly and vigorously, until the mixture looks soft like scrambled eggs. This will take 3–4 minutes so be on guard and don't overcook. Remove from heat immedately, sprinkle lightly with salt and pepper, and serve in warm, not hot serving-dish. Accompany it with thin corn bread and crisp bacon, or Canadian bacon.

## CARAWAY-SEED SOUFFLE
*[Pre-heat oven to 350°]*

6 tablespoons butter             6 egg whites
6 tablespoons flour              1 teaspoon caraway seeds
2 cups milk                      ¼ teaspoon pepper
6 egg yolks                      ½ teaspoon salt or more

SERVES 6–8

Butter 2 round 1½-quart-size baking-dishes. Melt 6 tablespoons butter in an enamel saucepan. In a separate pan heat 2 cups milk. Add 6 tablespoons flour to melted butter and cook this mixture over low heat, stirring constantly, for a few seconds. Then add to it 2 cups hot milk, making a smooth thick cream sauce. Remove from fire, season to taste with about ½ teaspoon salt and ¼ teaspoon pepper. Stir in 1 teaspoon caraway seeds. Beat 6 egg yolks until light and stir them into the sauce. Cool slightly. Beat 6 egg whites in a big bowl until stiff, then gradually fold them into the sauce. Place in the 2 buttered baking-dishes, dividing it equally. Place them in shallow pan of hot water on lowest rack of the oven and bake until well risen and a golden brown, 35–40 minutes. In the meantime, make a cheese sauce (page 56) and serve it with the soufflé.

## PETITE CHEESE SOUFFLES
### [Pre-heat oven to 375°]

| | |
|---|---|
| 6 tablespoons butter | ¼ teaspoon cayenne |
| 8 eggs | ½ cup heavy cream |
| ½ teaspoon salt | ¾ cup grated Parmesan cheese |
| ¼ teaspoon pepper | ¾ cup grated Swiss cheese |

SERVES 6–8

Butter 8 custard cups. Cream 6 tablespoons butter. Separate the yolks from the whites of 8 eggs. Stir the yolks gradually into the butter, and season with ½ teaspoon salt and ¼ teaspoon each of cayenne and pepper. Beat hard with rotary-beater and stir in gradually ½ cup heavy cream. Add ½ cup grated Parmesan cheese and ½ cup grated Swiss cheese. Beat vigorously. In separate bowl beat 8 egg whites. When stiff, fold into yolk mixture. Spoon into custard cups, and sprinkle tops with ¼ cup each of grated Parmesan and Swiss cheese mixed together. Bake 20–25 minutes and serve at once.

## CHEESE SAUCE

2 cups shredded sharp Cheddar      4 tablespoons flour
    cheese                                         2 cups milk
4 tablespoons butter                        salt, pepper

Melt 4 tablespoons butter in an enamel pan. Heat 2 cups milk
in separate pan. Stir 4 tablespoons flour into melted butter and
cook for a few seconds, stirring constantly. Add hot milk gradually, making a smooth cream sauce. Add 2 cups shredded sharp
Cheddar cheese and stir over low flame until cheese has melted
into the sauce. Remove from fire and season to taste with salt
and pepper. Heat over boiling water before serving.

## CHEESE SOUFFLE
[*Pre-heat oven to 350°*]

6 tablespoons butter                      6 eggs
6 tablespoons flour                        1 teaspoon salt
2 cups milk                                    ¼ teaspoon nutmeg
2 cups freshly grated Parmesan    ¼ teaspoon coarsely ground
    or Cheddar cheese                        pepper
                    SERVES 6–8

Make a thick cream sauce: melt 6 tablespoons butter, blend in 6
tablespoons flour, stirring constantly, and then add gradually 2
cups hot milk. When thick and smooth, stir in 2 cups grated imported Parmesan cheese (or Cheddar). Remove from fire, and
stir in 6 well-beaten egg yolks. Season to taste with about 1
teaspoon of salt, ¼ teaspoon grated nutmeg, and ¼ teaspoon
coarsely ground pepper. Fold in 6 stiffly beaten egg whites. Pour
into 2 well-buttered 1-quart-size baking-dishes, place them in shallow pan of hot water on lowest rack of oven, and bake 40–45
minutes. Serve at once accompanied by a sauce, such as tomato
sauce (page 305).

## CURRIED HARD-BOILED EGGS
*[Pre-heat oven to 400°]*

| Cream Sauce: | Hollandaise: |
|---|---|
| 6 tablespoons butter | 10 tablespoons butter |
| 6 tablespoons flour | 2 egg yolks |
| 2 cups hot milk | 2 tablespoons cider vinegar |
| salt, white pepper | salt, white pepper |
| ½ cup heavy cream | 1 tablespoon lemon juice |

8 eggs
3 teaspoons curry powder
salt, pepper
dash of cayenne
3 teaspoons cider vinegar
juice of ½ lemon

SERVES 6–8

Butter a round 2-quart-size earthenware or glass baking-dish. Make some smooth thick cream sauce by melting in a saucepan 6 tablespoons butter, then adding gradually 6 tablespoons flour, and finally adding 2 cups hot milk. Season to taste with salt and a little white pepper. Thin to desired consistency with about ½ cup heavy cream. Keep hot over hot water, stirring occasionally.

Make a small quantity of Hollandaise sauce in the following manner. Put 2 tablespoons butter in the top of an enamel double boiler. Separate the whites from the yolks of 2 large eggs, placing the yolks in a small bowl. In a small enamel pan mix together 2 tablespoons cider vinegar with a little salt and white pepper and reduce to 1 tablespoon by simmering on low flame. Remove from fire and add 1 tablespoon cold water.

Now beat the yolks with a rotary-beater and transfer them to the top of the double boiler containing the butter. Rinse out the egg bowl with the cooled vinegar and add this to the rest of the ingredients. Now place the pan over boiling hot water on a very low flame, but be sure the bottom of the pan does not come in direct contact with the hot water below. Stir very vigorously with a wire whisk until the butter melts into the eggs and the mixture is thick. Remove the double boiler from the fire entirely and continue, 1 tablespoon at a time, adding 8 tablespoons butter, stirring continuously with the whisk. Season to taste with about 1 tablespoon lemon juice. Remove the top of the double boiler from the bottom and allow the sauce to cool.

In the meantime hard boil 8 eggs by simmering them gently in boiling hot water for 15 minutes. Plunge into cold water and remove shells. Cut the eggs in two lengthwise and remove the yolks. Rub the yolks through a fine sieve into a small bowl. Sprinkle with about 3 teaspoons curry powder, a little salt and coarsely ground black pepper, a big dash of cayenne. Stir into this 3 tablespoons cream sauce. When well mixed stir in 3 teaspoons cider vinegar and the juice of ½ lemon. Stuff the empty whites level full and reassemble the halves making 8 stuffed eggs. Wipe them with a damp cloth and place them side by side in the bottom of the buttered dish. Spread over them the remainder of the cream sauce, being sure none of the eggs is exposed.

About 10 minutes before serving place eggs in the *pre-heated 400° oven* and cook until sizzling hot, about 9 minutes. Remove from oven and quickly spread the Hollandise sauce over the cream sauce. Now place the dish under the hot broiler not too close to the flame. Watch carefully until a beautiful golden-brown color appears, about 1 minute. Serve with pride at once.

## JELLIED EGGS

| | |
|---|---|
| 4 cups crystal-clear aspic | 1 cup mayonnaise |
| 8 eggs | 1 envelope gelatin |
| 24 fresh tarragon leaves | 3 2¼-ounce cans deviled ham |
| 3 lemons | |

SERVES 8

Make 4 cups clear aspic (page 60) and chill until ready to use. Place 8 fresh eggs in a deep-fat frying-basket. Heat water in a big saucepan (sufficient to cover the eggs); when it is boiling, plunge the basket of eggs into the water. Bring to a boil again, reduce heat, and simmer exactly 6 minutes. Remove basket from water and plunge immediately into cold water and let stand 10 minutes. Crack the eggs very gently all over and peel cautiously so as not to break the whites. The yolks should be soft as in soft-boiled eggs, and the whites firm as in hard-boiled eggs.

Set out 8 ½-cup-size soufflé or custard dishes with straight or slightly flaring sides. Heat the aspic in double boiler over hot water just long enough to soften; then put 2 tablespoons aspic into each dish. Place in coldest part of refrigerator to set firmly. In the meantime blanch 24 leaves tarragon, and pat them dry on paper towel. When the aspic has set firm in the little dishes, dip the leaves one at a time into the remainder of the aspic and lay 3 in each dish to form a 6-pointed star. Lay on this to hold the leaves in place a paper-thin slice of lemon, including the rind. Ladle over this sufficient aspic to cover the lemon and chill again until set. Lay 1 cooked egg in center of each dish. Now soak 1 envelope gelatin in ¼ cup cold water in top of small enamel double boiler 5 minutes. Place top over boiling water and stir until melted. Add this to 1 cup mayonnaise and stir well. Distribute over the 8 eggs, masking them with a thin coating of the mixture. Chill until set, about 10 minutes. Open 3 2¼-ounce-cans deviled ham and spread contents over the mayonnaise, dividing it equally. Now add sufficient aspic to fill each dish level full. Place in refrigerator until set, at least 2 hours.

To serve, run a knife carefully around edge of each dish, dip dish for a second into hot water to loosen, and turn contents out carefully onto individual plates. Garnish with quartered lemons.

## CRYSTAL-CLEAR ASPIC

4 cups beef broth
¼ teaspoon cayenne
2 egg whites

2 envelopes gelatin
1 small branch fresh tarragon
salt

Double the recipe for beef broth (page 29). Cool and strain into a deep enamel pan. Add 1 small onion, peeled and sliced, salt to taste (about 1 teaspoon), a sprig of fresh tarragon, and the whites of 2 eggs which have been beaten to a froth. Place on fire and stir vigorously with wire whisk until mixture comes to a lively boil. Remove from fire and allow to cool and settle for 5 minutes.

In the meantime soak 2 envelopes gelatin in 1 cup cold water. Strain the clarified broth through a fine sieve into a bowl, and while still hot add the soaked gelatin. Stir until gelatin is completely dissolved. Cool and chill in refrigerator at least 1 hour until ready to use.

## PETITS POTS DE CREME AU FROMAGE
### [Pre-heat oven to 350°]

2 cups grated imported Swiss
    cheese (½ pound)
6 eggs
3 cups heavy cream

¼ teaspoon cayenne
¼ teaspoon salt
¼ teaspoon grated nutmeg

SERVES 6–8

Grate imported Swiss cheese until you have 2 cups. Beat 6 whole eggs with fork or egg whisk, adding gradually 3 cups heavy cream. Season to taste with about ¼ teaspoon each of salt, cayenne, and nutmeg. Add 1 cup grated cheese, stir well, and pour into 8 little custard cups, being sure that part of the cheese goes into each. Place the cups in a shallow pan of hot water and bake until set, about 30 minutes. Just before serving, sprinkle the rest of the cheese over each dish.

## QUICHE LORRAINE
*[Pre-heat oven to 450°]*

| | |
|---|---|
| 1½ cups pastry flour | 2 cups cream |
| ½ teaspoon salt | pinch of nutmeg |
| ¼ pound butter | pinch of sugar |
| 4 tablespoons ice water | ¾ teaspoon salt |
| 1 cup grated Swiss cheese | pinch of cayenne |
| 18 strips bacon | freshly ground black pepper |
| 4 eggs | |

SERVES 6–8

Make a paste ahead of time in the following manner. Sift 1½ cups pastry flour with ½ teaspoon salt. Work into it with finger tips ¼ pound salted butter. Moisten with just enough ice water to make it hold together (about 4 tablespoons). Make a smooth ball of it, wrap in wax paper, and place in refrigerator for ½ hour or so before rolling it out thin on a lightly floured board. Line a very large tart or pie pan with it, trim the edges, and crimp them. Prick the surface with a fork and place in refrigerator while you prepare the following ingredients.

*Pre-heat oven.* Grate Swiss cheese until you have 1 cup. Fry or grill about 18 strips of bacon until crisp, but don't overcook. Break or cut bacon into small pieces. Break 4 whole eggs into a bowl and add to them 2 cups heavy or light cream, a pinch of nutmeg, a pinch of sugar, ¾ teaspoon salt, a big pinch of cayenne, and plenty of freshly ground black pepper. Beat with rotary-beater just long enough to mix thoroughly. Now rub a little soft butter over the surface of the pastry and sprinkle the bacon over the bottom; sprinkle the cheese over the bacon; and pour the egg mixture over all.

Place in oven and bake 10–15 minutes; then reduce the temperature to 325°, and continue cooking until an inserted knife comes out clean, showing the custard has set, 25–30 minutes. If not a light golden brown on top, place under a hot grill for a second before serving piping hot.

NOTE  Variations of this pie may be made by substituting for the bacon thinly sliced ham, sizzled in butter; or parboiled salt pork, cut in tiny squares and fried until a golden brown; or sizzled chipped beef. The cheese may be omitted, if you like; thinly sliced onions browned slowly in butter may be added.

## CANNELLONI

1 pound fresh Ricotta cheese
1 pound Manicotti (Italian egg-noodle paste in form of large tubes)
8 thin slices prosciutto (about ¼ pound)
1 tablespoon butter
1 cup light cream

2½ tablespoons salt
1 tablespoon olive oil
¼ teaspoon coarsely ground black pepper
1 egg
6 tablespoons grated imported Parmesan cheese
sauce Mornay (page 302)

SERVES 6–8

First make sauce Mornay (page 302), and keep it warm in top of double boiler over hot water. Next melt 1 tablespoon butter in a frying-pan and brown in it lightly for 1–2 minutes 8 slices Italian prosciutto (about ¼ pound). Remove from fire and put it through the meat-grinder, using the fine cutter. Butter lightly 2 rectangular, 10″ by 6″ by 1½″, glass baking-dishes.

Heat 6 quarts water in a very large heavy pan, or kettle, and when boiling rapidly, add 2½ tablespoons salt and 1 tablespoon olive oil. Drop in, one at a time, 2 dozen Manicotti (Italian egg-noodle paste in the form of large tubes, 1 inch in diameter, 3 inches long). Stir gently with a wooden spoon and cook until tender, 50–60 minutes. It will be necessary to give these constant attention and to stir them almost continuously, as they have a great tendency to stick to the bottom of the pan; also they break easily if handled roughly. When done, drain and spread them out on a clean damp cloth to wait while you mix the stuffing.

Place 2 cups fresh Ricotta cheese in a bowl, add ¼ teaspoon coarsely ground black pepper, a dash of salt, 1 well-beaten egg, 2 tablespoons grated Parmesan cheese, and the ground-up prosciutto. Mix thoroughly. Light your oven and set it at 400°.

Now slit the cannelloni down one side (some of them may well have slit open themselves during the cooking). Place length-wise down the center of the 16 most perfect ones 2–3 heaping tea-spoons Ricotta mixture and roll them up neatly. Place them side by side in the 2 buttered baking-dishes, smooth side up. Now stir your sauce well; if too thick to pour, thin with about 1 cup light cream. Pour over the cannelloni so as to completely cover them, dividing the sauce equally between the 2 dishes. Sprinkle lightly with 4 tablespoons Parmesan cheese, place in oven, and bake for 15 minutes, or until the sauce begins to bubble; at which time place under broiler for a minute or two until a light golden brown all over. Serve at once.

NOTE  If you prefer—and have time—a superior substitute for Manicotti noodles may be made at home of noodle paste (page 68).

Cut as directed and cook 8 at a time in at least 6 quarts boil-ing salted water in a very large pot until tender, about 10–12 minutes.

## SAUTEED HARD-BOILED EGGS

| | |
|---|---|
| 12 eggs | 2 tablespoons tarragon vinegar |
| ¼ pound butter | 1 tablespoon chopped parsley |
| 3 tablespoons capers | |

SERVES 6–8

Hard boil 12 eggs, cooking them gently for about 12 minutes. Shell them as soon as they are done, and cut them lengthwise in two. Melt ¼ pound butter in a frying-pan; add the eggs, yolk side down; and cook just long enough to brown the yolks lightly. Turn them over carefully with a spatula. When all have been turned, add 3 tablespoons capers. Continue cooking over low flame for just a few seconds, or long enough to warm the capers. Transfer the eggs to a hot serving-platter. Add 2 tablespoons tarragon vinegar to the butter and capers, and pour this mixture over the eggs. Sprinkle with finely chopped parsley and serve.

## CHARLES HAZARD DURFEE'S JOHNNY CAKE

3 cups white water-ground corn meal
1 teaspoon salt
½ cup granulated sugar

1 cup milk
4 eggs
bacon fat

SERVES 6–8

Grease heavily with bacon fat 2 1-quart-size baking-dishes, 2½ inches deep, preferably square. Stir together thoroughly 3 cups white water-ground corn meal, 1 teaspoon salt, and ½ cup granulated sugar. Add just enough boiling water to wet the meal, about 2 cups. Beat 4 eggs until very light and stir them into the meal. Thin with sufficient cold milk (about 1 cup) to make a batter that will pour out of the spoon. Pour into the 2 baking-dishes, dividing it equally. Place in cold oven, set control to 400° light, and bake 45 minutes. Place cake under broiler for the last 3 minutes. Serve at once with plenty of butter.

## ERMA'S CHEESE BREAD PUDDING
[*Pre-heat oven to 325°*]

16 slices white bread
butter
4 cups grated sharp Cheddar cheese

salt, pepper
8 eggs
7 cups milk

SERVES 6–8

Butter 2 baking-dishes or pans, 11″ by 7″ by 1½″. Cut crusts from 16 slices white bread, butter one side of each slice, then cut into four pieces. Arrange 16 bread squares, buttered side up, on the bottom of each dish and sprinkle with 2 cups grated cheese, a bit of salt, and a generous shower of pepper. Cover, making another layer, with remaining bread squares, and 2 cups grated cheese; add salt and pepper.

Beat 8 eggs slightly and stir in the milk; pour over bread-cheese combination. Let it rest 10 minutes so that milk soaks into the bread.

Bake 40 minutes, or until puffy and nicely browned. Makes a delicious supper, lunch, or dinner dish.

## GNOCCHI
### [Pre-heat oven to 475°]

| | |
|---|---|
| ¼ pound butter (and more) | 4 cups milk |
| ½ cup cornstarch | 1½ cups freshly grated imported Parmesan cheese |
| ½ cup farina | |
| ½ teaspoon salt | 4 egg yolks |

SERVES 6–8

Melt ¼ pound butter in the top of a double boiler over boiling water. Heat 4 cups milk in saucepan. Mix ½ cup cornstarch, ½ cup farina, and ½ teaspoon of salt together in a bowl and then add mixture to melted butter. Stir well and then add 4 cups hot milk gradually. Put pan directly on the flame and stir furiously with a wooden spoon. It will get very thick. Remove from direct heat and cook over boiling water 3 minutes. Keep stirring. Add 1 cup grated Parmesan cheese. Remove from fire and add 4 well-beaten egg yolks. Stir well and spread out to ¾-inch thickness in 2 oblong, buttered cake tins, 11″ by 7″. Let it get thoroughly cold, then cut in 15 equal pieces.

Butter a larger oblong baking-dish, 12″ by 7½″ by 1½″, and cover the bottom with 15 of the squares, placed neatly side by side, but not touching each other. Put a tiny dab of butter on each piece and sprinkle with grated cheese. Put a second layer of gnocchi on top of the first and repeat the butter-and-cheese process. Place the dish in a very hot oven and bake 15–20 minutes, or until brown. Serve at once.

## CURRIED GNOCCHI

[*Pre-heat oven to 450°*]

Gnocchi:
¼ pound butter
½ cup cornstarch
½ cup farina
4 cups milk
½ cup freshly grated imported Parmesan cheese
4 egg yolks
1 teaspoon salt
2 teaspoons curry powder
1 tablespoon cold milk

Sauce:
¼ pound butter
½ cup flour
3 cups hot milk
salt, pepper
½ cup grated imported Parmesan cheese
1 teaspoon curry powder
1 cup heavy cream (or more)

Topping:
1 pound fresh mushrooms
4 tablespoons butter
salt, pepper

SERVES 6–8

First make the gnocchi. Melt ¼ pound butter in top of large double boiler over boiling water. Grate 1 cup imported Parmesan cheese. Mix together in a little bowl ½ cup cornstarch and ½ cup farina. Heat 4 cups milk. Add the cornstarch and farina to the melted butter and cook over direct low heat for a minute or two, stirring constantly with wooden spoon; then add the hot milk gradually. Cook until well thickened, stirring constantly, then cover and continue cooking over boiling water for 5 minutes. Add ½ cup grated cheese, stir in, and remove pan from fire. Season to taste with 1 teaspoon salt and 2 teaspoons curry powder mixed with 1 tablespoon cold milk.

Beat the yolks of 4 eggs until light, add ¼–½ cup gnocchi to the yolks and stir well; add beaten egg yolks to the gnocchi and stir. Pour into 2 rectangular well-buttered pans, 11″ by 7″ by 1½″, dividing it equally. Set aside to cool until it sets while you make a cream sauce.

Make cream sauce by melting in saucepan ¼ pound butter, gradually adding ½ cup flour, and then 3 cups hot milk. When thick and smooth remove from fire and season to taste with about 1 teaspoon salt and 1 teaspoon curry powder. Remove from fire and stir in ½ cup grated Parmesan cheese. Thin with 1 cup heavy cream, or more. Keep warm in double boiler.

Butter a large shallow, round or oval baking-dish. By now the gnocchi should have set firm. Cut in neat squares, 15 from each pan. Spread these out on the buttered baking-dish and pour the sauce over all.

Wash and dry 1 pound fresh mushrooms. Discard tough part of stems and chop the rest fine. Sauté quickly for 5 minutes in 4 tablespoons butter in frying-pan. Season lightly with salt and coarsely ground pepper and then sprinkle them over the cream-sauce-covered gnocchi. Bake for 15 minutes, or until sizzling hot. If not browned on top, place briefly under the broiler. Serve at once.

## MACARONI PIE
*[Pre-heat oven to 500°]*

| Pastry: | Filling: |
|---|---|
| 3 tablespoons butter | 9 ounces macaroni |
| 3 tablespoons vegetable short-ening | 2 cups grated Cheddar cheese |
| 1½ cups pastry flour | 4 tablespoons butter (and more) |
| ½ teaspoon salt | 4 tablespoons flour |
| 3 tablespoons ice water | 2 cups milk |
| | ¼ cup heavy cream |

SERVES 6–8

Mix the pastry for the pie an hour or more ahead of time by working 3 tablespoons butter and 3 tablespoons vegetable shortening into 1½ cups pastry flour that has been sifted with ½ teaspoon salt. Moisten with not more than 3 tablespoons ice water. Form into a flat ball, wrap in wax paper, and chill while preparing the following ingredients.

Cook until tender 9 ounces macaroni, broken into short pieces, in plenty of boiling salted water, about 10 minutes. When done, drain well. In the meantime prepare 2 cups grated sharp Cheddar cheese. Make a smooth cream sauce in the usual way by melting 4 tablespoons butter in a saucepan, adding 4 tablespoons flour gradually, and then adding 2 cups hot milk. Season to taste with salt and coarsely ground black pepper and cook sauce until well thickened. Remove from fire and stir in ¼ cup heavy cream.

Line a medium-size pie plate with the pastry, rolling it out to fit the plate: crimp the edges prettily, and fill with layers of macaroni and cheese, saving out ½ cup grated cheese for the top. Pour the cream sauce over all and sprinkle with the remainder of the cheese. Dot well with butter and place in pre-heated oven and bake for 15 minutes. Then reduce heat to 400° and bake until the cream sauce is bubbling and the top is browned, about 10 minutes. Serve at once cut in pie-shaped pieces.

## HOMEMADE NOODLES

| | |
|---|---|
| 1½ cups all-purpose sifted flour | 1 egg |
| ¼ teaspoon salt | 1 tablespoon olive oil |
| | ⅜ cup warm water |

SERVES 6–8

Sift flour and salt together into a bowl. Make a depression in the center and break 1 egg into the hole, and add 1 tablespoon olive oil. Mix with small wooden spoon, adding gradually ⅜ cup warm water, making a stiff dough. Toss out onto floured pastry cloth and knead until smooth. Place in clean bowl, cover, and allow to stand ½ hour.

Roll out half of it at a time until paper thin, using a very little extra flour, if necessary, to prevent sticking. Allow the sheets to dry out a bit (about 15 minutes), fold and fold again and, using a sharp knife, cut in thin strips: ⅛ of an inch wide for thin noodles, ¼ of an inch for wide noodles. Or, if you want to use this for cannelloni, do not fold but cut in pieces 4″ by 5″.

## RAVIOLI WITH TOMATO SAUCE

### Paste:
3 cups all-purpose flour
¼ teaspoon salt
2 eggs
2 tablespoons olive oil
¾ cup warm water

### Filling:
1 cup chopped boiled chicken
1 10-ounce package frozen spinach
2 eggs
¾ cup soft bread crumbs
¼ cup heavy cream
½ teaspoon grated nutmeg
⅓ cup freshly grated imported Parmesan cheese
1 tablespoon chopped parsley
1 clove garlic, finely chopped
¼ teaspoon coarsely ground pepper
½ teaspoon salt

### Sauce:
1 2-pound, 3-ounce can Italian peeled plum tomatoes
1 6-ounce can tomato paste
3 cloves garlic
18 small white onions
12 shallots
3 cups strong chicken broth
1 teaspoon salt
½ teaspoon coarsely ground pepper
1 teaspoon granulated sugar
1 bay leaf
½ teaspoon dried oregano
¼ teaspoon dried basil
4 tablespoons olive oil

SERVES 6–8

First make the sauce. Peel and chop fine 18 small white onions, 12 shallots, and 3 cloves garlic. Sauté for about 10 minutes, or until lightly browned, in 4 tablespoons olive oil; stir frequently. Add 1 large 2-pound, 3-ounce can Italian peeled plum tomatoes, 1 6-ounce can tomato paste, and 2 cups strong chicken broth (preferably homemade). Season with 1 bay leaf, 1 teaspoon salt, ½ teaspoon coarsely ground pepper, 1 teaspoon granulated sugar, ½ teaspoon dried oregano, and ¼ teaspoon dried basil. Simmer gently for about 2 hours, stirring occasionally, skimming as necessary, and adding about 1 cup additional chicken broth as the sauce thickens.

In the meantime mix the filling for the ravioli. Cook 1 10-ounce package frozen chopped spinach, following directions on the label. Drain well. Prepare 2 cups freshly grated imported Parmesan cheese, 1 cup finely chopped cold boiled chicken meat, and 1 table-spoon chopped parsley. Pluck the white crumb from 2 slices white bread, discarding crusts. Beat 2 eggs, add the chicken, bread, spinach, and ⅓ cup grated cheese. Season with ½ teaspoon grated nutmeg, ¼ teaspoon coarsely ground pepper, ½ teaspoon salt, 1 clove garlic (peeled and finely chopped or put through a garlic press). Add 1 tablespoon chopped parsley; moisten with ¼ cup heavy cream; and mix well. Refrigerate until ready to use.

Now make the paste. This is the same as for homemade noodles (page 68). Sift 3 cups all-purpose flour with ¼ teaspoon salt, making a mound in the center of large shallow bowl. Make a well in the center and break into it 2 eggs. Add 2 tablespoons olive oil. Mix rapidly with small wooden spoon, adding gradually about ¾ cup luke-warm water to make a stiff dough. Toss out onto heavily floured cloth and knead until smooth. Cover with bowl and allow to stand for about 45 minutes.

You are now ready to make the ravioli—which is fun. You will need a ravioli-cutter, which is a wheel with a notched edge sold for the purpose. Cut the paste in 4 equal parts. Spread some wax paper conveniently near by the pastry cloth and sprinkle it with flour. Roll out the paste one section at a time, making a rectangle, paper thin, using extra flour if necessary to prevent sticking. Roll up on pin and unroll onto the floured paper. Now, using a tea-spoon, place 24 little mounds of the filling on the paste symmetrically about 1½ inches apart. Roll out another section of the paste, making it the same size as the first; and, rolling it up on the pin, unroll and drop it over the mounds so as to cover them with a blanket. Press gently but firmly between the rows up and down and across to seal the top and bottom sheets securely around the mounds. Now run the wheel dipped in flour between the mounds, making thereby neat little square cushions. Lift these carefully onto a floured cookie sheet and repeat the process until you have made 48 ravioli. Allow these to dry out for about ½ hour before cooking in the following manner.

Heat 8 quarts water in a very large kettle. Add 1 teaspoon salt and ½ teaspoon olive oil. When the water is boiling merrily, drop the ravioli, a few at a time, gently into the water, separating them with a wooden spoon to prevent sticking. When all have been added make a note of the time and cook until just tender, or about 10–15 minutes.

In the meantime heat the sauce over boiling water. Try one of the ravioli when you think they are done, and if they are *al dente*, or to your liking, remove them, a few at a time, from the boiling water, using a sieve, and slip them into a colander to drain thoroughly. Work quickly until all have been drained; then place them on a hot platter. Pour hot sauce over all and serve at once on hot plates. The remainder of the grated Parmesan cheese previously prepared should be served with the ravioli.


## RICE AND CHEESE SOUFFLE
[*Pre-heat oven to 325°*]

| | |
|---|---|
| 2 cups long-grain rice | 4 tablespoons butter |
| | 3 eggs |
| ¼ pound Cheddar cheese | 1 cup milk |

SERVES 6–8

Cook 2 cups of long-grain rice. Drain well. Butter a 2-quart baking-dish. Shred or grate ¼ pound Cheddar cheese. Sprinkle the dish inside with a little of the cheese, then fill it with alternate layers of rice and cheese, dotting with 3 tablespoons butter as you go along, ending up with cheese and butter. Beat 3 eggs with 1 cup milk until mixed, but not too frothy, and pour over the rice. Bake 20–25 minutes and serve piping hot.

## RICE PANCAKES WITH HAM SAUCE

Sauce:

24 shelled blanched almonds, slivered fine

¼ cup seedless white or black raisins

strained juice 3 lemons

3 tablespoons cognac, or brandy

4 generous tablespoons orange marmalade

2 tablespoons red currant jelly

2 ¼-inch-thick slices boiled ham (about ½ pound)

1 tablespoon butter

½ cup light-brown sugar

Pancakes:

½ cup long-grain rice

1 scant teaspoon salt

2 eggs

1 cup all-purpose flour

2 rounded teaspoons baking powder

1½ cups milk

3–4 tablespoons melted butter

SERVES 6–8

*Sauce:* Cut 24 blanched almonds into thin slivers. Wash ¼ cup seedless raisins and soak in cold water for ½ hour. Drain, cover with about 1 cup cold water, place on fire, and boil until plump and until no juice is left. In the meantime squeeze the juice of 2 lemons and strain. When the raisins are done pour over them 3 tablespoons cognac, or brandy, and add 4 generous tablespoons orange marmalade, 2 tablespoons red currant jelly, and the strained lemon juice. Bring gently to a boil. Remove from fire until ready to use.

Next cut 2 ¼-inch-thick slices (about ½ pound) boiled ham in small cubes. Melt 1 tablespoon butter in a small frying-pan, add the cubes of ham, and cook, stirring gently with a spoon, until lightly browned. Sprinkle over the ham ½ cup soft light-brown sugar; stir; and add raisin-brandy-jam sauce, simmering gently for a few minutes until slightly thickened. Add the sliced almonds. Keep hot until ready to serve on rice pancakes; then pour into a serving-bowl. Sauce is to be ladled over pancakes at table.

*Rice Pancakes:* Wash ½ cup long-grain rice and add it gradually to 3 cups boiling water (to which you have added 1 scant teaspoon salt). Cook until tender, about 20 minutes. Remove from fire. Do not drain. Cool slightly and either reduce it to a purée by rubbing it through a sieve, using a wooden spoon; or place it in an electric-blender for about 1 minute, using the low power at first and the high later. Put the resultant rice purée in a bowl. Separate the yolks from the whites of 2 eggs. Beat the yolks until very light, then stir in a little of the purée so that all the yolks are incorporated; then add this to the remainder of the rice purée. Beat until smooth. Sift into this 1 cup all-purpose flour to which you have already added 2 rounded teaspoons baking powder. You will have a very stiff batter. Thin it by adding gradually 1½ cups cold milk. Avoid overbeating. Now add 3 generous tablespoons melted butter. When ready to bake the pancakes, have the ungreased griddle (preferably a soapstone one) nice and hot. Beat the 2 egg whites until stiff, but not dry, and fold them gently into the batter. Make 6 cakes at a time, each about 3 inches in diameter. When the surfaces of the pancakes are covered with bubbles, turn them over carefully and brown other sides. Serve on hot plates with the ham sauce.

## TOMATO RISOTTO

*[Pre-heat oven to 400°]*

| | |
|---|---|
| 2¼ cups long-grain rice | 4 ripe tomatoes |
| 4 cans consommé Madrilène | salt, coarsely ground pepper |
| 6 tablespoons butter | 1 tablespoon chopped parsley |
| 4 tablespoons olive oil | 4 tablespoons grated imported |
| 2 sweet green peppers | Parmesan cheese |

SERVES 6–8

Remove stem end and seeds from 2 sweet green peppers and cut moderately fine. Peel 4 ripe tomatoes, extract as many seeds as possible, and cut in small cubes. Prepare 4 tablespoons grated imported Parmesan cheese. Prepare 1 tablespoon chopped parsley. Melt 4 tablespoons butter in a large iron cocotte, and add 4 tablespoons olive oil. Heat over moderate heat and add 2¼ cups unwashed long-grain rice. Stir constantly with wooden spoon until rice becomes white and opaque-looking. Then add the cut green peppers and tomatoes, season with ½ teaspoon coarsely ground pepper and about 1 teaspoon salt, and then add 1 cup canned consommé Madrilène. Stir mixture until it comes to boiling point. Cover tightly, place cocotte in moderately hot, 400° oven and bake for about 10 minutes.

Remove lid and add ½ cup of Madrilène, or just enough to moisten to level of rice. Cover and continue baking for about 25 minutes longer, adding about 1 cup Madrilène every 5 minutes, using in all 4 cans. Do not stir. Remove lid for the last 5 minutes to be sure that all the liquid has been absorbed by the rice. When done the rice should be flaky and almost dry. Remove from oven, add 2 tablespoons butter and 4 tablespoons grated Parmesan cheese, and toss lightly with 2 forks. Sprinkle with 1 tablespoon chopped parsley, tie two napkins around the pot, knotting them together, and serve at once; or, if you prefer, transfer to a serving-dish before adding parsley.

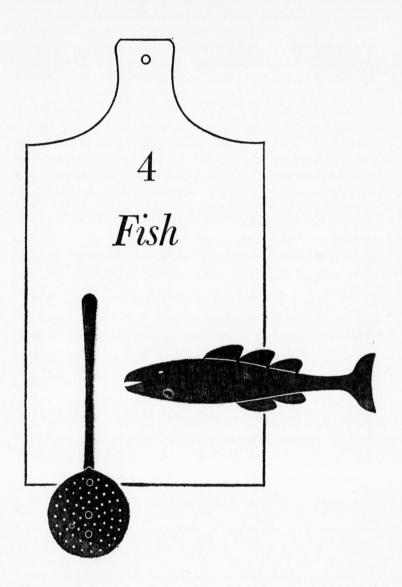

4

*Fish*

*P*rosper Montagné in his Grand Livre de la cuisine tells us that Heliogabalus, the famous Roman emperor of Antioch, would never eat fish when he was anywhere near the sea, but, to show how contrary he was, he would order it to be served abundantly at his table as soon as he found himself impossibly far away from all sources of supply. Montagné also tells us that Domitian, brother of Titus, son of Vespasian, husband of Domitia Longina, Emperor of Rome, last of the twelve Caesars, is said to have called a special meeting of the Senate in the middle of the night to deliberate over the momentous question of how best to cook a magnificent turbot that had been sent to him from Ischia, a volcanic island of Italy. In fact, so prized were fish in the feasts of Lucullus, Octavius, Apicius, and other Roman epicures that a sum amounting to one thousand dollars was often paid by them for a mullet (our sole) weighing two to four pounds.

## GARNISHES FOR FISH

Hot fish may be garnished with boiled potatoes, fried or plain parsley, slices or quarters of lemon or lime, or paprika.

Cold fish may be garnished with aspic, parsley, paprika, water cress, tomatoes, lemons or limes, hard-boiled egg, or with cucumbers, or with mayonnaise.

## HOW TO MAKE FRIED PARSLEY
## FOR DECORATING FISH

Select small sprigs of very green parsley and wash well in cold water. Drain well and squeeze it dry in a tea cloth. Lay it in a wire basket and plunge the basket into boiling deep fat (preferably olive oil). It will be crisp in just a second or two. Drain it thoroughly on absorbent paper and sprinkle it lightly with salt. Be careful not to break it, as it is very fragile.

## BOILED FISH

To boil fish, you must first make a *court bouillon* of sufficient liquid to cover the fish. To determine how much water or liquid will be required, put the fish to be boiled in the fish-boiler and, using a quart measure, pour cold water over it quart by quart, keeping track of how much is required to cover the fish completely. Remove the fish, pour off the water, and prepare the equivalent amount of court bouillon.

A de luxe court bouillon is made of equal quantities of dry white wine and water, simmered for about ½ hour with 3–4 sliced onions; 1–2 peeled carrots; some parsley; a bay leaf; some peppercorns; a pinch of thyme, if you like, or a bit of celery; and 1 teaspoon of salt to every 2 quarts of liquid. If you prefer not to use wine, use all water, adding, however, 1 tablespoon vinegar, or lemon juice, to each 2 quarts of water. After the court bouillon is cooked, allow to cool a bit before using.

When ready to boil the fish, place it with loving care on the rack of the enamel fish-boiler, wrapped in a cloth or not, as the case may be. Pour over it the hot, but not boiling court bouillon. Place on fire, bring to the boiling point, stand by, and skim the foam off carefully. Reduce the flame until water is barely trembling; cover; and cook gently until the flesh will leave the bone easily—about 10 minutes to the pound. When done, lift the rack carefully out of the court bouillon, transfer the fish to a hot platter, remove cloth and as much skin as possible without spoiling the shape of the fish, garnish with parsley, and serve with a delectable sauce.

Hollandaise, sauce mousseline, cream herb sauce, hard-boiled-egg cream sauce, curried hard-boiled-egg cream sauce are all suitable for boiled fish, and recipes for each of them will be found in this book. If boiled fish is to be served cold, cook it slightly less time, and allow it to cool in its own liquid before placing it on the serving-platter. Plain mayonnaise (page 320) mixed with a little whipped cream is good served with cold fish or lobsters; or mayonnaise mixed with plenty of finely chopped water cress is even better. Capers are an added joy, if you happen to like them. Tartar sauce (page 304) is also suitable for cold fish.

## BOILED DEEP-SEA STRIPED BASS

| | |
|---|---|
| 2 5-pound striped bass | 4 cloves |
| dry white wine | rock salt |
| 6 little white onions | ½ teaspoon peppercorns |
| 3 carrots | Sauce: |
| 2 branches celery | 8 shallots |
| 1 clove garlic | 3 teaspoons vinegar |
| 1 sprig thyme | salt, pepper |
| 1 bay leaf | 1 pound sweet butter |
| parsley | |

SERVES 6–8

Buy 2 5-pound striped bass; wash; and clean well. Lay them on the rack of your fish-boiler and cover entirely with a court bouil-

lon (page 77) made of half-water and half-dry-white-wine, 6
little white onions, 3 peeled and sliced carrots, 2 branches celery,
1 clove garlic, 1 sprig thyme, 1 bay leaf, some parsley, 4 cloves,
rock salt, and ½ teaspoon peppercorns. Put the pot on a good
fire and bring to a boil, skim carefully, and then reduce heat considerably so that it barely simmers for about 50 minutes. Remove
as much skin from fish as possible. Place on folded damask napkins
on 2 hot silver platters, garnish with boiled potatoes and parsley,
and serve with the following butter sauce.

Chop very fine 8 shallots, add 3 teaspoons vinegar, salt, and
pepper, and put all into an enamel saucepan with 1 pound sweet
butter. Place pan on a very low fire and stir constantly until butter is creamy and almost melted; then pour it into a sauce boat.

## BAKED STRIPED BASS
*[Pre-heat oven to 425°]*

| | |
|---|---|
| 1 5–7-pound fresh striped bass | salt, pepper |
| ½ pound butter, and more | parsley |
| 2 carrots | 2 lemons |
| 1 onion | ¼ teaspoon thyme |
| 3 stalks celery | |

SERVES 6–8

Buy a fine fresh striped bass weighing 5–7 pounds. Have the head
removed and ask the fishmonger to clean it for baking. Wash it
carefully and dry well. Lay it on a shallow baking-dish lined with
well-buttered aluminum foil.

Peel 2 carrots and 1 onion; remove strings from 3 stalks
celery. Chop all of these in coarse pieces and place them around
the fish. Make 3 gashes in the fish crosswise, and salt and pepper
the fish; then sprinkle with ¼ teaspoon thyme, rubbed to a powder. Dot with 10 tablespoons butter. Place in hot oven (400°
to 450°) and bake for about 1 hour and 15 minutes, basting frequently with the melted butter in the pan.

When done, lift fish carefully onto a hot fish platter and pour
the vegetables and butter around the fish, not over it. Garnish

with parsley and quartered lemons and serve at once with a separate bowl of melted butter.

## POISSON A LA MEXICAINE (PLUS OU MOINS)
*[Pre-heat oven to 425°]*

1 fine striped bass (weighing 7-8 pounds when cleaned
½ cup olive oil
2 lemons
1 6¼-ounce can pitted ripe olives
3 yellow onions
4 large green peppers
8 large ripe tomatoes
3 bay leaves
2 teaspoons thyme
2 teaspoons paprika
¼ teaspoon cayenne
½ teaspoon coarsely ground black pepper
2 teaspoons salt
1 small bunch parsley
1 6-ounce can tomato paste

SERVES 6–8

Ask the fishmonger to clean the fish and remove the head; ask him, however, to give you the head, but remove the eyes. Wash the fish carefully in cold water, then rub the inside with a cut lemon. Place the fish and the head in a shallow baking-pan, 15″ by 9″ by 3½″, preferably enamel-lined, the bottom of which you have rubbed with olive oil. Trickle over the fish ⅓ cup olive oil. Slice 8 large ripe tomatoes and completely cover the fish. Next add 3 onions, peeled and sliced fine. Also split 3 large green peppers in two and remove all the seeds. Wash, slice fine, and place on top of the onions. Add 1 6¼-ounce can pitted ripe olives, draining them first, however. Sprinkle with 3 bay leaves, crushed fine. Also sprinkle with 2 teaspoons thyme, 2 teaspoons paprika, ¼ teaspoon cayenne, ½ teaspoon coarsely ground black pepper, and 2 teaspoons of salt; tuck into one corner a small bunch of parsley.

Place in pre-heated oven and bake 1 hour, basting occasionally with its own juice. Remove from oven, lift fish tenderly onto a pretty fish platter using two spatulas, and carefully pull off the skin. Turn over and remove skin from other side. Now carefully lift meat off, exposing the back bone, which you pull away. Also pull out all the bones you can find, then replace the meat you took off and reshape the fish as neatly as possible on its platter. Drain any juice there may be on the platter and add it to the vegetables left in baking-dish. Also put all the skin and bones back in the vegetables and add 1 6-ounce can tomato paste. Fill this can with water, stir to get all the paste, and add this to the vegetables plus one more can of water. Place pan on low flame and simmer gently for 1 hour or a little longer. Stir occasionally to prevent sticking.

In the meantime, when the fish has cooled wipe edges of dish carefully and cover with wax paper to prevent the fish from drying out. When cold, chill fish in refrigerator.

Now make the sauce. Extract all the olives and put them aside. Also remove the large fish bone, then strain the vegetables through a large sieve placed over a large pan, pressing with wooden spoon or potato-masher, to extract all the juice and pulp possible. Cool and chill this sauce in refrigerator watching it carefully. When sauce is about to jell, skim off fat; spoon sauce over the fish. Refrigerate until the jelly has set, then garnish with the olives, thin rings of fresh green pepper, and quartered lemons. Serve with a crisp green salad, well tossed with a tart French dressing. Hot buttered French bread is good with this, and a good, not too dry, well-chilled white wine.

## BAKED BLUE FISH
*[Pre-heat oven to 450°]*

| | |
|---|---|
| 2 small 3–4-pound blue fish | 2 lemons |
| ¼ pound butter | parsley |
| salt, pepper | |

SERVES 6–8

Clean, wash, and dry 2 small blue fish weighing about 3–4 pounds each. Remove the heads and tails. Make 4 deep gashes on both sides of each fish and insert 1 tablespoon butter in each gash. Place on buttered aluminum foil in flat broiling pan. Sprinkle with salt and coarsely ground pepper. Place in oven and bake for 10 minutes. Reduce heat to 375° and continue baking ½ hour longer, basting occasionally. Garnish with 2 quartered lemons and parsley and serve with Maitre d'Hotel Butter (page 296) or with Cream Herb Sauce (page 292), and accompanied by little new potatoes that have been peeled, boiled, buttered, and sprinkled with chopped parsley.

## BAKED BONITA

*[Pre-heat oven to 450°]*

1 6–8 pound Bonita
1 fresh sweet red pepper
2 cloves garlic

¼ pound butter
salt, pepper
2 lemons

SERVES 6–8

Clean, wash, and dry thoroughly a good-size Bonita, about 6–8 pounds. Remove head and tail. Make 6 deep gashes on each side. Stuff these gashes with a mixture of 1 teaspoon salt, ½ teaspoon coarsely ground pepper, 1 large sweet red pepper, chopped very fine, and 2 cloves garlic (put through the garlic press), and ¼ pound butter. Set fish on buttered aluminum foil that you have placed in a shallow broiling-pan.

Bake in hot oven 15 minutes, reduce heat to 350°, and continue baking, basting occasionally, for about 45 minutes more. Garnish with 2 quartered lemons and serve with plain boiled potatoes, lightly buttered and sprinkled with paprika. Hard-boiled-egg Cream Sauce (page 297) is good with this.

## CALDILLO DE PESCADO

½ cup olive oil
2 large onions
2 large ripe tomatoes
8 medium-sized potatoes
3 pounds fresh fillet of cod

salt, pepper
½ teaspoon thyme
⅓ cup long-grain rice
chopped parsley

SERVES 6–8

Cover the bottom of an earthenware casserole with ½ cup olive oil. Peel and slice thin 2 large onions. Dip 2 large ripe tomatoes into boiling water, remove the skins, and slice thin; or substitute a 1-pound, 3-ounce can tomatoes. Peel 8 medium-size potatoes and slice them. Have ready 3 pounds fillet of fresh cod. Cover the bottom of the casserole with a layer of onions, and a layer of potatoes, using half of each. On this bed place the fish. Sprinkle with salt, coarsely ground pepper, and ½ teaspoon thyme. Cover with a layer of onions and a layer of potatoes, using the balance. Now sprinkle over this ⅓ cup unwashed long-grain rice, and cover with the sliced tomatoes and another sprinkling of salt and pepper. Place the casserole on very low flame, and cook for 5 minutes; then pour over it just enough boiling water to barely cover, about 2 cups. Place lid on dish and continue simmering slowly for 1 hour. Sprinkle with parsley and serve at once.

## COLD BOILED CODFISH
## WITH COLD SAFFRON SAUCE

1 4-pound slice fresh codfish
2 white onions, sliced
4 cups white wine
several sprigs parsley
½ teaspoon thyme
1 bay leaf
¼ teaspoon peppercorns
2 peeled carrots
1 teaspoon salt
4 cups water

Saffron sauce:
2 cloves garlic
2 leeks
2 medium-size onions
6 large ripe tomatoes
6 tablespoons olive oil
½ cup dry white wine
1 teaspoon genuine saffron
3 teaspoons salt
1 teaspoon coarsely ground pepper
2 quartered lemons
1 tablespoon chopped parsley

SERVES 6–8

Put the above ingredients, except the codfish, in enamel fish-boiler and boil about 30 minutes. Wash the fish in cold water, wrap in cheesecloth, and place it in this hot court boullion. Cook gently for about 40 minutes. Cool in the liquid. Discard cheesecloth, remove skin and all the bones, keeping the fish in as large pieces as possible. Arrange on platter. When cold, wrap platter in wax paper and refrigerate until ready to serve.

To make the saffron sauce, dip 6 ripe tomatoes in boiling water to remove skins. Remove green part from 2 leeks, split the white part in two lengthwise, and wash carefully. Peel 2 medium-size onions and 2 cloves garlic. Cut the tomatoes in two crosswise, and remove seeds. Place in wooden bowl and chop fine. Chop the onions and leeks very fine and cook in 6 tablespoons olive oil until just beginning to brown, stirring with wooden spoon. Add the juice from 2 cloves garlic (using garlic press) and the chopped tomatoes. Cook 2 minutes, then add ½ cup white wine and ½ cup water. Season to taste with about 3 teaspoons salt, 1 teaspoon coarsely ground pepper, and 1 teaspoon saffron. Simmer 10–15 minutes, stirring occasionally. Remove from fire and cool before placing in refrigerator to chill thoroughly.

Pour cold saffron sauce over fish, garnish with quartered lemons and parsley, and serve with crisp French bread, whipped butter, and a good imported well-chilled white wine.

## BAKED CRABMEAT

*[Pre-heat oven to 450°]*

| | |
|---|---|
| 1 pound cooked crabmeat | 4 hard-boiled eggs |
| ¼ cup sherry | salt, pepper |
| 7 tablespoons butter | ¼ teaspoon cayenne |
| 3 tablespoons flour | ½ teaspoon dry mustard |
| 2 cups light cream | 1 cup toasted bread crumbs |

SERVES 6–8

Have ready 1 pound cooked fresh crabmeat, carefully picked over. Pour over it ¼ cup sherry and let it soak for a few minutes. Make a cream sauce in the usual way by melting 3 tablespoons butter, gradually adding 3 tablespoons flour, and then adding 2 cups hot light cream. Hard boil 4 eggs; rub the yolks through a fine sieve and chop the whites. Add both to the cream sauce and season to taste with salt and pepper, ¼ teaspoon cayenne, and about ½ teaspoon dry mustard mixed in 1 teaspoon light cream.

Now fold in the crabmeat, and place in buttered baking-dish, or in 8 individual custard cups. Sprinkle the top with 1 cup toasted bread crumbs, and trickle over all about 3 tablespoons melted butter. Place in oven and bake until sizzling hot and lightly browned, 10–15 minutes. Serve at once.

## CREOLE CRAB CREPES
*[Pre-heat oven to 450°]*

| Filling: | Crêpes: |
|---|---|
| 1 pound crabmeat | 2 cups sifted all-purpose flour |
| 2 cups drained peeled canned tomatoes | 4 whole eggs |
| 4 onions | 1¼ cup milk |
| 2 green peppers | pinch of salt |
| 6 tablespoons butter | 2 tablespoons heavy cream |
| 1½ level tablespoons flour | 12 tablespoons butter |
| ½ teaspoon coarsely ground black pepper | 2 lemons |
| ¼ teaspoon cayenne | |
| ¾ teaspoon salt | |
| 2 tablespoons heavy cream | |

SERVES 6–8

Two hours ahead of time make the batter for the crêpes. Sift all-purpose flour and measure out 1 cup. Place in small bowl; make a hole in the center of flour and drop 2 unbeaten eggs in the hole. Stir with a wooden spoon, gradually incorporating the flour, to make a smooth paste; then add gradually 1¼ cup milk. Add a pinch of salt and last of all add 2 tablespoons heavy cream. Strain through a fine sieve into another bowl to be sure there are no lumps. Let stand for at least 2 hours.

In the meantime pick over carefully 1 pound fresh crabmeat.

Place temporarily in refrigerator while you make the creole filling. Wash 2 green peppers, remove stems, quarter, and remove all seeds. Cut in thin strips and again crosswise into tiny cubes. Peel 4 small onions, and cut also in tiny cubes. Melt 6 tablespoons butter in a frying-pan, add the onions and peppers, and cook slowly, stirring occasionally until they brown slightly, about 10 minutes. Sprinkle with 1½ tablespoons all-purpose flour, cook for a minute, stirring constantly; then add 2 cups drained, peeled canned tomatoes. Simmer gently until thick and well reduced, about 10 minutes longer. Season lightly to taste with ¾ teaspoon salt, ½ teaspoon pepper, ¼ teaspoon cayenne. Add 2 tablespoons heavy cream; set aside temporarily.

Butter 2 rectangular baking-dishes, 6″ by 10″ by 2″. Melt ½ teaspoon butter in 7½-inch frying-pan, stir the crêpe batter well, and ladle 2 tablespoons of it into the hot frying-pan. Tilt the pan so that entire surface of pan is covered with a thin coat of batter. Cook until set on bottom, turn with spatula, and cook lightly on second side; place on hot plate. Continue process until you have 12 crêpes piled carefully on top of each other. Spread some wax paper on the counter. Now add the crabmeat to the creole filling, folding it in carefully. Spread the crêpes out on the wax paper and pile in the center of each a heaping tablespoon or more of the filling, dividing it equally. Fold the two sides of crêpes over, then roll up neatly, making little oblong packages of them. Place side by side in 2 baking-dishes. Melt 6 tablespoons butter and trickle it over the crêpes.

Place in pre-heated oven and bake until sizzling hot, about 15 minutes. Place under broiler for 1 minute to brown and serve garnished with quartered lemons.

## SAUTEED SOFT-SHELLED CRABS, WITH OR WITHOUT ALMONDS

soft-shelled crabs        lemon
salted flour              almonds
butter

Wash the crabs (2 per person) in cold water, pat them dry, and roll them lightly in salted flour. Have ready plenty of hot melted butter in a heavy frying-pan and drop the crabs into the hot butter, then reduce the heat, and cook slowly until lightly browned on one side. Then turn over and brown the other side, by which time they should be cooked. Serve on hot platter, accompanied by a little melted butter, flavored with a few drops of lemon juice. A few blanched, slivered, well-dried almonds, sautéed separately in 1 tablespoon butter until a light brown and sprinkled over the crabs, add greatly to the dish.

## GOUJONETTES OF FLOUNDER
## WITH MUSTARD SAUCE

6 fillets of flounder
1 cup flour
1 cup fine toasted and sifted
     bread crumbs
salt, pepper

small bowl of milk
3 cups vegetable shortening
2 lemons
sprigs of parsley

SERVES 6–8

First make the mustard sauce (page 296). Next cut 6 raw large fillets of flounder on the bias in fingerlike pieces, being sure they are free from bones and skin. Roll each one slightly to give it a little shape. Mix together 1 cup flour and 1 cup fine, toasted and sifted bread crumbs and season with a little salt and coarsely ground pepper. Spread this out on wax paper. Have ready a small bowl of milk.

Now put 3 cups vegetable shortening in a deep frying-pan with straight sides and heat to 375°, or until a cube of bread dropped in it will brown in 1 minute. Have ready a pan lined with brown paper, to drain the fillets on as you fry them, and a hot platter on which to serve them when they are all cooked. Also have ready 2 quartered lemons and plenty of small sprigs of parsley, carefully washed and squeezed dry in a tea cloth. Lay parsley in a wire frying-basket or sieve.

Now dip a few of the fingerlike pieces of flounder into the milk; then roll them in the flour and bread crumbs; and place them on another piece of wax paper that has been lightly dusted with flour—repeating the process until all the pieces have been dipped and crumbed.

Drop about one quarter of them into the hot fat and cook until lightly browned, about 3 minutes. When done skim them out of the fat with a perforated spoon, repeat the process 3 more times.

When all the fillets are cooked, place them on a hot platter. At the very last minute plunge the basket containing the parsley quickly into and out of the hot fat, which will be time enough to cook the parsley to a crisp. Garnish the fish with the fried parsley and the quartered lemons. Serve at once accompanied by a bowl of warm mustard sauce (page 296).

## BAKED FILLETS OF FLOUNDER

*[Pre-heat oven to 400°]*

| | |
|---|---|
| 3 pounds flounder fillets | 3 tablespoons finely chopped |
| 1 cup dry white wine | shallots, or onion |
| salt, pepper | chopped parsley |
| ⅜ pound butter | 2 lemons |

SERVES 6–8

Butter an oblong baking-dish, sprinkle it with 3 tablespoons finely chopped shallots, or onions, and lay on this bed 3 pounds of flounder fillets that have been washed in cold water and well dried. Pour over the fish about 1 cup dry white wine, sprinkle with salt and plenty of freshly ground black pepper, and dot with about ⅜ pound butter.

Place in pre-heated oven and bake, basting occasionally, until opaque through, about 25 minutes. Then baste once more and place under hot grill to brown quickly and lightly. Sprinkle with finely chopped parsley, garnish with quartered lemons, and serve at once with plain boiled and buttered new potatoes.

## FISH AND MUSHROOM CUSTARD
*[Pre-heat oven to 450°]*

| | |
|---|---|
| 8 large fresh flounder | 1½ cups heavy cream |
| 8 shallots | ½ teaspoon cayenne |
| 2 tablespoons chopped parsley | ¼ pound butter |
| 1 pound fresh mushrooms | salt, pepper |
| 6 eggs | ½ cup dry white wine |

SERVES 6–8

Ask your fishmonger to fillet 8 large fresh flounder. Wash and pat dry on paper towel. Peel and chop fine 8 large shallots, or substitute 4 tablespoons chopped Bermuda onion. Prepare 2 tablespoons chopped parsley. Wash, stem, peel, and chop fine 1 pound fresh mushrooms. Butter 2 rectangular baking-dishes, 10″ by 6″ by 2″. Break 6 eggs into a small bowl, and pour over them 1½ cups heavy cream. Sprinkle with a scant ½ teaspoon cayenne.

Melt ¼ pound butter in frying-pan. Cook the shallots in this until just beginning to brown lightly, then add the mushrooms and cook slowly, stirring constantly, until they form their juice and boil down again (about 5 minutes). Season lightly with a very little salt and coarsely ground black pepper. Remove from fire and place in a small bowl until ready to use.

When ready to cook the fish, place 4 fillets in each buttered baking-dish. Cover equally with mushrooms, cover the mushrooms with the remaining fillets, and pour over each dish ¼ cup cold water and ¼ cup dry white wine. Sprinkle lightly with salt and pepper, cover with aluminum foil, and place in pre-heated hot oven. Cook until the fish is white and opaque, about 20 minutes. Remove from oven, discard the foil, and, disturbing the fish as little as possible, drain off or ladle off the juice into a small pan. Reduce this juice by boiling rapidly until only 1 cup.

Now, using a rotary-beater, beat the eggs and cream together and add gradually the reduced fish stock. Sprinkle the fish with the chopped parsley and pour over all the egg-and-cream mixture, dividing it equally. Place the dishes in a shallow pan of hot water and cook in oven until set through like custard and lightly browned on top, about 15 minutes. Serve at once.

## LEE ERICKSON'S FISH AND DILL SOUFFLE
*[Pre-heat oven to 375°]*

1 cup freshly grated imported Parmesan cheese

1½ pounds fresh halibut, or fillets of flounder

1 onion

1 tablespoon tarragon vinegar

10 peppercorns

1 large bunch fresh dill

salt, pepper

4½ tablespoons flour

4 tablespoons butter

1¾ cups milk

6 eggs

1 tablespoon Worcestershire sauce

SERVES 6–8

Butter a large round, 2½-quart-size, baking-dish. Remove tough stems from dill, keeping only perfect green feathery part. Wash and pat dry in paper towel. Cut fine with scissors. Wash fish in cold water and cook ever so gently for about 10 minutes in court boullion made of 2 cups water, 10 peppercorns, 1 teaspoon salt, and 1 tablespoon tarragon vinegar. Cool in its juice.

Separate yolks from whites of 6 eggs. Now make a smooth cream sauce, using 4 tablespoons butter, 4½ tablespoons all-purpose flour, and 1¾ cups hot milk. Season to taste with salt, coarsely ground black pepper, and 1 tablespoon Worcestershire sauce. Remove from fire and stir in 1 cup freshly grated imported Parmesan cheese, mixing well. Beat yolks of eggs until very light and stir into mixture. Last of all add the cut dill.

Drain fish, discard skin, and remove flesh carefully from bones. Place fish in baking-dish. Now beat the whites of eggs until stiff, but not dry, and fold carefully into dill mixture. Pour carefully over fish in baking-dish. Place dish in shallow pan of hot water and bake 40–45 minutes in pre-heated oven, by which time it should be a beautiful golden brown. Serve at once with creamed chopped string beans (page 265).

## LOBSTER MAYONNAISE COMME A PARIS

3–4 pounds cold boiled lobster
3 cups mayonnaise
1 cup chopped water cress

1 tablespoon chopped fresh
    tarragon
6 tomatoes

SERVES 6–8

Pack a glass bowl in another bowl of chopped ice. Arrange in it first a bed of 2 cups mayonnaise mixed with 1 cup very finely chopped water cress and 1 tablespoon chopped fresh tarragon. Then arrange 2–3 pounds cold boiled lobster that has been removed from shell and cut with silver knife in uniform pieces.

Cover with a coating of 1 cup plain mayonnaise and another layer of the most perfect slices of lobster, using the balance of the lobster (about 1 pound). Garnish with peeled and quartered tomatoes that have been well chilled. Serve with French or Italian bread and a very well-chilled white wine.

## LOBSTER MOUSSE SURPRISE

6 pounds (live) lobster
4 pounds fresh halibut
12 egg whites
1 pint heavy cream
2 carrots
bouquet of parsley, thyme,
    bay leaf
4 onions
4 cups water

14 tablespoons butter
1 cup olive oil
½ cup cognac
½ cup white wine
2 tablespoons tomato paste
2 cups fish stock
2 dozen fresh mushrooms
juice of 1 lemon
2 tablespoons flour

SERVES 6–8

Remove the skin and bones from 4 pounds fresh halibut and set them aside. Put the flesh through a meat-chopper, add the whites of 12 raw eggs, and put through a very fine sieve. Mix well with a wooden spoon until quite thick, then salt and pepper, and gradually add 1 pint heavy cream. Place this in the refrigerator.

Put the fish skins and bones into a little enamel pan, and add 2 carrots cut up fine, a little parsley, thyme, bay leaf, 2 onions, 4 cups water. Let simmer gently.

Cut up lobsters while still alive. This is done by inserting a sharp knife in their backs between the body and tail shells, severing the spinal cords. Then with a hammer and strong knife chop off the claws and split lengthwise. When this is accomplished, remove the stomachs and intestinal canals. Put 4 tablespoons butter into a large iron frying-pan and pour in 1 cup olive oil. When it is hot, put in the lobsters and their claws and cook until they turn red all over. Then add 2 onions, chopped fine, ½ cup cognac, ½ cup white wine, 2 tablespoons tomato paste, 2 cups of the liquid from the fish bones and skins, a pinch of thyme, another bay leaf, a sprig of parsley, and a little salt and pepper. Simmer for 18–20 minutes.

In the meantime, peel 2 dozen mushrooms, wash well, and slice fine. Put ¼ pound butter into an enamel pan and add the juice of 1 lemon and ½ cup water; cook the mushrooms in this 3 minutes. Drain the juice into the lobsters and save the mushrooms.

When the lobsters are done, carefully pick out all the meat and slice it in fairly large pieces. Take all the shells of the lobsters, pound in a mortar until well crushed, put in the sauce and continue to simmer while you start the finished sauce. Melt 2 tablespoons butter, add 2 tablespoons flour gradually, and then the strained lobster sauce. Simmer until quite thick, then add the lobster meat and the mushrooms.

Butter well a 2-quart mold and with a spatula carefully line the bottom and sides of the mold with an inch thickness of the halibut paste. Keep out enough paste to cover the top of the mold with an inch thickness also. Now carefully fill the center of the mold with the lobster and enough of the juice to fill the mold within 1 inch of the top. Take the rest of the paste and carefully spread it to completely enclose the lobsters. Now place the mold in a baking-pan of cold water and put it on the stove to heat. When it boils, place in a *pre-heated hot* 400°–450°

*oven* to set, 25–30 minutes. Empty it out carefully onto a hot platter and pour around it any of the sauce which you may have left over. Garnish with sprigs of parsley and serve at once.

## BANGKOK CURRIED LOBSTER

6–8 small 1¼-pound lobsters     saffron rice (page 218)
onion sauce (page 218)     genuine Madras curry paste
Side Dishes (page 218)

SERVES 6–8

This dish follows the same pattern of preparation as Brian's Bang-kok curried chicken (page 217). It is accompanied by the same saffron-flavored rice and the same side dishes. Buy 6–8 small live lobsters weighing about 1¼ pounds each and boil them in the usual manner. Cool and split; remove meat and remove intestinal vein from tail; and spread with a generous quantity of genuine Madras curry paste. Cut in bite-sized pieces. Make the same onion sauce as for the chicken recipe using ¼ pound butter, 2 generous cups chopped Bermuda onions, 3 tablespoons of cornstarch, and 2 cans clear chicken broth. When the sauce is cooked add the lobster coated with the curry paste, and simmer just long enough to heat thoroughly. Serve with saffron rice.

## LOBSTER AND SHRIMP
## WITH MUSHROOM-AND-DILL SAUCE

2 pounds fresh shrimp     1 teaspoon salt
2 1½-pound lobsters     1 tablespoon prepared mus-
1 large bunch dill         tard
1 pound fresh mushrooms     ⅔ cup olive oil
1 teaspoon cracked pepper     1 cup dry white Vermouth

SERVES 6–8

Boil lobsters and shrimp in the usual way (page 101). Shell and clean the shrimp and when cool refrigerate. Shell the lobsters, remove meat, and rinse off all the green with cold water, and refrigerate. Wash, dry, peel, and slice 1 pound small, fresh, firm mushrooms in not-too-thin slices. Wash, dry, and cut fine fresh dill until you have ½ cup. Now in small bowl place 1 teaspoon cracked pepper, 1 teaspoon salt, 1 tablespoon prepared mustard. Mix together and add gradually ⅔ cup olive oil; add the dill and stir; and last of all add gradually 1 cup dry white Vermouth. Pour over the sliced mushrooms and allow to marinate at room temperature at least 2 hours.

When ready to serve the shrimp and lobster, cut the lobster with silver knife in ½-inch slices and add to the shrimp. Place in chilled serving-dish and pour the mushroom sauce over all. Send to table to be eaten with plenty of hot crisp French bread and fresh whipped butter. This dish followed by gnocchi (page 65) or cheese soufflé (page 66), with fruit for dessert, would make a lovely lunch.

## LOBSTER THERMIDOR

[Pre-heat oven to 350°]

6–8 1½-pound live lobsters
2 cups crumbled cooked plain pastry
½ cup brandy
4 tablespoons butter
4 tablespoons flour

1½ cups milk
1 tablespoon imported prepared mustard
salt, pepper
¼ teaspoon cayenne

SERVES 6–8

First mix, roll out, and bake some plain pie crust—make half the recipe on page 362. When it cools, crumble it in not-too-small bits. Boil 6–8 live lobsters, weighing about 1½ pounds each. Cool and with a sharp knife slit center of thin undershell from head to tail. Spread open, remove the meat from the tail in 1 piece, and remove the intestinal vein. Remove claws, crack them, and remove meat. Wash out the lobster shells thoroughly. Cut the lobster meat in small pieces.

Pour over the lobster meat ½ cup brandy and refrigerate while you make a cream sauce in the usual way, melting 4 tablespoons butter, gradually adding 4 tablespoons flour, and then adding 1½ cups hot milk. Stir in 1 tablespoon prepared mustard, preferable imported, and season to taste with salt, freshly ground pepper, and about ¼ teaspoon cayenne. Fold in the lobster meat and brandy and fill the shells. Sprinkle copiously with crumbled pastry. *Pre-heat oven to moderate 350°–375°*. Place the lobsters side by side on broiling-pan which you have spread with aluminum foil. Bake in oven until heated through and lightly browned, 5–10 minutes, and serve.

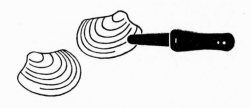

## SCALLOPED OYSTERS
*[Pre-heat oven to 400°]*

| | |
|---|---|
| 30 shelled oysters and their juice | 4 cloves |
| 2½ cups coarse, lightly browned bread crumbs | 1 bay leaf |
| | juice of 1 lemon |
| pinch of thyme | ¼ pound butter |
| pinch of ground mace | milk, if necessary |
| pinch of cayenne | 1 cup light cream |
| 2–3 tablespoons chopped parsley | salt, coarsely ground black pepper |

SERVES 6–8

Buy 30 freshly shelled oysters. Pick them over carefully to be sure there are no bits of shell; then strain the juice through a fine textured cloth to remove any sand.

Prepare 2½ cups coarse, lightly browned bread crumbs. Put ½ cup bread crumbs in a small frying-pan with 2 tablespoons butter; stir over low flame until the crumbs are well buttered.

Prepare 2 heaping tablespoons chopped parsley. Now butter a shallow 2-quart ovenproof glass or earthenware dish.

About ½ hour before serving the oysters, pre-heat oven. Now sprinkle about ⅔ cup *unbuttered* crumbs over the bottom of the buttered dish. Lay on this bed 15 oysters, cover with ⅔ cup *unbuttered* crumbs, sprinkle with half the chopped parsley, dot with 2 tablespoons butter; sprinkle with a very little salt, some coarsely ground black pepper, a pinch of cayenne, a pinch of thyme, and a pinch of ground mace. Lay 1 small bay leaf and 4 cloves in the center, and squeeze a little lemon juice over all. Make another layer of oysters, using the balance. Repeat the seasoning process. Cover with another ⅔ cup of *unbuttered* crumbs and dot with 2 tablespoons butter. Now pour over the oysters and crumbs the strained oyster juice (there should be 1½ cups; make up the difference with milk if insufficient). Besides this, pour over all 1 cup light cream, or rich milk. It will look too wet, but the crumbs will absorb it all. At the very last cover the top with the reserved *buttered* crumbs. Cover the dish with aluminum foil and place in oven. Bake until the oysters are bubbling hot through, 10–15 minutes, at which time remove the foil and allow to bake until lightly browned. The baking will take in all 20–25 minutes. Be careful not to overcook, which would toughen the oysters. Serve at once.

## HOT BOILED SALMON
## WITH HORSE-RADISH CREAM

| | |
|---|---|
| 1 4-pound cut of fresh salmon | pinch of sugar |
| Court Bouillon: | parsley |
| 2 cups dry white wine | 1 tablespoon vinegar |
| 1 teaspoon salt | 1 sliced white onion |
| 1 carrot | pinch of salt |
| 3 cups heavy cream | 6–8 tablespoons of horse-radish |

SERVES 6–8

Wrap a 4-pound cut of fresh salmon (preferably from the center of the fish) in a double piece of cheesecloth, and tie the ends with string. Place in pan just big enough to hold it, and cover it completely with warm (not hot) court bouillon (page 77), made of water, 2 cups dry white wine, 1 teaspoon salt, 1 carrot, a little parsley, 1 tablespoon vinegar, and 1 sliced white onion. Place fish in bouillon on fire, bring slowly to the simmering point, and simmer for about 30 minutes.

In the meantime put 3 cups heavy cream in an enamel pan and reduce it to 1 cup by letting it just barely simmer on a low flame. Stir it frequently. When it has reduced, place in double boiler on back of stove over low flame. When ready to serve, add a pinch of sugar, a pinch of salt, and 6–8 tablespoons grated horse-radish (preferably fresh).

When the salmon is cooked, drain it well and remove the cheesecloth. Pull off all the skin carefully, place on hot platter, garnish with lemon and parsley, and serve at once, accompanied by a sauce boat of horse-radish cream and, if possible, boiled potatoes. The same fish and the same sauce, served ice cold, are equally delicious. Canned salmon may be substituted for the fresh, but it must be drained of all its oil before using.

## BORSCH SALMON NATASHA

2 small 4½-ounce cans tomato paste
4 1-pound cans whole beets
2 12-ounce cans tomato juice
2 tablespoons Worcestershire sauce
juice of 2 lemons
celery salt and pepper
3 tablespoons olive oil
1 large bunch fresh dill
2 cups finely chopped radishes
2 cups chopped peeled cu-cumbers

2 cups diced peeled tomatoes
2 cups chopped parsley, spring onions, and chives *combined*
6 hard-boiled eggs, chopped fine
1 bottle capers
2 cups sour cream
8 slices thin-sliced pumper-nickel bread
5 pounds fresh salmon (center cut)
court bouillon (page 77)

SERVES 6–8

This especially good recipe was contributed by Marion Dorn, who says that I am the culprit who has made her conceited about her cooking. More of her recipes are scattered throughout this book—which proves that I think she is an inspired cook and has every right to be conceited. She goes on to say that advice as to timing is overlooked in many books—such advice is incredibly important to ladies who both work and cook. One of the joys of this dish—strictly a summer dish—is that it is practically a meal in itself and at least half of the work entailed may be done the day before. Briefly, it is a cold beet soup lavishly garnished with fresh salmon and a variety of chopped raw vegetables and topped with dill and sour cream.

The day before cook a 5-pound center cut of fresh salmon, following direction for boiled fish (page 77). Cool in its court bouillon and refrigerate until ready to serve. Next, blend 2 small cans tomato paste into the juice from 4 1-pound cans whole beets. Flavor with 2 tablespoons Worcestershire sauce, juice of 2 lemons, celery salt and coarsely ground black pepper to taste, 2 table-spoons pickled horse-radish, and 3 tablespoons olive oil. Add 2 cans beets, chopped very fine. Thin mixture to desired thick-soup consistency with about 2 cans tomato juice. Refrigerate until ready to serve.

The afternoon of the day you serve the dish, prepare 2 cups finely chopped radishes (do not peel), 2 cups chopped, peeled cucumbers, 2 cups diced, peeled tomatoes (minus seeds), 2 cups chopped parsley, spring onions, and cut chives *combined*. Wash, pat dry, and cut fine 1 large bunch fresh dill. Empty contents of 1 bottle capers into a small bowl. Refrigerate all of the above ingredients in separate containers until ready to serve. Also hard boil 6 eggs, which are to be shelled and chopped fine shortly before serving.

It is now time to describe how this pretty one-dish feast should be served. Required are a large soup tureen, ladle, and 8 extra-large soup plates (which ideally would be placed in even larger bowls that are filled with crushed ice). In any case, the dish must be served cold. The foundation soup of beets and tomato should be served from the soup tureen—the soup being covered at the last moment with a shower of cut fresh dill. The salmon should be placed in the center of a large oval serving-platter, all skin and bones having been previously carefully removed. Around this in neat separate piles place the chopped eggs; radishes; tomatoes; spring onions, parsley, and chives; cucumbers; and capers. A portion of the salmon is placed in the center of the soup in each soup plate and a selection of any or all of the accompaniments are then placed around the salmon. Pass a bowl of sour cream, which is the final touch, at this point, followed by a plate of thinly sliced pumpernickel bread.

## SALMON COULIBIAC

**Pastry:**

1 cup all-purpose flour
1 3-ounce package cream cheese
¼ pound sweet butter
1 egg yolk

**Filling:**

2 cups (1½ pounds) boiled fresh salmon
2 hard-boiled eggs
½ cup finely cut fresh dill

juice of 1 lemon
¼ pound fresh mushrooms
6 small shallots
2 cups flaky cooked long-grain rice
12 tablespoons butter
½ tablespoon cracked pepper
¼ teaspoon cayenne
2 teaspoons curry powder

The night before, mix the pastry. Sift 1 cup all-purpose flour into a bowl. Work into this with finger tips ¼ pound sweet butter. Add 3 ounces cream cheese, and using a large silver fork, work the cheese into the flour and butter until you can gather it all together in a ball. Wrap in wax paper, press into rectangle, and refrigerate overnight. When ready to make the Coulibiac, remove pastry from refrigerator and allow to remain at room temperature while you prepare the filling.

Remove tough stems from ¼ pound fresh mushrooms. Wash and dry caps and chop fine. Peel and chop fine 6 small shallots. Cook them gently in 2 tablespoons butter in small frying-pan for about 1 minute, then add mushrooms and simmer 5 minutes.

Season lightly with salt; cool. Prepare ½ cup finely cut fresh dill. Cook ½ cup flaky long-grain rice, following directions on box, which will give you about 2 cups. Boil 2 eggs gently for 12 minutes. Plunge into cold water, remove shells, and chop fine. Have ready 2 cups boiled salmon.

Now *pre-heat the oven to a very hot 500°*. Butter a cookie sheet lightly. Cut pastry in half and roll out separately into 2 rectangular sheets approximately 13″ by 9″, making one slightly larger than the other. Place smaller one over center of cookie sheet. Then spread about ¾ of the rice over pastry keeping within 1 inch of the edge. Place 2 cups boiled salmon in bowl and squeeze over it the juice of 1 lemon; season with ½ teaspoon cracked pepper, ¼ teaspoon cayenne, and a little salt. Spread salmon over the rice. Sprinkle with ¼ cup cut dill; then cover with chopped eggs, salt lightly, and dot with 4 tablespoons butter. Cover with mushrooms, another ¼ cup cut dill, and the remainder of the rice. Moisten edges of pastry on cookie sheet with water; then roll larger piece of pastry up on rolling-pin, and unroll over the whole. Press edges of top-and-bottom pastry together and roll up, making neat rolled edge. Mark edge with prongs of fork; cut 3 deep vents in top to allow steam to escape. Paint with beaten yolk of 1 egg. Place in pre-heated very hot oven and reduce heat immediately to slow 250°. Bake for 25 minutes, or until a golden brown and sizzling hot. Have ready 6 tablespoons melted butter, into which you have stirred 2 teaspoons curry powder. Pour this down into the 3 vents in pastry. Transfer with aid of spatula to hot platter and serve at once. Cut with sharp knife in 8 squares, and serve with pie knife.

## BAY SCALLOPS ALMONDINE

| | |
|---|---|
| 3 pounds small fresh bay scallops | salt, pepper |
| ¾ cup almonds | 1 cup flour |
| ¾ pound butter | 2 tablespoons chopped parsley |
| | 2 lemons |

SERVES 6–8

Wash 3 pounds bay scallops quickly in cold water and dry thoroughly on a tea cloth. Blanch ¾ pound almonds by pouring boiling water over them and letting them soak 3 minutes; drain and pinch off their skins; slice lengthwise in thin slivers and spread out to dry on paper towel. Clarify ¾ pound butter (page 290). Place ⅓ of the clarified butter in a small enamel pan, add the almonds, and let them cook over low flame until they begin to brown lightly. Remove from fire immediately.

When ready to cook the scallops place the remainder of the butter in 2 large, heavy iron frying-pans, dividing it equally. Season about 1 cup flour with a scant ½ teaspoon salt and ¼ teaspoon coarsely ground pepper; sift half of it over 2 sheets of wax paper. Spread the scallops out on these and sprinkle with other half of flour mixture. Avoid handling the scallops but coat them lightly all over with the seasoned flour by lifting the paper and rolling the scallops around. Heat the butter in the 2 pans to sizzling hot. Empty the scallops into a coarse sieve and gently shake off excess flour, and then distribute them equally over the bottoms of the frying-pans so that they are only 1 layer deep. Cook the scallops over moderate heat about 12 minutes, shaking the pans frequently so that the scallops brown on all sides. If they won't shake loose, use a spatula; but the less they are handled, the better. When done, place on hot platter, being sure to include all the nice brown crumbs from the pans. Reheat the butter and almonds quickly and pour over all. Garnish with 2 tablespoons chopped parsley and 2 quartered lemons, and serve at once.

## PLAIN BOILED SHRIMP

3-4 pounds fresh shrimp      parsley
salt, peppercorns      few stalks celery
pinch of thyme

SERVES 6-8

Wash 3-4 pounds shrimp in cold water. Have ready an enamel pan of boiling water flavored with salt, peppercorns, a pinch of thyme, a bit of parsley, and a few stalks of celery. Drop the shrimp into the boiling water and cook until they have turned pink, about 15 minutes. Drain and plunge into cold water. Pull off shells, and with a sharp little knife carefully remove the intestinal vein, which runs along the back from head to tail. As you clean them, dip them into a bowl of cold water and out again to wash off every last bit of black. Place in refrigerator in a covered crock until ready to serve.

## SHAD ROE MOUSSE

| Mousse: | Sauce: |
|---|---|
| 2 pounds fresh halibut | ¼ pound butter |
| 3 pair shad roe | ¾ cup flour |
| 10 tablespoons butter | 3 cups fish stock |
| 1 onion chopped fine | 2 egg yolks |
| bouquet of parsley | ¾ cup heavy cream |
| bay leaf | 1 cup sherry |
| pinch of thyme | juice of 1 lemon |
| 6 peppercorns | paprika |
| 1 cup white wine | |
| 6 egg whites | |
| salt, pepper | |
| 3 cups heavy cream | |
| 1 small can pimientos | |

SERVES 6–8

Remove the flesh only from 2 pounds halibut and put the bones, odd bits, and skin into an enamel saucepan with 2 tablespoons butter, 1 onion, chopped fine, a little bouquet of parsley, a bay leaf, a tiny pinch of thyme, 6 peppercorns, 3 cups water, and 1 cup white wine. Put on the fire to simmer—this liquid is to be used later in making the sauce. Put the raw fish through the meat-grinder, add the unbeaten whites of 6 eggs, and mash the combination through a very fine sieve. Add some salt and pepper and stir well until it thickens up a bit, then gradually add 2 cups heavy cream.

In the meantime cook for about 20 minutes 3 pairs shad roe slowly in a frying-pan with ¼ pound butter. Carefully remove the skin and veins. Mash the roe lightly and add it to the halibut paste. Mix well, add 1 cup heavy cream, and then season to taste.

Butter 2 medium-size fish-shaped molds and decorate the bottoms with strips of red pimiento. Fill the molds with the mousse, packing it well to get down into all the crevices. Set the molds in the refrigerator and keep there *until* 40 minutes before serving. At that time place the molds in a pan of hot water, cover with a piece of buttered typewriter paper, and set in a *pre-heated moderate 400° oven* to cook.

In the meantime, make the foundation for your sauce by putting ½ cup butter into an enamel pan to melt. Stir in ¾ cup flour and cook a minute or two without browning. Gradually add the strained fish stock (there should be about 3 cups). Continue to cook in top of double boiler until ready to serve. Then add 2 egg yolks that have been beaten up with ¾ cup heavy cream. Stir continuously and make sure it doesn't cook any more. At the last moment add salt and pepper to taste, a little paprika, and stir in 1 cup good sherry and juice of 1 lemon. Pour sauce around the mousses, which have been very carefully emptied from their molds onto warm platters. Garnish and serve at once.

## BROILED SHRIMP
### [Pre-heat broiler]

3 pounds shrimp
¾ pound sweet butter
1 cup olive oil
2 tablespoons chopped shallots
3 cloves garlic
juice 1 lemon
salt, freshly ground black pepper
1 cup dry white wine
chopped parsley

SERVES 6–8

Wash 3 pounds shrimp in cold water. Then with little scissors snip the shells open from head to tail, along the center of their backs, and devein, leaving the shells intact. This is definitely a bore, but absolutely necessary. When finished, rinse them once more in cold water and dry well. Now pour ¾ pound melted sweet butter mixed with 1 cup olive oil over the bottom of a flat ovenproof glass platter. Sprinkle the dish with 2 heaping tablespoons chopped shallots and 3 cloves garlic, also chopped fine. Now place the shrimps on the platter, rolling them over in the butter and oil so that they are well buttered and so that they are not one on top of each other. Squeeze the juice of 1 lemon over them.

Broil shrimp for 5 minutes; then sprinkle them lightly with salt and heavily with freshly ground black pepper; turn them over and broil them 5 minutes longer, being sure they are near enough the flame so that they actually brown lightly. Remove from broiler, sprinkle lightly with salt and heavily with pepper, and pour over them ½ cup dry white wine, reduced from 1 cup by simmering. Place under grill again for just a few seconds and then remove from grill and sprinkle with chopped parsley. Serve at once with plenty of French or Italian bread. Provide finger bowls with rose geranium or lemon, if possible, as the shrimp should be eaten with the fingers (the shells have to be removed) and are definitely messy—but, oh, so good!

## SHRIMP COOKED IN BEER WITH DILL

5 pounds fresh shrimp
2 cans beer
2 dozen peppercorns

1 large bunch fresh dill
home-made mayonnaise

SERVES 6–8

Wash 5 pounds fresh shrimp in cold water; place in large enamel pan. Wash a large bunch of dill, and shake and pat dry on a cloth. Cut off and save the feathery green part; cover the shrimp with the coarse stems of the dill. Pour over the shrimp 2 cans beer. Add 2 dozen whole peppercorns. Cover pan with folded towel and top with cover. Place over moderate heat and bring slowly to a boil. Continue cooking 10 minutes longer. Remove from stove, remove cloth, then cover partially, and allow the shrimp to cool in their juice.

When cold, place in refrigerator until ready to prepare them for serving. Have ready 2 tablespoons or more of the reserved feathery dill, cut fine with scissors, and a bowl of finely crushed ice. Drain the shrimp, remove shells and devein. Place on ice and sprinkle with the cut dill. Serve at once with home-made mayonnaise (page 320), into which you have stirred 2 scant teaspoons dry mustard and which you have thinned slightly with the strained juice of ½ lemon. Accompany with crisp French bread.

## SHRIMP IN CREAM WITH HOMINY

| | |
|---|---|
| 1 onion | 2 tablespoons salt |
| 1 clove garlic | 3–4 pounds shrimp |
| 1 bay leaf | 3–4 tablespoons butter |
| pinch of thyme | 2–3 cups heavy cream |
| ½ red-pepper pod | salt, freshly ground black pepper |
| 2 stalks celery | per |
| hominy grits (page 272) | 2 strips lemon peel |
| 1 tablespoon lemon juice | |

SERVES 6–8

Simmer together for 15 minutes 2 quarts water, 1 onion, 1 clove garlic, 1 bay leaf, a pinch of thyme, ½ hot red-pepper pod, 2 stalks celery, and 2 tablespoons salt. Cook in this bouillon 3–4 pounds well-washed shrimp for 10 minutes. Let the shrimp cool in the liquid, then shell them, and remove the black veins. Put them in a saucepan with 3–4 tablespoons butter. Heat until the butter has melted; add 2–3 cups of heavy cream, a little salt, plenty of fresh, coarsely ground black pepper. Add 2 strips lemon peel. Simmer 4 minutes and add 1 tablespoon lemon juice. When this boils up once, serve in a hot dish. Accompany with hominy grits (page 272); to be eaten from soup plates.

## SHRIMP WITH CUCUMBER JELLY

| | |
|---|---|
| 6–8 tender cucumbers | ½ teaspoon white pepper |
| 2 small white onions, grated | 2 envelopes gelatin |
| strained juice of 2 lemons | 3–4 pounds of cooked shrimp |
| 2 teaspoons salt | 1¾ cups boiling water |

SERVES 6–8

Peel 6–8 tender cucumbers (according to size). Score 2 cucumbers horizontally with the prongs of a fork, then slice them very thin. Place in a bowl of ice water (no salt please), cover tightly, and chill in refrigerator for several hours.

Grate the rest of the cucumbers until you have 4 cupfuls of pulp, including all the juice. Add to this the juice from 2 small grated white onions, the strained juice of 2 lemons; and season to taste with about 2 teaspoons salt and ½ teaspoon white pepper.

Soak 2 envelopes gelatin in ½ cup cold water, and when it has softened, add to it 1¾ cups boiling water. Cool and add the cucumber pulp, mix well, and pour into a ring mold large enough to hold it all (1½- to 2-quart size).

Cover with heavy wax paper and place in refrigerator to set firm for at least 2 hours. When ready to serve, turn out onto a large, round serving-plate and garnish the outer edge of the dish with the well-drained (now crisp) sliced cucumbers. Fill the center with 3–4 pounds carefully cooked and cleaned, well-chilled shrimp, dressed at the last moment with herb dressing (page 319), or water-cress dressing (page 318). Serve immediately on chilled plates. Accompany this dish with thin buttered slices of brown or pumpernickel bread.

## BRIAN CONNELY'S RICE AND SHRIMP WITH DILL

*[Pre-heat oven to 450°]*

| | |
|---|---|
| 2 cups uncooked long-grain rice | 2 pounds shrimp |
| 6 tablespoons butter | Hollandaise Sauce (page 300) |
| salt, pepper | 3 tablespoons finely cut dill |

SERVES 6–8

Boil, shell, and clean 2 pounds fresh shrimp. Split the shrimp in two lengthwise. Cook 2 cups long-grain rice in 3 quarts boiling water about 18 minutes until just barely tender through. Drain thoroughly. Season with 4 tablespoons butter and about ¼ tea-

spoon coarsely ground pepper. Make full quantity of Hollandaise
(page 300). Prepare 3 tablespoons finely cut fresh dill.

Bury the shrimp in alternate layers of rice in buttered baking-
dish, sprinkling as you go along with 3 tablespoons finely cut fresh
dill. Dot with 2 tablespoons butter. Cover with aluminum foil.
Bake the rice and shrimp for 25–30 minutes. Heat the Hollandaise over hot water, stirring constantly, until warm, but not
hot, pour over the rice and shrimp. Place under broiler for a
second or two to brown lightly and serve at once.

## BROILED FRESH SWORDFISH WITH
## BUTTER AND WORCESTERSHIRE SAUCE
*[Pre-heat broiler to 375°]*

|  | Sauce: |
|---|---|
| 4 pounds fresh swordfish, cut 1½″ thick | ⅜ pound butter |
| ¼ pound butter | 3 tablespoons Worcestershire sauce |
| ¼ teaspoon coarsely ground pepper |  |
| ½ teaspoon salt |  |
| 2 lemons |  |

SERVES 6–8

Line a shallow broiling-pan, 14" by 10" by 1¼", with aluminum foil. Grease foil with 2 tablespoons soft butter. Place on foil 4 pounds fresh swordfish, cut 1½" thick. Spread with 6 tablespoons butter and sprinkle with 1 teaspoon salt and ¼ teaspoon coarsely ground pepper. Place pan 3 inches away from broiling-unit and broil slowly for 35–40 minutes, or until opaque through, basting frequently with the butter drippings. Increase heat to 450° the last five minutes to brown fish well.

Lift carefully onto hot platter, pour drippings over the fish, garnish with 2 quartered lemons, and serve at once with potatoes and butter-and-Worcestershire sauce (made by melting ⅜ pound butter in a saucepan, then adding 3 tablespoons Worcestershire sauce, and heating both together for a few seconds).

## ELEANOR'S FRIED SWORDFISH STEAKS WITH PIMIENTO-AND-GREEN-OLIVE SAUCE

| | |
|---|---|
| 2 fresh 2-pound swordfish steaks, cut 1¼" thick | ¼ teaspoon coarsely ground pepper |
| 2 4½-ounce bottles pimiento-stuffed green olives | ¼ teaspoon salt |
| | 2 cups heavy cream |
| | ¼ pound butter, and more |

Drain 2 4½-ounce bottles pimiento-stuffed green olives. Chop moderately fine. Melt ¼ pound butter in large iron frying-pan, and when sizzling hot add two 1¼-inch-thick swordfish steaks, weighing approximately 2 pounds each. Cook 10 minutes over moderate heat, by which time the fish will have started to brown lightly. Cut each steak in two and turn carefully with spatula. Sprinkle lightly with about ¼ teaspoon coarsely ground pepper and ¼ teaspoon salt. Continue cooking for 10 minutes on second side. Add 2 additional tablespoons butter at this point if needed to prevent sticking. Turn once more and cook until well browned on bottom, about 5 minutes longer. Place fish on very hot serving-platter and keep warm. Add the chopped olives to brown  juice in pan and stir in 1 cup heavy cream. Bring to boiling point and stir in 1 cup heavy cream. Heat again to boiling point, stirring constantly, but do not allow to boil. Pour over the fish. Serve fish at once with boiled potatoes.

## ROSE VISHINO'S FRESH TUNA STEAKS
*[Pre-heat oven to 400°]*

8 fresh 6-ounce tuna steaks, cut 1 inch thick
3 dozen small, ripe red plum tomatoes (or 2-pound, 3-ounce can)
1 large Bermuda onion
1 cup of fish stock
3 tablespoons butter

¼ teaspoon dried basil
¼ teaspoon marjoram
¼ teaspoon savory
salt, pepper
⅛ teaspoon cayenne
1 cup white wine
1 tablespoon chopped parsley

SERVES 6–8

Wash and pat dry 8 individual fresh tuna steaks, weighing about 6 ounces each. Cut away skin and bones. Make 1 cup fish stock with the bones and skin. Butter a large earthenware or oven-proof glass casserole. Place the steaks in the casserole. Peel and chop coarsely 1 large Bermuda onion. Sprinkle it over the fish. Peel 3 dozen small ripe red plum tomatoes and cut them in half, or substitute a 2-pound, 3-ounce can. Cover the fish with the tomatoes. Season with about 1½ teaspoons salt, ½ teaspoon coarsely ground pepper, ¼ teaspoon cayenne, and ¼ teaspoon each of dried basil, marjoram, and savory. Dot with 3 tablespoons butter. Pour over this 1 cup fish stock.

Place uncovered in hot oven until it comes to boiling point, about 20 minutes; then pour over it 1 cup white wine. Cover the casserole, reduce heat to 375°, and continue cooking for about 1¼ hours longer. Remove the cover the last 20 minutes and allow the top to brown lightly. Garnish with 1 tablespoon chopped parsley. Serve with buttered string beans and little new potatoes (peeled, boiled, and sprinkled with paprika).

# FISH IN ASPIC WITH WATER-CRESS SAUCE

Aspic:

⅛ pound chopped onion
small bunch soup greens (parsley, chervil, tarragon, thyme, bay leaf)
1½ pounds shin of beef
1½ pounds knuckle of veal
¼ cup cognac
1 bottle dry white wine
1 calf's foot
½ pound ham
2 chicken giblets
1½ pounds lean beef

1 pound crabmeat
2 2½-pound lobsters
3 dozen medium size shrimps
1 tablespoon salt
2 peppercorns
salt, pepper
tart French dressing
chopped water cress

SERVES 6–8

The classic aspic must be made the day before. Also, lobsters, shrimp, and crabmeat should be ordered the day before, so that they may be delivered early on the day you are serving the dish.

Put in the bottom of large soup pot ⅛ pound chopped onion and a small bunch of soup greens, consisting of parsley, chervil, tarragon, thyme, and bay leaf. Add 1½ pounds shin of beef and 1½ pounds knuckle of veal, both cut in pieces. Put this on a moderate fire and sear lightly, then wet with ¼ cup cognac and 1 bottle dry white wine, and let simmer gently for a while. Then add 3 quarts water, 1 calf's foot that has been washed, cracked, and brought to a boil in a separate pot of water, and ½ pound ham that has also been brought to a boil separately. Before the liquid in the large soup pot actually boils, skim very carefully; when it does boil, cover and put it on the back of the stove on a low flame and let simmer for 5 hours, never letting it really boil. Next strain the mixture in the pot through a fine sieve and then let this stock get perfectly cold so that the fat may be removed.

Now pound 2 chicken giblets and 1½ pounds lean beef, cut in squares. Put into a big pot, then pour in the stock (previously strained through cheesecloth). This done, set pot on the fire and stir constantly with a beater until the stock boils. Put it on the back of the stove and let it simmer almost imperceptibly for 25 minutes or so. At the end of this time pass through a clean, wet linen napkin. (If aspic is then not clear enough, clear in this manner. For each pint of stock use 1 egg white. Beat the whites slightly until broken up or foamy, add 1 wineglass sherry, or dry white wine. Pour all this into the cool stock, place on the stove again and bring very slowly to a boil, stirring all the time with an egg whisk. Then allow it to simmer on the back of the stove for 10–15 minutes. Pour once more through a wet piece of linen. In other words, make a perfectly clear aspic.) A slightly less difficult clear aspic may be made (page 110), but double the recipe.

The fish part is easier. Order 1 pound crabmeat, 2 2½-pound lobsters, and 3 dozen medium-size shrimp. The lobsters should be washed, plunged into boiling water containing 1 tablespoon salt, and boiled gently 20 minutes. The shrimp are washed, plunged into boiling water in another pan, and cooked 12 minutes. The crabmeat is purchased already cooked and supposedly picked over by the fishmonger. It must be carefully picked over again, however, so that no shell particles or grit will be left.

When the shrimp are cooked, wash them in cold water, remove the shells, and take out the intestines, which are found along the middle of the back. When the lobsters are cooked, wash them in cold water and let them get cold. Then chop off the claws, split the lobster lengthwise, remove and throw away the stomach and the intestines, which run from the base of the tail to the stomach. Crack the claws and remove the meat. Take out the meat from the body and cut it in thin slices with a silver knife.

Have ready to use a bowl of lobster meat, 3 dozen clean shrimp, the crabmeat, and the stiffly jellied aspic. Now take 2 1½-quart-size molds that are shaped like fish. Put the stock on just enough fire to melt it. Put a peppercorn in each eye of the fish mold. Split the shrimp lengthwise with a silver knife; place them in the bottom of the molds to imitate the scales of the fish. Then pack in alternately the crabmeat, the lobster meat, and the rest of the shrimp until the molds are more or less filled. Then taste the aspic and season to taste with salt and pepper. Pour it into the molds until they overflow. Set them in the refrigerator until well set, at least 2 hours.

The best sauce to be served with this fish aspic is a delicious, tart French dressing poured over a bowl of very finely chopped water cress.

## LOBSTER AND SALMON PIE

*[Pre-heat oven to 450°]*

**Pastry:**

| | |
|---|---|
| ½ cup vinegar | 1½ cups pastry flour |
| 1 onion | ½ teaspoon salt |
| 1 carrot | 12 tablespoons butter |
| 2 bay leaves | **Sauce:** |
| thyme | 1 onion |
| parsley | 1 shallot |
| 3 live lobsters | 1 small carrot |
| 1 cup dry white wine | parsley |
| 1 teaspoon salt | 1 tablespoon butter |
| ½ teaspoon peppercorns | 1 teaspoon flour |
| 1 2½-pound slice fresh | 3 tomatoes |
| salmon | cayenne |
| 2 tablespoons butter | paprika |
| 1 egg yolk | freshly ground pepper |
| | nutmeg |

SERVES 6–8

Five or six hours ahead of time make the paste for the pie. Sift 1½ cups pastry flour with ½ teaspoon salt. Work in with the finger tips ¾ cup (12 tablespoons) butter, which has been previously worked in cold water to the consistency of putty and squeezed dry in a piece of linen. Moisten the flour and butter with tepid water, kneading lightly, and putting the moistened part aside until all is mixed. Roll into a ball, place in a bowl, cover with wax paper and a saucer, and chill thoroughly 5–6 hours.

In the meantime prepare a court bouillon (page 77) of

water, ½ cup vinegar, 1 onion, 1 carrot, a bay leaf, a pinch of thyme, and some parsley. When bouillon is boiling, plunge lobsters into the water and simmer 15 minutes. Remove from the fire and cool in the court bouillon. When cold, remove the meat from the claws and body, saving carefully the lobster coral. Place in the refrigerator. Now make another court bouillon in an enamel pan of 1 cup dry white wine, 2 cups water, a bouquet of parsley, thyme, and bay leaf, 1 teaspoon of salt, and ½ teaspoon peppercorns. When it is boiling, place in it the 2½-pound slice of fresh salmon, preferably from the middle of the fish, and on a low flame allow to barely simmer for 40 minutes. Remove from fire and cool in its juice.

Now make the following sauce. Peel and chop fine 1 onion, 1 good-size shallot, 1 small carrot, a little parsley. Cook for a minute or two without browning in 1 tablespoon butter; then add 1 teaspoon flour; stir; and add 1 cup stock from the salmon, the pulp only of 3 tomatoes, a pinch of cayenne, a dash of paprika, freshly ground pepper, salt, and a pinch of nutmeg. Simmer gently.

Now cream 2 tablespoons butter with the lobster coral and put it through a fine sieve. When the sauce has reduced to about 1¾ cups, strain it through a sieve, and stir into it the lobster butter.

You are now ready to assemble the pie. Butter a baking-dish, suitable for a deep-dish pie, which will hold about 3 pints of liquid. Lay in the center the salmon, from which you have carefully removed skin and bones, and place around this the lobster meat, which you have sliced with a silver knife. Pour the sauce over all. Now flour a board and the rolling-pin and take a little piece of the paste. Roll it into a 1-inch-wide strip long enough to go around the edge of the baking-dish. Paint the outer edge of the dish with a little slightly beaten egg yolk and press the paste securely around the edge. Paint the strip with more egg. Roll the rest of the paste and cover the pie. Trim the paste so that it hangs over the edge about 1 inch. Press it carefully to the narrow strip; then having dipped your fingers in flour, crimp the edges. Work quickly. Brush the top with more egg and cut a small hole in the center of the crust. Lay around this small diamond-shape pieces of paste to form a decoration. Cut another strip of pastry 1½″ by 8″. Wrap it loosely around your forefinger. Insert your finger into the center hole, and then withdraw it, leaving a pastry rose in center of pie, which makes a necessary vent.

Make small incisions around the edge of the pie and place in pre-heated hot oven. After 10 minutes reduce the heat to 350° and continue to cook slowly 30–40 minutes. Serve at once.

## ROSE VISINHO'S MARINATED PORTUGUESE FRESH TUNA

| | |
|---|---|
| 4 pounds 1½-inch-thick fresh tuna | 1 cup olive oil |
| juice of 3 lemons | 10 small white onions |
| ½ teaspoon pepper | 2 cups white wine, or more |
| 1 teaspoon salt | 2 tablespoons butter |
| 1 pound fresh mushrooms | 2–3 sprays of parsley |
| | 2 tablespoons chopped parsley |

SERVES 6–8

Marinate the tuna for 1½ hours in the juice of 3 lemons seasoned with 1 teaspoon salt, ½ teaspoon pepper, and 2–3 sprays of parsley. Peel, wash, and chop fairly fine 1 pound fresh mushrooms and 10 small white onions separately. Drain tuna and brown it lightly in 1 cup hot olive oil in large, preferably porcelain-lined, iron frying-pan, which should have a tightly fitting cover. When the tuna is brown on one side, about 5 minutes, turn and brown the other side.

Add the chopped onions; stir, and cook for a minute or two; then add the chopped mushrooms. Simmer for 20 minutes. Mix 2 cups white wine with 1½ cups water and pour as much as necessary over the fish to fill pan up to one third the height of the tuna. Cover tightly, turn heat way down, and simmer for about 40 minutes more, adding remainder of liquid as needed to keep from sticking. At this point, strictly speaking, one would strain the juice and discard the vegetables, but I personally like to leave them in. Place on hot serving-platter. Add 2 tablespoons butter to the sauce, stir until melted, and then pour over the fish. Garnish with 2 tablespoons chopped parsley.

## TRUITES AUX AMANDES
*[Pre-heat oven to 300°]*

6–8 brook trout
¾ cup sliced blanched almonds
1 cup flour
salt, pepper

½ pound butter
juice of ½ lemon
parsley

SERVES 6–8

Blanch ¾ cup almonds, slice very fine. Salt and pepper 6–8 small brook trout that have been properly cleaned. Roll them lightly in flour. Make an incision in the thickest part of the fillet. Heat ¼ pound butter in a large frying-pan over a moderate fire, and lay the trout carefully in the pan. Brown them well on both sides, which will take about 10 minutes. Put them on a platter, being careful not to break them, and place the platter in the oven to heat. Add the almonds to the butter in the frying-pan, and add another ¼ pound butter. Cook slowly until the butter and nuts brown slightly. Add the juice of ½ lemon. Pour mixture over the fish; sprinkle with parsley; serve at once.

## DUSTY'S MISSISSIPPI SEAFOOD GUMBO

½ pound diced ham
3 tablespoons olive oil
1 cup chopped celery
1 cup chopped white onions
2 medium-size cans cut okra (or 2 packages of frozen okra)
chopped parsley
2 tablespoons flour
2 small cans tomato paste

2 pounds shrimp
18 oysters and juice
1 pound crabmeat
4 bay leaves
2 tablespoons gumbo-filé seasoning
1 teaspoon coarsely ground pepper
salt
2 lemons

SERVES 6–8

Wash 2 pound fresh shrimp in cold water. Heat 1½ quarts water to which you have added the strained juice of 2 lemons. Add the shrimp when the water boils; cook the shrimp 10 minutes. Remove from fire until cool enough to handle. Strain, but save the water. Remove shells and devein. Rinse clean in cold water and place back in shrimp water until ready to use.

Prepare 1 cup diced ham, 1 cup chopped celery, 1 cup chopped white onions, 2 tablespoons chopped parsley. Heat 3 tablespoons olive oil in frying-pan, add ham and sauté it gently until beginning to brown. Transfer ham to large procelain-lined cocotte. Add to the oil in which the ham cooked the chopped onions and celery plus 2 cans sliced okra and their juice. Sprinkle with 2 tablespoons flour, stir well, add 2 small cans tomato paste, and 2 quarts of liquid made up of the juice from 18 oysters, the shrimp water, and more water if necessary. Stir well, add 4 bay leaves, 2 tablespoons chopped parsley, and pour the whole over the ham in pot. Season to taste with about 2 tablespoons gumbo-filé seasoning, 1 teaspoon pepper, and a little salt. Simmer gently 2 hours, adding more water if necessary. Thirty minutes before serving add the cooked shrimp, and 1 pound crabmeat (carefully picked over). Simmer gently 30 minutes, turn off heat, and add 18 oysters. Cover and allow to stand 5 minutes before serving. This should be ladled generously over flaky boiled rice in large soup plates to be eaten with soup spoons.

Followed by a plain tossed salad and a compote of fresh fruit for dessert, this in my opinion makes a perfect meal. Naturally a good white wine, possibly Vouvray, would add to the perfection of the whole.

## SEVICHE

1 3–4-pound red snapper  
2¼ teaspoon carraway seeds  
½ cup dry white wine  
3 small white onions  
4 ripe tomatoes  

2 limes  
1½ teaspoon salt  
¼ teaspoon cracked pepper  
chopped parsley  

SERVES 6–8

Buy a 3–4 pound red snapper, filleted, all skin and bones removed and discarded. Wash and pat dry on paper towel and cut in 1-inch squares. Look each piece over carefully for stray bones. Place 2 tablespoons carraway seeds in small enamel pan, add ½ cup dry white wine and ½ cup water. Bring gently to a boil, strain, and save the liquid. Peel and chop fine 3 onions. Place liquid in large earthenware casserole, add the onions, cover, bring gently to a boil, and simmer 1 minute. Add the fish, sprinkle with about 1½ teaspoons salt and ¼ teaspoon cracked pepper. Cover and bring gently to boiling point. Remove cover and baste the fish with the liquid. Continue simmering until fish is no longer transparent, about 7 minutes.

In the meantime scald 4 ripe tomatoes, peel, and cut in cubes. Cover fish with the tomatoes, and continue cooking about 5 minutes longer. Remove from fire, strain off, but save the juice. Add ¼ teaspoon carraway seeds to the juice, and reduce to ½ cup by boiling rapidly. Transfer the fish and tomatoes to a baking-dish 6″ by 9½″ by 2″. Pour the reduced juice and carraway seeds over all. Now add the strained juice of 2 limes. When cold, cover with aluminum foil and chill in refrigerator 12 hours. Sprinkle with chopped parsley and serve accompanied by a crock of sweet butter, French bread, and white wine. Followed by blue cheese and salad, this makes a perfect lunch.

## BAKED BONELESS SHAD
[*Pre-heat oven to 225°–250°*]

| | |
|---|---|
| **2** buck shad, weighing 3½ pounds each | 1 bunch of water cress |
| ½ pound bacon | salt, pepper |
| **2** lemons, quartered | aluminum foil |
| juice of 3 lemons, strained | (cooking time: 4½–5 hours) |

SERVES 6–8

It is possible to serve shad and have it completely boneless! This miracle is accomplished with incredibly long, slow baking of the fish—which is wrapped in aluminum foil.

Buy 2 fine fresh buck shad, weighing 3½ pounds each. Have them prepared for baking with the heads, tails, and center bones removed. Five hours before you will serve the dish, pre-heat oven to 225°–250°. Wash the fish inside and out and pat dry. Cut 2 large sheets of aluminum foil—large enough to wrap each fish securely. Cut ½ pound bacon in half; using half of it, make 2 beds of bacon on the sheets of aluminum foil and lay the fish to rest. Sprinkle fish lightly inside and out with salt and pepper and the strained juice of 3 lemons. Cover fish with the remainder of the bacon. Very carefully fold the foil, making double seams, so that the fish are completely and securely closed in with the seasoning. Lay them side by side on a large cookie sheet.

Bake shad slowly, without disturbing them, for at least 4½ hours. Ten minutes before you serve the fish, split the foil down the center to expose the fish. Allow to cook until the skins have crisped up a bit. Pour off all the fat and transfer to hot fish platter, discarding the foil. Garnish with quartered lemons and crisp water cress. Serve at once with boiled new potatoes and hot clarified butter (page 290).

NOTE   Olive oil may be substituted for the bacon, if preferred; in this case use about ⅓ cup olive oil in all.


## LOIS'S WILD-RICE AND SHELLFISH CASSEROLE
*[Pre-heat oven to 400°]*

| | |
|---|---|
| ½ pound cooked crabmeat | a few drops of Tabasco |
| ½ pound cooked shrimp | ⅓ cup almonds |
| ½ pound fresh mushrooms | ½ cup toasted bread crumbs |
| 1 small green pepper | ½ pound butter |
| ½ cup uncooked white rice | 2 tablespoons all-purpose flour |
| ½ cup uncooked wild rice | 1 cup milk |
| ½ cup chopped celery | 2 cups heavy cream |
| 1 onion | 2 tablespoons chopped parsley |
| salt, pepper | |

SERVES 6–8

Pick over the crabmeat carefully. Remove shells and clean shrimp; rinse them in cold water and split in two. Place in refrigerator while you prepare the rest of the ingredients.

Wash, stem, peel, and cut mushrooms in 8 pieces each. Remove seeds from green pepper and cut fine. Wash and remove strings from several stalks of celery and cut fine—you will need about ½ cup. Toast some stale white bread until crisp and lightly browned, then roll it fine, making ½ cup bread crumbs. Blanch ⅓ cup almonds, rinse in cold water, and cut lengthwise in fine slivers. Peel and cut fine 1 onion. Prepare 2 tablespoons chopped parsley.

Wash ½ cup long-grain white rice and cook in boiling salted water 18 minutes. Drain, allow cold water to run over it, drain, and set aside. In the meantime wash ½ cup wild rice and place it in a heavy saucepan, cover with 2 cups cold water, add ½ teaspoon salt, place on low flame, and cook gently without stirring until all the water has been absorbed, about 45 minutes. Watch carefully and shake occasionally to avoid scorching, especially toward the end of cooking.

Now melt 6 tablespoons butter in a frying-pan and sauté the onions, celery, green pepper, and mushrooms until just beginning to brown, about 5 minutes. Remove from fire, add white rice, and stir lightly with a fork. Now add all this to the wild rice, and last of all add the shrimp and crabmeat and mix lightly. Season to taste with ½ teaspoon coarsely ground black pepper and a few drops of Tabasco. Transfer to a well-buttered 2-quart-size casserole and pour over all 1 cup heavy cream. Melt 2 tablespoons butter in a small frying-pan, add ½ cup bread crumbs, and stir over a low flame until crumbs are well buttered. Sprinkle them lightly over the mixture in casserole. Dot casserole with 4 tablespoons butter, cover, and bake in pre-heated oven for about 30 minutes. Remove the cover the last 10 minutes to allow the crumbs to brown on top.

In the meantime sauté in small frying-pan the slivered almonds in 2 tablespoons butter until lightly browned. Make a medium-thick cream sauce (page 292) using 2 tablespoons butter, 2 tablespoons flour, and 1 cup hot milk. Season lightly to taste with salt and stir in 1 cup heavy cream. Keep hot over boiling water. When done, remove the casserole from oven, sprinkle lightly with chopped parsley, and serve accompanied by the cream sauce and toasted almonds. Plain buttered asparagus tips are good with this.

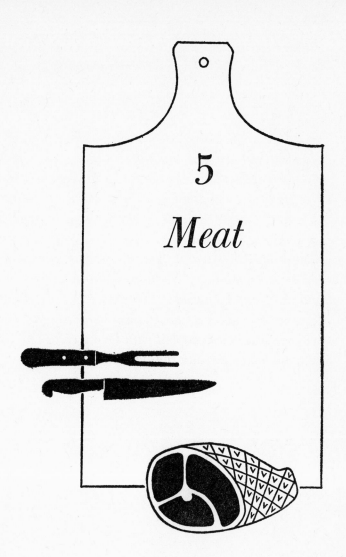

5

*Meat*

*W*e can plan a meal without soup; we can plan a meal without a sweet; but I defy you to plan a meal without meat and still please your lord and master. We all know that the way to a man's heart is through his stomach, but give him meat—beef, veal, lamb, ham, or pork—if you wish him to purr with contentment. Omit meat from the menu, and he will rightly feel that the backbone of his meal has been left out. Protein is all important in our diet, and meat unfortunately is the most expensive form of protein, so let's not only purchase it carefully and personally but also season and cook it with loving care. The following recipes should provide the necessary variety.

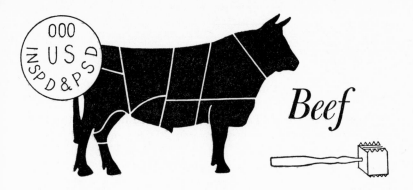

## MY ROAST BEEF WITH YORKSHIRE PUDDING

Not being the proud possessor of an electric rotating-broiler or a
wall oven, or even a meat thermometer, I still manage to roast
my meats in a rather battered aluminum roasting-pan in whatever oven happens to be around; and, without the aid of said
thermometer, I manage to roast the meat to our particular liking,
relying on past experience for the timing. I see to it that Joe and
I get the outside pieces, because that is the way we like it, and
I gladly give away the very rare center.

Speaking of beef, in particular, if you are going to have a
prime rib roast at all, I think you might as well be completely
extravagant and buy a 3- or 4-rib roast, but don't have it boned.
Be sure you know how much the roast weighs. Wipe it with a
damp cloth, and rub it with salt and pepper. Place it fat side up
in open roasting-pan. *Pre-heat oven to very hot 500°*. Place
roast in oven and cook until well browned and seared (20–30
minutes). Then reduce heat to 300°–350° and continue roasting,
basting frequently with fat in the pan, until done to your particular
fancy: well, medium, or rare. The general consensus of opinion
seems to be that one should count 18 minutes to the pound for
rare, 22–25 for medium, and 27–30 for well done. In any event,

only practice with your particular oven will solve the problem. Also, please don't put even one drop of water in the pan while roasting beef.

If you intend to make *Yorkshire Pudding* (and I hope you do), about ½ hour before you think the roast will be done, drain or ladle off about ½ cup of the rendered fat in roasting-pan and place it in a heavy iron frying-pan. Make room for it on the bottom shelf of your oven, and allow it to get hot while you quickly make the batter for the pudding. Beat 2 whole eggs very well with rotary-beater; add 1 cup milk; beat again; add 1 cup flour sifted with 1 teaspoon salt; beat with rotary-beater—and hope that it will be free from lumps. Pour immediately into the now hot iron frying-pan with the sizzling-hot fat. Close the door and hope for something sensational to happen. With luck, it will puff up all over, and by the time the roast is done it should be done too.

Place the roast on a hot platter and send to table to be carved and served. Cut the Yorkshire pudding in large squares, place it on separate hot platter, and serve immediately with the roast. If you wish to make a little clear gravy, pour off all of the remaining fat from roasting-pan into an earthenware crock (and keep it preciously for future use). Add 1 cup water to brown residue in roasting-pan and boil rapidly on top of stove, stirring well. When it is well reduced, it is ready to serve.

## POT AU FEU

4 pounds brisket of beef and bones
8 carrots
8 small white turnips
2 small onions
4 whole cloves
8 small tender leeks
bouquet of parsley, ½ bay leaf, and ¼ teaspoon thyme
1 tablespoon salt (preferably rock salt)
6 peppercorns

SERVES 6–8

Peel 8 carrots and 8 small white turnips. Peel 2 small white onions and stick 2 whole cloves in center of each. Cut the green part off 8 tender leeks, split them down the center, and wash well. Make a bouquet of parsley, ½ bay leaf, and ¼ teaspoon thyme. Wash the brisket of beef and bones and place them in large pot. Cover with 3 quarts cold water. Bring slowly to boiling point. Stand by and carefully skim off all the gray foam that rises to the surface. Add 1 cup cold water; when it comes to boiling point again, repeat the skimming process. Add another cup cold water, and once more skim carefully when it comes to boiling point—all this to assure a clear broth. Add the carrots, turnips, onions, and leeks; the bouquet; 1 tablespoon salt; and 6 peppercorns. Simmer gently, partially covered, for about 6 hours.

Remove pot from fire and cool. Pour the juice through sieve lined with cheesecloth into fresh pot. Discard bones, and place meat and vegetables in another fresh pot. Pour several cups broth over them and heat both pots on low flame until ready to serve. Serve the broth first in a hot soup tureen, accompanied by a basket of freshly toasted, lightly buttered French Bread. Serve the meat on a hot platter, carved, garnished with the vegetables, and sprinkled with rock salt, and accompany with a pot of French mustard and any other relish you happen to like. Boiled potatoes may also be served with this.

## FILLET DE BOEUF EN CROUTE

**Brioche Paste:**
3 cups all-purpose flour
1 teaspoon dry yeast
¼ pound butter
½ teaspoon salt
3 eggs
heavy cream

**Sauce:**
1 pound fresh mushrooms
6 shallots
1 tablespoon chopped parsley
1 can condensed consommé
¼ pound butter
3 tablespoons flour
½ cup Madeira or sherry

3 pounds center cut of fillet of prime beef, prepared for broiling or roasting, partially wrapped in a thin sheet of suet or pork fat back.

Prepare the brioche paste first. Sift 1 cup flour into a small bowl; make a hole in the center. Dissolve 1 rounded teaspoon dry yeast in ½ cup luke-warm water and place in hole. Stir with spoon, gradually mixing the yeast water into the flour. Scrape out onto lightly floured pastry cloth and knead until smooth. Form into a ball and drop into a bowl of luke-warm water. Cover with cloth and allow to rise in warm place until doubled in bulk, about 2½ hours. Have ready ¼ pound soft well-creamed butter and, in a separate bowl, 1 cup flour sifted with ½ teaspoon salt. Make a hole in the center of this flour and break into it 3 whole eggs. Stir with spoon gradually working the eggs into the flour. Next work in the softened butter and last of all the yeast sponge, from which you have drained the water. Toss out onto floured cloth and knead until smooth, working in 1 cup flour, or slightly more if necessary to keep it from sticking to the cloth. Form into a smooth ball, place in clean buttered bowl, cover, and allow to rise in warm place until doubled in bulk, about 3 hours.

In the meantime, make the sauce. Peel and chop fine 6 shallots. Prepare 1 tablespoon chopped parsley. Wash 1 pound mushrooms, remove tough part of stems, and chop the mushrooms reasonably fine. Melt ⅛ pound butter in frying-pan, add the shallots, and cook for a minute or two, stirring with wooden spoon. Then add the parsley and mushrooms and cook until mushrooms have formed their juice and cooked down and are about to brown lightly. Remove from fire temporarily. In a separate small frying-pan make a brown *roux* by cooking 3 level tablespoons flour in ⅛ pound butter stirring constantly with a wooden spoon until a golden brown, at which time stir in 1 can consommé to make a smooth sauce. Add the mushrooms and shallots and cook down for a minute or two. Season to taste with coarsely ground black pepper and salt, if necessary, and set aside to cool.

Have ready a shallow 2-quart-size baking-dish; grease it well with vegetable shortening. Sprinkle your fillet of beef lightly with pepper and salt and leave it at room temperature until ready to broil and wrap in its blanket of brioche paste. Once the above preliminaries have been accomplished, it will take about 1 hour to assemble and cook the fillet *en croute,* so plan accordingly.

*Pre-heat broiling unit to* 500°. Place the fillet on rack and broil 8 minutes on one side, turn, and broil 7 minutes on the other. Take it from oven and remove strings and fat; place back under broiler 3–5 minutes. Remove from broiler and allow to cool for about 15 minutes. Reduce heat of oven to 400°.

In the meantime roll out the brioche dough to a rectangular shape large enough to completely enclose the fillet. Spread the dough with about ½ prepared mushroom mixture, place the fillet on this bed, fold ends up and sides over, covering the fillet snugly. Place, smooth side up, in baking-dish. Make 3 good slits in top to allow steam to escape while baking. Brush the pastry with heavy cream and place in oven to bake until a golden brown and until it feels firm to the touch, 25–30 minutes. Place on hot platter, cut in ¾″-thick slices with a sharp knife, and serve accompanied by the remainder of the mushroom sauce, which you have heated over hot water and thinned to desired consistency with good Madeira, about ½ cup.

## BOEUF A LA BOURGUIGNONNE
*[Pre-heat oven to 325°]*

4 pounds top round of beef, cut in 1½″ cubes
4–5 pieces beef suet
½ pound lean salt pork, diced
2 cups strong veal broth, or consommé
1 bottle imported burgundy
1 medium-size onion
½ bay leaf
4 sprigs parsley
½ teaspoon thyme

2 tablespoons olive oil
3 tablespoons flour
1 bouquet garni (thyme, parsley, and bay leaf)
1 clove garlic, crushed
salt, coarsely ground pepper
24 small white onions
1 pound fresh mushrooms
¼ cup brandy
12 tablespoons butter

SERVES 6–8

This dish is not one to be tossed together in a hurry, but no self-respecting cookbook would be without it. It is well worth the trouble and may be made ahead of time and be reheated with only beneficial results. It's a perfect company dish, easy to serve.

The day before make the strong veal broth, or consommé. The night before put the beef to marinate in a glass or enamel dish: peel and slice fine 1 medium-size onion, spread half of it in the dish; lay on this bed the pieces of meat, preferably not on top of each other; and add ½ bay leaf, 4 springs parsley, ½ teaspoon thyme, ¼ teaspoon coarsely ground pepper, 1 teaspoon salt, and the remainder of the onion; pour over this a bottle of imported burgundy. Allow meat to marinate in a cool spot overnight, but do not refrigerate.

The next day, *pre-heat your oven to slow* 325°. Render 4–5 pieces beef suet in large heavy iron frying-pan, until you have at least 4 tablespoons melted fat. Remove the suet. Drain the meat, saving the marinade; wipe the pieces of meat on paper toweling. Add meat to the smoking-hot fat and brown lightly on all sides, turning pieces with spatula. Remove the meat as it browns and transfer it to a heated large, 3½-quart-size, earthenware casserole (with cover), containing 2 tablespoons melted butter. Pour ¼ cup heated brandy over the meat, light, and allow to burn itself out. Add 3 tablespoons butter to remaining fat in frying-pan and sprinkle with 3 tablespoons flour. Stir with wooden spoon over low heat to make a light brown *roux*, then add gradually 2 cups hot strong veal broth to make smooth gravy. Strain the marinade into this. Bring to a rapid boil, skim, and then pour over the meat.

Add to the meat a bouquet garni and 1 clove garlic, crushed (better still, put through a garlic press). Cover and bring to a simmer on low heat. Simmer 5 minutes. Place casserole in preheated oven and cook gently 3½ hours.

In the meantime prepare the garniture of salt pork and vegetables. Place ½ pound diced lean salt pork in pan, cover with cold water, bring to a boil, and simmer 5 minutes. Drain and pat dry on paper toweling. Melt 1 tablespoon butter in small frying-pan, add the pork, and brown lightly. Drain and set aside. Plunge 24 small perfect white onions into a saucepan of boiling water. Boil 2 minutes, drain; and when onions are cool enough to handle remove outer skins, melt 1 tablespoon butter in medium-size frying-pan and brown them lightly all over. Add them to the pork. Wash and remove tough stems from 1 pound fresh mushrooms. Dry on paper toweling and quarter each. Add 4 tablespoons butter to frying-pan in which you browned the onions and melt over low heat. Add the mushrooms, increase heat, and sauté mushrooms until lightly browned, shaking the pan occasionally. Do not cook too long. Set aside.

When the meat has been in the oven 3½ hours, remove it temporarily, and allow it to stand 10 minutes. Locate and remove the bouquet garni. Ladle off any excess fat. Taste and add more salt and pepper, if desired. Add pork and vegetables. Cover and return to oven and cook 45 minutes longer. Sprinkle with 1 tablespoon chopped parsley, and serve accompanied by a goodly supply of tiny peeled and boiled new potatoes.

NOTE  If this is to be reheated, place in moderate 400° oven and bake until sizzling hot, about 20 minutes.

## BEEF STROGANOFF

2–3 pounds tender beef (cut in thin strips ½″ by 2″ by ¼″ thick)
1 cup chopped onion
¼ pound butter
1–1½ cup beef consommé, or more
4 tablespoons flour

½ teaspoon dry mustard
1 teaspoon salt
½ teaspoon coarsely ground pepper
3 cups sour cream
2 tablespoons chopped parsley
2 tablespoons Worcestershire sauce

SERVES 6–8

Prepare 1 cup chopped onion and 2 tablespoons chopped parsley. Mix 4 tablespoons flour, ½ teaspoon dry mustard, 1 teaspoon salt, and ½ teaspoon coarsely ground black pepper together in paper bag; add 2–3 pounds tender beef cut in thin strips and shake well. Melt ¼ pound butter in iron frying-pan or cocotte and add the chopped onion. Cook slowly for about 6 minutes. Increase the heat, add the floured meat, and cook until the meat browns, about 5 minutes, turning the pieces over with a spatula.

Add gradually about 1 cup consommé stirring with wooden

spoon to incorporate the brown residue in bottom of pan. Also add 2 tablespoons Worcestershire sauce, and cook gently for 15–20 minutes longer, adding more consommé if necessary to keep it from becoming too thick. Reduce heat still further and gradually add about 3 cups sour cream, stirring constantly until hot; do not allow it to actually boil. Place in warm serving-dish, sprinkle with chopped parsley, and serve at once, accompanied by medium-wide buttered cooked noodles and a separate bowl of buttered crumbs. Fresh peas are also good with this.

## BOEUF EN DAUBE

4 pounds top round of beef (in 1 piece)
1 calf's foot, split in two lengthwise
1 2-ounce slice salt pork
6 tablespoons lard
6 tablespoons olive oil
14 medium-size white onions
4 carrots
4 ripe tomatoes
6 cloves garlic

3–4 branches parsley
3 small bay leaves
1 teaspoon thyme
12 peppercorns
1 strip orange peel
2 9-ounce packages macaroni
1 cup grated imported Parmesan cheese
1 teaspoon salt
1 bottle good burgundy

SERVES 6–8

Spread 6 tablespoons lard over bottom of large, heavy iron cocotte. Pour over this 6 tablespoons olive oil. Sprinkle with 2 ounces salt pork, cut in small cubes. Add 3 bay leaves, 1 teaspoon thyme, 6 cloves garlic, 12 peppercorns, 3–4 branches parsley, 1 onion (in which you have placed 2 cloves), 1 wide strip orange peel (minus all the bitter white part), and 4 peeled and quartered ripe tomatoes. Sprinkle with 1 teaspoon salt. Lay on this bed 1 calf's foot, cleaned and split lengthwise in two (being careful to wash it first thoroughly in cold water). Now add the 4-pound piece of top round of beef, just as it is. Place around it 13 peeled white onions, and 4 peeled carrots which you have cut in 2-inch lengths. Pour over this 1 bottle of good burgundy.

Cover cocotte tightly and bring rapidly to boiling point. Watch carefully and considerably reduce the heat at the exact moment it boils, skimming it carefully at this point. Now adjust the heat to produce a very gentle simmering, cover tightly, and let it cook evenly and very gently 6–8 hours on top of the stove. From time to time skim off as much as possible of the black part as it rises to the surface—this is caused by the red wine. Turn the meat over at least twice during the cooking period, using a spatula and spoon so as not to pierce the meat.

Forty-five minutes before dinner put water in top of a very large double boiler over direct flame, salt it to taste, and when it is boiling add 2 packages macaroni, which you have broken in fairly small pieces. Cook until the macaroni is well done, 15–20 minutes. Remove pot from fire and allow the macaroni to stand in the water for 5 minutes so that it will swell. Then strain it quickly through a colander and place it back in the pot in which it was cooked and over boiling water to keep warm. Place the meat upon a very hot platter. With a ladle, fish out any vegetables that are still somewhat presentable and place them around the meat, and strain some of the juice over the meat, dipping down deep to avoid the fat on the surface. Garnish with a big bunch of parsley and send to the table to be carved in thin slices.

In the meantime, holding a strainer over the macaroni, pour several ladles of the top part of the meat juice, using part of the fat, through the strainer. This takes the place of butter and gives a delicious flavor. Toss the macaroni around and remove from fire. Add 1 cup grated imported Parmesan cheese and toss with fork. Place in hot bowl and serve at once to be eaten with the meat. It is well to serve an extra gravy boat of the strained meat juice to moisten the meat, if desired. A very peasant dish, but a delectable one.

NOTE   If there is any left-over meat, place it in a suitable dish and strain over it all the remaining juice. When cold, place in the refrigerator. The next day, the juice will have become an aspic. Served cold with a mixed green salad, this version of the Daube is as good, if not better, than the hot one.

## BOEUF A LA MODE

⅛-pound piece beef suet
5 pounds boned pot roast (rump or eye of the round)
1¾ cups white wine plus ⅓ cup
1¾ cups Madeira plus ⅓ cup
¼ cup cognac
¼ pound bacon rind
1 calf's foot, cut in two
16 little carrots
8 little white onions
bouquet of parsley, bay leaf, and thyme

3 whole cloves
salt, pepper
¼ teaspoon powdered allspice
3¼ cups good beef stock, or canned consommé
2 egg whites
2 egg shells
2 lemons
1 head Boston lettuce
4 extra carrots (to be boiled separately)

SERVES 6–8

Ask your butcher to lard a 5-pound pot roast. Put it into a large bowl, salt and pepper it lightly, and sprinkle with ¼ teaspoon powdered allspice. Pour over it 1¾ cups white wine (sauterne, if possible) and 1¾ cups Madeira. Let this soak for 24 hours.

At the end of this time render a small piece of beef suet in an iron cocotte until you have 2 tablespoons melted fat. Add the roast and brown for 20 minutes, carefully turning it over and over. Then warm ¼ cup cognac in little pan and light it as you pour it over the meat (be careful). Allow it to burn itself out. Remove the roast from the cocotte and put ¼ pound bacon rind in bottom of cocotte, add a calf's foot, split in two, and place the roast on this bed. Surround with 12 peeled little carrots, 8 little white onions, a bouquet of parsley, a bay leaf, a pinch of thyme, and 3 whole cloves. Moisten with the juice in which the meat marinated, 3¼ cups home-made beef stock (or consommé), ⅓ cup white wine, and ⅓ cup Madeira. Salt and pepper lightly; cover; bring to boiling point; reduce heat; and simmer slowly for 5 hours.

When cooked, remove the meat and carrots, strain the juice, and take off all the grease. Clarify the juice by adding 2 slightly beaten egg whites and their crushed shells. Stir constantly over low heat until it comes to a boil. Remove from fire and strain through a sieve lined with heavy cheesecloth wrung out in cold water. Cut the beef in slices perpendicularly. Decorate the bottom of a suitable deep rectangular mold with some perfect rounds of the 4 carrots that you boiled separately. Pour over these 3–4 tablespoons meat juice and place in refrigerator to jell.

When set, arrange the slices of meat separately with the 12 carrots that you cooked with the meat, until all the meat and the carrots have been used, ending up with meat. Pour over this the meat juice until the mold is full. Place in refrigerator to jell. Unmold on large platter and decorate with washed and well-dried leaves of Boston lettuce and thin slices of lemon. Cut as if you were slicing a loaf of bread. Serve French mustard with this, and a big bowl of Boston lettuce with French dressing.

## FILLETINI ARROSTO
### [Pre-heat broiler to 450°]

8 ¾-inch-slices center cut of fillet of beef, prepared for broiling
10 ½-inch slices white bread
½ pound butter
salt, pepper

8 leaves fresh sage, or 1 teaspoon dried sage
8–10 large new potatoes
4 17-inch stainless-steel skewers

SERVES 6–8

Wash and boil 8–10 large new potatoes with their skins on until just tender, about 45 minutes. Drain, cool, and peel. Melt ¼ pound butter in bottom part of roasting-pan, 15″ by 10″. Lay on this the potatoes cut evenly in ½-inch slices. Dot with 4 tablespoons butter. Remove crusts from 10 slices good white bread, cut ½-inch thick, and trim to same shape as the fillets. Butter both sides of bread, using 4 tablespoons butter in all. Sprinkle 8 slices center cut of raw fillet of beef, prepared for broiling, with about 1½ teaspoons salt and ¾ teaspoon coarsely ground pepper. Arrange the meat and bread alternately on 4 17-inch stainless-steel skewers, using 2 skewers for each, placing 1 small leaf fresh sage between each slice of meat and bread (or substitute a pinch of dried sage). Balance the skewers lengthwise over the roasting-pan that contains the potatoes.

Broil the meat 15–25 minutes, depending on how well done you like your beef. Baste frequently with drippings in bottom of pan. Turn the skewers over once or twice for even cooking. Increase heat slightly toward the end. When broiled to your liking, remove pan from boiler. With a spatula lay the potatoes on a large ovenproof serving-platter. Pull out skewers from the beef and lay the beef and toast on the bed of potatoes. Pour drippings over all. Place platter under broiler for a few seconds and then serve immediately.

## PAUL'S BEEF STEW

| | |
|---|---|
| ¼ pound good lean bacon | 6 tablespoons flour |
| 3 pounds top round of beef | 4 teaspoons beef extract |
| 18 small white onions | ⅓ cup good brandy |
| 6 carrots | salt, pepper |
| ½ pound mushrooms | 2 bay leaves |
| 2 cans consommé | 3 whole cloves |
| 12 tablespoons butter | 2 tablespoons chopped parsley |

SERVES 6–8

Cut ¼ pound good lean bacon in small ½-inch strips. Remove all fat from 3 pounds tender top round of beef and cut in 1-inch cubes. Peel 18 small white onions. Make a light brown *roux* in a small saucepan using 6 tablespoons butter and 6 tablespoons flour; cook together stirring constantly for 4–5 minutes, using wooden spoon; remove from fire; heat 2 cans consommé and add them gradually to the *roux*, making a smooth thick sauce. Dissolve 4 teaspoons beef extract in 2 cups boiling water and stir into the sauce. This is the foundation for your stew.

Melt 4 tablespoons butter in large heavy iron frying-pan and brown the meat in it quickly on all sides. If the meat forms too much liquid, thereby preventing quick browning, pour off some of it—adding it to the foundation sauce. When the meat is lightly browned heat ⅓ cup good brandy in little saucepan and light it as you pour it over the meat, being careful not to burn yourself. Allow the brandy to burn itself out, then pour over it the foundation sauce. Stir and transfer the whole to a large iron cocotte. Season to taste with very little salt and pepper, and add 3 whole cloves, 2 bay leaves, and a big pinch of thyme rubbed to a powder between the fingers. Cover and simmer gently for 1½ hours, stirring occasionally.

In the meantime cook ¼ pound lean bacon, cut in ½-inch strips, slowly in a small frying-pan until a golden brown, but not crisp. Fish strips out and save. To the remaining bacon fat add 18 small peeled white onions. Sprinkle with 1 scant teaspoon granulated sugar and cook until a golden brown, about 10 minutes, stirring constantly. Remove onions from fire and drain off all the fat. Next, wash ½ pound small, tender, fresh mushrooms, remove tough part of stems, and cut in quarters. Sauté them lightly in 2 tablespoons butter until they begin to brown. Set aside temporarily. Peel 6 carrots, wash, and cut in 2-inch pieces. Cook in very little water for 20 minutes, by which time they should have boiled almost dry.

When the stew has cooked 1½ hours, remove it from fire for a few minutes and skim off all the fat. Add the mushrooms and their juice, the bacon strips, the carrots, and the onions. Continue cooking gently for about 30 minutes longer, or until the onions and carrots are just tender through. Transfer to large, 3-quart-size, earthenware casserole; sprinkle with 2 tablespoons chopped parsley; and serve with a bowl of peeled and boiled new potatoes, garnished with paprika.

## POT ROAST

| | |
|---|---|
| 1 4-pound top round roast of beef | 1½ dozen seedless raisins |
| 2 tablespoons flour, and more | parsley |
| salt, pepper | ½ cup hot water |
| beef suet | 6 carrots |
| 1 bay leaf | 8 white onions |
| | 4 tablespoons heavy cream |

SERVES 6–8

Wipe clean with a damp cloth a 4-pound roast of beef, top round. Sprinkle over it 2 tablespoons flour mixed with 1 teaspoon salt, and plenty of freshly ground pepper. Render a piece of beef suet in an iron pot slowly so as not to burn it. Then place your meat in the pot and brown on all sides, turning it over carefully without puncturing it. When nice and brown add 1 small bay leaf, 1½ dozen raisins, 1 sprig parsley, and ½ cup hot water. Cover and simmer ever so gently 3–3½ hours.

One hour before it should be done add 6 peeled whole carrots, 8 small onions, and a little more salt. When ready to serve, drain off the juice in the pan into a bowl, and as the fat rises to the surface, remove it by skimming it off with a spoon. To each cup of juice that you have in the bowl, put 2 level tablespoons of the fat in a little saucepan, add an equal quantity of flour, and cook fat and flour together for a minute or two before adding the hot juice from the bowl. Simmer this gravy a minute or two. Place meat on an earthenware platter that you have heated carefully; arrange the vegetables around the edge; garnish with parsley; and serve at once, accompanied by a bowl of fluffy mashed potatoes and the gravy, in which you have stirred at the last moment 4 tablespoons heavy cream.

## BOILED CORNED BEEF DINNER

| Boiled Dinner: | Pudding: |
|---|---|
| 5 pounds of brisket of corned beef | 6 tart apples |
| 6 carrots | granulated sugar |
| 6 parsnips | cinnamon |
| 6 little white turnips | mace |
| 6 potatoes | 2 cups pastry flour |
| 1 small white cabbage | 1 teaspoon cream of tartar |
| ½ pound salt pork | ½ teaspoon soda |
| ⅓ cup sugar | ½ teaspoon salt |
| | 2 tablespoons butter |
| | cold milk |

SERVES 6–8

Soak for 1 hour in cold water 5 pounds properly cured brisket of corned beef. Drain, cover with fresh cold water, bring briskly to a boil, skim carefully, reduce heat, and simmer gently for about 4 hours.

In the meantime, peel 6 carrots, 6 parsnips, 6 little white turnips, and 6 potatoes. Quarter a small white cabbage and remove the core. Scald ½ pound salt pork. Put the pork in a large pot and cover with plenty of cold water. Bring to a boil and simmer very gently. One hour before the dinner is to be served add the carrots, parsnips, and turnips to the pork and cook until tender. Twenty minutes before dinner add the cabbage to the pork and vegetables and put the potatoes on to boil separately. Add a little of the corned-beef water to the vegetables, if they need more water.

In the meantime you will have started to prepare the dessert, a boiled-apple pudding cooked in the corned-beef water while the dinner is being eaten. Butter and flour copiously a pudding-cloth. Peel and slice 6 tart apples. Sprinkle them copiously with granulated sugar, cinnamon, and a pinch of mace. Make a paste by sifting together 2 cups pastry flour with 1 teaspoon cream of tartar, ½ teaspoon soda, and ½ teaspoon salt. Work into this 2 tablespoons butter and moisten with cold milk. Roll out to about ⅛-inch thickness. Spread the pudding-cloth out flat on a table and lay the dough out on it in the center. Pile the apples in the center, trim the dough into an even square, and gather the 4 corners to meet in the center. Pinch the edges together, gather the 4 corners of the pudding-cloth together, and tie securely, leaving plenty of room for the pudding to swell.

Fifteen minutes before the dinner add ⅓ cup sugar to the corned beef. When ready to serve, place the meat on a hot platter and put the pudding immediately into the boiling corned-beef water, cover tightly—and don't remove the cover for 40 minutes. Garnish the meat platter with cabbage, potatoes, carrots, turnips and parsnips and rub a little butter over the beef. Serve at once with a pot of mustard. When the pudding is done, turn it out carefully and with it serve either hard sauce made in the usual way, or a pitcher of cream and a bowl of powdered sugar mixed with a little cinnamon.

## MOIST CORNED-BEEF HASH

8 cups diced raw potatoes
4 onions
salt, pepper
paprika
8 tablespoons butter

2 12-ounce cans of corned
  beef
½ cup heavy cream
3 cups milk

SERVES 6–8

Peel and dice in ⅓-inch squares 8 large potatoes (preferably new ones). You should have 8 cups. Wash and cover them with cold water, add 1 teaspoon salt, bring them to a boil, and cook just long enough to take away the raw taste—they must be only par-boiled. Drain well and put them into a large-size iron skillet (one with an iron handle), which you have first rubbed well inside with a raw onion. Pour over the potatoes about 3 cups milk, or enough to cover them. Add 3 tablespoons butter, ½ teaspoon salt, some freshly ground pepper, plenty of paprika, and 2 small whole white onions. Cook, stirring frequently, until the potatoes are tender, but not mushy, about 15 minutes—they must keep their shape.

In the meantime open 2 12-ounce cans corned beef and cut or chop it into tiny pieces. Do not grind it. When the potatoes are done, add the beef, cover, and continue cooking it very slowly, stirring frequently, for about 40 minutes. *Pre-heat broiler.* The hash at this point should still be moist, but not wet. Add more salt and pepper to taste, dot the surface with 5 tablespoons butter, and pour over it about ½ cup heavy cream. Put it under a hot grill just long enough to brown it beautifully. Serve at once right in the skillet. Chopped buttered spinach is perfect with this hash.

## MARINATED FRIED STEAK

4 small, 1½-pound, T-bone
  steaks, 1¼ inches thick
½ cup good soy sauce

2 cloves garlic, cut in two
1 tablespoon butter

SERVES 6–8

Rub 4 small T-bone steaks on both sides with 2 cloves garlic, cut in two, rubbing it in well. Place steaks on 2 shallow platters, and pour over each steak 2 tablespoons good soy sauce, leaving the garlic on each. Allow to stand 15 minutes; then turn steaks over to marinate 15 minutes on the other side. Heat a large, heavy iron frying-pan, add 1 tablespoon butter, and when sizzling hot add the steaks. Cook 5–6 minutes on each side depending on how well done you like steak. Place on hot platter, carve, and serve at once with Potatoes à la Crème (page 278).

## TAMALE PIE

2 pounds top sirloin, cut in 1-inch cubes

1 6¼-ounce can pitted ripe olives, drained and cut in two lengthwise

1 4-ounce can peeled green chiles, sliced

⅔ cup diced suet

1 large onion, peeled and coarsely chopped

2 cloves garlic, peeled but left whole

1 tablespoon chili powder

1 tablespoon paprika

2 teaspoons oregano

salt, pepper

1 teaspoon beef extract (dissolved in 1 cup hot water)

2 cups yellow corn meal

3 tablespoons butter

SERVES 6–8

Have ready, measured, and prepared the above ingredients. Start by rendering the suet in an iron cocotte over a moderate heat until the fat has melted and the remaining bits are a delicate yellow, about 5 minutes. Remove these bits with a slotted spoon. Add the beef and cook rapidly until lightly browned all over, about 10 minutes. Add the chopped onion and garlic and stir with a wooden spoon for a minute. Then reduce heat and add the chiles; stir; sprinkle with the paprika and oregano; stir; add a little salt and coarsely ground black pepper and the chili powder; stir; and moisten with the beef broth. Cover and cook very gently until the beef is very tender, about 2½ hours; at which time add the sliced

olives and simmer ½ hour longer. Stir occasionally while cooking and add 1 tablespoon hot water once or twice, if necessary,
to prevent juice from reducing too much.

Half an hour before the meat will be done, prepare the corn
meal in the following manner. Heat in saucepan to boiling point
6 cups water. Measure 2 cups yellow corn meal into top of large,
3-quart, double boiler. Add 2 teaspoons salt and 2 cups cold
water. Stir well and gradually add the boiling water. Place over
direct but moderate heat and stir constantly with a wooden spoon
until well thickened, about 10 minutes. Place pan over boiling
water and continue cooking about 15 minutes longer, stirring
occasionally. When done, add 3 tablespoons butter and stir until
melted. Remove from fire and cool about 10 minutes.

In the meantime butter lightly bottom and sides of a round
2-quart baking-dish (preferably an earthenware casserole), leaving unbuttered, however, the top inch of the sides to give the
corn meal something to cling to. You are now ready to line the
dish with a thick coating of the corn meal; to do this pour about
two thirds of the corn meal into the dish, and as it cools spread it
up the sides to the top with a spoon. Keep remaining corn meal
warm over hot water.

The meat by this time should be done. Remove it from the
fire and cool while the corn meal sets and cools in the dish.
*Pre-heat oven to 325°.* Now into this nest ladle carefully the meat
and all the precious juice. Cover the meat completely with the remaining one third of the corn meal. Be sure the corn meal touches
the rim of the casserole all around. Now make a generous 1-inch
hole in the center to act as a vent while the pie is baking.

Place in pre-heated oven and bake slowly for 1 hour. At the
last moment, if not already browned, place under the broiling-unit
for a few seconds until a delicate brown. Serve with a well-seasoned ripe-tomato salad.

NOTE   If you like more pepper heat, a few crushed Italian red
pepper seeds may be added to the meat while cooking, or you
may include, if procurable, 2–3 strips hot chile peppers, which
also come in a can.

## BROILED SIRLOIN STEAK DIPPED IN
## PEPPER-HOT WINE SAUCE

2 2½-pound sirloin steaks,
    1½–2 inches thick
6 shallots
3 cups red wine
¼ pound butter
1 teaspoon dry mustard

salt, pepper
1–2 teaspoons Worcestershire
    sauce
4 pickled hot peppers
1 tablespoon chopped parsley

Chop 6 shallots fine and put them into an enamel pan with 3 cups red wine. Simmer until wine reduced to 1 cup. While broiling the steak 12–14 minutes, melt ¼ pound butter in frying-pan and add to it 1 teaspoon dry mustard, salt, pepper, and 1 scant teaspoon of Worcestershire sauce. Then add 1 cup reduced wine, from which you have strained out the shallots. Simmer a second or two, stirring well, and then add 4 pickled hot peppers, green and red mixed, chopped fine, and 1 generous tablespoon chopped parsley.

Place the broiled steak (it should be on the rare side) on hot platter and send to the table accompanied by the sauce in a chafing-dish. Slice the steak in thin strips and dip each piece gradually in and out of the boiling-hot sauce before placing on hot plates.


## LE STEAK AU POIVRE

3 pounds ¾-inch-thick top sir-
    loin steak
1 tablespoon chopped parsley
1 tablespoon cracked pepper

½ cup white wine
¼ pound sweet butter
¼ cup brandy
salt

SERVES 6–8

Cut steak into 12 pieces of equal size, discarding fat and gristle. Cover breadboard with heavy wax paper. Lay steak out on paper and sprinkle with 1 tablespoon coarsely cracked pepper. Cover with more wax paper and pound with wooden mallet until ⅜-inch thick. Heat a large, heavy iron frying-pan until very hot, add ⅛ pound butter, and spread it over the entire surface of pan. Add steak and sear quickly on both sides; reduce heat and cook as desired until rare, medium, or well done, 1–4 minutes.

Place steak on large, sturdy hot platter and sprinkle with salt. Add 1 cup dry white wine to brown residue in pan and cook rapidly, stirring with wooden spoon, until reduced to syrupy consistency. Remove from fire and stir in ⅛ pound butter. Now pour ¼ cup heated brandy over steak, light it, and allow it to burn itself out, ladling the brandy over it with a spoon. Pour gravy from pan over all, sprinkle with parsley, and serve at once.

# *Lamb*

## ROAST LEG OF LAMB A LA FRANCAISE
*[Pre-heat oven to 500°]*

1 6–7-pound leg of lamb          salt, pepper
1 clove garlic

SERVES 6–8

Put the leg of lamb in a roasting-pan. Insert in the meat at the shank 1 clove garlic. Rub the roast all over with salt and pepper. Place pan in hot 500° oven for 15 minutes, then reduce heat to 350°, and continue roasting 15 minutes to the pound—no longer. The meat should still be pink when sliced. Add no water, but baste frequently with the melted fat in pan.

When done, place meat on platter and keep warm while you make a little clear gravy. Drain off fat in roasting-pan, add to the pan about 1 cup cold water, and cook over moderate flame, stirring well. When the gravy is reduced, pour it into hot sauce boat and serve with the lamb. Flageolet, or marrow beans, buttered and sprinkled lightly with chopped parsley, should accompany the roast.

## ROAST RACK OF LAMB PERSILLE

*[Pre-heat oven to 450°]*

2 3-pound racks of lamb (rib chops), trimmed for roasting
2 cups crumbs of white bread, plucked from loaf
1 clove garlic

3 lemons
½ cup chopped parsley
1 teaspoon salt
½ teaspoon cracked pepper
18 paper frills for chops

SERVES 6–8

Ask your butcher to prepare 2 racks of lamb for roasting. The exposed bones should be protected with cubes of fat or strips of aluminum foil to prevent charring. Interlace the bones so that the 2 roasts may prop each other securely in the roasting-pan. Prepare 2 cups crumbs, plucked from center of loaf of white bread. Chop sufficient parsley to make ½ cup. Peel 1 clove garlic. Place roasts in hot (400°–450°) oven and roast, basting frequently, until beginning to brown, about 15 minutes. Reduce heat to moderate 350°, sprinkle roasts with 1 teaspoon salt and ½ teaspoon cracked pepper, and continue roasting, basting occasionally, for 40–50 minutes longer, depending on how well done you like it.

Fifteen minutes before you figure the roasts will be done, toss together the crumbs and parsley and squeeze over them 1 clove garlic, using a garlic press. Sprinkle this over the two roasts; ladle some of the fat carefully over the crumbs so as not to wash them off. Return to oven to complete the roasting and until the crumbs are lightly browned. Transfer the standing roasts carefully to a hot meat platter, and surround with any of the crumbs remaining in the bottom of the pan. A sieve spoon is good for this process. Remove charred fat or foil from chop bones and replace with paper frills. Garnish with 2 quartered lemons, and just before sending to table squeeze the juice of 1 lemon over all. Carve at table and serve 2 chops to each person.

## LAMB WITH GARLAND OF VEGETABLES
*[Pre-heat oven to 450°]*

| | |
|---|---|
| 1 6–7-pound leg of lamb | 2 cans beef consommé |
| 8 green peppers | 6 tablespoons butter |
| 8 small zucchini, or yellow squash | salt, pepper |
| | 3 bay leaves |
| 2 large Bermuda onions | 1 teaspoon dried basil |
| 2 2-pound, 3-ounce cans Italian plum-shaped tomatoes | ½ cup olive oil |

SERVES 6–8

This dish was invented by me in a desperate effort to think up something delectable for my forever-dieting friends and family which would not be considered too fattening. We rose above the fact, however, that it contains ½ cup olive oil and almost as much butter—but heavenly it is!

Quarter 8 green peppers, remove stems and seeds, and wash carefully. Place them in a large porcelain-lined, cast-iron baking-dish, 15″ by 10″ by 3½″ (I hope you have one). Scrub clean 8 small zucchini, or yellow squash; peel, quarter, and, if you have used the yellow squash, scoop out and discard the seeds. Cut in chunks and spread over the peppers. Peel 2 large Bermuda onions, cut in half crosswise, and cut each half in 8 parts. Scatter over the squash. Open 2 large cans Italian tomatoes and pour over the other vegetables. Sprinkle with salt, pepper, and 1 teaspoon dried basil, and bury in the whole 3 bay leaves. Pour over this 2 cans of beef consommé. Dot with 6 tablespoons butter; trickle over all ½ cup olive oil.

Place in a pre-heated oven and bake for about 2 hours, basting with its own juice. Watch carefully and when the juice has boiled down and the vegetables are beginning to brown, reduce heat, cover with aluminum foil, and continue cooking, adding as necessary a little water at a time to prevent scorching (not more than 2 cups in all). Remove from oven and scrape down the sides to incorporate the nice brown residue into the remaining syrupy juice. This should be accomplished 2 hours before dinner is to be served.

It is now time to roast the leg of lamb in the usual way, 1½–2 hours, depending on how well done you prefer it. Be careful not to allow the fat to burn, and baste the lamb occasionally. A clove of garlic may be tucked into the shank before roasting, if you like. Fifteen minutes before you consider the lamb will be done, transfer it to the pan containing the cooked vegetables and place back in oven to warm the vegetables and complete the cooking of the lamb.

In the meantime pour off all fat from the roasting-pan, add 1 cup water to pan, and place it over moderate flame and simmer, stirring well with wooden spoon, to make a nice thick, syrupy clear gravy to be served separately with the lamb. When ready to serve this succulent dish, sprinkle copiously with chopped parsley and send to the table right in the baking-dish, which will keep it hot while the meat is being carved.

## BOILED LEG OF LAMB WITH CAPER SAUCE

|  | Sauce: |
|---|---|
| 6–7 pound leg of lamb | 8 tablespoons butter |
| 12 little white onions | 6 tablespoons flour |
| 12 medium-size carrots | 3–4 cups hot lamb broth |
| 12 tender small white turnips | 1 large bottle capers |
| salt | salt |
| bouquet of parsley | ¼ teaspoon coarsely ground black pepper |

SERVES 6–8

With a sharp knife trim a leg of lamb weighing 6–7 pounds, removing carefully all the dry skin, and some of the fat. Wrap it carefully and tightly in a piece of clean linen and sew it in securely. Peel 12 little white onions, 12 medium-size carrots, and 12 tender small white turnips. Leave all the vegetables whole.

Place the leg of lamb in a large roasting-pan. Pour enough

boiling water over the lamb to cover, and when it comes to the boiling point again, skim carefully and add all the vegetables. Cover and simmer gently for about 2 hours. Salt to taste after it has cooked 1 hour.

When done, make the sauce by melting 6 tablespoons butter in top of large enamel double boiler over direct heat; adding 6 tablespoons flour and cooking without browning over low flame; then adding gradually a sufficient amount of strained lamb broth to make a moderately thick sauce (3-4 cups). Simmer over direct heat, stirring constantly, until smooth and thick; then add 1 large bottle of capers and about half the liquid from the capers. Taste and season with very little extra salt and about ¼ teaspoon coarsely ground black pepper.

Now remove the cloth from the lamb and place it on a very large platter. Carve and place the boiled vegetables attractively around the edge; garnish with parsley. Serve the sauce separately in a large gravy boat, but just before serving it stir in a lump of butter the size of an egg. A bowl of plain boiled, peeled potatoes should accompany this very delicious and simple English dish.

## BRAISED LEG OF LAMB WITH OLIVES

| | |
|---|---|
| 5-6 pound leg of lamb | 1 teaspoon of thyme |
| 10 tablespoons butter | 1 heaping teaspoon beef ex- |
| 2 cloves garlic | tract |
| salt, pepper | 2 cups pitted green olives |
| bouquet of parsley and 3 bay leaves | 1 small bunch of parsley |

SERVES 6-8

Pare off all extra fat and dry skin from a small leg of lamb weighing 5-6 pounds. Melt ¼ pound butter in a roasting-pan on top of the stove. Stuff a clove of garlic at the small end of the leg, between the bone and the meat, until well hidden. Brown the roast slowly on top of the stove, turning it over and over until brown on all sides, then salt it lightly and pepper it well with coarsely ground pepper. Add a bouquet of parsley and 3 bay leaves and

sprinkle into one corner of the pan a scant teaspoon of thyme.
Put a big clove of garlic on end of fork and rub the roast all over
with it. Then add 1 heaping teaspoon beef extract that you have
dissolved in ½ cup hot water.

Cover tightly so that no steam escapes and let it simmer very
very slowly on a low flame on top of the stove for at least 3 hours.
When almost cooked, pour off most of the juice into a little saucepan and reduce it by simmering until thick and syrupy. Scald 2
cups pitted green olives, first removing the pimentos if you were
unable to purchase unstuffed ones. Drain well and add them to
the lamb with 2 generous tablespoons butter and let them simmer
with the meat, rolling them over so that they are well coated with
the remaining meat juice and butter. Remove all fat from the
reduced juice.

Carve the meat on a hot platter, garnish with olives and a
bunch of parsley and pour the clear reduced juice over all. Serve
at once with well-buttered lima beans garnished with chopped
parsley.

## GIGOT DE SEPT HEURES
## OR
## GIGOT A LA CUILLERE
[Cooking time—7 hours]

| | |
|---|---|
| 1 small 6-pound leg of lamb | 3 bay leaves |
| 1 ½-pound slice of pre-cooked smoked ham | 1 teaspoon thyme |
| ½ pound of salt pork | ¾ cup consommé |
| 6 onions | 3 whole cloves |
| 4 carrots | Large sprig of parsley |

SERVES 6–8

Ask your butcher to cut off all the fat from a 6-pound leg of lamb
and to bone and roll it. Then ask him to cut ½ pound salt pork
in strips and to lard the roast with half of this. Also ask him to
saw the lamb bones in several pieces. Also buy a ½-pound slice of
pre-cooked smoked ham cut ½ inch thick.

Peel 6 white onions and stud 1 onion with 3 whole cloves. Wash and peel 4 carrots and slice. Make a bouquet of parsley, 3 bay leaves, and 1 teaspoon thyme. Cut off all the fat from the slice of ham and cut the fat in cubes. Add these to ¼ pound salt pork cut in cubes and place both in an iron cocotte. Render this fat over a low flame until it is just beginning to brown lightly, then add the ham slice and brown it lightly on both sides. Remove the ham temporarily and place the lamb bones in the pot along with the onions and carrots and cook gently for a few minutes. Place the boned rolled lamb roast on this bed and cover it with the ham slice. Add the bouquet and pour over all ¾ cup consommé. Cover the pot tightly, place on very low flame, and simmer gently 7 hours on top of the stove. It will form plenty of juice and be remarkably tender.

Fifteen minutes before serving light your oven, setting the control at 450°. Lift the meat carefully onto an ovenproof serving-dish and cut and remove all strings; place in oven for a few minutes. Strain the juice into a small pan. Ladel off all the fat and pour several spoonfuls of this juice over the meat; place meat under the lighted grill (but not too close), and allow the meat to glaze 5–10 minutes, basting 3 times with a little additional juice. In the meantime reduce the juice in the saucepan by boiling it rapidly until syrupy.

Garnish the meat with parsley and serve at once, accompanied by the juice in a sauce boat; mashed potatoes are almost a must with this succulent dish, and buttered boiled carrots are lovely too. The meat will be so tender, it could really be eaten with a spoon.

### POACHED LEG OF LAMB
### WITH SAUCE BEARNAISE

7–8 pound leg of lamb
¼–½ cup ground white pepper
1 tablespoon salt

10 cloves garlic
12 juniper berries
bouquet of parsley
sauce béarnaise (page 298)

SERVES 6–8

We were having a cooking party. Mme. Pierre Brissaud offered to cook the lamb that I had expected to roast. She promptly took a sharp knife and calmly proceeded to remove every vestige of outer skin and fat from my nice leg of lamb. I was frankly worried. Next she wanted a piece of cloth, a needle, some thread, and a thimble. I brought her a clean old pillowslip, wondering what on earth she wanted it for. It seemed that the roast was to be sewn up in the cloth. I was bewildered but very interested. She didn't like the pillowslip—it wasn't linen—it had to be linen. I gave her one of my best linen napkins. She carefully boiled it and then hung it on the oven door to dry. Then she wrapped the leg of lamb ever so neatly, sewed it up securely, and said: "*Voila.*"

Next she wanted ½ cup pepper, 1 tablespoon salt, 12 juniper berries, and 10 cloves garlic. I said a silent prayer and good-by forever to my lovely leg of lamb, and concentrated on my praline soufflés, nevertheless keeping an eye on Mme. Pierre Brissaud. She next heated a large pot of water, and then asked for the scales. She carefully weighed the lamb. When the water boiled, she asked for a clock—I gave her one that my children hadn't taken apart. She then put all the pepper and cloves and garlic in the pot and then the leg of lamb. She then sat down to rest and watched me—the result being that my dessert was a definite flop. I really didn't care, however, because I knew her lamb was going to be even more of a flop.

Ray was to make the Béarnaise sauce for the lamb—everything was ready. He did it with perfect ease. The potatoes were pronounced cooked—by Jean. Joe had set the table—the plates were hot—we were ready. Mme. Brissaud stopped watching us and with incredible dexterity extracted her leg of lamb, carved it, and placed it on the table. The Béarnaise sauce didn't curdle, and never have I eaten anything as superbly delicate as Mme. Brissaud's leg of lamb. And here is how to make it:

Carefully trim off all the fat and dry skin from a 7–8 pound leg of lamb and then weigh the lamb again and make note of it. Wrap it in a piece of old white linen and sew it so that it is completely bound up. Choose a pan large enough to hold the leg comfortably. Partially fill with water and bring to a boil. Add ¼–½ cup ground white pepper, 1 tablespoon salt, 10 cloves garlic, and

12 juniper berries. Put in the leg of lamb. Allow to simmer ever so gently, partially covered, 15 minutes for each pound, and not a minute longer. When cooked the correct amount of time, remove from the water, cut away linen, and place on hot platter. Carve it as you would a roast of lamb; the lamb should be pink in the center. Garnish with parsley and serve at once with a large bowl of peeled and boiled new potatoes and sauce béarnaise (page 298).

## CURRY OF LAMB

3 pounds cubed shoulder of lamb (with all fat and gristle removed)
2 teaspoons salt
3 tablespoons flour
6 tablespoons curry powder
1/8–1/4 teaspoon cayenne
1/2 pound butter
2 bay leaves
2 onions
2 tart apples

4 tablespoons seedless raisins
6 carrots
6 stalks celery
saffron
juice of 1 lemon
2 cups drained pineapple cubes
1 pound long-grain rice
chutney
1–2 cups freshly grated coconut
tabasco

SERVES 6–8

Wash and remove strings from 6 stalks celery; cut in 2-inch pieces. Peel 6 carrots and cut in 2-inch pieces. Peel 2 onions and cut fine. Put the celery and carrots in a saucepan, cover with 3 cups water, and cook until tender, about 15 minutes. Put aside temporarily.

Mix together 2 teaspoons salt, 3 tablespoons flour, 6 table-spoons curry powder, and 1/4 teaspoon cayenne; dredge the 3 pounds cubed lamb in this mixture. Melt 1/2 pound butter in large heavy frying-pan. Add the 2 chopped onions and 2 bay leaves and cook gently until onion is soft, about 8 minutes. Add the floured meat, and fry gently for 10 minutes, stirring frequently with wooden spoon. Add 1 cup boiling water and stir well. Simmer 20 minutes, then add enough boiling water to barely cover the meat. Turn heat very low, cover the pan, and allow meat to simmer gently 45 minutes, or until tender.

At this point add the cooked carrots and celery, 4 tablespoons seedless raisins, 2 cups drained pineapple cubes (or substitute fresh pineapple cut in chunks). Peel 2 tart apples, core, and cut each in 8 pieces. Add apples to the lamb; add a big pinch of saffron and the strained juice of 1 lemon. Stir, add a little water if necessary, and simmer gently 20 minutes longer. If gravy seems too thin when done, thicken with 1–2 tablespoons of flour mixed smooth with water until consistency of cream. Be sure, however, to allow the gravy to cook long enough to thicken and to avoid the raw taste. Add a good dash of Tabasco if you like a very pepper-hot curry. Serve with plenty of flaky boiled rice (cooked with or without saffron), freshly grated coconut, and good chutney.

## CURRIED NOISETTES OF LAMB
*[Pre-heat oven to 425°]*

| | |
|---|---|
| 12–16 French lamb chops, cut 1″ thick | 1 heaping teaspoon good curry powder |
| 12–16 strips of bacon | 1 tablespoon chopped parsley |
| 12 small ripe tomatoes | salt, pepper |
| 10 tablespoons butter | |

SERVES 6–8

Order from your butcher 2 large French lamb chops, cut 1 inch thick, for each person. Ask him to cut the meat away from the bone, making what is known in France as *noisettes*. Ask him to wrap around each a strip of bacon, securing the bacon with toothpicks.

Wash 12 small ripe tomatoes and cut out stem ends. Slice each in three. Butter a large round ovenproof-glass pie plate with 1 tablespoon butter and lay the tomato slices in a circle around the edge overlapping each other regularly. In the center of the dish lay 3–4 slices to cover bottom of dish. Cream together 8 table-spoons butter and 1 heaping teaspoon good curry powder. Dot the tomatoes well with three quarters of the curried butter and sprinkle with salt and pepper. Bake the tomatoes in pre-heated oven about 25 minutes.

In the meantime heat a large, heavy iron frying-pan, add 1 tablespoon butter and sear the chops quickly on both sides, turning on bacon side and rolling them around a bit to cook the bacon a bit. When browned place them in the center of the ring of tomatoes, salt and pepper lightly, remove toothpicks, and put the dish back in oven to cook 6–8 minutes longer.

By this time the chops should be done and the tomatoes should have browned. If they haven't, place under direct flame for a second or two, then just before serving, dot with remainder of the curried butter, sprinkle with 1 tablespoon chopped parsley, and serve at once.

## PLAIN BUT GOOD LAMB STEW

| | |
|---|---|
| 4½ pounds shoulder of lamb, cut for stew | 1 tablespoon chopped parsley |
| 9 carrots | 2 bay leaves |
| 9 medium-size onions | 12–16 tablespoons butter |
| 2 large white turnips | 6 tablespoons flour |
| 12 small potatoes | ¼ teaspoon cracked pepper |
| | salt |

SERVES 6–8

Brown 4½ pounds shoulder of lamb in 6 tablespoons butter in large, heavy iron frying-pan. Make a white *roux* in saucepan using 6 tablespoons butter and 6 tablespoons flour; add gradually 4½ cups boiling water; stir until thickened. Transfer meat to large iron cocotte. Add 1½ cups water to frying-pan in which meat was browned. Bring to a boil, stirring well. Pour this clear gravy into the thickened sauce and then pour the whole over the meat. Add 2 bay leaves, ¼ teaspoon cracked pepper, and salt to taste. Cover and cook over low heat for 1 hour.

In the meantime wash and peel 9 carrots and cut in three; peel 9 medium-size onions; peel 2 large white turnips and cut in eight; and peel 12 little potatoes. Also wash and chop fine 1 tablespoon parsley. *Pre-heat your oven to moderate 375°.*

Transfer the stew to large ovenproof casserole, or baking-dish. Bury in the stew the carrots and onions, cover, and place in oven to cook gently for about 2 hours longer. Half an hour before the stew will be done, boil the potatoes and the turnips separately in lightly salted boiling water. When done, place the vegetables, well drained, in a serving-dish, side by side; dot with 4 tablespoons butter, if desired; and sprinkle with paprika. Ladle off any excess fat from the stew, sprinkle with parsley, and serve accompanied by the vegetables.

## HARICOT D'AGNEAU

2–3 pounds shoulder of lamb (for stew)
½ pound lean salt pork
4 tablespoons butter
1 big onion
8 little white onions
1½ cups canned consommé
¼ cup flour
½ glass dry white wine or dry sherry

salt, pepper
bouquet of parsley
1 clove garlic
¼ teaspoon marjoram
¼ teaspoon thyme
1 stalk celery
1 leek, white part
2 cups dried white beans (marrow or pea)
1 tablespoon chopped parsley

SERVES 6–8

The night before wash 2 cups dried white beans (preferably marrow) and put them to soak in luke-warm water overnight. When ready to make the Haricot d'Agneau, pour off the water in which the beans have soaked, cover them with fresh cold water, and bring them slowly to a boil; then reduce the heat and simmer until the skins will roll off when you blow on them.

In the meantime scald ½ pound lean salt pork cut in tiny squares; drain well. Peel 1 large and 8 small white onions. Slice the large onion fine and leave the others whole. Melt 2 tablespoons butter in a frying-pan, add the scalded salt pork and the sliced onion and cook slowly until lightly browned. Add the whole onions and when they have browned slightly, transfer them to a hot iron or earthenware cocotte containing 2 tablespoons fresh butter. To the sliced onion and salt pork left in the frying-pan, add 2–3 pounds shoulder of lamb, cut up as for stew, from which as much fat as possible has been removed. Brown the meat slowly on all sides transferring the pieces as they brown to the cocotte, along with the pork. Pour off all the fat in the frying-pan and add to the brown residue in the pan 1½ cups canned consommé, and stir until it comes to a boil. Next sprinkle ¼ cup flour over the meat in the casserole and stir with wooden spoon until the flour is well mixed. Then add ½ cup dry white wine or dry sherry, and stir well. Add the hot consommé. Stir until smooth; then season to taste with salt and coarsely ground pepper and add a bouquet of parsley, 1 clove garlic, 1 stalk celery, the white part of 1 leek (well washed), ¼ teaspoon marjoram, and ¼ teaspoon thyme.

Now drain the parboiled beans saving the water in which they cooked. Cover the meat with the beans, add just enough of the bean water to barely cover the whole. Cover tightly and simmer very gently until the meat is very tender, about 2 hours. Watch carefully and add more bean water if necessary to prevent sticking. The stew should be moist when served but not soupy. When done, set aside for 5–10 minutes, then skim off as much fat as possible. Reheat to boiling point, sprinkle with chopped parsley, and serve.

## SHISH KEBAB

| | |
|---|---|
| 5–6 pound leg of lamb | 2 cloves garlic |
| 1 teaspoon salt | 1 cup imported burgundy |
| 1 teaspoon thyme | 4 green peppers |
| 1 teaspoon coarsely ground pepper | 8 small ripe tomatoes |
| 1 teaspoon caraway seeds | 6 small onions |
| 1 teaspoon rosemary | 1 pound fresh firm mushrooms |
| 8 tablespoons olive oil, and more | 4 17-inch stainless-steel skewers |

SERVES 6–8

Ask your butcher to remove all fat from a small, 5–6 pound, leg of lamb and cut the meat in 1½-inch squares. Place meat in glass dish and pour over it 1 cup imported burgundy mixed with 4 tablespoons olive oil. Sprinkle with 1 teaspoon salt, 1 teaspoon coarsely ground pepper, 1 teaspoon caraway seeds, 1 teaspoon thyme, and 1 teaspoon rosemary. Also add 2 small onions, peeled and quartered, and 2 cloves garlic, peeled and cut in two. Allow the whole to marinate 5–6 hours, stirring occasionally to saturate meat on all sides.

Wash 8 small tomatoes and 4 green peppers. Peel and quarter 4 onions. Quarter the peppers lengthwise and cut again crosswise, making 8 pieces; discard seeds. Remove tough part of stems from 1 pound firm fresh mushrooms, wash if necessary, and peel— but leave whole.

*Pre-heat broiling-unit to maximum temperature.* Pour 4 table-spoons olive oil in bottom of large roasting-pan. Place on this bed the tomatoes. Then starting and ending with a mushroom, place the marinated meat alternately with the peppers and onions and mushrooms on 4 17-inch stainless-steel skewers, using all the prepared ingredients. Balance these lengthwise on end edges of roasting-pan over the tomatoes. Trickle olive oil over all and broil 15–20 minutes, turning skewers over to brown ingredients evenly. Have ready a large heated serving-platter and when the shish kebabs are done, slip them off the skewers in neat rows onto platter and garnish with tomatoes. Pour juice from bottom of roasting-pan over all and serve at once with Tomato Risotto (page 73).

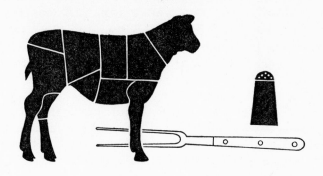

# Veal

## ROAST OF VEAL COOKED WITH CARROTS AND ONIONS

5-pound boned and rolled
  rump roast of veal
bones from the roast, and an
  extra one, if possible
1 large onion
2 whole cloves

14 carrots
12 little white onions
parsley
¼ pound soft butter
salt, pepper

SERVES 6–8

Buy a small rump roast of veal, weighing about 5 pounds. Have the butcher bone and roll it, but be sure he gives you the bones and an extra one, if possible. Wash the bones, place in large pan, and add enough water to cover well. Add 1 large onion, into which you have stuck 2 whole cloves, and 2 carrots, peeled and quartered. Simmer gently, skimming it carefully, for several hours, or until you have about 1½ cups strong veal broth.

About 2½ hours before you will be ready to serve the veal, light your oven to very hot 475°. Place the roast in your roasting-pan surrounded by at least 12 peeled little white onions and 12 peeled carrots, sliced crosswise. Spread ¼ pound soft butter over the meat, and place in oven until lightly browned, basting frequently. Be careful not to allow the butter to burn, turn the heat down a bit if necessary, and turn the meat over during the process so as to brown both sides. At this point sprinkle it lightly with about 1 teaspoon salt and ½ teaspoon coarsely ground pepper, turn the heat down to 350°–375°, and continue cooking slowly, basting frequently, until well done, about 2½ hours in all. The vegetables will be nice and brown by this time and will have collapsed (which is as it should be).

Transfer roast to another smaller roasting-pan, remove strings, and spoon over it as much buttery fat as possible, skimmed from the vegetables. Return to oven while you make the sauce. Add the strong veal broth to the vegetables and reduce by simmering until rich and syrupy. Carve the roast on a hot serving-platter, garnish with parsley, and serve at once accompanied by the sauce, collapsed vegetables, and all. Serve at the same time, to be eaten on the same plates, a well-tossed green lettuce or romaine salad with a tart French dressing (enhanced if possible with chopped fresh tarragon and parsley mixed).

## VEAL IN CREAM

| | |
|---|---|
| 2–3 pounds veal, cut very thin, from the top round from hind leg | 2 pounds butter |
| | 1 cup heavy cream |
| | salt, pepper |
| flour | 1–2 tablespoons good cognac |

Have the butcher cut 2–3 pounds top round of veal as thin as possible. Roll each piece lightly in flour, then lay them on a floured board, and pound with a mallet, or a wooden potato-masher. This process pounds the flour into the meat and also makes the slices thinner still. Brown these slices in about 2 tablespoons butter in a frying-pan, being careful not to crowd the pieces. As they brown, place them in a previously heated iron cocotte containing 2 tablespoons fresh butter. As you brown the meat, add more butter to the frying-pan, if necessary. A brown crust will form in the bottom of your frying-pan. Be careful not to let this get too brown.

Stop in the middle of the process of frying, add about 1 cup water to the pan, and stir with a wooden spoon until the brown part is melted and the water has reduced. This will form a syrupy brown gravy; add it to the browned meat in the cocotte. Wash the frying-pan, start again with a fresh lump of butter, and fry the rest of the meat, repeating the process of making the gravy again and adding it to the meat.

Now the veal must simmer quietly, tightly covered, for about 1 hour. It must be watched carefully. Add a little more boiling water, if necessary, to keep it from sticking. Salt and pepper to taste when half cooked. Fifteen minutes before serving, add 1 cup heavy cream, stir well, and continue cooking very, very slowly. Just before serving, season again to taste with salt, freshly ground pepper, and a tablespoon or more of good cognac.

## VEAL CHOPS WITH MUSTARD SAUCE

| | |
|---|---|
| 6–8 ¾-inch-thick veal chops | ¼ pound butter |
| 6–8 tablespoons finely chopped onions | salt, pepper |
| | 1 cup dry white wine |
| ⅛ pound butter | ½ cup heavy cream |
| flour | 2 teaspoons prepared mustard |

SERVES 6–8

First cook slowly, without browning, 6–8 tablespoons finely chopped onions in ⅛ pound butter. Wipe surface of 6–8 ¾-inch-thick veal chops clean with a damp cloth. Sprinkle them very lightly on both sides with flour. Heat a little less than ¼ pound butter, previously clarified if possible, in a heavy, not-too-large frying-pan, and when sizzling hot, add the chops and sauté quickly to a golden brown on both sides; then reduce the heat and continue cooking slowly about 10 minutes.

When the chops are cooked, salt and pepper them well, place them in a small hot earthenware or glass baking-dish. Add to the butter in which chops were cooked about 1 cup dry white wine; stir while it reduces to a syrupy consistency; then pour this over the chops. Place around the chops the cooked onions. Cover tightly with well-buttered wax paper and the lid of the dish, and continue cooking slowly in a *pre-heated 400° moderate oven* 20–30 minutes, or until the chops are very tender. Remove the chops temporarily while you add about ½ cup heavy cream to the onions. Bring to a boil for a second; then add 2 heaping teaspoons prepared mustard to the cream and stir well, but do not let it boil again. Replace the chops and serve at once, accompanied by mashed potatoes.

## BRAISED VEAL CHOPS EN GELEE

| | |
|---|---|
| 8 veal chops | ¾ cup chicken or veal stock |
| salt, pepper | 1 pint quick aspic (page 309) |
| clarified butter | fresh tarragon leaves |

SERVES 6–8

Brown 8 neatly trimmed veal chops in a little sizzling-hot clarified butter in a cocotte, so that they are a golden brown on both sides. Salt and pepper them; pour over them ¾ cup hot stock, preferably veal or chicken; cover tightly and let simmer for about 1 hour. Place the chops on a platter, and pour the juice left in bottom of pan through a fine sieve into a small bowl. Place in refrigerator to hasten the rising of the fat to the surface. Skim off this fat carefully and pour the remaining juice over the chops.

In the meantime make 1 pint clear aspic. Pour one third of the aspic on a shallow platter and place in refrigerator to set. Lay the chops on this aspic bed when they are perfectly cold and decorate with plenty of fresh tarragon leaves, dipping the leaves first in the aspic—which is about to set. Place platter in refrigerator for a few minutes, then carefully pour the rest of the aspic on the chops and replace in refrigerator to set firm. Serve ice cold on chilled plates, accompanied by a delicious green salad.

## BRAISED QUASI DE VEAU

4-pound rump roast of veal, boned and rolled
1 extra veal bone, weighing about 1 pound
3 large carrots
6 large mushrooms
10 tablespoons butter
1 large onion
4 shallots

3 tablespoons flour
1 teaspoon salt
¼ cup parsley
¾ teaspoon coarsely ground pepper
1 bay leaf
¼ teaspoon thyme
1 quart milk
1 teaspoon beef extract

SERVES 6–8

First make the sauce. Wash and peel 3 large carrots. Cut in chunks. Peel 1 large onion and 4 shallots and cut in quarters. Wash and remove tough part of stems from 6 large mushrooms and quarter. Wash some parsley and pluck green from stems to make ¼ cup. Place shallots, onion, carrots, parsley, and mushrooms in enamel pan. Add 1 bay leaf and ¼ teaspoon thyme and pour over all 1 quart milk. Bring to a boil on low flame, protect with asbestos mat, cover and simmer gently, stirring occasionally, until milk reduces to about 3 cups, about 1 hour. Strain and discard vegetables. Melt 4 tablespoons butter in top of enamel double boiler over low flame, add 3 tablespoons flour, stir for a minute or two, and add gradually the hot seasoned milk to make a smooth sauce. Place over warm water, stirring occasionally to prevent skin forming.

In the meantime brown lightly on all sides a 4-pound roast of veal, and the extra veal bone with some meat attached, in 6 tablespoons butter in a heavy iron pan. Transfer to a large heavy casserole (preferably porcelain lined). Melt 1 teaspoon beef extract in ½ cup boiling water and add to pan in which you browned the meat; stir well and reduce slightly; and then pour over meat. Sprinkle with 1 teaspoon salt and ¾ teaspoon coarsely ground pepper. Cover tightly and cook gently until meat is very tender, 1½–2 hours. Remove meat and bones temporarily and keep warm while you complete the sauce.

Add the milk sauce to the remaining buttery juice in casserole; stir constantly over low heat until very hot, but do not allow to boil. Strain through fine sieve back into top of double boiler. Keep hot over boiling water while you remove strings from roast. Place roast on hot platter, cut with sharp knife in thick slices, pour hot sauce over all, and serve at once.

## BLANQUETTE OF VEAL

3 pounds solid veal, horseshoe cut, cut in 1-inch squares
salt, pepper
1 small peeled onion
1 whole clove
1 large carrot, peeled
bouquet: parsley, celery leaves, 1 bay leaf, ¼ teaspoon thyme

½ pound small white mushrooms
1 lemon
⅜ pound butter
12 small white onions
½ cup flour
1 tablespoon chopped parsley
2 egg yolks
¼ cup heavy cream
pinch of nutmeg

SERVES 6–8

Soak 3 pounds solid veal (horseshoe cut) cut in 1-inch squares, in enough cold water to cover for 2 hours. Drain and place the meat in a deep enamel pan. The top of a large 3-quart double boiler is ideal. Pour over it 1 quart fresh cold water, or as little more as possible, so that the meat is well covered. Add 1 teaspoon salt, place on low heat, and bring very slowly to boiling point. This is a slow process and will take about ½ hour. Stand by and skim carefully. Add 1 small peeled white onion that you have studded with 1 whole clove, 1 large peeled carrot, cut in chunks, also a little bouquet, securely tied, of a few celery leaves, parsley, ¼ teaspoon of thyme, and 1 bay leaf. Cover partially and simmer gently for 1½ hours.

In the meantime remove the stems from ½ pound fresh small white mushrooms. Wash them carefully. Have ready an enamel saucepan containing ¼ cup cold water, the juice of ½ lemon, and 1 tablespoon butter. Peel the mushrooms one by one, quarter them, and place immediately in the sauce pan containing the water, lemon, and butter. When all are prepared, place the pan on the fire, cover, and bring to a brisk boil. Cook 4–5 minutes, shaking the pan occasionally. Watch carefully, so that they don't boil dry. Remove from fire and keep warm.

Now place 12 little white onions of uniform size in a sieve and dip the sieve down into a pan of boiling water. Let it stay for 1 minute. This is to facilitate the removal of the outer skin. Drain and with a little knife cut off as little as possible from each end of the onions and peel. Place the onions in a little pan just big enough to hold them comfortably, then add 1 tablespoon butter and ¼ cup broth from the veal. Cover and place on low heat and cook gently about 35 minutes or until just tender through. Watch carefully and add a spoonful of hot water if necessary to keep them from boiling completely dry.

When the veal is done remove the bouquet, carrots, and the onion, and strain off most of the broth into another little pan. Dot the meat with 2 tablespoons butter, place over boiling water, cover, and keep warm while you make the sauce.

Melt ¼ pound butter, add ½ cup flour, cook together a minute or two, stirring constantly to make a white roux, then add the hot broth gradually, of which there should be 3 cups (if there is not enough, add boiling water to make up the difference). Now add the mushrooms and their juice and the onions and their juice to the meat. Chop fine some parsley. Break 2 egg yolks into a little bowl, add ¼ cup heavy cream, beat it together, and add to it gradually a little of the hot sauce, and in turn add this mixture gradually back to the sauce. Do not allow to boil. Season to taste with salt, coarsely ground pepper, a pinch of nutmeg, and the juice of ½ lemon. Also drain into it all the remaining juice on the meat. Pour the sauce over the meat. Place into a deep hot serving-platter. Garnish with chopped parsley and serve at once accompanied by a big bowl of flaky, boiled white long-grain rice.

## CURRIED VEAL CHOPS

8 1-inch-thick veal chops
2 juicy apples
8 tablespoons butter
2 cans consommé
2 tablespoons cornstarch
¼ teaspoon cayenne
¼ teaspoon coarsely ground
    pepper
3 tablespoons genuine Madras
    curry paste
1 tablespoon chopped parsley
½ cup finely chopped shallots

Accompaniments:
1 cup shredded coconut
1 cup raisins
juice of 2 lemons
1½ cups chutney
1 pound rice

SERVES 6–8

Buy 8 1-inch-thick veal chops. Ask the butcher to trim them carefully, and cut off most of the rib bone so that they won't be too long. Prepare ½ cup peeled, chopped shallots (onions may be substituted but will not be as delicate). Peel, core, and chop moderately fine 2 large juicy apples. Melt 4 tablespoons butter in a medium-size frying-pan and add the shallots. Cook slowly for about 5 minutes, stirring constantly with wooden spoon. Add the apples and continue cooking for about 5 minutes more, stirring lightly to avoid crushing the apples. Have ready 2½ cups (2 cans) hot consommé. Sprinkle the apples and shallots with 2 tablespoons of cornstarch and when well stirred in, add the consommé, stirring constantly. Reduce the heat and simmer ever so gently for about 15 minutes.

In the meantime melt 3 tablespoons butter in large, heavy iron frying-pan, and when sizzling hot, add 8 veal chops and cook slowly, turning occasionally until a golden brown both sides, about 15 minutes. Be careful not to allow the butter to burn. Have ready a large earthenware casserole with a cover, in which you have melted 1 tablespoon butter. Place the casserole on an asbestos mat over a very low flame. When the chops are brown, transfer them temporarily to a plate and spread the top of each with a generous coating of genuine Madras curry paste, using about 3 tablespoons of the mixture. Place the chops, curry side up, in the casserole. Add ½ cup water to pan in which you browned the chops and reduce to a syrupy consistency, by simmering over a low flame. Add this to the apple-and-shallot sauce. Pour this over the chops. Cover the casserole and simmer gently until the chops are very tender, about 1½ hours. Prepare 1 tablespoon chopped parsley. Remove casserole from fire and allow to stand until excess fat rises to surface. Ladle this off. Reheat, sprinkle with parsley, and serve at once accompanied by boiled rice, chutney, coconut, and seedless raisins that have been washed, soaked until plump, then drained, and covered with strained juice of 2 lemons.

## ESCALOPES DE VEAU A L'ESTRAGON

3 pounds veal cutlets, pounded
    thin and cut in 2-inch
    squares
½ cup olive oil
1½ cups dry white wine
4 cups chicken broth

1 large bunch tarragon
2 level teaspoons arrowroot
    powder, or cornstarch
small bunch of parsley
salt, pepper

SERVES 6–8

Wash the tarragon and pat it dry. Then reserve 2–3 dozen of the most perfect leaves. Add to the remaining bunch of tarragon a small bunch of parsley and make a little bouquet of it.

Now pour ½ cup olive oil into a large heavy frying-pan and place over moderate heat until it is just beginning to smoke; at which time add the pieces of meat one at a time, distributing them over the bottom so that they are not on top of each other. Cook for about 3 minutes or until they are a beautiful golden brown. Then turn them over one by one and brown the other sides. Reduce the heat a little if necessary, as it is important not to allow the brown particles at the bottom of the pan to become too dark in color. When the meat is browned on both sides, drain off and discard every bit of the olive oil and pour over the meat

1½ cups dry white wine; stir well. Add gradually, stirring with a wooden spoon, 4 cups chicken broth. When all the brown residue has been melted into the liquid, transfer to an earthenware casserole. Season to taste with a little salt and pepper. Add the bouquet of parsley and tarragon stems, cover tightly and place over low heat to simmer gently for about 1 hour. Turn the meat over when it is half done. Watch carefully toward the end, adding a little more broth and wine if necessary so that there will be at least 2 cups of syrupy clear gravy left.

Five or ten minutes before it is done, stir in gradually 2 tablespoons arrowroot or cornstarch dissolved in 4 tablespoons water; stir with a wooden spoon until thickened.

Now cut the tarragon leaves that you have saved, but not too fine, and place them in a sieve. Drop the sieve into a small pan of boiling water to blanch the leaves, drain, and add leaves to the meat. Stir and serve at once, accompanied by buttered boiled new potatoes.

## TENDRONS DE VEAU A L'ESTRAGON

| | |
|---|---|
| 4 pounds solid veal (horseshoe cut), cut in inch cubes | 4 teaspoons dried tarragon, or 6 teaspoons fresh tarragon |
| 2 teaspoons salt | 2 medium-size onions |
| ⅓ cup flour | 4 egg yolks |
| ¼ pound butter | 1½ cups heavy cream |
| 3½ cups boiling water | 4 tablespoons tarragon vinegar |
| | ¼ cup chopped parsley |

SERVES 6–8

Melt ¼ pound butter in large heavy iron frying-pan and when sizzling hot add 4 pounds solid veal, horseshoe cut (part just above the knuckle) which has been cubed. Brown lightly, turning pieces over with pancake turner. If too much juice forms, preventing browning, drain off some of it, but keep it. When the meat has browned very lightly, sprinkle with ⅓ cup flour, stir with wooden spoon, and add gradually 3½ cups boiling water. When well mixed and smooth and sauce has thickened, pour back into the sauce any juice you may have drained off, sprinkle with four teaspoons dried tarragon, or 6 of fresh, and 2 teaspoons salt. Add 2 medium-size onions, peeled and quartered. Transfer to large earthenware casserole or porcelain-lined Dutch oven. Cover tightly and simmer gently on top of stove until meat is tender, at least 2 hours. Stir occasionally to prevent sticking.

When done, stir in 4 tablespoons tarragon vinegar. Remove from fire and stir in gradually 4 egg yolks beaten with 1½ cups heavy cream. Place back on low flame and stir constantly just long enough to heat and thicken the sauce, but be very careful not to allow it to actually boil. Sprinkle with ¼ cup chopped parsley and serve right in the dish in which it was cooked. Serve with carrots, peas, or string beans and French bread. This is also delicious served cold with salad the next day.

## VEAL BIRDS
*[Pre-heat oven to 500°]*

| | |
|---|---|
| 3 pounds veal cutlet, sliced thin | ¼ teaspoon marjoram |
| 1½ tablespoons chopped parsley | ¼ teaspoon thyme |
| 1½ cups soft bread crumbs | 3 whole eggs |
| 3 tablespoons chopped celery | 10 tablespoons butter |
| 8 shallots chopped fine | ½ cup flour |
| 4 strips bacon | 3 small carrots |
| salt, pepper | 1 medium-size onion, chopped fine |
| ¼ teaspoon cayenne | 2 stalks celery |
| | 1 can consommé |

SERVES 6–8

Buy 3 pounds veal cutlet, sliced very thin. Prepare 1½ tablespoons chopped parsley, 1½ cups soft white-bread crumbs, 3 tablespoons finely chopped celery, and 8 shallots, chopped fine.

Spread the meat out onto wax paper on a large breadboard, cover with more wax paper, and pound until very thin. With sharp scissors cut off all the odds and ends of pieces, leaving 16 large pieces about the size of the palm of your hand. Run all the scraps twice through your meat-grinder using the medium blade; also put through the grinder 4 strips bacon. Place the meats in a big bowl and add the soft bread crumbs and the chopped parsley, shallots, and celery, and season with a little salt, a little coarsely ground black pepper, ¼ teaspoon each of cayenne, mace, marjoram, and thyme, the latter two well rubbed between your finger to reduce them to a powder. Now break 3 whole eggs into the mixture and stir well until thoroughly mixed.

Now place 1 tablespoon of this stuffing on each piece of veal, and roll them up nice and neatly, enclosing as much of the stuffing as possible. Tie each roll securely like a little package, using a fine string. Butter copiously the bottom of a large rectangular shallow baking-dish or pan, approximately 16″ by 8″. Melt a little butter in a small pan, and using a pastry brush paint each little bundle with a coating of butter on both sides. Then roll each one lightly in a saucer containing about ½ cup flour seasoned lightly with a little salt and pepper. Place the little birds side by side in the baking-dish, cover with wax paper, and chill until ready to bake.

At this point, dot with 6 tablespoons of butter and sprinkle with 3 small carrots and 1 medium sized onion chopped fine and 2 stalks of celery likewise chopped fine. Place in pre-heated 500° oven and bake for about 20 minutes; then pour over them about ½ cup hot consommé, and continue cooking 10 minutes. At this moment cover, reduce heat to 400°, and continue cooking slowly for 45 minutes. Remove cover and continue cooking, basting frequently until a beautiful golden brown, about 30 minutes longer, adding from time to time a little additional hot beef consommé so that at no time are the birds allowed to get completely dry.

When done remove from oven and with the help of scissors carefully remove all the strings. Place the birds on a hot platter and keep warm while you once more add a little hot consommé to the residue in the pan. Place on low flame and stir well to incorporate all the brown part, then pour it over the birds. Garnish with chopped parsley and serve at once.

## OSSO BUCCO

8 3-inch-thick pieces knuckle of veal
1 cup chopped raw carrots
1 cup chopped celery
1 cup chopped onion
bouquet garni, (parsley, bay leaf, ½ teaspoon thyme)
1 1-pound, 4-ounce can Italian peeled tomatoes
8 tablespoons butter
1 tablespoon of flour
4 thin strips lemon peel
½ cup good dry white wine
¾ cup clear chicken or veal broth
4 tablespoons of olive oil
1 tablespoon of chopped parsley
1 teaspoon grated lemon peel
salt and pepper to taste

SERVES 6–8

Ask your butcher to saw 8 slices knuckle of veal about 3 inches thick, being sure he gives you the part where there is some meat on the bone.

Prepare, 1 cup *each* of finely chopped raw carrots, celery, and onion. Also prepare a bouquet garni, consisting of parsley, 1 bay leaf, and ½ teaspoon thyme tied in a little bundle. Drain but save the juice from 1 small can of Italian peeled tomatoes and rub the tomatoes through a fine sieve; discard the seeds, add the pulp to the juice, which should give you about 1½ cups of thick juice. Cream together 2 tablespoons butter with 1 tablespoon flour, and cut 4 thin strips of peel from a lemon, avoiding the white bitter part. Measure out ½ cup good dry white wine, and ¾ cup clear broth, preferably veal or chicken.

Place 4 tablespoons olive oil in a large, heavy iron frying-pan, and place on low flame. Add the chopped carrots and celery and cook slowly for about 10 minutes, stirring constantly until vegetables are just beginning to brown; then add the onions and continue cooking, stirring constantly for 10 minutes longer. At this point add the 1½ cups tomato juice and pulp and ½ cup wine. Add the flour and butter, and stir until thickened.

Remove from fire temporarily while you brown the meat quickly in 4 tablespoons butter in a seperate large frying-pan. When a golden brown all over place the meat in a heavy iron pot containing 2 tablespoons fresh butter and pour over them the sauce. Add ¾ cup clear broth to the pan in which you browned the meat, and stir well to dissolve the brown residue into the broth. Add this to the meat and add the prepared bouquet garni. Sprinkle lightly with salt and coarsely ground pepper, and add the 4 strips thin lemon peel. Cover and simmer about 1¾ hours, or until the meat is tender. Watch carefully so that it does not stick on the bottom.

In the meantime prepare 1 tablespoon finely chopped parsley and 1 teaspoon freshly grated lemon peel. When the meat is done tie a pretty towel around the pot, sprinkle the meat with the grated lemon peel and chopped parsley, and serve at once, accompanied by freshly cooked broccoli and plenty of crisp French or Italian bread.

## JON STROUP'S VEAL-AND-HAM ROLLED ROAST WITH MUSHROOM SAUCE
*[Pre-heat oven to 475°]*

| | |
|---|---|
| 1 boned loin of veal, weighing 4½ pounds dressed | 14 tablespoons butter |
| 4 ¼-inch-thick slices boiled ham | 2 cups heavy cream |
| | 2 lemons |
| 1½ pounds firm fresh mushrooms | salt, pepper |
| | 1 cup chicken broth |
| | 2 long, thin meat skewers |

SERVES 6–8

Rub the roast (which should be long in shape) with a little coarsely ground pepper. Dot with ¼ pound butter. Roast, basting occasionally, until lightly browned, about 25–30 minutes. Reduce heat to 350°, and continue roasting slowly for 1¾ hours more, basting occasionally. Transfer to another pan and strain over the roast the fat in which it was cooked. To the brown residue in first pan add 1 cup clear chicken broth or water; stir with wooden spoon over moderate heat and simmer until well reduced and syrupy in consistency. Place in small double boiler over hot water, until ready to serve the roast.

When the roast has cooled sufficiently to handle, place on wooden board, remove strings, and cut in even ½-inch slices, leaving them in place. Cut the ham in two, making 8 pieces and place them between the veal slices. With the aid of 2 long thin skewers and white string, reform the roast. With scissors trim the ham slices so that they conform to the shape of the roast. Return to second pan until ready to reheat, preferably within an hour or so.

In the meantime wash and dry carefully 1½ pounds firm fresh mushrooms and chop very, very fine. Do not grind them. Melt 6 tablespoons butter over low heat, add mushrooms and cook very slowly for 10 minutes—the aim being to heat rather than to cook the mushrooms. In top part of double boiler over boiling water heat 2 cups heavy cream. Add the mushrooms and season lightly with salt. Keep warm.

Reheat the roast in 400° oven for ½ hour, basting once or twice. Remove the roast from the oven and transfer carefully to deep, hot, serving-platter. Remove the skewers and strings, and squeeze the juice of 1 lemon over all. Now be sure the mushroom sauce is hot, but do not allow it to boil. Add the juice of ½ lemon, stir, and pour half of it over and around the roast. Serve roast at once, accompanied by the remainder of the mushroom sauce and the hot clear gravy in separate bowls. This is a very festive dish. I suggest serving also plain boiled potatoes, buttered fresh green peas, and white wine.

## VITELLO TONATO

2½ pounds round of veal
    without bone
2 teaspoons salt
3 stalks celery
3 carrots
3 onions
1 bay leaf
a few peppercorns

parsley
2 cloves
1 4-ounce-can tuna fish
juice of 2 lemons
1 cup olive oil
salt, pepper
1 lemon

SERVES 6–8

Make a bouillon of 2 quarts water, 2 teaspoons salt, 3 carrots, 3 small onions peeled and sliced, 1 bay leaf, a few peppercorns, a sprig of parsley, and 2 cloves. Boil 5 minutes, and add a small piece of solid round of veal without the bone, weighing about 2½ pounds. Simmer very gently, skimming carefully, for about 1½ hours. Cool in its juice.

Drain, slice thin, and arrange in overlapping slices on oblong serving-dish. Cover with the following sauce.

Crush 4 ounces canned tuna fish, well drained of its protective oil; add juice of 2 lemons, 1 cup olive oil, a little coarsely ground pepper, and a little salt. Marinate the veal in this sauce for at least 24 hours in the refrigerator. When ready to serve, garnish with thin slices of lemon, minus all peel, and sprinkle copiously with chopped parsley. Serve crisp Italian or French bread with this. This is also good as an hors d'œuvre.

# *Pork*

## ROAST LOIN OF PORK
### [*Pre-heat oven to 450°*]

2 2½–3 pound half loins of pork, rib ends
3 teaspoons salt
1 teaspoon coarsely ground black pepper
1 teaspoon thyme
½ teaspoon mace or nutmeg
4 whole cloves
3 bay leaves
bouquet of celery leaves and parsley
1¼ cups dry white wine
1 can beef consommé
juice of 1 lemon, strained
2 large onions, sliced fine
2 small cloves garlic
1 bunch of parsley
2 carrots

SERVES 6–8

Buy 2 half loins of pork, rib ends, 2½–3 pounds each, nicely trimmed. Wipe with damp cloth and dry. Mix together 3 teaspoons salt, 1 teaspoon coarsely ground black pepper, 1 teaspoon thyme, and ½ teaspoon of mace or nutmeg. Rub this well over the roasts. Place in enamel-lined roasting-pan; and place around them 2 peeled carrots cut in thick slices, a bouquet of parsley and celery tops, 3 bay leaves, 4 whole cloves, 2 cloves crushed garlic, and 2 large onions, peeled and sliced. Pour over all ½ cup dry white wine and ½ cup beef consommé. Place in oven and roast for 20 minutes or until a golden brown. Reduce heat to 350° and continue roasting, basting occasionally, until well done, about 3 hours. If necessary add a small quantity of hot water to the vegetables in the pan from time to time to prevent their burning. Fifteen minutes before the roasts will be done, transfer them to another pan and squeeze over them the juice of 1 lemon. Return to oven while you make the gravy from the residue in the first pan.

Add ½ cup water, ¾ cup white wine, and the remainder of the can of consommé. Boil this down rapidly, scraping the brown part down from the sides of the pan and cook until thick and syrupy. Strain into a small pan and set aside until fat rises to the surface. Discard the vegetables. Ladle off the fat from the clear gravy and keep hot over boiling water until ready to serve. Place the roasts on a hot platter, garnish with parsley, and serve accompanied by the sauce in a sauce boat. Mashed sweet potatoes are delicious with this.

For variety, cook this in advance and serve cold, garnished with the clear gravy, which jells beautifully when cold.

## JON STROUP'S PORK TENDERLOIN
## WITH APRICOTS

| | |
|---|---|
| 3 pounds pork tenderloin or boned loin | flour |
| | salt, pepper |
| 1 pound dried apricots | ¾ cup heavy cream |
| 4 tablespoons butter | 2½ cups Bordeaux |

SERVES 6–8

Wash 1 pound dried apricots. Place in enamel pan and cover with 2 cups Bordeaux diluted with 2 cups water. Cook uncovered for 15–20 minutes or until tender. Keep warm.

Meanwhile remove all the fat from 3 pounds pork tenderloin

or boned loin. Cut in ½-inch-thick slices, making 10 slices. Sprinkle lightly with salt and coarsely ground pepper and dust both sides with flour. Melt 2 tablespoons butter in a large iron frying-pan and brown the pork slowly on both sides, which will take about 20 minutes. Cover tightly and continue cooking slowly for another 20–25 minutes or until well done, turning occasionally to prevent sticking. Arrange in a circle around a hot platter and keep warm in hot oven.

Heat the apricots. Drain but save the juice and pile the apricots in center of meat. Pour off any fat there may be in the frying-pan and add to the brown residue the apricot juice and an additional ½ cup Bordeaux. Stir and boil down rapidly until thick and syrupy. Add gradually ¾ cup heavy cream, and when syrup is hot remove from fire and stir in 2 tablespoons butter. Pour over the meat and apricots and serve at once with plain, unbuttered, peeled, boiled new potatoes.

## PORK CHOPS AS THEY COOK THEM IN THE AUVERGNE

8 pork chops
2 small fine, white cabbages
2 cups heavy cream
salt, freshly ground pepper

6 tablespoons butter
1 cup dry white wine
freshly grated imported Parmesan cheese

First wash, quarter, core, and cut up fine 2 small white cabbages. Soak in salted water; drain; cover with salted boiling water; and cook until tender, about 10 minutes—but do not overcook. Drain; rinse off in cold water; then put it in an enamel pan with 2 cups heavy cream, salt, and freshly ground pepper; and let it simmer gently for about ½ hour.

In the meantime fry to a golden brown in 2 tablespoons butter 8 choice pork chops from which you have cut off some of the excess fat; salt and pepper them adequately and cook them thoroughly, but do not let them burn. When cooked, remove from pan and keep warm while you add a good pinch of crumbled sage and about 1 cup dry white wine to the butter in the pan in which they were cooked. Stir well to dissolve all the nice brown part in the pan: then add this juice to the cabbage, taste, and add more salt and pepper if necessary (it must be highly seasoned), and mix well together.

Now put a layer of the cabbage in a glass or earthenware baking-dish and lay the chops on this bed. Then cover the chops completely with the rest of the cabbage; over all pour the cream from the cabbage. Sprinkle the top lightly with freshly grated Parmesan cheese and pour over it 4 tablespoons melted butter. Put the dish in a *pre-heated* 350° *oven* to cook slowly for about 45 minutes until a golden brown on top. Serve accompanied by French bread and red wine.

## PORK CHOPS EN CASSEROLE
[*Pre-heat oven to 425°*]

| | |
|---|---|
| 10 fine loin pork chops | salt, pepper |
| 11 tablespoons butter | 1 tablespoon chopped parsley |
| 18 small white onions | |

SERVES 6–8

Peel 18 small white onions and brown in frying-pan in ⅛ pound butter. At the same time in a separate large iron frying-pan brown slowly on both sides 10 fine loin pork chops in 3 tablespoons butter. While you are browning the onions and chops, place in the oven a large earthenware casserole with ⅛ pound butter, and allow it to heat gradually.

When the chops and onions are browned, place the chops first in the casserole and cover with the onions. Add ½ cup water to each frying-pan, and stir over low heat until you have a little clear brown gravy in each; pour both all over the chops. Sprinkle lightly with about 1 teaspoon salt and ½ teaspoon coarsely ground pepper. Cover and cook slowly for 1½ hours, reducing heat to 375° after the first 15 minutes. Remove from oven, drain off juice into little pan, and allow it to stand until fat rises to surface; then skim this off, and pour the clear gravy back over chops. Return casserole, uncovered, to oven and cook 5 minutes longer. Sprinkle with 1 tablespoon chopped parsley and serve at once accompanied by carrots and mashed potatoes.

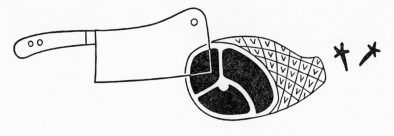

# Ham

## BAKED HAM IN CRUST OF DOUGH
*[Pre-heat oven to 450°]*

<table>
<tr><td>Ham:</td><td>Crust:</td></tr>
<tr><td>12-pound pre-cooked ham</td><td>4 cups all-purpose flour</td></tr>
<tr><td>24 whole cloves</td><td>⅔ cups cider vinegar</td></tr>
<tr><td>6 tablespoons light-brown<br>    sugar</td><td>1⅓ cups cold water</td></tr>
<tr><td>1 teaspoon dry mustard</td><td>1 tablespoon dry mustard</td></tr>
<tr><td>4 tablespoons cider vinegar</td><td>½ cup extra flour</td></tr>
</table>

**Bottom of pan:**
⅓ cup vinegar mixed with ⅔ cup water

SERVES 6–8

Buy a 12-pound pre-cooked ham; trim off the brown part of the fat, removing as little as possible. Score the fat neatly with a sharp knife, forming a diamond pattern. Place it, fat side up, in a large roasting-pan. Stud with 24 cloves. Pour over it 4 tablespoons cider vinegar, then pat over the surface 6 tablespoons light brown sugar mixed with 1 teaspoon dry mustard. Cover top and sides with blanket of dough made in the following manner.

Mix 4 cups all-purpose flour in a bowl with 1 tablespoon dry mustard, and add enough vinegar diluted with water (about ⅔ cup vinegar and 1⅓ cups water) to make a stiff dough. Roll out on floured pastry cloth, using about ½ cup extra flour to prevent sticking, making the blanket large enough to cover top and sides of ham. Hold your breath, and with the help of a trusted friend roll it up on the pin and drop it on the ham, hoping it will land safely without tearing. If it does tear, don't worry, just patch it with a bit from the sides. Pour ⅓ cup vinegar mixed with ⅔ cup water in bottom of pan. Place in pre-heated oven for about 20 minutes to the pound, about 4 hours.

By the time the ham is done, the crust will be very hard and dark brown, but will have held the moisture in the ham and absorbed some of the excess fat. The crust is discarded, of course. Give it a crack with a mallet and remove carefully before serving. This is my favorite way of preparing pre-cooked hams.

## ROBERT'S BOILED HAM AND GREENS

| | |
|---|---|
| ½ pre-cooked tenderized ham (bone left in, weighing about 6 pounds) | salt, pepper |
| | parsley |
| | English mustard |
| 4 bunches tender white tur-nips, leaves attached | French mustard |
| | 1 jar bread-and-butter pickles |
| 5 bunches tender fresh mus-tard greens | 6 ripe tomatoes |
| | 1 Bermuda onion |
| 4 pounds new potatoes | whipped butter |

SERVES 6–8

Wash the mustard greens, leaf by leaf, cutting or pulling away all of the tough stems. Do likewise with the turnip tops. Wash again in several waters, keeping the turnip greens separate from the mustard leaves.

Wash and peel the turnips (there should be at least 2 dozen), and cut them into uniform-size oval shapes. Wash and peel 4 pounds potatoes of uniform size and put them into cold water until ready to cook.

Wash the ham and place it in the bottom half of a big roasting-pan and cover with 4 quarts cold water. Bring gently to boiling point, skim carefully, reduce heat even more, cover, and simmer very gently for 1 hour. By this time the ham should be well done, but not falling apart. Remove it temporarily to a platter and trim off the brown part of the fat. Place it in a smaller deep pan and pour over it half of the ham water. Cover and allow to cool in its juice.

Now blanch the turnip greens by pouring boiling water over them and allowing them to come to a boil; then drain off the water. Add the mustard greens just as they are to the remaining ham stock in the roasting-pan, bring to a boil, add the blanched turnip greens, and cook gently for about 1 hour, or until tender. At this point add the drained white raw turnips, a little salt if necessary, about ½ teaspoon coarsely ground black pepper. Cook for 1 hour more, or until the turnips are tender.

In the meantime, ladle off some of the excess juice from the greens, placing it in an enamel pan, add most of the juice from the ham; and boil it down until well reduced, or until you have about 1 quart left. Put the ham with the rest of its juice over a very low flame and let it heat through gently, but be sure not to let it boil. Twenty minutes or so before the turnips will be done, boil the potatoes in the usual way until done. When ready to serve the whole, place the ham on a deep hot platter. Carve it in thin slices, garnish with parsley, and serve, accompanied by the greens, garnished with the turnips and the well-drained potatoes (dotted with plenty of sweet butter, sprinkled with chopped parsley).

Collect the juice from the ham and the greens, add it to the reduced juice, and put it into a pitcher. This is the precious pot liquor, and it should be served in cups and be sipped while eating the ham and vegetables.

This succulent dish should be accompanied by small pots of English mustard and French mustard, bread-and-butter pickles, plenty of thin corn bread (page 180), and a bowl of very cold peeled and sliced tomatoes (arranged in alternate layers in a serving-dish with paper-thin slices of Bermuda onion—over which you have poured the juice from the bread-and-butter pickles) and last but not least a dish of whipped or sweet butter for the corn bread.

## THIN CORN BREAD

*[Pre-heat oven to 500°]*

1 cup of water-ground corn meal
1 cup of flour
3 teaspoons baking powder
1 tablespoon sugar
1 teaspoon salt
2 eggs
1½ cups milk
4 tablespoons melted butter

Butter copiously two round layer-cake pans. Sift together 1 cup water-ground corn meal, 1 cup all-purpose flour, 3 teaspoons baking powder, 1 tablespoon granulated sugar, and 1 scant teaspoon salt. Beat 2 eggs until light; add to them 1½ cups milk; add the flour mixture and beat with spoon just long enough to mix; then stir in 4 tablespoons melted butter, and spread into the 2 buttered tins. Bake for about 20 minutes or until a golden brown, reducing heat to 450° if it browns too quickly. Turn out onto hot plates, cut in pie-shaped pieces, and serve at once.

## HAM STEAKS AND HOMINY IN CREAM

*[Pre-heat oven to 350°]*

2 ¾-inch-thick slices raw tenderized ham
2 teaspoons prepared mustard
½ teaspoon coarsely ground pepper
2 cups milk
2 cups heavy cream
2 1-pound cans white whole hominy
1 tablespoon butter

SERVES 6–8

Butter 2 rectangular ovenproof glass dishes, 7¼″ by 12″ by 2″. Trim off any brown fat there may be on 2¾-inch-thick slices raw tenderized ham; leave, however, the white fat, slashing the edges to prevent curling. Spread over each 1 teaspoon prepared mustard. Place mustard-side-down in dishes and pour over each 1 cup milk. Place in oven and bake 50 minutes, basting frequently—drain off the milk which will have curdled due to the salt in the ham.

Open 2 1-pound cans whole hominy, drain, and place around both slices of ham. Pour over each ½ cup heavy cream. Sprinkle each with ½ teaspoon coarsely ground pepper. Return to oven and bake 10 minutes, basting once. Add another ½ cup cream to each dish and bake 10 minutes more. Remove from oven, and put under hot broiler for a minute or two to brown lightly. Cut and serve with fresh green peas.

## FRESNO HAM STEAKS
*[Pre-heat oven to 375°]*

| | |
|---|---|
| 2 1-inch thick slices of tender-<br>    ized ham | 1 navel orange |
| | 2 lemons |
| 1 cup raisins | paprika |
| ⅔ cup light brown sugar | 18 pitted ripe olives |
| juice of 1 orange | |

SERVES 6–8

Soak 2 slices tenderized ham, cut at least 1 inch thick, in cold water for 2 hours. Pour off the water, trim off a little of the fat, and cut gashes in the remaining fat to prevent curling while cooking. Wash 1 cup seedless raisins and soak 15 minutes in cold water. Slice one navel orange in thin pieces and cut in half. Moisten ⅔ cup light brown sugar with ¼ cup cold water. Add the strained juice of 1 orange. Bring to a boil, add the well-drained raisins and simmer 5 minutes. Put the 2 slices ham in a large, shallow earthenware or ovenproof glass casserole and pour the sauce over them. Lay the sliced orange over all.

Bake the ham slowly, tightly covered, for about 2 hours. Baste occasionally and turn the slices over. By the time the ham is cooked the sauce should have become nice and syrupy. Fifteen minutes before it will be done, add 18 pitted ripe black olives. Transfer to hot platter, cut in inch-thick strips, garnish with quartered lemons dipped in paprika. Pour sauce over all and serve.

# *Other Meat Dishes*

## CASSOULET

1 3-pound loin roast of pork
1 2½-pound boned and rolled
   shoulder of lamb
bones from the lamb
1 shank of ham
½ pound lean salt pork
½ pound of Salsicietta or
   Luganica sausage
1 pound dried white beans
   (preferably marrow)

bouquet of parsley, 1 bay leaf,
   and ½ teaspoon thyme
10 small white onions
½ teaspoon coarsely ground
   pepper
1 clove garlic
toasted buttered crumbs
   (page 268)
tomato sauce (page 305)
2 tablespoons chopped parsley

SERVES 6–8

The night before, salt and pepper lightly 3 pounds loin of pork (the meat partially cut away from the bone lengthwise, but not crosswise). Refrigerate overnight. Also pick over and wash carefully 1 pound dried white beans (preferably marrow, though pea beans will do), cover well with cold water, and soak overnight.

The day of the party, wash a shank of ham, cover with cold water, bring gently to a boil, and drain. Do the same with ½ pound salt pork. Prepare a bouquet of parsley, ½ teaspoon of thyme, and 1 bay leaf. Make tomato sauce (page ooo). Drain the beans, cover with 4 quarts luke-warm water, bring to a boil, skim carefully, and reduce heat to a bare simmer. Add the scalded ham, scalded salt pork, and bouquet; and simmer gently for 1½ hours. Now add 5 little white onions, peeled and left whole; and after washing it first add ½ pound Salsicetta or Luganica sausage. Continue simmering for 1 hour or so until the beans are tender but not falling apart.

In the meantime *pre-heat the oven to moderate* 350° and roast the loin of pork slowly, basting frequently, cooking it in all about 2½ hours.

On top of the stove start cooking the lamb in the following manner. Melt 1 tablespoon butter in an iron cocotte and add 5 small white onions, peeled and left whole. When lightly browned, add the boned and rolled shoulder of lamb, weighing about 2½ pounds, and its bones. When the lamb has browned on all sides, drain off excess fat, add 1 clove garlic, peeled and chopped, and place uncovered in the oven to continue cooking slowly along with the pork for about 2 hours. A half-hour before it will be done pour the tomato sauce over the lamb and continue cooking until done.

When the beans are done and you are ready to assemble the cassoulet, drain the beans but save preciously their juice. Slice the ham in uniform pieces, discarding rind and bone. Cut the salt pork in uniform pieces, too; also the sausage. Remove the lamb from the cocotte, discard strings, and cut in bite-size pieces, discarding excess fat. Loosen pork from bone and cut it, too, into neat pieces. Strain the tomato sauce through coarse sieve, thereby removing bones. Add the bean juice to this and allow to stand until excess fat rises to surface. Skim carefully. Arrange the beans in alternate layers with the meat in a large earthenware casserole, reserving some of the sausage for the top layer. Moisten with the combined bean and tomato juices or sauce. Put back into a slow oven and continue cooking about 1 hour longer. In the meantime prepare 2 tablespoons chopped parsley and 1 cup buttered crumbs (page 268). When ready to serve, sprinkle with the hot crumbs and chopped parsley.

NOTE In case you think this is a complicated dish just be thankful I didn't include any *Confit d'Oie* as they do in the South of France.

## GALOTSIE POLONAISE

*[Pre-heat oven to 375°]*

1 pound boneless fresh pork, cut in thin slices

½ pound sliced boiled ham, cold

1 pound thinly sliced bacon

½ pound frankfurters, sliced in little pieces

1 pound mushrooms, peeled, washed, and sliced

1 8-ounce bottle green pitted olives, sliced fine

¼ pound butter

1 pound tomatoes, peeled and cut

1 pound sauerkraut, washed in cold water and juice drained out

1 can tomato juice (2 cups)

2 juicy apples, peeled, cored, and sliced

4 white onions, peeled and sliced

1 small cabbage, sliced and parboiled in salted water

salt, freshly ground black pepper

2 bay leaves

1 heaping teaspoon of sugar

2 cups sour cream

3 heaping tablespoons imported mustard

SERVES 6–8

Line a big earthenware baking-dish with part of the bacon, and put into it the different ingredients, layer by layer, leaving plenty of cabbage and tomatoes for the top, and lay several slices of bacon over all. Then pour the tomato juice over it and dot well with part of the butter. The rest of the butter should be buried lower down in the ingredients. Put the cover on the co-cotte and place it in a moderately hot (375°–400°) oven and cook for at least 2 hours. Remove cover toward the end to allow it to brown on top lightly. Serve with a big bowl of boiled new potatoes, peeled or not, and a bowl of mustard sauce.

*Mustard Sauce:*

Fold 3 heaping tablespoons prepared mustard into 2 cups sour cream. Sprinkle the top with plenty of finely cut fresh tender chives, and serve with the above Galotsie Polonaise.

NOTE   If the Galotsie Polonaise shows signs of boiling down too dry, moisten with more tomato juice or canned consommé as it cooks down.

### GABRIELLE'S CABBAGE, POTATO, AND SAUSAGE DISH

| | |
|---|---|
| 2 big green cabbages | salt, pepper |
| 16–18 small old potatoes | parsley |
| 2 pounds small pork sausages | |

SERVES 6–8

Gabrielle was old and fat and cross, but she could make a cabbage, potato, and sausage dish that tasted like something straight from heaven; but she couldn't make cake, so I undertook to teach her how. I mixed the cake, put it in the oven, which was just the right temperature, and went out in the garden to pick flowers. For some mysterious reason the cake was a dismal failure, all sunken in the middle. Gabrielle looked suspiciously gleeful. The next day I made another cake; and this time I only pretended to pick flowers. In a little while I saw her come innocently to the door to see where I was, then I saw her deliberately open the oven door wide with a diabolical smile on her face. We soon parted, but not before I learned how to make her cabbage dish.

Cut in quarters and remove cores from 2 large green cabbages; soak in salted water 30 minutes. Shred fine and boil in salted boiling water for 10 minutes. Drain well. Boil 16–18 small old potatoes with their skins on. Cool and peel. Cut in ½-inch squares. Brown 2 pounds small pork sausages slowly in a big iron frying-pan. Pour off the grease and cover with alternate layers of potato and cabbage. Salt and pepper lightly and simmer for

30–40 minutes until well browned on the bottom. Cover pan with a large round serving-platter, protect your hands with dry towels, and turn out upside down. Garnish with parsley and serve.

## LAMB KIDNEYS

| | |
|---|---|
| 8–10 lamb kidneys | 1 cup heavy cream |
| ¼ pound butter, and more | salt, pepper |
| 2 tablespoons imported pre- | fresh tarragon |
| pared mustard | parsley |

SERVES 6–8

Remove the fat from 8–10 lamb kidneys. Wash them, remove membrane, and slice them thin. Melt 8 tablespoons butter in a frying-pan; add the kidneys; simmer on low flame for 10 minutes, stirring well. Add 1 tablespoon butter and 2 tablespoons of imported prepared mustard, and stir until well mixed. Then add gradually 1 cup heavy cream. Season to taste with salt, freshly ground pepper, and a few chopped fresh tarragon leaves. Simmer a second or two longer, sprinkle with chopped parsley, pour into a warm serving-dish, and serve at once.

## BAKED WHOLE CALF'S LIVER
### [Pre-heat oven to 325°]

| | |
|---|---|
| 1 3½-pound calf's liver | 1 small clove garlic |
| ⅛ pound salt pork, cut in tiny squares | 3 tablespoons butter |
| | salt, pepper |
| 8 carrots | pinch of nutmeg |
| 8 little white onions | 1 can consommé |
| 8 whole cloves | ¼ cup white wine |
| bouquet of parsley, thyme, and bay leaf | ¼ cup Madeira |
| | 3 lemon slices |

SERVES 6–8

Buy a fine calf's liver weighing about 3½ pounds. Ask the butcher to lard it for you (as he would to prepare a pot roast). Also buy ⅛ pound salt pork cut in tiny squares. Peel 8 young carrots and cut each in four. Peel 8 little white onions and stick a whole clove in each. Make a bouquet garni of parsley, a pinch of thyme, 1 small bay leaf, and 1 small clove garlic. Brown the pieces of salt pork in 1 tablespoon butter, and place them in the bottom of an iron cocotte with 1 tablespoon fresh butter. Add the carrots, onions, bouquet, and liver. Sprinkle with salt, coarsely ground pepper, and a pinch of nutmeg. Pour over it 1 can of consommé, ¼ cup white wine, and ¼ cup Madeira. Top it all off with 3 thin slices lemon from which you have removed seeds and rind. Cover and place on low heat. Bring gently to a simmer.

Place cocotte in oven and continue cooking, basting frequently, about 2 hours or until very tender. Remove the bouquet. Pour off most of the juice and skim off as much fat as possible, strain juice and reduce by simmering until quite thick. Carve the liver in thin slices and place in heated earthenware casserole surrounded by the vegetables and pour over all the reduced juice into which you have stirred 1 tablespoon fresh butter. Return to oven for a few minutes to be sure it is hot, then serve accompanied by mashed potatoes.


## MEAT LOAF

*[Pre-heat oven to 450°]*

1¼ pounds top round of beef
1¼ pounds veal cutlet
1¼ pounds fresh pork (minus all fat)
1 cup finely rolled cracker crumbs
2 small onions, chopped fine
1 heaping tablespoon chopped parsley

½ teaspoon coarsely ground pepper
1 scant teaspoon salt
3 eggs
2 tablespoons butter
3 strips bacon, cut in two
1 can beef consommé
few sprigs of parsley

SERVES 6–8

Ask your butcher to put through the meat-grinder twice 1¼ pounds top round of beef, 1¼ pounds veal cutlet, and 1¼ pounds fresh pork minus all fat. Place in large bowl and add to it 1 cup finely rolled cracker crumbs, 2 small onions, peeled and chopped fine, 1 heaping tablespoon chopped parsley, ½ teaspoon coarsely ground pepper, 1 scant teaspoon salt, and 3 whole eggs. Work together with your hands until well mixed. Butter copiously a large bread pan, measuring approximately 10″ by 4¼″ by 3″, and lay over the bottom 3 half-strips of bacon. Fill the pan with the meat mixture, packing it in firmly and evenly. Lay 3 half strips of bacon over the top, and place in preheated oven and bake until lightly browned. At this point, pour over it about ¼ can beef consommé and reduce heat to 375°. Continue baking, basting with the remainder of the can of consommé every 15 minutes, until done. It should cook 2 hours in all.

As soon as it is done, run a knife around the edge and turn out onto hot platter, garnish with parsley and serve accompanied by buttered string beans and baked tomatoes. If you prefer to serve the meat loaf cold, turn out immediately as above, and cool. When completely cold wrap in wax paper and refrigerate before serving. Accompany with a green salad dressed with a tart French dressing and sprinkled with chopped parsley and fresh tarragon.

## PATE "VIEU-LOGI"

*[Pre-heat oven to 375°]*

| | |
|---|---|
| 2 pounds veal scallopini (pounded thin) | 1 scalded calf's foot, cut in four |
| 2 pounds ground shoulder of pork | 2 bay leaves |
| ⅛ pound pork fat back, pounded thin | 1 teaspoon thyme |
| ½ cup chopped parsley | ½ cup chopped shallots |
| | salt, pepper |
| | ½ cup brandy |

SERVES 6–8

Line the bottom of a covered baking-dish, 10″ by 4½″ by 4″, with the pork fat back. Cover with layer of veal cut in small pieces. Mix together the shallots and parsley and sprinkle part of it over the veal. Next add a layer of pork, and sprinkle lightly with salt and pepper. Repeat the process until all the ingredients have been used, being careful to press the meat firmly and evenly into the corners. Sprinkle the top with 1 scant teaspoon thyme and pour over all ½ cup brandy. Lay 2 bay leaves on top of the meat, and cover with the 4 pieces of calf's foot.

Cover the dish and place in pre-heated oven to bake slowly for 3 hours. Remove from oven, discard the calf's foot, and when cold, place in refrigerator overnight. When ready to serve turn out carefully onto serving-platter, slice, and garnish with chopped aspic and parsley. This is a good dish for a hot summer night.

## AUTRE PATE "VIEU-LOGI"

*[Pre-heat oven to 375°]*

| | |
|---|---|
| 2-pound slice leg of veal | ½ teaspoon dried rosemary |
| 3 strips pork fat back | ¼ teaspoon cracked pepper |
| ½ pound uncooked bacon, chopped fine | 2 tablespoons chopped parsley |
| 1 pound mushrooms | 1 calf's foot, split and cut into 4 pieces |
| 1 cup dry white wine | |

Ask the butcher to cut a 2-pound slice from a leg of veal, and ask him to pound it out thin, about ⅓ of an inch thick (as veal scaloppini) but to leave it in 1 piece instead of cutting it up. Place the veal on wax paper, and sprinkle evenly with the un-cooked chopped bacon. Next sprinkle it with 2 tablespoons chopped parsley, about ½ teaspoon dried rosemary, and ¼ tea-spoon of cracked pepper. Wash 1 pound fresh mushrooms, cut off the tough part of stems, and then chop the remaining stems and caps until moderately fine. Spread these evenly over the veal. Now roll the veal up, like a jelly roll, and tie it carefully, making as neat a roll as possible. Cover with the 3 strips of pork fat back and secure with more string. Place in iron cocotte and surround with a calf's foot, split and cut in 4 pieces. Pour 1 cup of dry white wine over all, place in pre-heated oven and bake gently for about 2½ hours, basting occasionally.

Remove from oven, transfer the meat to an oval-shaped dish that will hold it comfortably, and remove all strings. Add 2 cups water to the bones and brown residue in bottom of pan, stir well, and cook until slightly reduced, about 5 minutes. Strain this juice over the meat and allow to cool thoroughly. Chill in refrigerator until ready to serve. Run knife around the edge. Dip bottom of dish in very hot water for a second or two and turn out on serving-platter. Scrape off some of the excess fat around the sides. Garnish with parsley or water cress and send to table to be cut in ¼-inch slices and to be eaten with French bread and a good green salad.

## ROGNONI ALLA VENESIANA

| | |
|---|---|
| 4 veal kidneys | ½ cup Marsala wine |
| 1 large Bermuda onion | salt, pepper |
| 9 tablespoons butter | 1 teaspoon butter |

SERVES 6–8

Remove the fat and thin veil-like skin from 4 veal kidneys. Next slice in small pieces, being careful not to include any of the hard white substance in the center. Place on towel and squeeze lightly to remove any excess juice. Chop up fine 1 large Bermuda onion. Sauté the onion slowly in 4 tablespoons butter until a beautiful golden brown.

At this time add another 4 tablespoons butter and when sizzling hot, add the kidneys and cook quickly for about a minute, stirring the whole well. Then add ½ cup Marsala wine, reduce the heat, and simmer gently just long enough to cook the kidneys through, about 5 minutes. Then season well with salt and lots of coarsely ground black pepper. Remove from fire, add 1 teaspoon butter, stir until melted, and serve at once with red wine and mashed potatoes.

## SMOKED TONGUE GARNI WITH
## SOUR-CREAM HORSE-RADISH SAUCE

|  | Sauce: |
|---|---|
| 2 3-pound smoked tongues | 2 cups sour cream |
| 2 onions | 1 4-ounce bottle pickled |
| 6 cloves | horse-radish |
| 1 tablespoon whole mixed | |
| pickling-spices | |
| 6 onions | |
| 2 small heads cabbage | |
| 3 pounds new potatoes | |
| ¼ cup caraway seeds | |

SERVES 6–8

Prepare small cheesecloth bag containing 1 tablespoon whole mixed pickling-spices. Peel 2 medium-size onions and stud with 6 whole cloves. Peel 3 pounds new potatoes and soak them in cold water. Remove outer leaves from 2 small heads of cabbage; cut each in 8 parts down through the core; soak in a big pot of cold water. Remove stockinet covering from 2 small smoked tongues, weighing approximately 3 pounds each; wash the tongues thoroughly; then soak 1 hour in cold water. Drain, cover with cold water, and bring very slowly to boiling point—this should take about 1 hour.

Drain, cover with fresh boiling water; bring to boiling point. Skim carefully, add the bag of pickling-spices and 2 onions. Place on low flame, cover, and simmer very gently for about 3 hours. Insert a cake-tester, and if it goes in easily, the tongues are done. Remove from liquid, and as soon as the tongues are cool enough to handle, with the help of a sharp knife, pull off all the skin, and trim away all root tissue. Place in clean enamel pan, and cover with part of the liquid in which it was cooked. Keep below boiling point on lowest of flames.

Now put the potatoes on to boil in cold water. In 15–20 minutes they should be done. In the meantime bring the original pot of liquid to boiling point and 10 minutes before the potatoes will be done, add the drained cabbage. Watch and when it comes to boiling point, skim carefully. Add 1 teaspoon caraway seeds. Cook until just barely tender, or for not more than 8–10 minutes.

Place the 2 tongues on a large hot platter, cut in thin slices, garnish with the cabbage (lifted from the water with a pancake-turner). Drain the potatoes and place in separate hot vegetable dish. To make the sour-cream horse-radish sauce, drain all the liquid from the horse-radish and fold it into 2 cups sour cream. Serve shortly after mixing. Serve at once, accompanied by the sour-cream horse-radish sauce and a shaker (with large holes) containing caraway seeds—to be sprinkled over all, if desired (personally, I do). May I suggest a Rhine wine with this.

## SWEETBREADS HOLLYWOOD A LA BELLE MEUNIERE

| | |
|---|---|
| ⅔ cup shelled almonds | 3 cups milk |
| 3 avocados | 6 egg yolks |
| 6 pairs sweetbreads (about 2¼ pounds) | ¾ cup sherry |
| | 1–2 teaspoons salt |
| ¾ pounds fresh mushrooms | ½ teaspoon coarsely ground pepper |
| 3 tablespoons flour | |
| 6 tablespoons butter | ⅛ teaspoon cayenne |

SERVES 6–8

First blanch ¾ cup shelled almonds and slice them thin. Wash and cover with cold water and refrigerate until ready to use. Wash 6 pairs calves' sweetbreads carefully, place in enamel pan, sprinkle with 1 teaspoon salt, and cover with boiling water. Cover and cook gently for 20 minutes. Drain, cover with cold water, and soak until cold. Take them one by one and with the help of a small knife remove the very thin transparent membrane with which they are protected and the thin black bits running through the center. Cut into small pieces. Place in refrigerator while you make the sauce.

Wash, peel, and slice ¾ pound fresh mushrooms and sauté

them in 6 tablespoons butter until juice has reduced but do not allow to brown. Heat 3 cups milk and drain into it the juice from the mushrooms. Sprinkle mushrooms with 3 tablespoons flour and stir well. Add gradually the hot milk making a smooth sauce. Transfer to top of enamel double boiler and season to taste with about ½ teaspoon coarsely ground black pepper, additional salt, and about ⅛ teaspoon cayenne. Add the prepared sweetbreads, place over boiling water and heat thoroughly. Beat the 6 egg yolks with ¾ cup sherry and pour gradually into the sweetbreads and sauce. Continue cooking until thickened like custard, about 5 minutes.

Remove from fire and quickly peel 3 ripe avocados, split, remove seed, and slice crosswise in ½-inch slices. Pour sweetbreads into warm serving-dish, garnish lavishly with the avocado, and last of all sprinkle the drained, crisp blanched almonds over all. Serve at once accompanied by warm crisp French bread or rolls.

## VEAL KIDNEYS IN MUSTARD

| | |
|---|---|
| 6–8 veal kidneys | ½ pound sweet butter |
| imported prepared mustard | 1 heaping tablespoon cut |
| salt, pepper | chives |
| ¾ cup cognac | 2 teaspoons chopped parsley |

SERVES 6–8

Skin and cut up 6 veal kidneys, being careful not to include any of the white membrane. Prepare a large tray containing the chafing-dish, salt, pepper grinder, a pot of imported prepared mustard, ¾ cup cognac, ½ pound sweet butter, 1 heaping tablespoon cut chives, and 2 teaspoons finely chopped parsley.

The kidneys are sautéed in the kitchen and brought to the table in a hot dish with their juice in a cup. To sauté them, put 3 tablespoons butter in a very hot frying-pan, and when it is sizzling hot, add the kidneys and shake them around until lightly browned. They should cook very quickly or they will be tough.

At table put ¼ pound butter in the chafing-dish, and when

it has melted, add the juice from the kidneys, 4 tablespoons prepared mustard, the cognac, and some freshly ground pepper and
salt. Light the cognac as soon as it begins to boil and let it burn
until the flame starts to turn yellow and green. At this moment
extinguish the flame by putting on the cover. Now add the kidneys and chives and simmer a minute or two. Then stir in another good lump of butter, sprinkle the parsley over it all, and
pass at once.

# 6

# *Poultry*

*A*t the mere mention of guests, chicken is likely to pop up in one's mind as the best company dish—and it probably is. The trouble is, however, that in this country we almost always encounter it either broiled or roasted, which gets to be a bit of a bore. There are almost as many ways of cooking chicken as there are recipes for eggs, so there is no excuse for not being more imaginative.

Next in popularity are the barnyard cousins the duck and the turkey. It is almost impossible to do anything unusual about turkeys except to discover a new stuffing. They are certainly very handsome—roasted to a golden brown—and ideal for a big party. The recipe I have given for a boiled turkey doesn't succeed in making it look at its best, but is very good. The duck has five definite affinities—applesauce, oranges, peas, turnips, and olives.

Game birds are more complicated. There is always the question of how long they should hang; they are dreadfully expensive; they are never in market when you want them; somebody is always sending one to you when you have a date for every day in the week and have no idea how to cook it, anyway. I still have to discover, however, anything better than pheasants in cream, the recipe for which I have included in this chapter.

# Chicken

## BOILED CHICKEN

2 4½–5-pound roasting-
  chickens
8 whole peeled carrots
1 bunch celery
4 large leeks, white part only

4 medium-size onions
6 peppercorns
2 teaspoons or more of salt
1 small bay leaf

SERVES 6–8

Peel and wash 8 carrots. Remove tops from bunch of celery, wash thoroughly, and tie in bundle. Remove green part from 4 large leeks, split white down centers, and wash well. Peel 4 medium-size onions. Make a bundle of the leeks. Wash 2 fine plump roasting-chickens, weighing 4½–5 pounds each, and dry. Singe and truss. Place side by side in large enamel pan (preferably rectangular in shape). Add just enough warm water to cover (not more than 3 quarts), place on low heat and stand by until the water comes to boiling point. Skim carefully, and add the carrots, leeks, onions, 6 peppercorns, and 1 small bay leaf. Simmer gently, and when it has cooked 1 hour, season to taste with about 2 teaspoons salt. Continue simmering gently until tender but not falling apart, 1½–2 hours. Turn the chickens over once while cooking.

When done, remove pan from fire, lift chickens carefully out of their broth, and pull off as much skin as possible without causing them to lose their shape. Place them in a clean pan and strain the broth back over them again. Keep hot until ready to serve, at which time place them on a hot deep platter, remove strings, carve the breasts, and loosen the joints, leaving meat on carcass. Garnish with 2 neat bundles of parsley inserted in cavity of each. Surround with the carrots and onions and leeks (minus strings), and serve at once accompanied by a bowl of chive-and-butter sauce (recipe below) and plenty of tiny boiled potatoes. Also send to the table at the same time in a big hot soup tureen the broth in which the chicken cooked. The broth should be ladled into cups and sipped while eating the chicken.

## COLD BOILED CHICKEN, YORKSHIRE STYLE

| | |
|---|---|
| 2 5-pound roasting-chickens | 4 cups light cream |
| 12 peeled whole carrots | thin peel of ½ lemon |
| 6 little white onions | dash of mace |
| 3 stalks celery | juice of ½ lemon |
| parsley | 12 slices lean bacon |
| ¾ cup butter | paprika |
| ¾ cup flour | 3 level tablespoons gelatin |
| 2 cups strained chicken broth | |

SERVES 8

When I was seven years old, we lived with a charming English family in Yorkshire. My sister and I ate, of course, in the nursery with the other children, and consequently did not at the time have the pleasure of eating this delicious dish. But I used to watch the cook making it in the kitchen on Sunday mornings.

Clean 2 5-pound roasting-chickens inside and out carefully. Tie up for roasting; then put them into a big deep pot and barely cover with warm water. Add 12 peeled whole carrots, 3 stalks celery, 6 little white onions, and a little parsley. Boil gently until chickens are quite tender, but not falling apart, about 2 hours. Remove from the fire and allow the chickens to remain in their broth until quite cold.

When cold, remove from the broth, place chickens on a deep platter, and be sure that all the juice is drained out of them. Then carefully remove as much of their skin as you possibly can without spoiling the form of the chicken; also remove all the strings.

Now make a thick cream sauce. Melt ¾ cup butter and cook in it 3 minutes without browning ¾ cup flour. Add to this 2 cups hot strained chicken broth and 4 cups light cream in which you have put the thin peel of ½ lemon and which you have heated to boiling point. Stir well until perfectly smooth; then continue to cook in a double boiler for at least 10 minutes.

In the meantime soak for 10 minutes 3 level tablespoons gelatin in ½ cup cold water. Add to the cooked cream sauce and stir until well dissolved. Salt to taste and add a dash of mace and the juice of ½ lemon. When slightly cooled, pour it carefully over the cold chickens little by little with a spoon until you have completely coated the chickens and the bottom of the platter. Decorate the platter with the whole carrots from the broth and place in the refrigerator to chill. Just before serving, fry 12 slices lean bacon until crisp and place them around the chickens and sprinkle a little paprika on the breast of the chickens.

## CHIVE-AND-BUTTER SAUCE

| | |
|---|---|
| ¾ pound butter | pinch of nutmeg |
| grated rind of 2 lemons | 2 heaping tablespoons finely |
| salt, pepper | cut chives |

Clarify ¾ pound butter by letting it melt very slowly over a low flame; carefully skimming off the foam that rises to the surface; then pouring off the clear butter into another pan, avoiding the milky sediment in the bottom. Just before serving, heat and add the grated rind of 2 lemons, being careful not to include any of the white bitter part. Also add a pinch of salt; a little freshly ground black pepper; a pinch of nutmeg—if you like it—and last of all 2 heaping tablespoons finely cut chives.

## ROAST CHICKEN
## WITH CLEAR OR CREAM GRAVY

*[Pre-heat oven to 500°]*

2 4½-pound roasting-chickens    1 cup heavy cream (or 1 cup
½ pound sweet butter            clear chicken broth)
                              salt, pepper
                              pinch of curry

SERVES 6–8

Clean inside and out 2 fine roasting-chickens, weighing about 4½ pounds each; singe; wash and dry well. Insert in the cavity of each ⅛ pound sweet butter, and sprinkle them inside with salt and pepper. Place side by side in a roasting-pan, breast side up, dot with ¼ pound butter, place in oven to brown quickly, basting frequently. When breasts are browned, salt and pepper the birds lightly, turn the birds and brown on other side before reducing heat to about 400°. Continue roasting, basting frequently and turning them over occasionally, until well done, allowing about 25 minutes to the pound, or about 2 hours.

When ready to serve, remove the birds from the roasting-pan and place temporarily in an ovenproof dish in the oven, with the heat turned off, to keep warm while you make the gravy. Pour off all the juice in the roasting-pan into a little pan and let the fat come to the surface; then skim off all the fat and pour it back over the birds in the oven to keep them from drying out.

If you prefer a *clear gravy*, add to the sediment in the little pan 1 cup clear chicken broth made by simmering together in 2 cups water 1 carrot (sliced fine), a bit of celery, the chicken necks, livers, and gizzards (if you like the flavor of gizzards), until broth reduced to 1 cup. Place the little pan on the fire and bring to a boil, stirring to melt the brown sediment, then pour the whole into the roasting-pan and simmer, stir to melt all the sediment in the roasting-pan, then strain the whole back into the little pan and simmer until reduced to a syrupy consistency. This will give you a rich *clear gravy*.

If you prefer a *cream gravy* add ½ cup heavy cream to the sediment in the pan, blend thoroughly, pour into the roasting-pan, and simmer gently for a few minutes. At the last moment, add another ½ cup cream and heat just to the boiling point. A pinch of curry added to the *cream gravy* will give a delicate flavor.

Place the birds, carved or not, on a hot serving-platter, garnish with parsley, and send to table accompanied by the gravy in a sauce boat.

## ROAST CHICKEN, SAUCE PIANI
### [*Pre-heat oven to 450°*]

| | |
|---|---|
| 2 4–5-pound fine roasting-chickens | ½ cup heated cognac |
| | ½ cup white port |
| ½ pound sweet butter, and more | 2 cups heavy cream |

SERVES 6–8

This is one of my favorite dishes. Prepare 2 fine 4–5-pound chickens in the usual manner for roasting. Salt and pepper the insides well and insert ¼ pound sweet butter in each. Sew the chickens up just as though they had been stuffed. Spread a little butter over the bottom of a small roasting-pan; place the birds on the butter. Put in a very hot oven to brown; in about 12 minutes, if they have browned, remove the pan from the oven and place it on top of the stove.

Pour over the birds ½ cup heated cognac and light it (be careful). Let it burn a bit; then extinguish the flames by pouring over them ½ cup good port, preferably dry (white). Baste well with the resulting sauce. Salt and pepper well and put back in the oven to continue roasting, but reduce the heat to 400°. Allow 15–20 minutes to the pound. Every 5 minutes until the chickens are cooked baste and pour over them 2 tablespoons heavy cream. Carve and serve immediately on a hot platter, accompanied by the sauce in separate gravy boat. Just before serving the sauce, place it over a low flame and stir until bubbling hot, then turn out the light, stir in remainder of cream, and serve.


## ROAST CHICKEN STUFFED WITH NOODLES
### [Pre-heat oven to 450°]

|  | Sauce: |
|---|---|
| 2 5-pound roasting-chickens | 1 peeled carrot |
| 2 quarts chicken broth | 2 little onions |
| 2 8-ounce packages wide noodles | 1 heart of celery |
| 1 pound mushrooms | 4 tablespoons flour |
| ½ pound butter | 4 tablespoons butter |
| 1 cup grated imported Parmesan cheese | 1 quart hot milk |
| ½ pint heavy cream | parsley |
| salt, freshly ground pepper | thyme |
| 2 carrots | bay leaf |
| 2 onions | ½ cup heavy cream |
|  | 1 cup grated imported Parmesan cheese |

SERVES 6–8

Singe and clean 2 5-pound roasting-chickens inside and out. Wipe with a dry cloth. Stuff them with the following stuffing. Heat 2 quarts chicken broth and when boiling, add 2 packages wide noodles, broken in little pieces. Cook for about 5 minutes (the noodles should be only about half cooked). In the meantime wash, dry, peel, and chop fine 1 pound fresh mushrooms. Sauté them in ¼ pound butter until cooked, but not browned. Prepare 2 cups grated imported Parmesan cheese. Drain the noodles well, add the mushrooms and their juice, salt and freshly ground pepper, 1 cup grated Parmesan cheese, and ½ pint heavy cream. Mix well, and stuff the chickens with this. Sew them securely and truss for roasting.

Place 2 cut-up carrots and 2 whole onions in a large roasting-pan with ¼ pound melted butter. Place the birds in the pan and roll then around until buttered all over. Place the pan in oven and baste frequently until roasted to a golden brown, adding from time to time a little hot chicken broth. Turn the chickens breast-side-down, being careful not to puncture them. Reduce the heat to 325°, baste frequently, and cook for about 1 hour longer. When almost done, salt and pepper lightly.

In the meantime make the following sauce Mornay. Chop 1 peeled carrot very fine, 2 little onions, and 1 heart of celery. Cook them in 4 tablespoons butter until a golden brown, then sprinkle them with 4 tablespoons flour. Cook together for 1–2 minutes, and then add gradually 1 quart hot milk and a bouquet garni of parsley, thyme, and bay leaf. Cook in a double boiler, stirring from time to time, for at least ½ hour. When ready to serve the chickens, put them on a hot platter, remove all strings, carve them, and pour over them the chicken gravy (from which you have removed all fat and which you have strained through a fine sieve).

Add ½ cup heavy cream to the sauce Mornay, remove the bouquet, and add the other cup of grated imported Parmesan cheese. Salt and pepper to taste, and serve with the chickens.

## CHICKEN EN COCOTTE A LA BONNE
## A TOUT FAIRE
*[Pre-heat oven to 400°]*

| | |
|---|---|
| 2 4-pound roasting-chickens | 12 little peeled carrots |
| 2 onions | 3 tablespoons dry white wine |
| ¾ pound butter | 1 wineglass Madeira |
| ¼ pound salt pork | 1 tablespoon beef extract |
| salt, pepper | 20 little potato balls |
| 12 little white onions | olive oil |

Clean and tie up as for roasting 2 small tender roasting-chickens, weighing about 4 pounds each. Place 1 onion, chopped fine, and 1 tablespoon butter in each chicken, and sprinkle them inside with salt and pepper. Brown them in 4 tablespoons butter in an iron frying-pan on top of the stove until a delicate brown all over. Place 4 tablespoons butter in an earthenware casserole and add to it ¼ pound salt pork, cut in tiny squares. Place in the oven, and when the butter has melted and the casserole is hot, add the chickens. Salt and pepper lightly. Cover them with buttered typewriter paper. Fit the lid of the casserole on tight and cook in the oven slowly for ½ hour.

In the meantime brown lightly in 2 tablespoons butter in a separate frying-pan 12 little white onions and 12 little peeled carrots. Now take the chickens from the casserole for an instant and remove the strings. Pour the juice in the cocotte through a fine sieve and replace the birds and the strained juice. Add the browned carrots and onions. Pour over it 3 tablespoons dry white wine, 1 wineglass Madeira, and 1 tablespoon beef extract dissolved in a little hot water. Taste and season, cover, and place back in the oven for another ½ hour to cook slowly.

In the meantime scoop out of some big peeled potatoes about 20 little potato balls; wash and dry them carefully. Put them into a frying-pan with some hot olive oil and fry to a delicate brown and until they are thoroughly cooked. When the chicken is ready add the potatoes, garnish with parsley, and serve at once (to be carved at the table in the casserole).

## CHICKEN BREASTS BAKED
## WITH CORN AND CREAM

| | |
|---|---|
| 4 whole chicken breasts, cut in two lengthwise | 4 tablespoons butter |
| 1½ teaspoons salt | 3 cups of heavy cream |
| 8–10 large fully developed but tender ears fresh corn | 1 tablespoon good paprika |
| | coarsely ground pepper |

SERVES 6–8

Singe, wash, and dry thoroughly 4 whole chicken breasts, cut in two lengthwise. Place them in a pan (large enough so that they are not piled too much on top of each other) and pour over them 4 cups cold water. Place on low heat and allow to come to simmering point, skim carefully, cover, and cook gently until tender, about 1 hour, adding 1½ teaspoons of salt when half done. Remove from fire and let them cool in their juice.

Husk 8–10 ears of corn and remove all the silk. Score each row of kernels with a sharp knife and then cut them from the cob. Next with the dull side of the knife scrape off the milky residue. This should give you about 3–4 cups cut corn. Butter a large rectangular baking-dish 12″ by 7½″ by 2″. Spread the corn evenly over the bottom of the dish. Sprinkle with coarsely ground black pepper and dot with 4 tablespoons butter.

When the chicken has cooled enough to handle, remove all the skin and bones and place the meat on the bed of corn. *Preheat oven to 400°*. Reduce the remaining chicken broth by boiling it down rapidly until you have only ¼ cup. Pour this over the chicken and corn. Next pour over all 3 cups heavy cream and sprinkle evenly with 1 scant tablespoon paprika. Place dish in oven and bake 20–25 minutes. Serve at once.


## BONED STUFFED CHICKEN BREASTS OLIVETTE
*[Pre-heat oven to 425°]*

| | |
|---|---|
| 4–5 boned chicken breasts, halved | 2½ tablespoons Hungarian paprika |
| 1 pound fresh mushrooms | salt, coarsely ground black pepper |
| 4 shallots (or onion) | juice of 2 lemons |
| ¾ pound butter | ½ cup chopped parsley |

SERVES 6–8

Have ready 4–5 uncooked boned, chicken breasts, halved (or 8–10 pieces). Remove skins. With a sharp knife slice in two lengthwise, being careful, however, not to cut all the way through. Wash, stem, peel, and slice fine 1 pound fresh mushrooms. Peel and chop fine 4 shallots or substitute the equivalent amount of chopped onion. Cook the shallots a minute or two in ¼ pound butter, then add the mushrooms, and cook until the mushrooms have formed their juice and boiled down and are just beginning to brown. Season lightly to taste with salt and pepper.

Stuff the chicken breasts with the mushrooms and place in a buttered baking-dish large enough to hold them without crowding. Melt ½ pound butter and sprinkle it copiously with Hungarian paprika, about 2½ tablespoons, plenty of salt, and coarsely ground pepper and then add the juice of 2 lemons and a lot of finely chopped parsley (at least ½ cup). Pour over the chicken. Place dish in preheated oven and bake, basting frequently, until well done but not dried up, about 1 hour, or slightly more.

## MY VERSION OF CHICKEN GUMBO

1 5-pound roasting-chicken, cut as for fricassee
1½ pounds tenderized ham hock
1 onion
1 carrot
1 parsnip
1 white turnip
2 stalks of celery
1 pound of solid veal, cut in large cubes
1 Bermuda onion
1 green pepper
3 slices lean bacon
3 tablespoons chopped parsley
4 cloves garlic

2 bay leaves
2 hot dried peppercorns
1 2-pound, 3-ounce can peeled Italian tomatoes
pinch of thyme
salt, coarsely ground black pepper
1½ teaspoons sugar
5 tablespoons butter
2 10-ounce packages frozen whole baby okra
Tabasco
Worcestershire sauce
3 teaspoons gumbo-filé powder
juice of 1 lemon

SERVES 6–8

Wash, dry, and singe carefully a 5-pound roasting-chicken cut up as for fricassee. Wash a tenderized ham hock weighing about 1½ pounds. Peel 1 onion, 1 carrot, 1 parsnip, and 1 whole white turnip; and remove strings from 2 stalks of celery. Place the chicken in a deep 4-quart-size enamel pan and surround it with the prepared vegetables. Add just enough water to cover the chicken well. Place on low flame, bring gently to boiling point, skim well, cover, and simmer for 1½ hours, or until the chicken is tender. Then add the ham hock and continue simmering until the ham may be readily pierced with a fork, or about 1 hour longer. Cool, and when cold place in refrigerator overnight.

The next morning remove as much fat as possible with a spoon, extract the ham, discard the skin and fat, and cut the ham meat in bite-size pieces. Place the fat and bone in another pan temporarily. Remove the chicken from the jellied stock, and remove the meat from the bones, cutting it into large bite-size pieces. Place the chicken bones and discarded chicken skin into the new pot with the ham bone. Extract the vegetables and discard them, then strain the jellied soup without heating it over the chicken and ham. The jelly will go through a coarse sieve if rubbed with a wooden spoon. Place in refrigerator until ready to use.

Now cover the ham bone and chicken bones with sufficient water to cover and simmer for about 15 minutes before straining, making thereby an additional weaker broth to be used later (there should be 3 cups).

Wash and pat dry 1 pound solid veal, cut in large cubes. Peel and dice 1 medium-size Bermuda onion. Remove stem and seeds from 1 green pepper and cut fine. Cut 3 slices lean bacon into small pieces. Prepare 3 tablespoons chopped parsley. Fry the bacon slowly until crisp; fish out the bacon and set it aside. Add the chopped onion to the bacon fat and cook slowly until it begins to brown lightly. Add 4 cloves peeled garlic and continue cooking 1 minute, then add the chopped green pepper and parsley, and cook together 5 minutes, stirring constantly. Add 2 bay leaves, 2 hot dried peppercorns from which you have removed the seeds, 1 2-pound, 3-ounce can peeled Italian tomatoes with basil leaf, a generous pinch of thyme, a little coarsely ground black pepper, 1½ teaspoon sugar, a very little salt. Bring to boiling point stirring occasionally. Transfer to a large enamel pan, place on low heat over an asbestos pad, and simmer gently for 1 hour. Remove from fire when done.

In the meantime melt 2 tablespoons butter in a separate frying-pan, and when it is sizzling hot add the veal cubes and cook until they begin to brown, turning them over occasionally with a fork. Do not allow the butter to burn. Meanwhile heat the weaker broth and when it is hot pour it over the veal. Stir well to melt the brown residue then transfer to a small enamel saucepan, cover, and simmer gently for 1½ hours or until tender. Add the veal and broth to the tomato sauce. Then add the chicken and the ham and the jellied broth to the sauce, and heat until it comes to simmering point. Remove from fire until ready to add the finishing touches.

Half an hour before you will be ready to serve the gumbo, open 2 10-ounce packages frozen whole baby okra. Pull them apart and cut in ½-inch pieces. Drop them into 1 cup boiling water. Add ½ teaspoon salt, cover, bring to a boil and cook gently 6 minutes. In the meantime heat the soup or stew to boiling point. Add the cooked bacon and the cooked okra and season highly to taste with additional salt, 2–3 dashes of Tabasco, 2–3 teaspoons gumbo-filé powder, if procurable, and 2–3 table-spoons Worcestershire sauce.

In the meantime, cook 1 pound flaky white long-grain rice. When ready to serve the gumbo, be sure it is scalding hot. Tie 2 large pretty napkins, knotted together, around the pot, add 3 tablespoons butter, and squeeze into the gumbo the juice of 1 lemon. Serve at once in large soup plates ladling it generously over piles of white rice. A hearty and delectable treat, a meal in itself. Well-chilled Pouilly Fuissé adds to the festivity.

## BAKED CHICKEN CUSTARD

| | |
|---|---|
| 2  small  roasting-chickens | 7 egg yolks |
| 2 onions | 3 eggs |
| 2 carrots | 1 cup heavy cream |
| 2 pieces celery | pinch of cayenne |
| salt, pepper | 1 cup buttered toasted bread |
| 3 tablespoons butter | crumbs |
| 8 little white onions | parsley |

SERVES 6–8

Place 2 small roasting-chickens, cut up as for fricassee, in a pan, and add 2 onions, 2 carrots, 2 pieces of celery, salt and pepper,

2 tablespoons butter, and just enough warm water barely to cover. Place on the fire, bring slowly to a boil, skim, and simmer gently until very tender, 1½–2 hours, until the meat falls away from the bones. Remove from the fire and cool in the broth.

In the meantime peel and slice very thin 8 little white onions. Cook them without browning until tender in 1 tablespoon butter and 1 tablespoon water. When the broth is cool, strain it from the chicken through a piece of cheesecloth. Remove the skin from the chickens and pick meat from the bones in as large pieces as possible.

Butter a baking-dish, put the dark meat in the bottom, then the onions, and then the white meat. Beat the 7 egg yolks lightly and then beat them into 3 whole eggs. Add 2½ cups broth, 1 cup heavy cream, taste, and season with more salt and a pinch of cayenne. Strain over the chicken. Place baking-dish in a pan of hot water sufficient to reach to half its height. Set on the fire and bring to a boil; then place in a *pre-heated 325° oven* for about 1¼ hours. When firm to the touch, sprinkle the top copiously with buttered toasted bread crumbs. Garnish with parsley and serve at once.


## FRIED CHICKEN WITH CREAM GRAVY
*[Pre-heat oven to 400°]*

| | |
|---|---|
| 3 3-pound frying-chickens, cut as for fricassee | milk |
| flour | 3–4 tablespoons flour |
| salt, pepper | fat left in pan |
| ½ pound butter | 2 cups rich milk |
| | ½ pound bacon |

Singe and wash quickly and dry well 3 tender chickens cut up as for fricassee. Salt and pepper them and place in refrigerator for a while. Fry ½ pound bacon slowly until crisp. Remove the bacon and keep it warm. Add ½ pound butter to bacon fat. Now roll the pieces of chicken in flour to which you have added a little salt and pepper. Dip the pieces one by one in milk, then roll again in flour, and put immediately into the bacon fat, which must be bubbling hot, but not smoking. Start with the dark meat and finish with the white. Don't crowd them; use 2 pans if possible. Turn them over carefully so that they brown evenly all over. Put the pieces as they are cooked into a pan in pre-heated oven to continue cooking. In 15 minutes they should be completely cooked through.

When the last piece of chicken is cooked sprinkle the fat left in the frying-pan with 3–4 tablespoons flour and stir it well. Don't let it scorch. Then pour in enough of a mixture of half milk and half cream to make a fairly thick gravy, about 2 cups. Serve the chicken on a hot platter, garnished with the bacon, and accompany with a sauce boat of the gravy.

## POULET FONDUE A LA CREME

2 4½-pound roasting-chickens, cut as for fricassee
¼ pound butter
3–4 small onions
salt, pepper

½ cup cognac
½ teaspoon curry powder
3 cups heavy cream
1 tablespoon chopped parsley

SERVES 6–8

Singe, clean, wash, and dry 2 tender roasting-chickens, weighing about 4½ pounds each, cut as for fricassee. Melt ¼ pound butter in large iron cocotte, and when sizzling hot add the chicken and 3–4 small onions, peeled and sliced fine. Sprinkle lightly with salt and coarsely ground pepper. Turn chicken over when lightly browned, and cover cocotte tightly. Simmer gently until chicken is tender, about 1¼ hours.

Then add ½ cup cognac, ½ teaspoon curry powder, and 3 cups heavy cream. Simmer for 5–10 minutes longer. Remove the chicken and place on a hot platter. Pass the sauce through a fine sieve, pressing hard on the onions. Heat sauce without boiling, stir in 1 tablespoon butter, and pour over the chicken. Sprinkle with 1 tablespoon parsley and serve at once.

NOTE  We once had a vegetable garden in which we had planted far too many onions. In our enthusiasm to use them up, we made the above recipe, but instead of using only 4 onions, we literally smothered the chickens with 7–8 sliced onions, filling our big iron pot. We allowed the chickens to cook until the onions had completely melted, which took considerably longer than 1¼ hours. We found that the onions had produced far too much juice, but we rose above it and added the cognac and were more generous with the curry powder, although we added the same amount of cream. We decided not to bother passing the onions through a sieve, and, tying two big damask napkins around the black pot, sent it to the garden to be served in soup plates to be devoured by our starved guests. With a bowl of mashed potatoes to accompany it, this became a family favorite.

## REVISED POULET FONDUE A LA CREME RECIPE

| | |
|---|---|
| 2 4½-pound roasting-chickens, cut up as for fricassee | 10 tablespoons butter |
| 7–8 large onions | ½ cup cognac |
| salt, pepper | 3 cups heavy cream |
| ½ cup water, or chicken broth | 1 teaspoon curry powder |
| | 1 tablespoon chopped parsley |

SERVES 6–8

Peel and slice very fine 7–8 large onions, cutting slices again in half. Singe, wash, and dry thoroughly 2 tender roasting-chickens cut as for fricassee, weighing about 4½ pounds each. Brown the chicken very lightly both sides in 8 tablespoons butter in heavy iron frying-pan. Transfer to iron cocotte containing 2 tablespoons butter. Add ½ cup water or chicken broth to pan in which chicken was browned and stir well. Cover the chicken with the sliced onions, which will completely bury it. Pour the clear gravy over all. Sprinkle lightly with salt and coarsely ground pepper, cover tightly, and simmer gently for at least 1½ hours, or until the onions have melted and the chicken is falling off the bones.

Cool sufficiently to pull off as much skin as possible from the chicken and extract any large bones that may have found their way out of the chicken. Pour off most of the juice into an enamel pan and boil it rapidly to reduce it considerably. In the meantime pour ½ cup cognac over the chicken and allow it to simmer gently while you complete the sauce.

Mix 1 teaspoon of curry powder with ¼ cup heavy cream and pour over the chicken. Now add 2¾ cups heavy cream to the reduced chicken juice and heat, but do not allow to boil. Empty the chicken and onions into a hot soup tureen and pour over it the hot cream-and-chicken broth. Sprinkle with 1 tablespoon chopped parsley and serve at once in soup plates on fluffy mashed potatoes.

## COLD CHICKEN CURRY

2 young 4–5-pound roasting-chickens, cut as for fricassee
2 large Bermuda onions
10 tablespoons butter
1 jigger brandy

salt, pepper
2 tablespoons curry powder
2 cups heavy cream
parsley
tarragon
2 quartered lemons

SERVES 6–8

Singe, wash, and dry thoroughly 2 young roasting-chickens cut up as for fricassee. Peel 2 large Bermuda onions, quarter, and slice thin. Melt 8 tablespoons butter in large frying-pan and brown chicken lightly both sides, transferring the pieces as they brown to an iron cocotte containing 2 tablespoons butter. The cocotte should be on a very low flame or, better still, on an asbestos mat over a low flame. When all the chicken has been transferred heat 1 jigger brandy, pour over the chicken, and set ablaze, being careful not to burn yourself. When it has burned itself out, cover the chicken with the sliced onions and sprinkle with salt and pepper.

Add ½ cup water to the big frying-pan and stir over low flame to melt the brown residue in pan, making a small amount of clear gravy. Pour this over the chicken, cover tightly, and simmer gently until the chicken is cooked through and about to fall off the bones, about 1¼ hours. By this time the onions should have collapsed and the chicken should be swimming in plenty of strong broth. Now sprinkle the chicken with 2 tablespoons good curry powder and baste well. Remove from fire and cool until the chicken may be handled, at which time be prepared for the messy job of removing the meat from the bones.

Discard skin, gristle, and bones. Cut breasts in two lengthwise and lay these symmetrically over the bottom of an oblong glass baking-dish, 6″ by 10″ by 2″. Then add the rest of the meat, distributing it evenly over the breasts. Now add 2 cups heavy cream to the onions and buttery juice remaining in the cocotte; stir well, place on low flame, and heat to boiling point. Taste and add more salt if necessary. Do not allow the cream to boil. When it is heated through strain out the onions, using a colander placed over a large pan. Press gently with wooden spoon to extract all the cream. Pour the resulting cream sauce over the chicken in the dish. There should be plenty to cover the chicken completely and to fill the dish. When cold, cover with aluminum foil and place in refrigerator for several hours or overnight until jelled and set through like custard.

When ready to serve, run a knife carefully around the edge. Dip the dish into shallow pan of hot water for a few seconds to loosen the bottom, then turn out carefully onto a large oval platter. Garnish prettily with quartered lemons and crisp parsley. Serve accompanied by a bowl of crisp romaine broken in small pieces and dressed with a good French dressing, seasoned if possible with finely chopped fresh herbs, preferably parsley and tarragon.

## CURRY OF CHICKEN

| | |
|---|---|
| 2 small 4-pound roasting-chickens | ½ pound butter |
| | 2–4 tablespoons curry powder |
| 2 carrots | 4 egg yolks |
| 2 stalks celery | 1 cup heavy cream |
| 4 onions | |

SERVES 6–8

Put 2 small roasting-chickens, cut up as for fricassee, into a sauce-pan with 2 carrots, 2 stalks of celery, and a little salt. Add just enough water barely to cover the chicken. Simmer until tender, approximately 1½–2 hours, keeping the pan carefully covered. Remove from the fire, take out the chicken, and pour the broth into a bowl. Chop 4 onions fine, put them in a frying-pan with ½ pound butter, and fry them until a golden brown. Then skim out the onion and fry the pieces of chicken in the same fat 3–4 minutes until slightly browned. Then sprinkle over chicken from 2–4 tablespoons good curry powder (depending on how much you like curry) and some salt. Then pour over this the chicken broth and simmer for 5–10 minutes. Beat 4 egg yolks and add to them 1 cup heavy cream. Put into a double boiler and add the chicken broth. Cook until thick, stirring all the while; it must not boil.

Pile the chicken in a bowl and pour over it the curry sauce. Serve with this dish a big bowl of hot flaky rice and a tray of as many different accessories as you like, such as shredded coconut, pine nuts, pickled onions, spiced currants, chutney, ginger preserves, caramelized bananas, quince jelly, and poppadums (which come packed in tin boxes with dried leaves between the wafers).

## CARAMELIZED BANANAS

1 cup granulated sugar                6 bananas
SERVES 6–8

Place 1 cup granulated sugar in a large deep heavy aluminum pan. Moisten with 2 cups cold water. Stir, bring to a boil, and cook 3 minutes. In the meantime peel 6 bananas and cut them in 1½-inch pieces. Drop these into the syrup and cook gently 10 minutes or until they are shiny and transparent. Sprinkle once or twice with cold water as they cook, skimming off the grayish foam that forms. When done, remove them temporarily from the syrup using a sieved spoon or spatula. Continue cooking the syrup until it begins to brown lightly, 3–4 minutes.

Then slip the bananas back into the syrup and continue cooking until the syrup is caramelizing and the bananas are browning on the bottom, about 2 minutes. Shake the pan occasionally and remove from the fire the instant they are done. Place the bananas brown-side-up on a hot serving-plate and pour over them the small amount of remaining syrup. Serve with curried meat or chicken or as a dessert accompanied by heavy cream and grated coconut.

## POULET A L'ESTRAGON

| | |
|---|---|
| 2  4½-pound  roasting-chickens | ⅝ pound of butter |
| 2  tablespoons  chopped  fresh tarragon, or 2 teaspoons dried tarragon | salt, pepper |
| | 1½ cups chicken broth (made of necks and giblets) |
| 2  branches  of  fresh  tarragon, or 2 teaspoons of dried | 2 cups heavy cream |

SERVES 6–8

Clean, singe, wash, and dry 2 roasting-chickens, weighing about 4½ pounds each. Sprinkle the cavities lightly with salt and coarsely ground pepper, and insert in each ⅛ pound butter and a branch of fresh tarragon, or substitute 2 teaspoons dried tarragon. Make 1½ cups strong chicken broth, using necks and giblets. Melt ¼ pound butter in large iron frying-pan and brown in it slowly the 2 chickens, turning them over on all sides. This process should take at least 15 minutes. Transfer to large iron cocotte, or roasting-pan, containing 2 tablespoons butter. Add the chicken broth to the frying-pan and stir to melt brown residue, then pour half of it over the chickens. Cover tightly and simmer gently 1–1¼ hours, or until very tender. Turn the chickens over once or twice while cooking and add the remainder of the broth as needed to prevent sticking.

When the chickens are done, pour over them 2 cups heavy cream and sprinkle around them 2 tablespoons chopped fresh tarragon or substitute 2 teaspoons dried tarragon. Baste the chickens with the cream while it heats to boiling point, then remove from heat immediately to prevent curdling. Place chickens on hot platter, pour a little of the tarragon sauce over them, and send to table to be carved. Serve the remainder of the sauce in a gravy boat. Fresh buttered peas and tiny peeled boiled new potatoes are the perfect accompaniment.

## POULET PATRON

2–3 small roasting-chickens, or large broilers, cut up as for fricassee
1 pound fresh mushrooms
3 shallots, or 3 small white onions
1 pint heavy cream
4 egg yolks
6 truffles
parsley
1 cup white wine, or sherry
salt, pepper
½ cup olive oil
1 tablespoon chopped parsley, or chervil
1 cup chicken broth
¼ cup cognac
10 tablespoons butter

SERVES 6–8

Cut up 2 or 3 broilers, or small roasting-chickens, using only the legs, second joints, and breasts. Boil the other parts with a few soup greens to make a small quantity of strong chicken broth.

Singe and wipe clean the choice pieces to be used. Remove tough stems from 1 pound fresh mushrooms, wash, dry, peel, and chop the caps very fine. Peel and chop fine 3 large shallots, or 3 small white onions. Prepare 1 tablespoon chopped parsley, or chervil. Simmer 6 small truffles in ½ cup white wine, or sherry, 5 minutes. Peel if necessary and chop fine. Beat the 4 egg yolks with 1 cup cream just long enough to mix well.

Season the chicken lightly with salt and coarsely ground pepper. Fry until a golden brown in ½ cup olive oil. Remove from pan temporarily and pour off any oil that may remain. Replace the oil with 4 tablespoons butter and put the chicken back into the pan. Pour over this ½ cup sherry, or white wine, and ¼ cup cognac, and let it simmer.

In a separate pan melt 4 tablespoons butter and brown in

it very lightly the onions, or shallots. Add the mushrooms, pour over all 1 cup strong chicken broth, and simmer 10–15 minutes. Set aside until ready to use.

In about 1 hour the chicken should be tender and thoroughly cooked—but not falling off the bones. When you think it is done pour the juice off into an enamel saucepan, add 2 tablespoons butter to the chicken, and keep hot. Now add the mushrooms and their juice to the chicken juice, and pour into this 1 cup heavy cream. Simmer for a few minutes over direct heat, then place over boiling water. Season to taste with salt and pepper and add the truffles and 1 tablespoon chopped parsley. Pour a little of the hot sauce gradually into the previously beaten together yolks and cream; then add this gradually, stirring constantly, back to the sauce. Cook until thickened like custard, never ceasing the stirring. When done, remove from hot water and fire. Place the chicken on a hot platter and pour the sauce over all. Decorate with parsley and serve at once.

## BRIAN CONNELLY'S BANGKOK SIAMESE CHICKEN CURRY

8 whole chicken breasts, cut in two lengthwise
2½ cups Bermuda onion, finely chopped
18 tablespoons butter
3 cans clear chicken broth (5 cups)
salt, pepper
4 tablespoons cornstarch
genuine Madras curry paste
2 teaspoons imported saffron
1 pound rice

½ cup slivered almonds
2 cucumbers, peeled and cubed
2 cups fresh or canned grated coconut
2 cups diced peeled tomatoes
½ cup chopped parsley
1½ cups chutney
grated rind 4 navel oranges
3 ripe bananas
juice 2 lemons

SERVES 6–8

Buy 8 whole chicken breasts and ask the poultry man to cut them in two lengthwise. Singe, wash, and dry the chicken breasts thoroughly. Sauté in 8 tablespoons butter (¼ pound) until both sides lightly browned. Transfer as they brown to an iron cocotte containing 2 tablespoons butter. Add ¾ cup chicken broth to the buttery residue in frying-pan and stir over low heat until dissolved, forming a little clear gravy. Pour this over the chicken. Sprinkle lightly with salt and coarsely ground pepper. Cover tightly and simmer gently until tender, about 1–1½ hours, depending on size.

In the meantime prepare 3 cups chopped Bermuda onion. Cook the onions very slowly in 8 tablespoons butter without browning until transparent, about 20 minutes, stirring frequently. Sprinkle with 4 tablespoons cornstarch and add the remainder of the opened can of chicken broth and 2 additional cans. Simmer gently, stirring frequently, for about ½ hour.

When the chicken is done, remove from fire and spread the pieces out on a large platter until cool enough to handle, at which time remove and discard both skin and bones. Spread each piece copiously with genuine Madras curry paste. Place the chicken back into the iron cocotte with the remaining juice and pour over all the onion sauce. Simmer gently another 15 minutes. Set aside until ready to reheat and serve.

In the meantime prepare the following dishes to accompany the curry: ½ cup chopped parsley; ½ cup slivered almonds; 2 cucumbers, peeled and cubed; 2 cups diced and peeled ripe tomatos (minus as many seeds as possible); 2 cups moist grated coconut, canned or fresh; 1½ cups good chutney, 3 ripe bananas, peeled, sliced not too thin, and sprinkled with juice of 2 lemons to prevent discoloration; and in another dish grate just before serving the rind of 4 navel oranges. Arrange all of these attractively in separate dishes, or on a condiment tray.

Twenty-five minutes before serving the curry, cook 2 cups long-grain rice in a big pot following directions on the box, but add 2 teaspoons imported saffron tied in a little bag to the boiling water and remove when the rice is done. Reheat the curry itself on low flame. The curry may be transferred to a hot serving-dish, if it is to be passed, or left right in its black pot, if it is to be served buffet style (knot 2 large napkins together and tie them around the pot in this case).

## POULET A L'OSEILLE

2 4½–5-pound roasting-chickens, cut up as for fricassee
1½ cups strong chicken broth
½ pound boiled ham cut in cubes (minus fat)
¾ pound butter
2 cups heavy cream
2 large onions, peeled and sliced fine

2 13-ounce cans Belgian sorrel, or 3 cups chopped fresh sorrel
2 tablespoons flour
½ pound fresh mushrooms
extra flour for flouring chicken
several sprigs parsley
strained juice of 1 lemon
salt, pepper
2 bay leaves

Wash, singe, and dry thoroughly 2 roasting-chickens cut up as for fricassee. Make 1½ cups strong chicken broth using necks, backs, and giblets. Melt ¼ pound butter in top of large 4-quart enamel double boiler. Stir in 2 tablespoons of flour and add 2 large onions peeled and sliced fine. Stir in 1½ cups hot chicken broth, seasoned with 2 bay leaves, 2 teaspoons of salt, and several sprigs of parsley. Add the cut-up chicken. Cover tightly and cook for 2½ hours, replacing boiling water in bottom pan as it boils down. When it has cooked 1 hour, it is well to put the top pieces on the bottom and vice versa, so that the chicken cooks evenly.

When done, remove from fire and drain off all the juice into a little pan; there should be about 3 cups of very strong chicken essence. Spread the pieces of chicken out on wax paper and sprinkle lightly with flour, turning pieces over so that they are floured on both sides. Now in a large iron frying-pan melt ½ pound of butter and brown in it lightly ½ pound boiled ham, cut in little cubes. Fish out the ham and set it aside while you brown the chicken lightly on both sides in the remaining butter. Transfer the chicken to a heavy cocotte, preferably enamel-lined. Add 1 cup water to remaining brown residue and boil down, stirring well, and pour back over the chicken. Now skim off excess fat from the essence of chicken before pouring it over the chicken. Sprinkle with the bits of ham and ½ pound washed, partially stemmed, and quartered fresh mushrooms. Sprinkle lightly with about ¼ teaspoon coarsely ground pepper, and add the contents of 2 13-ounce cans Belgian sorrel, or substitute 3 cups very finely chopped, fresh raw sorrel.

Place over low flame and simmer gently for 30–45 minutes, stirring frequently to mix sorrel down into the broth and to prevent sticking. When done, turn heat very low and stir in gradually 2 cups heavy cream. Allow to heat thoroughly but do not allow to boil. At the very last stir in the strained juice of 1 lemon. Send to table accompanied by plenty of boiled lightly buttered noodles. White wine is almost a necessity with this scrumptious dish.

## CHICKEN SAUTE ARCHIDUC

*[Pre-heat oven to 350°]*

| | |
|---|---|
| 2 plump 3½-pound frying-chickens, cut in 8 pieces each | 1 jigger white wine |
| | 1 jigger brandy |
| | 1 jigger bourbon |
| ¼ pound butter | 3 egg yolks |
| 1 jigger Kirsch | 1½ cups heavy cream |
| 1 jigger port | salt, pepper |
| 1 jigger Madeira | 2 tablespoons chopped parsley |

SERVES 6–8

Do not be frightened by the outrageous mixture of spirits. The alcohol evaporates in the simmering, leaving an alluring fragrance.

Singe and wipe clean 2 plump chickens cut in 8 pieces each. Save the backs and necks for soup. Melt ¼ pound butter in large iron frying-pan over low flame, add the chicken, and sauté gently, turning the pieces over with a spatula from time to time. Do not allow the chicken to brown too much. Salt and pepper lightly and cook in all about 1 hour, or until done. To test, pierce a second joint and if the juice that comes out is white, the chicken is done. At this point mix together the 6 liqueurs listed above and pour them over the chicken. Simmer for a minute or two, then transfer the chicken *only* to a heated earthenware or ovenproof casserole. Cover, place in oven and continue cooking gently for about 10 minutes while you complete the sauce.

Add 1 cup heavy cream to the 3 egg yolks and beat with rotary-beater just long enough to mix well. Now add ½ cup heavy cream to the liqueurs remaining in the frying-pan. Stir well over very low flame and strain into top of enamel double boiler. Place over boiling water and add the egg-and-cream mixture. Cook, stirring constantly, until thickened; it must not boil. Pour sauce over the chicken, sprinkle with chopped parsley, and serve at once, accompanied by mashed carrots.

## A VERY FANCY CHICKEN TART

**Filling:**

3 plump 5-pound roasting-
   chickens, cut as for fricassee
6 whole carrots
6 stalks celery
1 onion
salt
½ teaspoon peppercorns
1 pound small fresh mush-
   rooms
1 pound small white onions
½ pound butter
6 tablespoons flour
½ cup heavy cream
1 teaspoon tarragon vinegar
1 teaspoon strained lemon
   juice
⅛ teaspoon cayenne
1 tablespoon chopped parsley
3 egg yolks
paprika

**Pastry:**

¼ pound butter
1½ cups pastry flour
4 tablespoons ice water
½ teaspoon salt

SERVES 6–8

The day before buy 3 plump roasting-chickens, weighing about 5 pounds each, and have them cut up as for fricassee. The breasts should be split in two lengthwise, and the wings should be severed from the breasts. Clean and wash all the pieces and dry them carefully. Put the breasts and wings in a bowl, cover with wax paper, and refrigerate until the next day.

Place the rest of the chicken in a large enamel pan and cover with about 2½ quarts water. Place on fire and bring slowly to boiling point; skim very carefully; reduce heat to a bare simmer and add 6 whole peeled carrots, 6 stalks celery, 1 onion, salt to taste, and ½ teaspoon peppercorns. Cover partially and simmer gently for about 2½ hours to make a good strong broth. Drain, and when the chicken is cool enough to handle, pull the meat from the bones, discarding bones and skin. Place the meat back in the broth and when it is completely cold, refrigerate until next day.

On the afternoon, start by mixing the pastry. Using your finger tips work ¼ pound butter into 1½ cups pastry flour that has been sifted with ½ teaspoon salt. Moisten with not more than 4 tablespoons ice water. Form into flat ball, wrap in wax paper, and refrigerate at least 1 hour.

Now peel 1 pound small fresh mushrooms, discarding the stems (or save them for future use as seasoning). Wash quickly and slice fine. Heat the chicken you cooked the day before just long enough to be able to drain off the broth, but leaving enough on the chicken to prevent its drying out (this chicken will not be used for the tart but may be used for chicken salad or croquettes for another meal). Melt 6 tablespoons butter in a frying-pan, add the mushrooms, and cook for 10 minutes, or until the juice has boiled down and the mushrooms are just beginning to brown, at which time sprinkle with 2 tablespoons flour and cook, stirring well, for 1 minute. Then add gradually about ¾ cup hot broth, season to taste with salt and freshly ground pepper, and cook for a minute or two. Remove from fire and stir in about ¼ cup heavy cream—enough to make them a nice creamy consistency, but not too runny. Place in top of double boiler over hot water and keep warm until ready to use.

*[Pre-heat oven to 400°]*

You are now ready to cook the breasts and wings. Melt 4 tablespoons butter in a big heavy frying-pan and when it is sizzling hot, add the chicken and brown lightly all over. Transfer the pieces as they brown into a warm iron cocotte containing 2 table-spoons fresh butter. When all the chicken has been transferred, add ½ cup chicken broth to the frying-pan, stir it well to melt all the nice brown residue, and pour the whole back over the chicken. Salt and pepper lightly, cover cocotte tightly, and place it in oven to cook until chicken is done, about 1 hour. When done, cool until you can handle the chicken. Remove the skin; then pull the bones away from the breasts, keeping them as whole as possible; and remove all the meat from the wings. Place the breasts and wing bits in an enamel pan and pour all the juice left in the cocotte over the chicken. Place the bones and skin back in cocotte, add 1 cup broth, bring to a boil, and cook for a few minutes; then drain through sieve over the chicken. It should now have enough juice over it to keep it from drying out until ready to use.

At this point you make the foundation for the sauce. Melt 4 tablespoons butter in the top of a small double boiler over low flame. Add 4 tablespoons flour gradually and cook together for a minute or two without browning. Then add gradually 1½ cups hot chicken broth. Cook over low flame, stirring constantly, until thickened and smooth. Place over boiling water and continue cooking, stirring occasionally.

Now peel 1 pound small white onions. Cover with boiling water and cook 25–30 minutes until just tender through; do not salt them. Remove from fire, but do not drain, as the water will be used to warm them in later.

*[Pre-heat oven to 500°]*

At this point remove the pastry from the refrigerator, and when it has softened up at room temperature enough to roll out, place on pastry cloth or board that you have lightly sprinkled with flour and roll it out to right size to line a large 12-inch ovenproof glass pie plate. Crimp the rolled-under edge prettily, then cut the pastry in 8 equal-size pie-shaped pieces, prick them with the prongs of a fork all over, and bake for a few minutes until just beginning to brown a little. Reduce heat to 325° and continue cooking until a delicate brown all over. Remove from oven and keep warm.

Have ready the 3 egg yolks beaten into ¼ cup heavy cream. Put onions and chicken on low flame to come to boiling point. Place the mushrooms on the fire, too, in their double boiler to heat. Now complete the sauce, which has been cooking gently over boiling water. Add to it, stirring constantly, the eggs and cream, and continue cooking until the yolks have had time to thicken the sauce well. When done, remove from fire entirely and season well to taste with a very little tarragon vinegar (about 1 teaspoon), the same of strained lemon juice, ¼ teaspoon cayenne, and salt and pepper, if necessary.

Now drain the chicken thoroughly (saving the juice, of course, for future use), and distribute the white meat equally over the 8 sections of the tart, tucking in the wing bits around here and there. Now look at the mushrooms; if they are too thick, soften them with a little of the juice drained from the breasts. Spread them over the chicken. Place tart in oven to keep warm. Drain the onions thoroughly. Reheat the yellow cream sauce slightly and pour over all, covering the chickens and mushrooms completely. Pile the onions in the center of the tart, sprinkle lightly with paprika and 1 tablespoon chopped parsley, and serve at once, accompanied by a pie knife and serving-spoon.

## PERSIAN CHICKEN

| | |
|---|---|
| 3 4½-pound roasting-chickens, cut as for fricassee | 1 cup granulated sugar |
| 1½ pounds long-grain rice (3¾ cups) | 1 cup salt |
| | 1 tablespoon Spanish saffron |
| 8 navel oranges | ¾ pound butter |
| 1¼ cups shelled almonds | 1 tablespoon chopped parsley |

SERVES 6–8

This is a heavenly dish. Don't be frightened off by the cup of salt. I guarantee it isn't too much.

Clean 3 young roasting-chickens, cut up as for fricassee, weighing about 4½ pounds each. Place in large enamel pan and cover with about 3 quarts cold water. Bring gently to boiling point, skim carefully, and simmer until tender and falling from the bones, about 1½ hours. Cool in its broth. Remove skin and discard. Pull meat from bones making 4 pieces of each breast; use only the choice pieces of dark meat minus all gristle and veins. Cover with broth until ready to use.

Blanch 1¼ cups shelled almonds and cut in thin slivers. With sharp knife cut rind from 8 navel oranges in thin slivers, avoiding bitter white part. Slice fine, cover with cold water, bring to a boil, drain, repeat process twice more. Moisten 1 cup granulated sugar with 1 cup cold water, bring to a boil, skim, and boil 5 minutes. Add orange rind and almonds and simmer 5 minutes longer. Set aside.

Wash 1½ pounds long-grain rice in several waters, rubbing well between your hands. Drain and place in large pan. Cover with 2 quarts luke-warm water, and, believe it or not, add 1 cup table salt. Soak 3½ hours. Place 1 tablespoon genuine Spanish saffron in a small jar, add 3 tablespoons cold water, cover, and allow to soak until ready to use.

One hour before dinner *pre-heat oven to hot 450°*. Place ¾ pound sweet butter in small pan and melt by pouring over it 1½ cups boiling water. Heat 6 quarts water to boiling point in 2-gallon pot. Now pour off slowly and with care the salt water in which the rice has been soaking. Empty the rice into the actively boiling water, stir with wooden spoon, cover, and as soon as the water comes to the boiling point again remove cover and stir. Repeat the process twice more, which should take in all about 5 minutes. Next drain the partially cooked rice in a sieve, shaking it to remove all adherents of starch water. Now pour half of the melted butter and water into a large iron or earthenware casserole, and gently empty the rice into this pot in such a way that it will spread evenly and not stick together in rice balls. Cover and place in hot oven. In about 5–6 minutes pour the remainder of the melted butter and water over the rice, cover, reduce heat to 300°, and continue cooking until rice is done, about 15 minutes longer.

In the meantime heat the chicken in its broth, but do not allow to boil. Heat a large oval serving-platter. When the rice is done spread about one third of it over the platter and lay on this bed the well-drained chicken meat. Drain off the syrup from the orange peel and almonds and add them to the remaining two thirds of the rice in the casserole. Add also the water from the soaked saffron and mix lightly with fork to color evenly. Pile this over the chicken, sprinkle with 1 tablespoon chopped parsley, and serve at once with a well-chilled white wine.

## BONED ROAST STUFFED CAPONS

| | |
|---|---|
| 2 boned 7–8-pound capons, or roasting-chickens | 1 pound tender lean boiled ham |
| 2 4-pound chickens, cut up | 1 tablespoon onion juice |
| celery | 1½ cups bread soaked in milk |
| carrots | ½ cup pistachio nuts |
| parsley | salt, pepper |
| onions | ½ pound butter, or more |

SERVES 6–8

Ask the butcher to bone 2 good capons, or, if you prefer, 2 good roasting-chickens; or bone them yourself, using directions for boning a turkey as a general guide (page 232). All you really need is a sharp knife, plenty of time, and the urge. Also buy 2 chickens cut up as for fricassee, not boned; boil these and the bones from the capons until tender, 1½–2 hours, in water to cover containing celery, carrots, a little parsley, and several small onions (page 197). Cool in their juice. Then pick off all the meat, discarding all skin and gristle. Save out the breast and put the rest through the medium-fine meat-grinder.

Also put through the grinder 1 pound tender lean boiled ham. Add to this 1 tablespoon onion juice, 1½ cups bread that has been soaked in milk and squeezed dry, 1 tablespoon chopped parsley, 1 tablespoon chopped celery, ½ cup pistachio nuts, if obtainable, and salt and pepper to taste. Moisten with stock. Stuff the 2 capons nice and full with this, inserting the boiled breasts in the center. Sew the capons up front and back and shape them as nearly as possible into their original shape, tying them with white string so that they will keep their form.

*Pre-heat oven to 450°.* Brown lightly in 4 tablespoons butter in a large roasting-pan 2 carrots and 2 onions, chopped fine, and then lay the birds on this bed. Rub them with salt and pepper and ½ pound soft butter, and roast to a golden brown in a hot oven, about 20 minutes. When brown, reduce the heat and cook slowly about 1¾ hours more, basting frequently with their own juice, adding butter and chicken stock as necessary. Remove from oven. Lay on platter. Pour the juice (from which you have removed the fat) over all and serve at once.

# *Turkey*

## GENERAL DIRECTIONS FOR ROASTING
## A TURKEY

Choose a young, 6-month-old, plump-breasted turkey, either a hen or a tom, but weighing preferably not more than 14–16 pounds. Personally, I like a 12-pound hen turkey best. It depends, however, upon how many people you must serve. Allow ¾–1 pound per person. Be sure the poultry man pulls out the sinews from the legs and have him split the back part of the skin of the neck and cut off the neck close to the body. This will permit you to stuff the breast as well as the body of the bird if you so desire. Clean, singe, wash, and dry the turkey thoroughly inside and out. Rub the inside of the bird well with salt and pepper before stuffing. Stuff the breast of the turkey, fold the skin of the neck back over it securely, and sew or skewer it down carefully. Stuff the body not too fully, as most stuffings swell during the roasting process. Truss and sew securely, or use the convenient aluminum pins (sold for the purpose) and lace the pins with white string and tie securely.

Place the turkey breast side up in a roasting-pan containing at least ¼ pound butter. Also rub the turkey all over with another ¼ pound soft butter.

Place in *pre-heated very hot 475°–500° oven* for about 30 minutes, or until the breast is light golden brown, basting occasionally with the melted butter in the pan. Turn the bird over carefully breast side down and continue roasting until the back is browned lightly too. Then salt and pepper the back, turn the bird breast side up again, and salt and pepper the breast. Add more butter if necessary for basting, reduce heat to 350°, and continue roasting slowly, basting occasionally, allowing 15–20 minutes to the pound in all.

When done, to make clear gravy add 1–2 cups boiling water or, better still, turkey or chicken broth, to the buttery residue in pan, place over low flame, and cook, stirring continuously with a wooden spoon, until the gravy has reduced to a thin syrupy consistency. Strain into hot gravy boat and, with a spoon, skim off as much fat from the top as you think necessary. Opinions vary on this; if all butter is used in the roasting I prefer to leave some of the fat.

## ROAST TURKEY WITH RAY'S STUFFING

Stuffing:
30 chestnuts
1 pound mushrooms
butter
4 peeled onions
¼ pound fresh sausage meat
juice of 1 lemon
few drops tarragon vinegar
salt, pepper
¼ cup French vermouth
¼ cup cognac
1 teaspoon chopped parsley
½ pound Grapenuts

10–12-pound turkey
¾ pound butter
2 sliced carrots
1 whole onion
salt, pepper

SERVES 6–8

With a sharp knife make an incision in about 30 chestnuts, plunge them into smoking fat for a few seconds, then remove and cool. Peel off the outer and inner shells. Boil them until quite tender in salted water. Drain, and break them up into quite small pieces.

Now peel 1 pound washed and dried mushrooms and chop them very fine. Place 6 tablespoons butter in a pan, add the mushrooms, cover tightly, and simmer for 15 minutes. Then remove the lid and continue to cook until almost dry. Take a large frying-pan and put into it 2 tablespoons butter, 4 peeled onions, chopped fine, and ¼ pound fresh sausage meat. Cook together, stirring with a fork, until slightly browned. Now mix the chestnuts, mushrooms, and sausage meat together. Add the juice of 1 lemon, a few drops tarragon vinegar, salt and pepper, ¼ cup French vermouth, ¼ cup cognac, 1 teaspoon chopped parsley, and last of all ½ pound grapenuts.

Clean a fine 10–12 pound turkey. Stuff with the above dressing, truss, and sew up securely. Rub the turkey with ¼ pound soft butter. Place it in a roasting-pan, containing ¼ pound butter, 2 sliced carrots, and 1 whole onion. Put into a *pre-heated hot 450° oven* for ½ hour, basting carefully, and adding from time to time a little chicken broth or water, so that the pan is never quite dry. Now reduce the heat to 350°, salt and pepper the turkey lightly. Continue to roast for 2½–3 hours, basting frequently, and keeping the bird breast down as much as possible; add broth from time to time.

Pour off the juice, and remove as much grease as possible. Remove strings, garnish, and send to the table to be carved. Pass the strained gravy separately.

## WILD-RICE STUFFING FOR ROAST TURKEY

¾ cup finely chopped celery
3 tablespoons chopped onion
3 tablespoons chopped parsley
3 cups wild rice
2 tablespoons salt

¾ cup butter
salt, freshly ground pepper
3 tablespoons gumbo-filé powder
2 cups heavy cream

The gumbo filé in this, if you have never tasted it before, will be a real treat, for it has a delightfully different flavor.

First prepare ¾ cup finely chopped celery. Next chop fine enough onions to make 3 tablespoonfuls. Also chop fine 3 tablespoons parsley. Now wash 3 cups wild rice thoroughly in several waters. Put rice in a large heavy pan with 4 quarts cold water and 2 level tablespoons salt. Bring to a boil and cook, without stirring (shaking the pan occasionally to prevent sticking), for 15 minutes, counting from the time it first actually boils. Drain well in a colander, then place it again in the pan, and shake it over a low flame to dry the rice a bit.

Now melt ¾ cup butter in a small frying-pan and cook in it slowly the chopped onions for 5 minutes, stirring constantly, so that they do not brown. Add the celery and cook a minute longer, then add the whole to the wild rice, stirring lightly with a fork. Also add the chopped parsley, a little freshly ground pepper and salt to taste (about 1½ teaspoons), and 3 level tablespoons of genuine Creole gumbo filé. Mix well, then stuff both the body and the breast of the turkey. Truss, sew, or lace securely and roast as usual (page 228).

When well cooked, place the turkey on a hot platter, remove the strings, and keep warm while you make the cream gravy. Pour off some of the fat from the juice in the roasting-pan, then stir in gradually 2 cups heavy cream. Place on low fire and stir constantly, to melt all the brown, crusty part into the cream, but don't allow the cream actually to boil. Taste, add a little salt, if necessary, and a little freshly ground black pepper, and serve in a gravy boat.

## ORANGE-FLAVORED SWEET-POTATO STUFFING FOR ROAST TURKEY

6–8 large yams, or sweet potatoes
grated rind of 1 lemon
grated rind of 1 orange
pulp of 3 navel oranges
salt

freshly ground pepper
¼ pound butter
2 tablespoons cognac
1 cup of orange juice for gravy

The orange in this recipe permeates the whole turkey, giving it, I think, a distinct and delectable flavor.

Peel 6–8 large yams, or sweet potatoes. Cut in quarters and cook in boiling salted water until just tender through. Don't over-cook them. Put them through the potato-ricer into a large bowl. Add to them the grated rinds of 1 lemon and 1 orange, being sure not to include any of the bitter white part. Cut 3 navel oranges in half crosswise, scoop out the pulp, and add it to the potatoes. Add a little salt and freshly ground black pepper. Also cut into the potatoes ¼ pound butter. Sprinkle 2 tablespoons cognac over all, and toss with a large fork just enough to mix the whole, but do not mash the potatoes. Stuff the body of the bird with this and truss and sew or lace securely.

Roast the turkey in usual way (page 228). When done, re-move it to a hot platter. To the juices in the roasting-pan add 1 cup chicken broth and 1 cup strained orange juice. Stir well and simmer, dissolving all brown residue in pan, until gravy is re-duced and syrupy. Strain into gravy boat, and skim off any ex-cess fat before serving.

## BONED STUFFED TURKEY

| | |
|---|---|
| 12–14-pound turkey | 2 cups milk |
| 5-pound fowl | 1 cup pecan meats |
| 10 carrots | ½ cup chopped parsley |
| 6 leeks, or onions | 2 tablespoons grated onion |
| 1 bunch celery | 2¼ cups chicken broth |
| salt, pepper to taste | 1 large onion |
| 3 cups ground boiled or baked | ⅜ pound butter |
| ham | 1 bunch parsley |
| 16–20 slices bread | |

The day before singe a dressed turkey weighing about 14 pounds, then remove all pinfeathers. Next, working on a wooden board, chop off the tips of the wings, using a strong knife or cleaver and a hammer. Now, wash the bird carefully, inside and out, and dry thoroughly. Split the bird open down the back, like a broiler, and remove all the bones except the drumsticks and small bones in lower halves of wings. What you must not do is to cut through the outer skin and flesh of the breast.

Keeping this always in mind, lay the bird breast down on the board and, starting at the furthermost end of the neck, slit the skin of the neck and back, then cut through the backbone. This accomplished, pull the skin away from the neck, being careful not to tear it, and then chop off the neck, close to the body. Next, cut away the backbone from skin and flesh, and, with caution, cut the rest of the carcass away from the bones, running a sharp knife between the bones and the flesh.

As you come to the joints in wings and legs, break them by bending them backwards before trying to cut through them. Do not attempt to remove the small bones in lower wings, nor the drumsticks. Don't worry if you tear the flesh as you scrape it away from the bones. It's the outside that must remain intact.

Place the bones as you remove them in a big enamel pan. When finished, put the boned bird in the refrigerator while you prepare the stuffing. This concoction of ground-up boiled chicken, ham, bread, pecans, celery, and seasonings is made in the following manner:

Wash and clean a 5-pound fowl and place it on the bed of turkey bones. Add 5 or 6 whole peeled carrots, 6 well-washed leeks, or 6 onions, and 1 bunch washed celery. Pour over the chicken just enough boiling water to barely cover it. Bring to a boil, skim meticulously, cover partially, and simmer gently for about 2 hours, or until legs are tender through. Season with salt and pepper when half done.

Next drain the broth from the bones and chicken (saving it of course), and when the chicken is cool enough to handle, pull off all the skin and throw it away. Then pull off all the breast, leaving it as whole as possible, and put it aside—for the moment. Now pull off the rest of the meat from the chicken and any scraps that may have clung to the turkey bones. Put all this, except the breast, through the meat-grinder. Now take 3 cups ground boiled or baked ham, including a little of the ham fat. Soak 16–20 slices bread, crusts removed, in 2 cups milk. Break up lightly with a fork and add it to the ground chicken and ham.

Also add 1 cup celery, chopped fine, 1 cup pecan meats, chopped fine, ½ cup parsley, 2 tablespoons grated onion, and ½ teaspoon ground black pepper. Mix all together well, moistening it with 3–4 tablespoons chicken broth.

You are now ready to stuff the turkey. Spread it out flat, skin down, on the table and sprinkle lightly with salt and pepper. Cover with layer of stuffing, using about half the quantity. On this lay the whole reserved chicken breast and cover with remaining stuffing. Get someone to hold the 2 sides of the turkey together again, while you sew it up securely from base of neck to tail, using a poultry or curved upholstery needle and strong, fine, white string. Pull the remaining flap of loose skin from neck down over back and sew it carefully in place. Turn bird breast side up and sew up slit in apron. At this point the turkey will look very flat and odd indeed. It is now up to you to give the bird a proud shape by pushing the legs up and close to the body, thereby forcing a goodly amount of stuffing up into the breast. Secure the legs and wings close to the body, lacing all with string as you have seen the butcher tie up a boned, rolled roast, but avoid pulling the strings too tight directly over the breast. Now wrap the bird in wax paper and place in refrigerator until ready to roast the next day.

It will take about 3 hours and 45 minutes to cook the turkey so plan accordingly. *Pre-heat the oven to 500°.*

Cut 1 large onion in fairly small pieces and brown lightly in 4 tablespoons butter. Add 2–3 peeled sliced carrots and place the whole in bottom of large roasting-pan. Lay on this bed the turkey, breast side up. Spread over all at least ½ cup soft butter. Place in pre-heated, very hot oven and roast, basting frequently, until lightly browned, about 20 minutes. Then reduce heat to 450° and continue roasting, basting frequently for about 1 hour longer. At this point salt and pepper the bird well all over, cover with top of roaster, leaving vent open, and continue cooking, basting occasionally for about 1¼ hours longer. Remove the cover and continue roasting until the bird is rich brown and well done, or for about 1¼ hours longer. Turn cover of roasting-pan open side up, close vent, and place turkey in it, transferring it carefully with the aid of a big spoon or firm spatula and fork and 2 extra

strong hands protected against the heat. Now skim off most of
the fat from the gravy in the roasting-pan and put it back over
the turkey. Return the turkey to the oven while you make the
following clear gravy:

Add to the remaining brown juice in roasting-pan 2 cups
chicken broth. Place on fire and stir well to incorporate all the
nice brown bits clinging to sides of pan. Boil down until syrupy,
then strain into hot gravy boat; if you prefer, leave the vegetables
right in the gravy.

Place the turkey on a hot platter, carefully. Working quickly,
cut off and pull out as much of the string as possible. Garnish at
tail end with a great big bunch of parsley. Serve at once to be
sliced at table, accompanied by the hot gravy.

## ROAST TURKEY AND CREAM GRAVY
*[Pre-heat oven to 450°]*

| | |
|---|---|
| a 10–11-pound hen turkey | ½–¾ cup sherry |
| ¾ pound sweet butter | 2 cups heavy cream |
| salt, pepper | parsley |
| ½ cup cognac | juice of ½ lemon |

SERVES 6–8

Clean, wash, and dry thoroughly, inside and out, a fine plump
hen turkey, weighing 10–11 pounds. Salt and pepper it well inside and insert 1 scant cup butter. Sew, just as though it had been
stuffed. Spread a little soft butter in the bottom of your roasting-
pan, place the bird in the pan, breast side up, and spread the
breast with about ¼ pound sweet soft butter. Place in hot oven
and roast, basting frequently, until a beautiful golden brown all
over, turning the bird on its sides and upsidedown to brown
evenly all over.

When well browned, remove pan from oven and pour over
the bird ½ cup heated cognac. Light it, and when it has burned
out, pour over it 1 cup heated sherry. Reduce heat to 400° and
continue roasting until it has been in oven about 1 hour, then
salt and pepper the turkey, reduce the heat a bit more, and continue roasting until done (about 2½–3 hours in all).

During the cooking period, every 15 minutes pour a little heavy cream over the bird. The cream will curdle and cook, forming a dark brownish black sediment in the fat, some of which will stick to the bird as you baste it. (Don't worry about it, for it is as it should be.) Shortly before the turkey is done, shift it to a baking-dish and place back in oven to finish roasting while you carefully strain from roasting-pan all the juice and fat into a little saucepan. There should be quite a lot of it. Let it stand until the fat rises to the surface, skim off the fat, and pour some of it back over the turkey, to keep it from drying out. To the remaining dark brown clear gravy, add 1 cup heavy cream and simmer gently while you make a *roux* of 1 heaping teaspoon flour and 1 heaping teaspoon butter. Cook a minute or two without browning, then add the hot gravy gradually, blending it smooth and free from lumps.

In the meantime heat in a separate pan 4 tablespoons sherry and a dash of cognac, light it (away from the fire), and when it has burned out, add it to the gravy and simmer gently while you place the turkey on a hot serving-platter. Garnish turkey with parsley and send it to the table to be carved immediately. Just before serving the gravy in a sauce boat, stir into it the juice of ½ lemon.

## BOILED TURKEY WITH
## CHIVE-AND-BUTTER SAUCE

10-pound hen turkey
4 carrots
3 small white onions
6 stalks celery
2 white leeks
parsley
pinch of thyme
½ bay leaf
small slice salt pork

Sauce:
½ pound butter
grated rind of 2 lemons
dash of nutmeg
salt, pepper
2 tablespoons chopped chives

SERVES 6–8

Choose a hen turkey weighing not more than 10 pounds. Have the butcher draw the sinews from the legs. Clean the bird well and tie securely so it will not fall apart while boiling. Place in a large pot, add 4 peeled and cut-up carrots, 3 small white onions, 6 stalks celery, 2 white leeks, some parsley, a pinch of thyme, ½ bay leaf, and a small slice of good salt pork. Cover with warm (not hot) water and let come to a boil slowly. Skim carefully and let simmer about 2½ hours, or until quite tender but not falling apart. Remove the bird carefully to a platter. Strain the juice and remove all the grease; but work quickly, as the turkey shouldn't be out of the juice long enough to dry. Put turkey into a clean pot and pour the broth back on it.

When ready to serve the turkey, put it on the fire to heat in its broth. When it is boiling hot, put the turkey on a large platter, remove as much of the skin as possible, and then decorate with large bunches of parsley. Pour a spoonful or so of broth over it and send it to the table to be carved. Pour the rest of the hot bouillon into cups and serve it to be sipped while eating the turkey. Serve the following sauce with the turkey:

Clarify ½ pound butter by melting slowly. Skim any foam that rises to the surface, let stand a minute, then pour off the clear part, being careful not to take in any of the milky sediment. Put the clarified butter into a saucepan and add the grated rind of 2 lemons, a dash of nutmeg, salt, and pepper. Heat, and when ready to serve, add 2 tablespoons chopped chives.

# Duck

## BRAISED CANARDS AUX NAVETS
### [Pre-heat oven to 375°]

2 ducks
½ pound butter
1 cup dry white wine
3 dozen little white turnips
1 dozen little white onions
1 tablespoon sugar

salt, pepper
bouquet of parsley
½ bay leaf
2 carrots
2 tablespoons of beef extract

SERVES 6–8

Clean 2 fine ducks well, inside and out. Brown them in 4 table-spoons butter in a big iron pan on top of the stove. When brown, draw off the fat and pour over them 1 cup dry white wine and let them simmer gently.

In the meantime peel 3 dozen tender little white turnips and 1 dozen little white onions and brown them in ¼ pound butter in a big frying-pan on top of the stove; when they begin to brown, sprinkle them with 1 tablespoon sugar to caramelize them. Now take 2 separate iron cocottes and put into each 4 tablespoons butter. Place a duck in each one, salt and pepper them, and smother with the turnips and onions. Add a little bouquet of parsley, ½ bay leaf, and 1 carrot to each bird.

Melt 2 good tablespoons beef extract in ½ cup boiling water and put it into the pan in which the ducks were browned. Bring to a boil and strain over each bird. Cover tightly and place the casseroles in a *pre-heated medium 375° oven* to cook slowly for 1½ hours, or more.

When thoroughly cooked, place the ducks on a large hot platter, cover them and surround them with the turnips and onions. Remove any excess grease from the juice, and then pour the gravy over all. Garnish with parsley and serve at once.

## CANARDS AUX OLIVES
*[Pre-heat oven to 450°]*

2–3 ducks
¼ pound butter
cognac
2 8¼-ounce cans large ripe
    olives
1-pound fillet of raw veal
5 shallots
salt, pepper
10 little carrots
10 small white onions
2 thin slices salt pork

2 cloves garlic
small bit of fennel tops
2 small bay leaves
½ teaspoon thyme
parsley
dash of nutmeg
2 cups chicken broth
6-ounce glass green pitted
    olives
1 heaping teaspoon beef extract

SERVES 6–8

Clean 2–3 ducks well, inside and out, with a damp cloth and stuff with a small quantity of dressing made as follows:

Sauté the livers slightly in 4 tablespoons butter to a golden brown, then pour over them ½ cup of cognac, and light it. Let it burn out. Next remove the pits from 2 8¼-ounce cans large ripe olives and chop them fine. Also chop the livers very fine and add

them with their juice to the olives. Then add to this 1 pound of
the fillet of raw veal, put through the grinder twice, and 3 shallots,
chopped or grated very fine. Salt and pepper to taste, mix
lightly together, stuff the ducks, and sew them up.

Place the ducks in a large roasting-pan for which you have an
airtight cover; but don't put the cover on. Place the pan in a hot
450° oven and roast until the ducks become a golden brown,
20–30 minutes. In the meantime, peel and slice thin 10 little
carrots, and peel but do not slice an equal quantity of small white
onions and 2 shallots. When the ducks are brown, remove from
the pan, pour off all grease, and wash the pan. Now put 4
tablespoons butter into the pan, 2 thin slices salt pork, cut in
little squares, and then the onions and shallots. Set on the fire
and brown the onions carefully. Then add the carrots and a little
cheesecloth bag containing 2 cloves garlic, 1 teaspoon chopped
fennel tops, 2 small bay leaves, ½ teaspoon thyme, and a little
parsley. Lay the ducks on this bed, salt and pepper them, sprinkle
with a dash of nutmeg, and pour over all 2 cups hot chicken broth.

Now cover the pan and simmer very gently on top of the
stove for 1½ hours, adding more bouillon if necessary. Watch
carefully, so that the carrots do not burn. Half an hour before
serving, sprinkle with several teaspoons of good cognac and a
dozen or so green pitted olives. Put into a moderate 350° oven,
uncovered, and continue to cook for another ½ hour. Drain off
almost all of the juice and remove as much grease as possible
from it. Add to it 1 heaping teaspoon beef extract and reduce
almost to a glaze. Put the ducks on a hot platter, pour the glaze
over them, carve them, and put the carrots and olives around the
edge. Decorate with parsley and serve at once.

## CANETON AUX PETITS POIS

| | |
|---|---|
| 2 4½-pound Long Island ducklings | salt, pepper |
| 5 pounds fresh peas | 4 tablespoons butter |
| 2 pounds little white onions | pinch of soda |

SERVES 6–8

First shell 5 pounds green peas and cook them in a small quantity of salted boiling water with a tiny pinch of soda until tender, about 15 minutes. When cooked, drain and rub through a sieve using wooden spoon or potato-masher. This should give you 2 generous cups puréed peas. In the meantime, place 2 pounds small white onions in large sieve, and dip the sieve down into a large pan of boiling water so that the onions are covered with water. Allow to stand 1 minute. This facilitates the removal of outer skins. Drain and with sharp knife cut off as little as possible from each end of onion and peel. Place the onions in pan and add 2 tablespoons butter and 1 cup boiling water. Cover, place on low heat, and cook gently until just tender, about 35 minutes. Watch carefully and add a few spoons of hot water if necessary to keep them from boiling completely dry. Drain, but save the juice. Add the purée of peas to onions, season lightly with salt and coarsely ground pepper, and mix in lightly 2 tablespoons butter. This is the stuffing for the ducks.

Clean 2 fine Long Island ducklings inside and out, wiping them with a clean cloth or paper toweling. Sprinkle the inside of each with a little salt and coarsely ground pepper. Make a small quantity of broth using the 2 necks and giblets; you should have 1¼ cups of it. When done, strain and add the onion juice.

*Pre-heat oven to moderate 350°.* Stuff the 2 ducks with the onions and peas. Fold back neck skins over backs and secure with skewers or toothpicks. Close cavities with toothpicks or steel pins made for the purpose and lace securely with fine strong string. Place side by side in roasting-pan and roast slowly until very tender, about 2½ hours. Pour off all the fat in pan after the first hour. Watch carefully toward the end of cooking time so that the brown residue in bottom of pan will not burn. When done, transfer the ducks to another pan and keep warm in oven while you make the gravy. Pour off all the fat in roasting-pan and add the broth and onion juice. Stir with wooden spoon over moderate heat and simmer down until thick and syrupy. Strain and keep warm. Place ducks on hot platter, remove strings and toothpicks or pins, and serve. The ducks should be carved at table. Remove any fat remaining on gravy, heat, and serve with the ducks.

## JELLIED DUCK A L'ORANGE
*[Pre-heat oven to 350°]*

| | |
|---|---|
| 2 large 5–6-pound Long Island ducks | 1 can clear chicken broth |
| 3 navel oranges | 1 lemon |
| salt, pepper | 1½ tablespoons gelatin |
| 1 12-ounce can Madrilène | 1 bunch water cress |

SERVES 6–8

Clean 2 large Long Island ducks; wipe inside and out with damp cloth or paper toweling. Sprinkle cavities with salt and coarsely ground pepper. Place side by side in roasting-pan. Roast ducks until very tender, 2½–3 hours. Pour off the fat after they have cooked one hour and again in another hour. Remove from pan when done and cool; at which time remove all the meat from the bones in as large pieces as possible, discarding all skin and fat and undesirable pieces. Sprinkle lightly with salt, cover with a plate, and chill.

In the meantime remove the thin outer rind from 1 navel orange, using a sharp knife. Place it in a cup and pour over it the juice from 1 large lemon. Cover and place in refrigerator until ready to use for flavoring the aspic. Now cut off every bit of white skin left on the orange and cut off the rind and white part from 2 more. Then using a sharp knife, cut between the sections of the 3 oranges so as to form perfect half-moon-shaped pieces of the pulp. Chill these.

Next heat together 1 12-ounce can Madrilène and 1 12-ounce can clear chicken broth. Soak 1½ tablespoons plain gelatin in 3 tablespoons cold water. Add to the heated broth and stir well, then strain into it the orange-flavored lemon juice held in reserve. Add more salt, if necessary, and cool. Arrange the orange sections around the edge of a large glass pie plate, and pour just enough of the cooled aspic over them to cover the bottom of the plate with ¼-inch-thick coating. Place in refrigerator to set.

Now garnish the center of the aspic-covered plate with a pattern of water-cress leaves and cover the whole with the pieces of duck, cutting the breasts to make 4 pieces of each. Place the most perfect pieces in the center and the bits around the edge and on top. Pour the rest of the aspic over all and refrigerate until set firm. When ready to serve, run knife around the edge, dip bottom of dish in hot water, and turn out on large round serving-platter. Serve at once accompanied by a water-cress salad dressed with lime or lemon juice, salt, and a very little olive oil, or peanut oil.

# Goose

## ROAST GOOSE WITH SAGE-AND-ONION STUFFING

1 10–12-pound goose
Stuffing:
6 large onions
6 fresh leaves sage
1 teaspoon salt
1 teaspoon sugar
1 teaspoon prepared mustard
pepper
1 large or 2 small apples
dash of nutmeg
4 cups fine bread crumbs
4 tablespoons butter
1 small lemon
strip of pork
salt, pepper
flour

1 teaspoon of dry mustard
pinch of cayenne
3 tablespoons port wine

Gravy:
1 large onion
butter
1 pound beef, cut in little
squares
parsley
pinch of thyme
1 clove
3 peppercorns
Roux:
1 teaspoon butter
1 teaspoon flour

SERVES 6–8

In the first place, it is essential to choose the goose with great care. Geese live to be incredibly old and tough, and we want a young one, big enough, however, to have some meat on its bones. The skin should be white; the breast plump; the feet yellow, smooth, and limber; the windpipe easily broken; the goose weighing 10–12 pounds. It must be carefully singed, picked, the plugs of feathers pulled out, and well washed and dried inside and out.

For the stuffing: Boil 6 large onions until tender. Drain and chop fine. Then add 6 fresh leaves sage, 1 teaspoon salt, 1 teaspoon sugar, 1 teaspoon prepared mustard, a little pepper, 1 large or 2 small apples, pared and chopped fine, a dash of nutmeg, if you like it, 4 cups fine bread crumbs, and 4 tablespoons melted butter. Mix lightly together and put into the stomach of the bird.

Now, with a very sharp knife, peel 1 small lemon, removing all the yellow rind, but leaving as much of the thick white part as possible. Place the lemon, yes, the whole lemon, in the center of the dressing, sew up the bird, and truss well. Cover the breast with a strip of pork. Place in roasting-pan and put in *hot preheated 500° oven* for 45 minutes. Remove from oven, pour out all the fat, sprinkle the bird with salt and pepper, dredge with flour, and return to oven. Reduce the heat to 350°. When the flour has browned, add 1 cup hot water and baste the goose often. It should cook at least 3 hours.

When ready to serve, mix 1 teaspoon dry mustard with water until smooth, add a pinch of cayenne and 3 tablespoons port wine. Heat gently. Make a slit in the apron of the goose. Remove the lemon, being careful not to puncture it, and pour the hot port into the body. Garnish and serve at once with gravy that you have made separately.

For the gravy: Slice 1 large onion and fry it in butter with 1 pound beef, cut in little squares, until slightly browned. Then pour over it 1 pint boiling water. Skim and add a little parsley, a pinch of thyme, 1 clove, and 3 peppercorns. Simmer for 1 hour, or until well reduced. Strain and add the drippings from the goose. Skim off all the fat. Make a *roux* of 1 teaspoon butter and 1 teaspoon flour. Cook together for several minutes, then add the gravy. Simmer a minute or two, and then serve with the goose.

# Guinea Hen

## GUINEA HENS STUFFED WITH
## BLACK-WALNUT-AND-BREAD STUFFING

2–3 fine plump guinea hens
1 small white onion
1 loaf stale white bread
½ pound butter
1 cup milk
2 whole cloves
½ nutmeg

1 cup black-walnut meats
salt, pepper
3 branches celery
1 large carrot
2 teaspoons beef extract
parsley

SERVES 6–8

Peel 1 small white onion and cut in two. Stick 1 whole clove in each half. Place the onion in a little pan and add 1 cup milk. Place on low heat and bring to scalding point. In the meantime remove crust from loaf of stale white bread and crumble it into fine crumbs. Add ¼ pound butter, cut in little pieces; then pour over it the scalded milk. Sprinkle lightly with salt and coarsely ground pepper and grate over all ½ of a small nutmeg. Also add 1 cup carefully picked over, broken black-walnut meats. Toss the whole together lightly, using a large fork.

Clean 2–3 fine plump guinea hens, wash and dry thoroughly inside and out. Sprinkle them lightly inside with salt and a little coarsely ground pepper, then stuff the birds, dividing the stuffing equally. Sew up the cavities using fine string, or substitute toothpicks, and lace securely. Place side by side in roasting-pan, and dot with ¼ pound butter. *Pre-heat oven to very hot 450°.* Brown the birds lightly in this hot oven, then reduce heat to moderate 375°, and continue roasting, basting frequently, for ½ hour. In the meantime peel 1 large carrot and slice, and remove strings from 3 branches celery. Wash and add the vegetables to the birds. Continue cooking, basting frequently, until the birds are very tender, 1¼–1½ hours longer.

When done, transfer the birds to another pan and pour over them some of the fat from the roasting-pan; then place them back in oven to keep hot while you make a clear gravy. Add to the vegetables and juice in pan 2 scant teaspoons of beef extract dissolved in 1 cup boiling water. Stir well and reduce by boiling rapidly until nice and syrupy. Strain and keep hot while you remove string from birds. Place on hot platter. Garnish with parsley and send to table to be carved. Grape conserve or black-current preserves go well with this.

## CURRIED GUINEA HENS

Accompaniments:

3 fine guinea hens

1 bunch celery

1½ teaspoons salt

½ teaspoon peppercorns

¼ pound butter

6 tablespoons flour

1½ cups heavy cream

3–4 teaspoons good curry powder

1 can shredded coconut

1 glass quince jelly

1 cup, or more, chutney

1 pound boiled rice

SERVES 6–8

Clean, wash, singe, and dry thoroughly 3 fine guinea hens. Fill the cavity of each with celery cut in small pieces. Place in a pot just large enough to hold them, and pour over them 4 cups hot water. Bring slowly to boiling point, skim carefully, reduce heat to simmer, and cook gently until very tender, about 2 hours.

When they have cooked ½ hour add 1½ teaspoons salt and ½ teaspoon whole peppercorns. When done, cool in their own juice. When cool enough to handle, remove the birds from the broth, pull off the skins, and remove meat from bones. Strain the broth through a fine sieve and let it stand until the fat rises to the surface. You should have about 3–4 cups good broth.

Now cut the meat in small squares. Skim off the fat from the broth and pour the broth over the meat. Place in top of double boiler until ready to make the curried sauce for the meat.

In the meantime place the bones, skin, and celery back in the pot and pour over them 4 cups cold water. Place on fire, cover, and simmer for 1 hour. (This broth will not be used for the curried guinea hens, but will make an excellent broth for another meal.) Strain when done, cool, and refrigerate until ready to use.

When ready to make the curried sauce, place the meat covered with broth over boiling water, and heat until the broth is hot. Melt ¼ pound butter in an enamel saucepan, add 6 tablespoons flour. Stir well over low flame; then add gradually, so as to make a smooth sauce, 1⅔ cups hot broth, poured off of the hot meat. When thick and smooth, place over boiling water, stir in gradually 1 cup heavy cream, and season to taste with salt. Place 3–4 teaspoons of good curry powder in a little bowl and stir into it gradually ½ cup heavy cream. Pour off most of the remaining broth from the meat and pour over it instead the thickened sauce. Cover and keep hot over boiling water until ready to serve, at which time stir in the curried cream, taste, and add more salt if necessary. Serve at once with plain, flaky rice, a bowl of shredded coconut, a glass of quince jelly, and chutney.

# Pheasant

## ROAST PHEASANT
### [Pre-heat oven to 475°]

3 3-pound hen pheasants        salt, pepper
¾ pound sweet butter

### SERVES 6–8

Singe 3 fine hen pheasants, weighing about 3 pounds each, clean, wash and dry thoroughly inside and out. Rub the inside of each with salt and pepper, and insert in the cavity of each at least ⅛ pound sweet butter. Place side by side in small roasting-pan. Rub each bird copiously with plenty of soft butter, using at least ¼ pound of butter, and preferably more. Place in pre-heated oven and roast, basting frequently, until a golden brown; then salt and pepper the birds, turn them over, and continue roasting until brown on the back. Turn them right side up, reduce the heat to about 375°, and continue roasting, basting frequently, until the legs feel tender to the touch, about 1 hour in all.

Remove from roasting-pan, place temporarily in a baking-dish containing a little fresh butter, and replace in oven with the heat turned off while you make a clear gravy. Add to the roasting-pan about 1 cup clear chicken broth, place on the fire, stir until all the brown part in bottom of pan has melted, then strain it into a small pan. Let the butter come to the top, and skim off most of it, then simmer until reduced to a more syrupy consistency. Place the birds on a serving-platter, garnish, and send to the table. Accompanied by the reduced juice, and black-currant sauce (page 289), bread sauce (page 289) a bowl of buttered crumbs (page 268) the pheasants are just that more delightful.

## ROAST PHEASANTS BASTED WITH GIN AND JUNIPER BERRIES

We were discussing one day, with a sculptor in Paris, different ways of cooking pheasants. He told us that it is a well-known fact that pheasants found in parts of the country abounding in juniper berries have a particularly delicate flavor. Living in a part of the country once where there were no juniper berries to be had except in drugstores, he decided to make an experiment. If juniper berries were what flavored gin, why not baste the pheasant with gin? He tried it and found it especially good. We tried it and agree.

*[Pre-heat oven to 500°]*

Sauce:

| | |
|---|---|
| 3 pheasants | 1 small glass red-currant jelly |
| 6 strips bacon | grated rind of 1 orange |
| ⅜ pound butter | pinch of salt |
| salt, pepper | ¼ teaspoon cayenne |
| 9 juniper berries | juice of 2 oranges |
| ¼ cup gin | 1 tablespoon prepared mustard |

SERVES 6–8

For 6–8 people you really should have 3 pheasants, but perhaps 2 plump ones could be made to do. To roast, they must be young and tender. Ask the butcher to lard them carefully with a little fat salt pork and truss them nicely. Line the bottom of your roasting-pan with 6 strips bacon, ¼ pound butter, and salt and pepper. Wipe the birds, inside and out, with a damp cloth. Place 2–3 juniper berries inside each bird, salt and pepper them lightly, and rub them over with a little soft butter; lay in the roasting-pan. Place in pre-heated hot oven for 15 minutes; then pour over them ¼ cup gin mixed with ¼ cup hot water. Baste frequently, reducing the heat to 350°. Cook for another 45 minutes, or until nice and brown all over. Serve on a hot platter, carve, and pour the strained juice over them. Serve the following sauce with them:

Empty a small glass of red-currant jelly into a bowl and break it up well with a silver fork. Add the grated rind of 1 orange, a pinch of salt, and ¼ teaspoon cayenne. Then add the juice of 2 oranges in which you have dissolved 1 tablespoon good pre-pared mustard.

## PHEASANTS IN CREAM
*[Pre-heat oven to 425°]*

| | |
|---|---|
| 3 plump pheasants | salt, pepper |
| 6 strips bacon | 2 cups veal or chicken broth |
| 6 tablespoons butter | 1 quart heavy cream |
| 8 shallots | ¼ cup pickled grated horse- |
| ¼ cup cognac | radish |

SERVES 6–8

Clean well 3 plump pheasants, cover their breasts with strips of bacon, and tie them up. Brown carefully in an iron cocotte with 6 tablespoons butter and 8 shallots. Pour over them a little cognac and light it. Salt and pepper them, add 2 cups veal or chicken broth, and cook in a pre-heated moderately hot oven for ½ hour.

Then add 1 quart heavy cream and ¼ cup of pickled grated horse-radish. Let all this cook for another 20–30 minutes, continuing to baste with the sauce. Season to taste. Place the birds on a platter, carve, and serve with the cream gravy.

## GOGI'S PHEASANTS OR CHICKENS
## WITH WALNUTS

2 fine pheasants, or 2 large
   broilers
1 pound shelled walnuts
2 bay leaves
4 small carrots
½ bunch Chinese parsley (the
   feathery variety)
20 black peppercorns
3 tablespoons butter

2 pounds onions (preferably
   Bermuda)
3 egg yolks
¼ teaspoon cayenne
2½ teaspoons salt
1 teaspoon paprika
2 tablespoons tarragon vinegar
3 scallions

SERVES 6–8

Singe, pick over carefully, wash and dry well 2 fine pheasants, or large broilers, cut up as for fricassee. Place in deep enamel pan and add just enough cold water to cover. Add 4 peeled carrots, 2 bay leaves, the stems only of a few sprigs of parsley, 20 black peppercorns, 2 onions, 3 scallions. Bring gently to simmering point, skim carefully, season to taste with about 2 teaspoons salt, and cook gently until tender, about 1½ hours.

In the meantime peel and put through the meat-grinder, using medium cutter, 2 pounds onions (preferably Bermuda, as they are milder). Wash and chop fine the leaves only of ½ bunch of Chinese parsley. Now put 1 pound shelled walnuts through the nut-grater. This makes about 5 cups powdered nuts. Place in a mortar or sturdy bowl and pound with wooden pestle until they bring forth some of their oil.

Melt 3 tablespoons butter in a frying-pan and add the chopped onions. Cook gently until transparent, but without browning, about 5 minutes. Remove from fire, add the nuts, chopped parsley, and 3 cups broth strained from the birds. Season to taste with about 1 teaspoon paprika, ¼ teaspoon cayenne, and additional salt if necessary. Set aside while you arrange the cooked pieces of pheasant or chickens in a shallow rectangular glass baking-dish, 12″ by 7½″ by 2″. Remove as much skin as possible, and any stray bones, without destroying the shape of the pieces.

Now place the nut mixture on a low flame and bring very slowly to boiling point, but do not let it boil. Remove from fire. Beat the 3 egg yolks with ½ cup additional broth; add this gradually to the nuts. Place back on low flame to thicken, stirring constantly to just under the boiling point, lest it curdle. At the last moment, blend in 2 tablespoons tarragon vinegar and pour the sauce over the birds, filling the dish almost level full. When completely cold, place in refrigerator for several hours, or even overnight, covering first with aluminum foil.

This fancy dish is not to be served cold, as you might think. Instead it is to be thoroughly heated through before serving. Place dish, still covered with aluminum foil on a cookie sheet in *pre-heated 375° oven* for 40–50 minutes. Watch carefully, and when it starts to sizzle remove from oven. Remove foil, sprinkle with freshly chopped parsley, and serve accompanied by boiled and buttered fresh, or frozen baby lima beans.

7

*Vegetables*

$M$ost vegetables are at their best simply boiled and well seasoned with salt, freshly ground black pepper, and plenty of fresh sweet butter. The same amount of loving care should go into the selection and preliminary preparation of vegetables as is required for the cooking and seasoning processes. Shopping personally is the answer to the selection problem, and the proverbial "capacity for taking great pains" the one and only answer to the preparation situation. Overcooking seems to be the greatest pitfall connected with the actual cooking, although lately I seem to have encountered an avalanche of undercooked vegetables (away from home), which, in my opinion, is almost as bad, if not worse. This is probably the natural result of the prevalent desire not to kill any precious vitamins.

And here is where I differ from some people, because I do recommend a pinch of soda when cooking green vegetables especially, unless they have just come out of a garden, which, alas! they seldom have. Back to the wall, obstinately, I do it simply because the vegetables look prettier and taste none the worse for it. If you are reckless enough to follow in my footsteps, please use a glass or enamel pan for the best results.

To go back to the seasoning question, once the vegetables have been cooked to the "just done" degree, drain them carefully (saving the water for soups, except water from strongly flavored ones). Next put 1–2 tablespoons fresh sweet butter for each 1 cup vegetables into the bottom of the pan in which they cooked, and put the vegetables back into the pot on top of the butter. Shake over the fire just long enough to melt the butter, but not long enough to let the butter sizzle or cook. Taste, season to taste with more salt and freshly ground black pepper, toss the vegetables around with a fork, so that they are uniformly buttered, put them into a hot vegetable dish, and serve at once. A little thick cream added to the butter makes a change, but in that case add the cream to the vegetables and let them simmer in it a second or two until the cream is hot, but not boiling; then remove from fire, add the butter and salt and pepper, and toss lightly with a fork until the butter has melted. Place in hot serving-dish and serve at once.

Cream sauce, Hollandaise sauce, and browned butter are also used on some vegetables when they are to be served hot. French dressing, boiled dressing, and mayonnaise are served with cold vegetables. You will find recipes for all of them in chapters VIII and IX.

Vegetables require very little garnishing: finely chopped parsley or chervil being permissible, but not essential. White vegetables may be given a dash of color by sprinkling them with paprika, but do be sure the paprika is fresh before you use it. For some reason buttered croutons seem indicated for creamed spinach, the alternative being sliced hard-boiled eggs.

## HOT BOILED ASPARAGUS

2–3 bunches asparagus          salt
pinch of soda                  sauce (see below)

SERVES 6–8

Peel and wash 3 bunches fine asparagus. Peeling asparagus may seem a nuisance, time-consuming, and even wasteful, but the asparagus tastes so very much more delicate that it is worth taking the trouble. It is almost invariably done in the best restaurants.

Cut off the tough ends and tie in 3 bunches, top and bottom, with white string. Place heads down in cold water to soak until ready to cook. Plunge into a big enamel pan full of boiling water, add a tiny pinch of soda and a little salt, and cook until tender but not limp, 15–20 minutes.

Drain well, place on hot platter, sprinkle with chopped chervil, and serve at once, accompanied by good tart French dressing (page 318); or omit the chervil and serve with sauce mousseline (page 303); or with browned butter (page 289); or with browned butter to which a few capers have been added; or with sauce Hollandaise (page 300); or with plain clarified butter (page 290).

## ASPERGES EN PETITS POIS

6 pounds fresh asparagus       1 cup heavy cream
4 tablespoons butter           1 tablespoon granulated sugar
8 tiny onions                  salt, pepper
3 egg yolks

SERVES 6–8

Peel and wash 6 pounds fresh asparagus. Cut in ½-inch slices crosswise, discarding tough ends. Place in enamel pan, cover with 6 cups boiling water. Skim carefully when they come to a boil; cook 2 minutes. Drain thoroughly. Peel 8 tiny white onions, place in enamel pan, add 1 tablespoon granulated sugar, and

4 tablespoons butter. Cover with drained asparagus. Add 1 cup boiling water and bring to boiling point, cover, reduce heat to simmer point, and cook slowly for 30 minutes. Place 3 egg yolks in top of enamel double boiler, add 1 cup heavy cream, and beat with rotary-beater just long enough to mix well.

When the asparagus is done, drain, saving the juice. Add juice gradually to cream and egg, stirring constantly; place over boiling water; and cook, stirring constantly, until well thickened, about 2½ minutes. Season to taste with salt and coarsely ground pepper, add the asparagus, and serve as vegetable course alone or with an entree.

## BOILED WHITE MARROW BEANS GARNISHED WITH TRUFFLES

2 cups dried white marrow
    beans
6 tablespoons butter
½ cup heavy cream

2 truffles (1 can containing 2)
salt, coarsely ground pepper
½ cup white wine

SERVES 6–8

Look over carefully 2 cups dried white marrow beans, discarding imperfect ones. Wash with care, cover with cold water, and soak overnight. Drain, put them into 2 quarts luke-warm water, and bring gently to boiling point. Skim carefully. Simmer very gently until tender but not falling apart, 2½–3 hours, adding hot water as necessary to keep the beans just covered with water.

When almost done, open a small can of truffles which contains at least two, peel if necessary, and chop moderately fine. Cover with white wine and heat gently. When the beans are done, drain (but save the water for soup). Place 6 tablespoons butter in bean pan, cover with the drained beans and pour over them ½ cup heavy cream. Season lightly to taste with salt and coarsely ground pepper. Shake over low flame until butter has melted and cream is hot. Place beans and juice in hot vegetable dish. Drain the truffles and sprinkle over the beans. Serve at once.

## PUREE OF DRIED WHITE BEANS

2–3 cups dried white-pea or
    marrow beans
1 cup diced peeled old pota-
    toes

salt, pepper
4 tablespoons butter
2–3 tablespoons heavy cream

SERVES 6–8

Wash and soak for 12 hours in cold water 2–3 cups dried white-pea or marrow beans. Drain off the water in which they soaked and cover with fresh cold water. Bring slowly to a boil, skim carefully, and reduce heat. Simmer gently for about 1½ hours, at which time add 1 cup peeled diced old potatoes. Cook until the potatoes are done, by which time the beans should be done too. Drain (saving the juice for soup). Mash the beans through a sieve using a wooden potato-masher or spoon.

    Place 4 tablespoons butter in top of enamel double boiler. Add the purée, season to taste with about 1 teaspoon salt and ¼ teaspoon coarsely ground pepper and beat well with spoon, adding a small quantity of heavy cream to soften, if necessary. Keep hot over boiling water until ready to serve.

## DRIED RED KIDNEY BEANS COOKED IN RED WINE

1 pound red kidney beans
1 white onion
½ pound scalded salt pork

2 cups California red wine
salt, pepper

SERVES 6–8

Wash well and soak overnight 1 pound kidney beans. The next morning drain well, put them in an enamel pan, and just barely cover them with cold water. Add 1 white onion, bring them slowly to a boil, and then simmer gently for 45 minutes. Scald ½ pound salt pork, add it to the beans, and cook for another 45 minutes very slowly, adding from time to time, little by little,

2 cups warm California red wine. Salt and pepper lightly just before serving.

## PUREE OF FROZEN LIMA BEANS

4 packages large frozen lima beans
¼ cup heavy cream

4-6 tablespoons butter
chopped parsley

Cook lima beans, following directions on wrapper. Place large sturdy sieve over a saucepan and rub the beans and their juice through the sieve, using a heavy wooden spoon or potato-masher. An electric-blender may also be used, but do a small portion of the beans at a time. It may be necessary to moisten them with a little cream as you go along. If the blender has been used, it may still be necessary to rub the resultant purée through a sieve. Transfer the purée to top of enamel double boiler in which you have placed 2 tablespoons butter. Keep warm over hot water, pouring a little cream over the top to prevent the purée from drying out.

When ready to serve, beat well with spoon, adding a little more cream if necessary, to the consistency of mashed potatoes. Place in hot vegetable dish, make a depression in the center with back of serving-spoon, and place a fresh lump of butter in the depression. Sprinkle with chopped parsley and serve.

## MARION'S SPICED SPANISH BEANS
### [Pre-heat oven to 300°]

6 1-pound cans kidney beans
2 large Bermuda onions
½ teaspoon ground cloves
1 teaspoon ground ginger
1 teaspoon dry mustard
2 teaspoons of Worcestershire sauce

4 tablespoons of chili sauce
¼ teaspoon Tabasco
¼ teaspoon coarsely ground pepper
2 cups very strong black coffee
2 cups brandy
1 pound of bacon

SERVES 6-8

Make 2 cups very strong black coffee. Empty contents of 6 1-pound cans kidney beans into a large 4-quart earthenware casserole. Add 2 large Bermuda onions, peeled and cut moderately fine. Sprinkle with 1 teaspoon dry mustard, 1 teaspoon ginger, and ½ teaspoon of powdered cloves. Mix together 4 tablespoons of chili sauce, 2 teaspoons Worcestershire sauce, ¼ teaspoon coarsely ground pepper, and ¼ teaspoon Tobasco; pour over the beans and mix lightly with fork. Pour over all 1 cup very strong black coffee and 1 cup brandy. Stir once more and bake uncovered slowly for 3 hours.

Remove from oven and allow to cool. An hour and a half before you will be serving the beans, pour over them another cup of very strong black coffee and another cup of brandy and bake slowly in 300° oven. Just before serving fry 1 pound lean bacon slowly until crisp, drain on paper towel, and cover the beans.

## MARION'S MEXICAN BEAN LOAF

| Loaf: | Trimmings: |
|---|---|
| 3 cups black Mexican beans, or 3 cups dried red kidney beans | ¼ pound freshly grated imported Parmesan cheese |
| 2 large white onions | ½ cup cut chives *mixed* with ½ cup chopped parsley |
| 1 teaspoon dry mustard | 8 sweet red pimientoes, chopped medium fine |
| 1½ cups good olive oil | 8 hot chilis (pickled hot red peppers), chopped fine |
| 5 large yellow onions | grated rind 4 oranges |
| 5 cloves garlic | 2 cups good chili sauce |
| 2 tablespoons chopped parsley | |

Wash 3 cups black Mexican beans, or substitute dried red kidney beans. Cover with plenty of cold water and soak overnight. Change the water in the morning and put the beans on to simmer gently with enough cold water to cover, 2 white onions, peeled and cut in two, and ½ teaspoon dry mustard. Cook gently for 8 hours, changing the water 3 times (using boiling water to replace water poured off), and adding each time another ¼ teaspoon dry mustard. When beans are done, do not drain them.

Cover the bottom of a great big iron frying-pan (2½″ deep, 13″ across the top) with good olive oil ¼ inch deep (about 1½ cups). Add to this 5 large peeled and sliced yellow onions and 5 cloves peeled garlic, left whole. Heat and pour the whole bean mixture, including the juice, into the pan and cook 65 minutes longer; watch carefully and stir frequently. At this point start mashing the beans with a potato-masher or a large wooden spoon, and as the mixture thickens build it up with an omelette spatula or pancake-turner to form an oblong loaf-shaped pile in the center of the pan. This sounds complicated but it really isn't; all that is needed is patience and time.

When the whole becomes a solid and neat loaf shape, and has become dry enough to retain this shape, transfer it onto an ovenproof platter—if it should break in the process, don't worry about it; just reshape it. Place in slow 300° oven to keep warm until ready to serve, at which time garnish with 2 tablespoons chopped parsley and send to table to be cut in slices. Serve with it: a bowl of freshly grated imported Parmesan cheese, ½ cup of chopped parsley mixed with an equal quantity of cut tender chives, 8 sweet red pimientoes, chopped medium fine, 8 hot pickled red peppers (chilis), cut fine, 2 cups good chili sauce, and the freshly grated rind of 4 navel oranges. The bean loaf should be eaten with a little of each of the above trimmings.

## STRING BEANS ALMONDINE

| | |
|---|---|
| 3 pounds fresh string beans | ½ cup shelled almonds |
| ½ pound butter | 1 tablespoon chopped parsley |
| pinch of soda | |

SERVES 6–8

First prepare the almonds. Cover ½ cup shelled almonds with boiling water and let stand 5 minutes. Pinch off skins, wash, and slice lengthwise. Spread out on paper towel to dry out thoroughly.

Wash 3 pounds string beans in cold water. With a sharp knife, remove strings and cut fine lengthwise. This is known as "Frenching the beans." Cook them in plenty of boiling salted water to which you have added a large pinch of soda to keep them green. Be sure to skim them. Do not overcook; 10–12 minutes should be sufficient.

In the meantime melt ½ pound butter in deep pan and add the almonds. Place on low flame and cook until the almonds and the butter begin to brown, about 5 minutes. Stir frequently with wooden spoon. Watch carefully, as the butter foams way up. Be sure to remove pan from fire the second they are done.

Drain the string beans thoroughly, place in hot vegetable dish, and pour the almonds and butter over all. Sprinkle with 1 tablespoon chopped parsley and serve.


## MOTHER'S MOONLIGHT CABBAGE

| | Sauce: |
|---|---|
| 1 large head tender green cabbage | ¼ pound butter |
| ¼ teaspoon soda | ½ cup flour |
| 1 teaspoon of salt | 2 cups hot milk |
| | ¼ cup heavy cream |
| | salt, pepper |

SERVES 6–8

First make 2 cups thick cream sauce (page 292) and keep hot over boiling water. Remove outer leaves from 1 large head of new green cabbage. Quarter, core, and shred very, very fine. Place in large colander and allow cold water to run over it. Place in large 3-quart enamel pan; sprinkle with 1 teaspoon salt and ¼ teaspoon baking soda. Heat 2 quarts water to boiling point and when it is bubbling pour it over the cabbage. Cook until just barely tender, or for not more than 7 minutes, skimming it carefully. Drain thoroughly. Return to the pot. Thin the cream sauce slightly with ¼ cup heavy cream, then pour it over the cabbage. Taste, and season to taste with additional salt and a very little coarsely ground pepper. Place in hot serving-dish and serve at once.

## STRING BEANS CHOPPED AND CREAMED

3 pounds string beans
2 tablespoons butter
2 tablespoons flour
1½ cups milk

½ cup heavy cream
salt, pepper
pinch of bicarbonate of soda

SERVES 6–8

Remove both ends from beans, wash in cold water, and French them (page 264). Cook in enamel pan in salted boiling water with a pinch of soda until just barely tender, about 10 minutes. Remove from fire, pour off hot water, rinse in cold water, and drain thoroughly. Chop coarsely, and place them in top of large enamel double boiler over boiling water.

In the meantime make a smooth cream sauce (page 292), using 2 tablespoons butter, 2 tablespoons flour, and 1½ cups hot milk. Season to taste with salt and coarsely ground black pepper and thin with about ½ cup heavy cream. Keep sauce hot over boiling water. When ready to serve pour off from the beans any remaining juice that may have formed. Add cream sauce, stir lightly with fork, and serve in hot vegetable dish.

## HARVARD BEETS DIVINE

1½ dozen sliced cooked beets
½ cup granulated sugar
½ cup vinegar
1 scant tablespoon cornstarch

2 heaping tablespoons ginger
     marmalade
2 tablespoons butter

SERVES 6–8

Mix together ½ cup sugar and 1 scant tablespoon cornstarch. Stir in ½ cup of vinegar, and boil until clear. Remove from fire, stir in 2 tablespoons of butter and 2 heaping tablespoons of ginger marmalade. Pour over hot sliced beets. If you use canned beets, drain them well before adding the sauce.

## FROZEN BRUSSELS SPROUTS WITH CARAWAY SEEDS

| | |
|---|---|
| 4 10-ounce packages frozen Brussels sprouts | 1 teaspoon salt |
| 1 tablespoon caraway seeds | ¼ pound butter |

SERVES 6–8

Heat 2 cups water to boiling point. Open 4 packages frozen Brussels sprouts. Add 1 tablespoon caraway seeds and 1 teaspoon salt to boiling water and add the Brussels sprouts, separating them with a fork. Bring quickly to a boil again, reduce heat, cover, and cook gently 5–6 minutes. Drain well, add ¼ pound butter, and shake over low heat until butter has melted. Serve at once.

## CARROTS VICHY

| | |
|---|---|
| 3 bunches carrots | 1 teaspoon granulated sugar |
| ½ pound butter | ⅓ cup cognac |
| ½ teaspoon salt | |

SERVES 6–8

Peel and wash about 3 bunches tender young carrots and cut them in tiny thin slices. Melt ½ pound butter in an enamel baking-dish and add ½ teaspoon salt and 1 teaspoon sugar. Mix well. Add the carrots and pour over all ⅓ cup cognac. Cover the dish

and place in a *moderate 375° oven* to cook for 1 hour. Do not
stir, but watch carefully to be sure they do not cook too long and
get hard or brown.


## SPANISH CARROTS

3 bunches carrots
1 clove garlic
6 tablespoons butter

2 4-ounce cans pimientos
2–3 tablespoons chili sauce
salt, pepper

SERVES 6–8

Peel 3 bunches carrots, wash, and cook in enough salted water to
cover until tender, about 45 minutes. Drain and chop fairly fine.
Drain and chop 2 cans pimientos. Melt 6 tablespoons butter, add
1 clove garlic cut in two, simmer without browning for 3 minutes.
Discard garlic, add chopped carrots and pimientos, and season
to taste with salt and coarsely ground pepper. Last of all stir in
2–3 tablespoons chili sauce and serve.


## MASHED CARROTS

3 bunches carrots
¼ pound butter
1 teaspoon salt

coarsely ground black pepper
1 teaspoon granulated sugar

SERVES 6–8

Wash and peel 3 bunches of carrots. Slice not too fine. Cover with
cold water to which you have added 1 teaspoon salt and 1 teaspoon granulated sugar and boil until tender and until they have
absorbed all the water. Watch carefully toward the end and be
careful not to burn them. Add ¼ pound butter cut in several
pieces and mash with a wire potato-masher until well crushed.
Sprinkle with coarsely ground black pepper to taste and add a
little more salt if you think it necessary. Place in hot vegetable
dish, sprinkle with chopped parsley, and serve.

## CAULIFLOWER WITH CREAM SAUCE AND BUTTERED CRUMBS

2 medium-size white cauliflower
2 cups milk
1 cup heavy cream

8 tablespoons butter
6 tablespoons flour
salt, pepper
1 cup toasted bread crumbs

SERVES 6–8

Remove tough stem and leaves from 2 medium-size cauliflower. Soak in salted cold water for 20 minutes. Plunge into rapidly boiling, lightly salted water, and cook until tender, about 25 minutes. In the meantime make a medium-thick cream sauce in the usual way (page 292), using 6 tablespoons flour, 6 tablespoons butter, and 2 cups hot milk. Place over hot water and thin with 1 cup heavy cream. Season to taste with salt and coarsely ground black pepper.

Drain the cauliflower thoroughly, place in hot vegetable dish, and cover with the cream sauce. Cover with 1 cup fine toasted bread crumbs that you have heated in 2 tablespoons butter in small frying-pan. Serve at once.

## BAKED CORN
*[Pre-heat oven to 375°]*

24 large ears fresh picked corn
1½ teaspoons salt

¼ teaspoon coarsely ground
pepper
1 tablespoon granulated sugar
½ pound butter, and more

SERVES 6–8

Butter copiously 2 9½-inch ovenproof glass pie plates. Husk 24 large ears fresh picked corn. With a sharp knife score each row of kernels, then slice off a thin layer, and then scrape well with the dull side of the knife to extract all of the remaining milky pulp. You should have about 8 cups of pulp. Season to taste with about 1½ teaspoons salt, ¼ teaspoon coarsely ground pepper, and 1 tablespoon granulated sugar. Cut ½ pound butter in thin slices and mix it with the corn. Fill the 2 pie plates and spread it out evenly then bake for 40–50 minutes, or until sides and top are a crusty golden brown. Remove from oven and serve.

## CORN PUDDING WITH BUTTERED CRUMBS
*[Pre-heat oven to 300°]*

| | |
|---|---|
| 1 1-pound, 1-ounce can whole-kernel corn | 5 eggs |
| 1 1-pound, 1-ounce can cream-style corn | 1 tablespoon granulated sugar |
| | 1 teaspoon salt |
| 1 cup milk | ½ teaspoon cracked pepper |
| 1 cup heavy cream | 3 teaspoons melted butter |
| | 2 cups hot buttered crumbs |

SERVES 6–8

Butter copiously a large 2-quart-size rectangular baking-dish, 12″ by 7½″ by 2″. Beat 5 whole eggs until well mixed, but not too long. Add 1 cup milk and 1 cup heavy cream, 1 can whole-kernel corn, 1 can cream-style corn, 3 tablespoons melted butter, 1 tablespoon granulated sugar, 1 teaspoon salt, and ½ teaspoon cracked pepper.

Mix well, pour into baking-dish, place in oven, and bake until set through like custard, about 30 minutes. Watch carefully and reduce heat to 250° if custard shows signs of bubbling. When an inserted knife is placed in center of pudding and comes out clean, the pudding is done. Sprinkle the entire top with 2 cups buttered crumbs and serve at once—especially good with fried chicken.

## DRIED FLAGEOLETS

| | |
|---|---|
| 1 pound of flageolets (imported French dried green-colored beans) | 1 white onion |
| | 1 teaspoon salt |
| | butter |

SERVES 6–8

Wash and soak 1 pound dried flageolets for 2 hours in plenty of luke-warm water. Drain off the water in which they soaked. Place them in enamel pan, cover again with 6 cups cold water, and bring gently to boiling point (which should take at least 1 hour). Skim carefully, turn light way down, cover, and simmer ever so gently for 1 hour. Add 1 teaspoon salt and 1 peeled onion and continue cooking until done, 2–3 hours longer, adding additional water as needed to keep water just above the level of the beans.

When done, drain off most of the juice, but not all of it— and be sure to save the juice. Add a big lump of butter and shake pan over low flame until butter has melted. Season to taste with salt and pepper, sprinkle with chopped parsley, and serve at once, with roast lamb. Make soup the next day of the juice you drained off and any beans that are left over.

## BRAISED ENDIVES ON A BED OF MUSHROOMS
*[Pre-heat oven to 400°]*

18 stalks of endives
juice of 1 lemon
1 pound fresh mushrooms
1½ cups clear chicken broth
¾ pound butter
1 small onion
1 stalk celery
1 small carrot
1 tablespoon chopped parsley

1 bouquet of parsley and a bay leaf
3 tablespoons flour
2 cups hot milk
2 tablespoons grated imported Parmesan cheese
2 tablespoons grated imported Swiss Gruyère cheese
⅓ cup heavy cream
salt, pepper

SERVES 6–8

Trim and remove outer leaves of 18 stalks of endives. Wash carefully, allowing cold water to run into their centers. Shake and dry well on tea cloth. Butter copiously 2 rectangular dishes, 10″ by 6″ by 2″. Butter both sides of 4 sheets of typewriter paper. Lay the endives side by side in the 2 dishes. Sprinkle with the strained juice of 1 lemon, and a little salt and pepper, and dot with 2 tablespoons butter for each dish. Pour ½ cup chicken broth over each dish. Cover with buttered typewriter paper and bake until tender through and beginning to brown lightly, about 1½ hours. Remove from oven, discard paper, and while still hot, pour ¼ cup hot chicken broth into each dish; stir mixture in dishes into brown buttery residue to make a small quantity of clear gravy. Keep warm.

Now make a sauce béchamel. Wash and peel 1 small carrot and cut in tiny cubes. Peel and chop fine 1 small onion. Remove strings from 1 stalk crisp celery, and cut it in fine cubes like the carrot. Melt 3 tablespoons butter in top of enamel double boiler directly over low flame. Add chopped vegetables and cook slowly over low heat for 10 minutes, stirring frequently. Sprinkle with 3 tablespoons flour, stir, and add gradually 2 cups hot milk. Cook, stirring constantly, until thick; then place over boiling water. Add a bouquet of parsley and 1 bay leaf, and season to taste with salt and pepper. Cover and cook, while you prepare the mushrooms.

Wash and dry 1 pound fresh mushrooms. Cut off and discard tough stems. Chop the caps and tender stems until very fine. Melt 4 tablespoons butter in frying-pan, add the mushrooms, and cook over moderate heat until all the juice has evaporated, about 10 minutes. Now remove the parsley and bay leaf from the béchamel sauce; add the mushrooms. Stir in 2 tablespoons grated Parmesan cheese and 2 tablespoons grated Swiss Gruyère cheese. Add more salt if necessary and thin with about ⅓ cup heavy cream.

Pour into large buttered 2-quart-size rectangular baking-dish, 12″ by 7½″ by 2″. On this bed place the braised endives crosswise in 2 rows. Pour over all the brown gravy from both dishes. Sprinkle with chopped parsley and serve at once. This is especially wonderful and well worth the trouble; it should be served as a separate course.

NOTE This dish may be prepared ahead of time, if more convenient, but in this case, do not place the endives on the mushrooms until you are ready to assemble and heat the dish. Place in a pre-heated moderate 400° oven until heated through, about 20 minutes. Sprinkle with parsley just before serving. Celery may be braised in the same manner, and served plain or on a bed of mushrooms.

## BOILED HOMINY GRITS

1½ cups hominy grits          lump of butter
1½ teaspoons salt

SERVES 6–8

Add to 6 cups water in top of double boiler 1½ teaspoons salt and bring to an active boil over direct flame. Then add gradually, stirring constantly, 1½ cups hominy grits. Cook 5 minutes, stirring frequently, then place pan over boiling water, and continue cooking, tightly covered, 2–3 hours. Place in hot vegetable dish, make a hole in the center, add a large lump of butter, and serve at once.

## OKRA DAUBE

¼ pound bacon                 salt, pepper
5 cups okra                   rice water or tomato juice, if
6 cups ripe, peeled, pitted to-    necessary
  matoes, or canned toma-
  toes

SERVES 6–8

Cut into small strips ¼ pound bacon and fry it until it begins to get crisp. Then add 5 cups okra, washed and cut into ¼-inch slices, and fry until the okra browns. Then add 6 cups ripe, peeled, pitted tomatoes, or an equal quantity of canned tomatoes. Simmer the whole very gently for 3 hours, stirring occasionally. Season well with salt and freshly ground pepper. If it boils down too much, add a little gruel from boiled rice, or a little tomato juice, to thin it out slightly.

## ONIONS, SPICED AND CREAMED

| | Sauce: |
|---|---|
| 3–4 dozen white onions | 1 tablespoon butter |
| ⅛ pound butter | 1 teaspoon flour |
| 1 teaspoon granulated sugar | 1 cup light cream |
| 2 dozen whole cloves | |
| salt, pepper | |

SERVES 6–8

Peel 3–4 dozen small white onions. Parboil them until almost tender in salted boiling water. Drain; let the cold water run over them a second; then when they have drained again, place them in a frying-pan containing ⅛ pound butter. Sprinkle them with 1 teaspoon granulated sugar and let them brown slowly, shaking the pan frequently, so that they roll over and over, becoming a beautiful golden yellow. Don't let them burn. Place them in a shallow baking-dish. Add to the frying-pan ¼ cup cold water and place it over fire, stirring until you have about 2 tablespoons nice, brown, syrupy liquid left, which should then be poured over the onions. Now stick a whole clove in every other onion, sprinkle them with freshly ground black pepper and a little salt, and pour over them a thin cream sauce, made of 1 tablespoon butter, 1 teaspoon flour, and 1 cup light cream. Place in *preheated 350° oven*, bake slowly about 20 minutes, and serve.

## MASHED PARSNIPS

| | |
|---|---|
| 3–4 pounds young parsnips | salt, coarsely ground pepper |
| ⅛ pound butter | |

SERVES 6–8

Wash, peel, and split in two lengthwise 3–4 pounds fresh young parsnips. Split once more and cut out pithy core. Cover with small quantity of boiling water and season with about 1 teaspoon salt. Cook until tender, about 30 minutes. Drain well, add ⅛ pound butter, and mash well. Add a little coarsely ground pepper, if you like, and serve at once.

## ONION TART

| Filling: | Crust: |
|---|---|
| 5 large onions | 1¼ cups pastry flour |
| 5 slices bacon (¼ pound) | 3 tablespoons butter |
| 1 teaspoon caraway seeds | 3 tablespoons vegetable short- |
| 2 tablespoons chopped parsley |    ening |
| 4 large eggs | 3 tablespoons water |
| 1½ cups milk | ½ teaspoon salt |
| 3 tablespoons butter | |
| 1 teaspoon salt | |
| ¼ teaspoon pepper | |

SERVES 6–8

Make half the recipe for plain pastry (page 362). Chill for ½ hour, or longer. Prepare 2 tablespoons chopped parsley. Peel 5 large onions, slice crosswise in thin circles, and then cut once more making half-circles. Place in enamel pan and cover with boiling water. Cook 6 minutes, then remove from fire, drain in sieve, and plunge them immediately into cold water. Drain again thoroughly and pat dry on clean tea cloth.

Cut 5 slices bacon in little squares. Place in little pan, cover with cold water, place on low flame, and bring to boil. Simmer 5 minutes, drain in sieve, and plunge into cold water. Drain and pat dry on tea cloth. *Pre-heat oven to hot 450°.* Roll out chilled pastry and line a 10-inch ovenproof glass pie plate. Roll the edges under and crimp prettily. Chill while you make the filling.

Melt 3 tablespoons butter in frying-pan and add the bacon and sauté for a minute. Then add the onions and cook very slowly, without browning, for 15 minutes, stirring frequently. Remove from fire, add 2 tablespoons chopped parsley, and cool slightly while you beat 4 whole eggs with rotary-beater but not too long. Add 1½ cups milk and mix well, season with 1 scant teaspoon salt, ¼ teaspoon coarsely ground pepper, and 1 teaspoon

of caraway seeds. Stir in the onion and bacon and whatever butter there is on them, and mix well. Pour into prepared pastry
shell, put pie plate on cookie sheet and place in oven to bake for
about 10 minutes or until pastry begins to brown lightly. Then
reduce heat to slow 325° and continue baking until set through
like custard, 20–25 minutes longer or until a golden brown on top.
Serve at once.

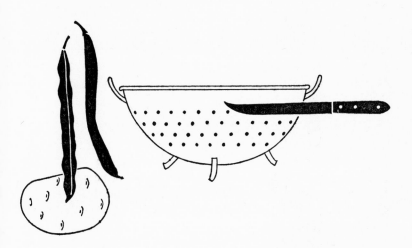

## PETITS POIS A LA FRANCAISE

4 pounds fresh green peas, or 12 tablespoons butter
   4 packages frozen peas    pinch of nutmeg
8 little white onions    ½ teaspoon salt
1 small head Boston lettuce    ¼ teaspoon pepper
2 lumps sugar    several sprigs of parsley

SERVES 6–8

Shell 4 pounds fresh green peas, and wash in cold water. Discard
outer wilted leaves of a small head of Boston lettuce and pull it
apart, saving heart for salad. Wash the leaves carefully, and shred.

Peel 8 little white onions and quarter them. Place 6 tablespoons butter in a pan, cover with the shredded lettuce, add the onions, 2 lumps sugar, and a few sprigs of parsley, minus stems. Season with about ½ teaspoon salt, pinch of nutmeg, and ¼ teaspoon coarsely ground pepper. Now add the peas and moisten with ½ cup cold water.

Cover the pan, place on moderate heat, and shake occasionally. Watch carefully and when the lettuce has formed a juice, decrease heat and cook slowly for 20–30 minutes. When the peas are tender, drain off most of the juice into a separate little pan, and keep the peas warm. Reduce the buttery juice by boiling it rapidly for about 5 minutes. Add 6 additional tablespoons butter to the peas and shake over low heat until melted. Place peas in hot serving-dish, pour the reduced juice over them, and serve.

## DEEP-DISH TART OF PEAS

| Crust: | Peas: |
|---|---|
| 1½ cups pastry flour | 8–10 pounds of peas |
| ½ teaspoon salt | ¼ pound butter |
| ¾ cup sweet butter | salt, pepper |
| very little tepid water | pinch of bicarbonate of soda |
| 1 slightly beaten egg | |

SERVES 8

I once read in a magazine in France that one of Anatole France's favorite dishes was a deep-dish pie of petits pois. Fascinated by the idea I worked out the following recipe, which is now a great favorite of ours.

To make this dish, first make the pastry. Sift together 1½ cups pastry flour with ½ teaspoon salt. Work into it with finger tips ¾ cup butter that has been previously worked in cold water to the consistency of putty and then squeezed dry in a piece of linen. Moisten the flour and butter with a few drops of tepid water, and mix with a big fork until it holds together. Form a flat ball of it, wrap in wax paper, and chill several hours.

In the meantime shell the peas, discarding any big tough ones. Wash them, place in large enamel pan, add a pinch of soda and 1 teaspoon of salt, and cover with rapidly boiling water. Skim carefully. Cook until very tender, 20–25 minutes, being sure that the peas have enough water to cover them during the whole cooking process, but no more. When done, drain, but save the juice. Put the peas temporarily in a 2-quart-size dish in which you have already placed ¼ pound butter; then pour over the peas just enough of the reserved juice barely to cover the peas. Season to taste with salt and freshly ground black pepper. Stir lightly with a fork. Allow the peas to cool in their juice.

When ready to assemble and bake the pie, roll out a small piece of the pastry so as to form a band about 1 inch wide and long enough to edge the rim of the dish in which the pie is to be cooked (a round 1½-quart-size baking-dish should be the right size). First paint the rim of the dish with beaten egg, then press the strip of pastry securely around the edge. Now fill the dish level full with peas and the juice. Reserve a small piece of the remaining pastry, then roll the rest to form a circle large enough to cover the dish and overhang about ¾ inch. Paint the strip of pastry around the dish with more egg. Then rolling the pastry up on your rolling-pin, unroll it so that it will fall in the right place to cover the dish. Press the edges together and, using your floured fingers, crimp the edges prettily. Work quickly. Brush the top with more egg, and make a hole in the center of the crust. Lay around this 5 small diamond-shape pieces of paste crust from the remaining rolled-out scraps to form a decoration. Also cut a narrow strip of pastry and roll it around your finger—to form a rose—and insert it in the hole, being sure to leave a hole for the steam to escape. Paint the rose and the diamonds with egg and place the dish in the refrigerator for a few minutes to chill until ready to bake.

*Pre-heat oven to 450°.* Bake pie; in about 15 minutes the crust should be a beautiful golden brown. Reduce the heat a little. Continue cooking about 15 minutes longer, or until the juice in the pie is boiling hot and the crust is cooked through. Serve at once.

## POTATOES ANNA

*[Pre-heat oven to 450°]*

12 medium-size new potatoes          salt, pepper to taste
1 tablespoon chopped parsley          ½ cup sour cream
¼ pound butter, and more

SERVES 6–8

Butter a large 12-inch ovenproof glass pie plate. Peel, wash, and slice fine about 12 medium-size new potatoes. Cover the bottom of the plate with a symmetrical layer of overlapping slices, starting in the middle and working around and around to the edge. Next fill the plate to the top with potatoes, sprinkling with a little salt and coarsely ground pepper as you go along and packing the potatoes in evenly and tightly. Melt at least ¼ pound butter; pour over the potatoes. Cover with another ovenproof plate of the same size, place dish in hot oven, and bake until the potatoes feel tender when poked with a fork, about 30 minutes. At this time remove cover, reduce heat to 325°, and continue cooking until potatoes are brown on the bottom, about 25 minutes longer. Remove from oven and cool for a few minutes. Loosen the potatoes with a spatula if sticking around the edge. Turn out upside down on large, round, hot serving-dish. Place ½ cup sour cream in center, sprinkle with 1 tablespoon chopped parsley, and serve.

## POTATOES A LA CREME

3 pounds small new potatoes          1½ cups heavy cream
1½ cups milk                         ¼ teaspoon grated nutmeg
3 tablespoons butter                 salt, pepper

SERVES 6–8

Wash 3 pounds small new potatoes. Place in large pan, cover with cold water, bring to a boil, and cook until almost tender through, about 20 minutes. Drain, and when cool enough to handle, peel and cut in thick slices.

Place 1½ cups milk in heavy enamel pan, add 3 tablespoons butter and bring to a lively boil. Add the sliced potatoes and simmer gently until the milk has reduced about half, 10–15 minutes. Watch carefully to avoid scorching. Add 1½ cups heavy cream, ¼ teaspoon of grated nutmeg, and a little coarsely ground black pepper. Place pan on asbestos mat on low flame and continue cooking 15 minutes longer, shaking the pan occasionally. Add salt to taste, and serve. Wonderful with steak or chops.

## POTATOES, BOILED
[Served with Cottage Cheese and Sour Cream]

3–4 pounds hot boiled pota-
    toes
2–3 cups cottage cheese
1 pint thick sour cream

1 cup chopped onion
salt, freshly ground pepper
caraway seeds

SERVES 6–8

This dish consists of a big bowl of freshly boiled peeled white potatoes, accompanied by a big bowl of cottage cheese, a big bowl of thick sour cream, a small bowl of chopped white onion, a pepper mill, a salt cellar, and a dish of caraway seeds. Each person serves himself to potatoes, puts on top of them some cottage cheese, covers this with sour cream, and then sprinkles the whole to taste with onion, salt and pepper, and caraway seeds. One of my favorite dishes.

## BUTTERED BOILED NEW POTATOES
## WITH DILL

3 pounds new potatoes
6 tablespoons butter

2 tablespoons fresh dill, cut
    fine
salt, pepper

SERVES 6–8

Wash and peel 3 pounds little new potatoes. Cook in boiling salted water until just tender through, 25–30 minutes. Prepare 2 tablespoons fresh dill, cut fine. Melt in a separate pan 6 tablespoons butter. Drain the potatoes well, place in hot vegetable dish, sprinkle lightly with about ¼ teaspoon coarsely ground pepper, and then pour the butter over all. Sprinkle with the cut dill and serve.

## LEMON-FLAVORED MASHED POTATOES

| | |
|---|---|
| 12 medium-size potatoes | 2 tablespoons butter |
| ½ lemon | 1–1½ cups hot light cream |
| salt | |

SERVES 6–8

Peel, wash, and quarter 12 potatoes. Place them in an enamel pan with ½ lemon. Cover well with water, salt lightly, and boil until tender, but not falling apart, 20–25 minutes. Drain well, remove lemon, and put potatoes through a ricer. Add a lump of butter and a little salt, and place pan on low fire. Beat well until perfectly smooth. Then add, little by little, a cup or so of hot light cream, beating furiously meanwhile with a wire or wooden masher, or electric-beater, until light and fluffy.

## NEW POTATOES COOKED IN CONSOMME

| | |
|---|---|
| 2 pounds new potatoes | 1 can consommé |

SERVES 6–8

Peel 2 pounds new potatoes, leaving them whole. Wash, place in heavy aluminum pan, and pour 1 can undiluted consommé over all. Bring to a boil, cover, and cook gently on low heat until potatoes are tender through and all the consommé has been absorbed, 35–40 minutes. Watch carefully toward the end to avoid sticking. Serve piping hot with any roasted meat.

## PROVINCIAL POTATOES

3 pounds new potatoes
⅛ pound butter
3 tablespoons olive oil
grated rind of ½ lemon
¼ teaspoon nutmeg

½ teaspoon flour
salt, pepper
1 tablespoon chopped parsley
1 tablespoon chopped chives
juice of 1 lemon

SERVES 6–8

Wash and boil in their skins 3 pounds new potatoes. Put ⅛ pound
butter in a saucepan. Cut it up and pour over it 3 tablespoons of
olive oil, and grate into this the rind of ½ lemon. Add 1 tablespoon chopped parsley, 1 tablespoon chopped chives, ¼ teaspoon
freshly grated nutmeg, ½ teaspoon flour, and some salt and pepper. When the potatoes are cooked, peel, cut into quarters or
eighths, and put them into the butter mixture. Heat, but don't
let the butter boil. When ready to serve, add the juice of 1 lemon.

## POTATOES SHALMAAR

Irish bacon
chopped onion
potatoes

sweet butter
salt, pepper
heavy cream

This delectable treat is an Irish dish from Ballinasloe Athlone.
Strange as it may seem, it is served there at teatime, accompanied
by a large cup of English tea with cream and sugar; and to be
truly Irish the tea should be served so strong "you could walk a
cat on it."

The dish itself consists of, first, plenty of piping-hot Irish
bacon—and it must be Irish, dry-cured, turf-smoked—that has
been cut in little squares and along with several chopped onions,
freshly fried until crisp. Secondly, it consists of baked potatoes,
piping hot and snowy and fluffy, broken open the second they
are baked and scraped out lightly with a fork onto individual
heated plates, allowing at least 3 potatoes for every 2 people. A

lump of sweet butter, with salt and pepper, is then crushed lightly into the potato on each plate with a fork, and a mound is made of the potato. The well-drained bacon and onions are sprinkled generously over all. A hole is poked in the center of each mound and filled to overflowing with plenty of luscious heavy cream. All of this must be accomplished as quick as a flash and eaten then and there immediately. Nothing could be simpler and nothing could be better!

## RUTABAGAS MASHED

3-pound rutabaga          ¼ cup heavy cream
⅛ pound butter            1 teaspoon salt

SERVES 6–8

Wash, peel, and cut in dice a large 3-pound rutabaga. Place in cold water until ready to cook. Pour off water in which it has soaked, cover with fresh cold water, add 1 teaspoon salt, and boil until tender, about ½ hour. Drain thoroughly, add ⅛ pound butter and mash thoroughly with wire-masher. Add ¼ cup heavy cream, beat well, and serve at once.

## SUMMER SQUASH IN CREAM
[*Pre-heat oven to 400°*]

4 white summer squash     ½ pint heavy cream
salt, pepper              chopped parsley
6 tablespoons butter

SERVES 6–8

Butter a deep glass baking-dish. Peel 4 white summer squash and remove the seeds. Slice the squash into the dish, sprinkle with salt and pepper, and add here and there 6 tablespoons butter in little dabs. When the dish is full, place in a hot oven and cover with an inverted pie tin. As the squash becomes tender, add ½ pint heavy cream and let cook without the cover until perfectly done, in all about 45 minutes. When slightly browned, sprinkle with parsley and serve in the baking-dish.

## SUMMER SQUASH CUSTARD A LA VIOLA
*[Pre-heat oven to 350°]*

2 pounds summer squash
½ pound American cheese
salt, pepper
2 eggs

¾ cup milk
corn flakes
1 tablespoon butter

SERVES 6–8

Remove seeds and cut up in fairly small pieces 2 pounds green summer squash. Boil until very tender, drain well, and put into a deep baking-dish. Add ½ pound American cheese, cut in small pieces—saving out, however, a little to sprinkle over the top. Sprinkle with salt and freshly ground pepper. Beat 2 eggs just long enough to blend the yolks and whites, add ¾ cup milk to them, and pour over the squash. Sprinkle the remaining cheese over the top, then cover with crushed corn flakes, and dot with 1 tablespoon of butter. Bake slowly for 30 minutes, or until top becomes a delicious brown and the custard is set. Test with an inverted silver knife; if it comes out clean and the top is brown, serve at once.

## SWEET POTATOES WITH MARRONS GLACES

4 pounds sweet potatoes
⅛ pound butter

1 13-ounce bottle French marrons glacés vanillés
½ cup light cream

Peel, wash, and cut into medium-size pieces 4 pounds sweet potatoes. Cook until tender in boiling, slightly salted water. Drain well. Add ⅛ pound butter and mash, using a potato-masher or electric-beater. Moisten gradually with about ½ cup hot light cream. When nice and fluffy, keep warm in double boiler until ready to serve, at which time fold into them 1 13-ounce bottle French marrons glacés vanillés, syrup and all—having, however, first broken the marrons into medium-size pieces. Be sure the potatoes are piping hot before serving. If you like, reserve 1 spoonful of syrup and marrons to garnish a hole in the center of the mound of potatoes heaped into a hot vegetable dish.

## GLAZED TURNIPS

24 small white turnips      chopped parsley
6 tablespoons butter      1 teaspoon beef extract
1 tablespoon granulated sugar

SERVES 6–8

Peel 24 tender white turnips, wash well, and boil in salted water until almost done. Then drain well and put in a frying-pan with 6 tablespoons butter. Brown them carefully and season with salt and pepper and 1 tablespoon granulated sugar. Drain off the butter and add 1 teaspoon beef extract that you have dissolved in ¼ cup water. Let the turnips simmer until almost dry or until the juice is reduced to a glaze. Sprinkle lightly with chopped parsley and serve at once.

## YAMS AND ORANGES

5–6 large yams      grated rind of 1 orange
3 navel oranges      1 cup unsweetened pineapple
¼ pound butter      juice
1 cup light-brown sugar

SERVES 6–8

Slice 5 or 6 peeled raw yams in thin slices and arrange them in a buttered baking-dish with 3 peeled and sliced oranges in alternate layers, until the dish is three quarters' full, dotting each layer as you go along with, in all, ¼ pound sweet butter creamed with 1 cup light-brown sugar. Add the grated rind of 1 orange to 1 cup unsweetened pineapple juice and pour over the yams. Cover the dish and bake slowly for 1 hour, or until the yams are tender through and the juice is reduced to a thick syrup. These—served with roast duck, ham, or chicken—are divine!

## COLACHE

4 small summer squash, or 4 Italian squash (zucchini)
4 tablespoons butter and bacon fat *mixed* (or 2 tablespoons olive oil, instead of bacon fat)
1 large onion

2 green peppers, seeded and quartered
4 peeled tomatoes
salt, freshly ground black pepper
cayenne
3 ears fresh corn, or 1 package frozen corn

SERVES 6–8

This dish is a kind of vegetable stew which was made by the Spanish in early days in California. Cut into ½-inch squares 4 small summer squash (round, scalloped, light green) or 4 long green Italian squash (known as zucchini). Melt 4 tablespoons butter and bacon fat *mixed*—or use 2 tablespoons olive oil, instead of the bacon fat—and fry the squash in it until partly browned. If too much juice is formed, pour off some of it and put it back in the colache later on.

Next add 1 large onion, sliced thin, and 2 green peppers. Fry a bit, then add 4 peeled tomatoes, or an equal amount of canned ones. Season well with salt, freshly ground black pepper, and cayenne to taste. Add corn cut from 3 ears fresh corn, or 1 package frozen corn, and cook ½ hour. Be sure to season the colache well, for it should be quite hot and peppery. This goes very well with chicken dishes.

# 8

# *Sauces for Meat, Vegetables, and Fish*

*The French have a saying:* "La sauce fait manger le poisson. Avec elle on peut même se passer de poisson." *In other words, the sauce makes the fish; with it, we can even do without the fish!*

## BLACK CURRANT SAUCE FOR ROAST PHEASANTS

⅔ cup black currant jam
3 tablespoons strained lime
  juice

½ cup of blanched walnut
  meats, cut in quarters

Heat ⅔ cup black currant jam in a double boiler with 3 tablespoons lime juice. When hot, add ½ cup blanched walnut meats
that you have cut in quarters, and serve at once.

## BREAD SAUCE FOR GAME

3 heaping cups cubed soft
  bread (minus crusts)
1½ cups milk
2 tablespoons heavy cream
2 small peeled onions

2 cloves
⅛ bar butter, or 1 tablespoon
salt, pepper
nutmeg, or powdered mace

Put 2 small peeled onions, with a clove stuck in each one, into
top of large enamel double boiler and add 1½ cups milk. Bring to
a boil over direct heat, then place over boiling water, and add 3
cups cubed soft bread (no crusts). Cover and cook for 20 minutes, stirring lightly occasionally with a fork. Remove onion and
season to taste with salt and pepper. Add ⅛ bar, or 1 tablespoon,
butter, 2 tablespoons heavy cream, toss lightly with a fork, and
serve at once. A pinch of nutmeg or powdered mace may be
added, if you like the flavor.

## BROWNED BUTTER

Put the required amount of butter in a saucepan, place over
moderate flame, and cook slowly, skimming off the white foam
as it forms. Continue cooking until brown specks begin to form
on the bottom of the pan. Watch carefully and remove from
fire when well browned—but don't let it burn, for it will be bitter.
Use a deep pan if you are browning very much butter, for it foams

way up and might overflow and catch fire. If browned butter is to be used for fish or string beans, a few capers may be added. Browned butter may also be served on asparagus, calves' brains, fried eggs, and skate fish.


## CLARIFIED BUTTER

To clarify butter, place it in a small pan over low flame and let it melt slowly. When melted, skim off the foam that rises to the surface. Remove from fire, let it settle a few minutes, and then ladle off the clear butter, being careful not to include any of the milky sediment in the bottom of the pan. This makes a clearer and more attractive sauce.

Clarified butter is helpful in frying, especially omelettes and meats.


## COLD SAFFRON SAUCE FOR COLD BOILED FISH

2 cloves garlic                 ½ cup dry white wine
2 leeks                         ½ cup water
2 medium-size onions            2 teaspoons saffron
6 large ripe tomatoes           2 teaspoons salt
6 tablespoons olive oil         1 teaspoon pepper
2 lemons

Dip 6 ripe tomatoes in boiling water and remove skins. Remove green part from 2 leeks, split the white part in two lengthwise, and wash carefully. Peel 2 medium-size onions and 2 cloves garlic. Cut the tomatoes crosswise in two and remove seeds. Place in wooden bowl and chop fine. Chop the onions and leeks very fine and cook in 6 tablespoons olive oil until just beginning to brown, stirring with a wooden spoon. Add the juice from 2 cloves garlic (using a garlic press). Add the chopped tomatoes. Cook 2 minutes, then add ½ cup dry white wine, and ½ cup water. Season with about 2 teaspoons of salt, 1 teaspoon of coarsely ground black pepper, and 2 teaspoons of genuine saffron. Cook 10–15 minutes. Stir occasionally.

Remove from fire and cool before placing in refrigerator to chill thoroughly. Serve on cold boiled fish.

## COLD SAUCE FOR SHRIMP, LOBSTER OR CRAB MEAT

| | |
|---|---|
| 1 cup chili sauce | 1 tablespoon celery |
| 1 cup mayonnaise | ½ tablespoon imported pre- |
| ¼ cup Indian relish | pared mustard |
| 1 hard-boiled egg | 1 teaspoon A.-I. sauce |
| ½ teaspoon chopped chives | dash of paprika |
| ¼ green pepper, chopped fine | coarsely ground black pepper |

Mix together 1 cup of chili sauce, 1 cup mayonnaise, ¼ cup Indian relish, 1 chopped hard-boiled egg, ½ teaspoon chopped chives, ¼ green pepper, chopped fine, 1 tablespoon chopped celery, ½ teaspoon imported prepared mustard, a little coarsely ground black pepper, 1 teaspoon A.-I. sauce, and a dash of paprika. Chill well and serve with shrimp, lobster, or crab meat.

## CREAM SAUCE

To make cream sauce (also known as white sauce), make a *roux* by cooking together the required amount of butter with the required amount of flour over a low flame, stirring constantly, for 1–2 minutes; then add gradually the required amount of hot milk, stirring continuously and furiously, to make a smooth sauce. Place over boiling water, cover, and continue cooking about 15 minutes longer. Season to taste when cooked. If a richer sauce is desired, make a slightly thicker sauce than required and thin it at the end with little heavy cream.

*Thin cream sauce:* To make a thin cream sauce, follow directions as given, but use 1 tablespoon flour and 1 tablespoon butter to each cup of hot milk.

*Medium-thick cream sauce:* To make a medium-thick cream sauce, use 2 tablespoons flour and 2 tablespoons butter to each cup of hot milk.

*Thick cream sauce:* To make a thick cream sauce, use 4 tablespoons flour and 4 tablespoons butter to each cup of hot milk.

## CRANBERRY SAUCE DE LUXE

4 dozen blanched almonds
1 pound fresh cranberries
2 cups granulated sugar
1 cup cold water

6 generous tablespoons orange marmalade
strained juice of 2 lemons

SERVES 6–8

Blanch 4 dozen almonds by pouring boiling water over them. Let them stand 2–3 minutes, then pour off the water, and the brown skins should pinch off easily. Cover with cold water and place in refrigerator for several hours.

Wash and pick over 1 pound fine cranberries. Moisten 2 cups granulated sugar with 1 cup cold water, stir, bring to a boil, skim carefully, and boil 5 minutes. Then add the cranberries and cook 3–5 minutes longer, or until they have all popped open and become transparent. Remove from fire and add 6 generous tablespoons orange marmalade; stir, and add the strained juice of 2 lemons. When cold, add the blanched almonds, which have been well drained. Serve well chilled with roast chicken, turkey, or pheasant.

## CREAMED HERB SAUCE

4 shallots
1 tablespoon flour
1 tablespoon butter
1 cup hot milk
2 egg yolks
½ cup of heavy cream

4 dozen tarragon leaves
1 tablespoon chopped parsley, or chervil
grated rind of 1 lemon
juice of 1 lemon
salt, pepper

SERVES 6

Chop 4 shallots very fine and cook them slowly in 1 tablespoon butter, being careful not to brown them at all; add 1 tablespoon of flour; cook together a minute or two, then add gradually 1 cup hot milk. When smooth and slightly thickened, place over boiling water; cook awhile longer. When ready to serve beat the yolks of 2 eggs with ½ cup of cream and stir into them a little of the hot sauce; then add the eggs to the cream sauce gradually and continue cooking over boiling water, stirring constantly, until thickened. Season to taste with salt and freshly ground pepper, then add the grated rind of 1 lemon, being sure not to include any of the white part of the rind, which would give the sauce a bitter taste. At the last add 1 tablespoon of chopped parsley or chervil, 4 dozen tarragon leaves, chopped fine, and the juice of 1 lemon. Serve with boiled cauliflower, string beans, boiled fish, or boiled chicken.

## MADEIRA SAUCE

| | |
|---|---|
| 1 onion | 3¾ cups canned consommé |
| 1 carrot | ½ cup Madeira wine, and 1 |
| 2 tablespoons ham fat | tablespoon |
| bouquet of parsley, bay leaf, | 1 teaspoon beef extract |
| thyme | salt, pepper |
| 7½ tablespoons butter | ½ lemon |
| ½ cup flour | |

SERVES 6–8

Have ready 1 onion and 1 carrot, chopped fine, and 2 tablespoons of ham fat, cut in little pieces. Prepare a bouquet of herbs consisting of parsley, bay leaf, and a big pinch of thyme.

Melt 6 tablespoons butter in an aluminum saucepan, over a low flame; then add ½ cup of flour and stir until smooth. Continue cooking, stirring constantly, using a wooden spoon, until the mixture, known as the *roux*, becomes a rich golden brown. It must be dark enough to give the sauce a rich color, but great care must be taken not to allow it to burn and turn black on the bottom, for this would make the sauce bitter. In about 10 minutes it should have become the right color, at which time remove pan from the fire and gradually stir into the *roux* 3¾ cups of luke-warm canned consommé.

When smooth, place back on fire and bring to a boil; skim carefully. Reduce the flame and let it simmer while you brown the prepared ham fat in 1 teaspoon butter in a small frying-pan. When butter is brown add the chopped onion and carrot and cook until they are brown; then add the whole to the simmering sauce. Also add the bouquet of herbs. Continue cooking gently for 2 hours, being sure to skim the sauce carefully and frequently.

When done, strain carefully and cool, stirring it occasionally so that no skin will form on it. Place in tightly covered glass jar in the refrigerator until ready to finish the sauce, at which time place it in a double boiler over hot water. When it is scalding hot, add to it ½ cup good Madeira that you have reduced to ¼ cup by simmering it in an enamel pan in which you have melted 1 teaspoon beef extract. Just before serving, season to taste with plenty of coarsely ground black pepper, a little salt, a little lemon juice and 1 tablespoon Madeira. Remove from fire and add little by little 2 teaspoons butter. Stir until melted and serve with Boeuf en Croute (page 125).

## CURRIED HARD-BOILED-EGG CREAM SAUCE

| | |
|---|---|
| 2 cups medium-thick cream sauce | 6 tablespoons heavy cream, or more |
| 4 hard-boiled eggs | 2 teaspoons good curry powder salt |

SERVES 6–8

Make a cream sauce in the usual way, using 4 tablespoons butter, 4 tablespoons of flour, and 2 cups of hot milk. When thick and smooth, place over boiling water and continue cooking awhile longer. When ready to serve, dissolve 2 teaspoons of curry powder in 6 tablespoons heavy cream and stir it into the cream sauce. Add salt to taste, then add 4 hard-boiled eggs, chopped or sliced, and serve at once on boiled fish or fish soufflé.

## GINGER SAUCE

¾ cup preserved ginger
¾ cup light-brown sugar
rind of ½ a lemon

1½ teaspoons powdered ginger
1½ cups water
1½ tablespoons lemon juice
3 tablespoons brandy

SERVES 6–8

Prepare ¾ cup preserved or candied ginger cut in little squares. Simmer together for 15 minutes, ¾ cup of light brown sugar mixed with the rind of ½ a lemon cut in thin slivers, and 1½ teaspoons of powdered ginger, moistened with 1½ cups of water. Add the prepared ginger, 1½ tablespoons of strained lemon juice, and 3 tablespoons good brandy. Bring again to a boil. Serve at once with hot baked or boiled ham, or serve well chilled with cold ham.

## MARCHAND DE VIN SAUCE FOR STEAK

6 shallots
1 cup red wine
1 tablespoon chopped parsley, or chervil

¼ pound butter
¼ lemon
salt, pepper
1 teaspoon beef extract

Chop 6 shallots fine and put them in an enamel pan with a cup of red Bordeaux (claret). Reduce one half by boiling hard. In the meantime prepare 1 tablespoon finely chopped parsley, or, better still, chervil; also cream ¼ pound butter and stir into it the juice from ¼ lemon. Add a pinch of salt and some freshly ground pepper to the wine and 1 teaspoon beef extract dissolved in 1 teaspoon hot water. Let it simmer until the steak is done. Add the parsley to the butter and stir both gradually into the wine. Pour over the carved steaks (sufficient for 2 steaks), and serve at once.

## MAITRE D'HOTEL BUTTER

¼ pound butter
1 tablespoon finely chopped
    parsley
¾ teaspoon salt
dash of freshly ground pepper

2 tablespoons strained lemon
    juice
¼ teaspoon dry mustard (op-
    tional)

Cream the butter well, add the parsley, salt, pepper, and mustard
(if desired), mix, and stir in the lemon juice. Serve spread on
grilled fish, steak, chops, or boiled vegetables.

## MINT SAUCE

1 bunch fresh mint
1 cup cider vinegar
¼ cup water

¾ cup granulated sugar
½ teaspoon salt
½ glass green mint jelly

Boil together until syrupy 1 cup cider vinegar, ¼ cup water,
¾ cup granulated sugar, and ½ teaspoon salt. Remove from fire
and pour it over about 3 tablespoons finely chopped fresh green
mint. Cover and when cooled place in refrigerator to chill.

When ready to serve, place ½ glass mint jelly in a serving-
bowl and break it up with a fork. Add the mint sauce and mix
just long enough to break the jelly into fairly small pieces; then
serve at once with hot roast leg of lamb.

## MUSTARD SAUCE FOR GOUJONETTES
## OF FLOUNDER

juice of 1 lemon
4 tablespoons vinegar
salt, white pepper
2 tablespoons cold water
4 egg yolks

16 tablespoons butter (½
    pound)
2 level tablespoons dry mus-
    tard
coarsely ground black pepper

Squeeze and strain the juice of 1 lemon. Put 4 tablespoons vinegar in top of enamel boiler with a pinch of salt and a little white pepper; reduce it by simmering directly over low flame until only 2 teaspoons. Add 2 tablespoons cold water and the slightly beaten yolks of 4 eggs. Add 4 tablespoons butter, cut in pieces. Place pan directly on very low flame and beat constantly with wire whisk until the mixture thickens slightly. Remove from fire immediately. Place pan over hot (not boiling) water and add little by little 12 tablespoons butter, stirring vigorously all the while. When all the butter has been added, stir in 2 level tablespoons dry mustard and the juice of 1 lemon. At this point taste, and add more salt if necessary and about ¼ teaspoon of coarsely ground black pepper. Remove top of double boiler from the bottom until ready to serve, at which time place top again over hot water on low flame until warm (not hot), stirring constantly.

Serve at once with Goujonettes of Flounder (page 87).

## PLAIN HARD-BOILED EGG CREAM SAUCE

4 tablespoons flour
4 tablespoons butter
2 cups of milk
6 tablespoons heavy cream

4 sliced or chopped hard-
  boiled eggs
salt, pepper

Make a medium-thick cream sauce in the usual way, cooking 4 tablespoons butter and 4 tablespoons flour together for a minute or two, then adding 2 cups hot milk gradually, stirring constantly. When thick and smooth, continue cooking for a while over boiling water. When ready to serve, add about 6 tablespoons heavy cream, season to taste with salt and pepper, and add 4 chopped or sliced hard-boiled eggs. Serve with vegetables or fish.

## SAUCE BEARNAISE

| | |
|---|---|
| ¾ cup tarragon vinegar | 4 egg yolks |
| 3 shallots | ⅝ pound butter |
| 5 whole peppercorns | 1 tablespoon chopped tarragon |
| ¼ teaspoon salt | leaves |

Put ¾ cup tarragon vinegar into top of a small enamel double boiler directly over flame, add 3 shallots, chopped fine, 5 whole black peppercorns, crushed, ¼ teaspoon salt, and boil until reduced to ¼ cup. Remove from fire and, when cold, add the slightly beaten yolks of 4 eggs and ⅛ pound butter. Set the pan over boiling water and stir furiously with a wire whisk, until thick. Remove from fire and pass through a fine sieve. Put back into the top of the double boiler and place again over hot (not boiling) water, this time entirely remove from the fire, and add little by little ½ pound soft butter, stirring all the while with the wire whisk. Just before serving stir in 1 tablespoon or more chopped tarragon—which, by the way, may be bought pickled in certain food-specialty shops.

There will be enough sauce for 2 big steaks. It may be put directly onto the carved steaks, or it may be passed separately in a bowl. Do not put the sauce in a very hot bowl, for it will curdle; and, above all, don't try to serve the sauce hot. It should be just luke-warm.

Sauce béarnaise may also be served on other grilled meats or fish.

## ELECTRIC-BLENDER SAUCE BEARNAISE

¾ cup tarragon vinegar
3 shallots, peeled and chopped
5 whole peppercorns, crushed
½ teaspoon salt
¾ pound butter

4 egg yolks
1 teaspoon powdered dried
   tarragon
1 tablespoon cut fresh tarragon
   leaves

FOR 6–8

Place in enamel pan ¾ cup tarragon vinegar, 3 shallots, peeled and chopped, 5 whole peppercorns, crushed fine, ½ teaspoon salt, and 1 teaspoon powdered dried tarragon. Place on low flame and reduce by simmering until you have only about ¼ cup liquid. Cool. Place yolks of 4 eggs in glass container of electric-blender, add cooled vinegar mixture, and cover. Heat ¾ pound butter over low flame until bubbling hot, but do not brown. Turn on blender and run at low speed while you count five; uncover, turn motor to high speed, and add the hot butter in small steady stream. When all the butter has been added continue blending while you count five. Turn off power, transfer mixture to top of small enamel double boiler.

When ready to serve the sauce, place over small quantity of boiling water on low flame, being sure the bottom of pan containing the sauce, does not come in direct contact with boiling water. Stir furiously until sauce is warm, not hot. Stir in 1 tablespoon finely cut fresh tarragon leaves and serve in warm sauce boat.

## SAUCE FOR BOILED AND BAKED HAM
## OR COLD VENISON

3 tablespoons brandy, or cognac
4 tablespoons marmalade
juice of 2 lemons

2 tablespoons currant jelly
¼ cup seedless raisins
2 dozen blanched almonds

Wash ¼ cup of seedless raisins and soak in cold water ½ hour. Drain, cover with cold water, boil until plump and until no juice is left. Add 3 tablespoons cognac, 4 tablespoons marmalade, juice of 2 lemons, and 2 tablespoons currant jelly. Bring gently to boiling point, add ¼ cup blanched split almonds, and serve.

## SAUCE DIJONNAISE

| | |
|---|---|
| 4 hard-boiled eggs | juice of 1 lemon |
| 4 tablespoons prepared imported mustard | 1 tablespoon chopped capers |
| | 1 tablespoon chopped parsley |
| salt, pepper | 1 tablespoon chopped fresh |
| 1 cup olive oil | tarragon |

Hard boil 4 eggs. Put the yolks through a fine sieve; add 4 tablespoons prepared mustard, and salt and pepper to taste. Then add gradually, drop by drop, about 1 cup olive oil and the juice of 1 lemon. Before serving add 1 tablespoon chopped capers, 1 tablespoon chopped parsley, 1 tablespoon chopped fresh tarragon, and the egg whites, chopped fine. Serve on cold salmon, or any other cold boiled fish.

## SAUCE HOLLANDAISE

| | |
|---|---|
| juice of ½ lemon | ⅛ teaspoon white pepper |
| 4 tablespoons vinegar | 2 tablespoons cold water |
| pinch of salt | 4 egg yolks |
| pinch of cayenne | ⅝ pound butter |

SERVES 6–8

We once had a little cook in Paris who made faultless Hollandaise. We were given to ordering it at the least provocation, but Gabrielle never complained. Then one fine day in the middle of August we ordered it for lunch and were surprised to see a look of utter panic flitter across her usually smiling countenance. It seemed that little Gabrielle had never made Hollandaise in her life but had managed to hide the fact by having her friend, the cook across the hall, make it for her whenever it was ordered. Being the *Quinze Août*, her friend was *en vacance*, so we had *Beurre Noisette* instead and all was serene.

Squeeze and strain the juice of ½ lemon. Put 4 tablespoons vinegar in top of enamel double boiler over direct low flame with a big pinch of salt and about ⅛ teaspoon white pepper (coarsely ground black pepper may be substituted, but it will show). Reduce the vinegar by simmering until only 2 teaspoons of it are left. Add 2 tablespoons cold water and the 4 egg yolks, being sure not to include any of the whites. Beat well with wire whisk or rotary-beater, and add ⅛ pound butter cut in little pieces.

Place the pan directly on a very, very low heat (or to be safer still, place over boiling water on low flame and be sure that the bottom part of the top pan does not actually touch the boiling water), and beat constantly with wire whisk until the mixture has thickened. At this point, remove the pan from the fire entirely, and add little by little, beating constantly with wire whisk, ½ pound butter. When all the butter had been added, stir in the lemon juice, and season to taste with salt, pepper and cayenne. Serve in warm, not hot bowl.

Hollandaise is especially good on boiled vegetables, fish, and eggs.

## ELECTRIC-BLENDER SAUCE HOLLANDAISE

| | |
|---|---|
| ⅝ pound butter | 1 tablespoon cold water |
| 4 egg yolks | ½ teaspoon salt |
| juice of ½ lemon | ⅛ teaspoon white pepper |
| 4 tablespoons cider vinegar | ¼ teaspoon cayenne |

SERVES 6–8

Squeeze and strain juice of ½ lemon. Reduce 4 tablespoons vinegar to 2 teaspoons by simmering on low flame. Remove from fire. Add 1 tablespoon cold water and lemon juice. Separate the yolks from the whites of 4 eggs. Heat ⅝ pound butter in small saucepan over low heat until bubbling hot, but do not let it brown. Into the glass container of your electric-blender place the mixture of lemon juice, water, and vinegar. Add the 4 egg yolks and ½ teaspoon salt, ⅛ teaspoon white pepper, and ¼ teaspoon cayenne.

Cover container, turn on motor, and count five. Remove cover and run at high speed while you add the hot butter in a fine steady stream. When all the butter has been added, turn off motor, and empty contents into top of small enamel double boiler. When ready to serve, place over small quantity of boiling water on low flame, being sure the bottom of pan containing the sauce does not come in direct contact with boiling water. Stir furiously until sauce is warm, not hot, and serve in warm sauce boat.

## SAUCE MORNAY

2 small onions
1 small carrot
1 stalk celery
6 tablespoons butter
3 cups milk
bouquet of bay leaf, pinch of thyme, parsley
salt, pepper
cayenne

pinch of nutmeg
6 tablespoons butter for *roux*
6 tablespoons flour for *roux*
⅓ cup of grated imported Swiss cheese
⅓ cup of freshly grated imported Parmesan Cheese
heavy cream

SERVES 6–8

Chop very fine 2 small onions, 1 small carrot, and 1 stalk of celery, minus all strings. Place in top of large enamel double boiler with 6 tablespoons butter and cook directly over low flame, stirring constantly, for about 5 minutes. Then add 3 cups milk, and a bouquet garni consisting of 1 bay leaf, a pinch of thyme, and a few sprays of parsley. Add a very little salt, some coarsely ground black pepper, and a pinch of nutmeg; and place over boiling water. Cover and cook for about 15 minutes, stirring occasionally. At this point strain through a fine sieve and discard the vegetables.

Make a *roux* in the top of an enamel double boiler by cooking 6 tablespoons flour in 6 tablespoons butter directly over a low flame, stirring constantly, without browning, for about 1 minute; then adding gradually 3 cups hot milk to make a smooth sauce free from lumps. Cook over boiling water stirring occasionally for 30 minutes longer. Add ⅓ cup of grated Swiss cheese and ⅓ cup grated Parmesan cheese and stir until cheese has melted. Season to taste with salt, pepper, and a pinch of cayenne; and just before serving stir in 1–2 tablespoons butter, or thin to desired consistency with a little heavy cream. This sauce is used on eggs, fish, vegetables, and other dishes that are to be served gratinéed, such as cannelloni. Pour sauce over ingredients, sprinkle with a little more cheese, and brown lightly under a hot grill.

## SAUCE MOUSSELINE

| | |
|---|---|
| juice of ½ lemon | 4 egg yolks |
| 4 tablespoons cider vinegar | ⅝ pound butter |
| salt, pepper | cayenne |
| 2 tablespoons cold water | ⅓ cup heavy cream |

Make exactly as for Sauce Hollandaise, but fold into it just before serving ⅓ cup heavy cream, beaten stiff. Serve in warm, not hot bowl. This sauce is for boiled vegetables or fish.

## SAUCE NEWBURG

| | |
|---|---|
| 4 tablespoons butter | 2 teaspoons salt |
| ⅔ cup dry sherry | 1 teaspoon paprika |
| 2 cups heavy cream | 6 egg yolks |

SERVES 6–8

Melt 4 tablespoons butter over boiling water in top of enamel double boiler. Add ⅔ cup good dry sherry. When hot, stir in 2

cups heavy cream. Season with about 2 teaspoons salt and 1 teaspoon paprika. Cook for a minute or two, then pour hot mixture
over the well-beaten yolks of 6 eggs. Return to top of double boiler
and cook, stirring constantly, until smooth and thick like custard,
about 5 minutes. Serve with lobster, shrimp, crab meat, and
scallops.

## TARTAR SAUCE

1½ tablespoons chopped capers
1½ tablespoons chopped pitted olives
1 tablespoon chopped chives

1½ tablespoons chopped gherkins
1½ tablespoons chopped parsley
1½ cups mayonnaise
1 teaspoon grated horse-radish

SERVES 6–8

Prepare 1½ tablespoons chopped capers, 1½ tablespoons chopped
green pitted olives, 1½ tablespoons chopped gherkins, 1½ tablespoons chopped parsley, and 1 tablespoon chopped chives.
Combine just before serving with 1½ cups mayonnaise into which
you have stirred 1 teaspoon freshly grated horse-radish (if procurable; if not, substitute the same quantity of pickled horse-
radish).

## SAUCE REMOULADE

3 hard-boiled eggs
3 tablespoons chopped capers
3 sweet pickles
12 leaves of fresh or pickled
tarragon
2 tablespoons prepared mustard

1½ teaspoons grated onion
coarsely ground black pepper
1½ tablespoons chopped parsley
1½ cups mayonnaise
½ teaspoon lemon juice
salt

Hard boil 3 eggs. Chop the whites very fine and rub the yolks
through a sieve into a bowl. Chop fine 3 tablespoons capers, 3

sweet pickles along with 12 leaves fresh tarragon (pickled ones will do). Add to the egg yolks 2 tablespoons of prepared mustard and mix; then add the chopped capers, tarragon, and sweet pickle. Also add 1½ teaspoons grated onion and a little coarsely ground black pepper. Now add 1½ cups mayonnaise and last of all add 1½ tablespoons finely chopped parsley and the chopped egg whites. Mix lightly. Chill thoroughly. Taste, add more salt and pepper if necessary, and stir in ½ teaspoon lemon juice just before serving with fish.

## TOMATO SAUCE

| | |
|---|---|
| 2 pounds luscious ripe tomatoes | 1 cup dry white wine |
| 2 white onions | 3 tablespoons butter |
| bouquet of parsley, thyme, and bay leaf | 1 teaspoon flour |
| 2 whole cloves | 1 teaspoon beef extract |
| | ¼ cup hot water |
| | salt, pepper |

Peel 2 pounds luscious ripe tomatoes and cut in little pieces. Place in saucepan with 2 peeled and sliced white onions; a bouquet of parsley, 1 bay leaf and ½ teaspoon thyme; 2 whole cloves; and 1 cup dry white wine. Simmer for 1 hour; then pass through a fine sieve.

Now melt 2 tablespoons butter and add 1 teaspoon flour. Cook together without browning for several minutes, then add the tomato sauce. Add 1 teaspoon beef extract dissolved in ¼ cup hot water. Season to taste with salt and pepper and continue to simmer gently until of the right consistency. Remove from fire and stir in 1 tablespoon butter. Serve with spaghetti, onion meat dishes, meat loaf, and eggs.

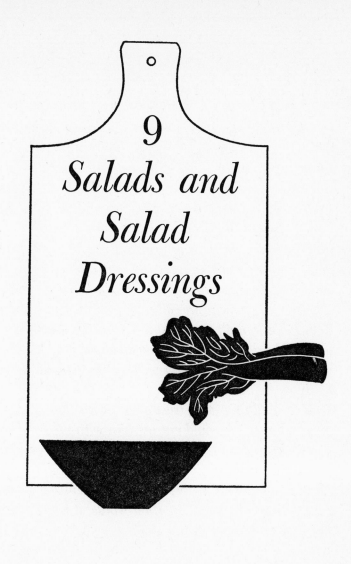

# 9
# *Salads and Salad Dressings*

*S*trictly speaking, the simpler the salad the better it will be, its success depending rather on the masterful seasoning of a simple dressing than on the artistic amalgamation of too many varied ingredients. There are exceptions to the rule, but a word to the wise should be sufficient.

The next time you are stuck with a hopelessly silent dinner partner, be he young and handsome, or in his prime and formidably impressive, or old and cross (I mean tired), start the conversation by asking him how he makes his salads. The chances are, although he may not look it, he does pride himself on his ability to make a salad dressing, and will be delighted to tell you all about it in detail. Listen carefully while he tells you why his way is best, because it really is the best.

I wouldn't exactly trust a man with the making of an angel cake, but I would entrust him with my carefully prepared greens, and a salad bowl, and a tray of condiments, and other salad-dressing ingredients, and count on him to produce a salad infinitely superior to one mixed by the fairest hands in the world. In other words, it is my sincere belief that men excel in the art.

# *Salads*

## ASPARAGUS SALAD, SAUCE VINAIGRETTE

3 bunches asparagus        chervil, or parsley
sauce vinaigrette (page 321)

SERVES 6–8

Cook 3 bunches asparagus (page 258). When tender, but not floppy, lift them out of the water and lay them on a platter. Let the cold water run over them a second, draining them well again. Sprinkle with salt. When cool, place on serving-platter, first removing strings. Place in refrigerator to chill until ready to serve, then pour over them a sauce vinaigrette (page 321), and sprinkle with shopped chervil, or parsley. Serve at once on ice-cold salad plates.

## QUICK ASPIC

1 heaping tablespoon plain      2 cups hot bouillon
    gelatin (2 packages)       1 teaspoon lemon juice
½ cup cold stock (bouillon or   sherry to taste (optional)
    water)

SERVES 6–8

Soak gelatin in cold water or stock for 5 minutes. Heat 2 cups bouillon and add the gelatin. Stir until dissolved. Flavor with lemon juice and sherry to taste, about 1 tablespoon.

This can be added to cold fish, chicken, or vegetables for molded salads. Chill for 2–3 hours, or until well set, before turning out on crisp lettuce leaves for a summer salad.

## COLE SLAW WITH CREAM DRESSING

4 cups finely shredded white cabbage
1 cup heavy cream
1 egg yolk
2 tablespoons strained lemon juice

2 tablespoons pickled horse-radish
¼ teaspoon paprika
2 teaspoons prepared mustard
½ teaspoon granulated sugar
1 teaspoon salt

SERVES 6–8

Mix together 1 teaspoon salt, ½ teaspoon sugar, 2 teaspoons prepared mustard, ¼ teaspoon paprika, 2 tablespoons pickled horse-radish, and 2 tablespoons strained lemon juice. Beat the yolk of 1 egg with 1 cup heavy cream, and when almost stiff, fold in the mixed ingredients. Chill while you shred very fine 4 cups crisp white cabbage. Place cabbage in a chilled bowl, pour the dressing over it, and toss well before serving.

## CURRIED EGG AND WATER-CRESS SALAD

8 eggs
¼ pound sweet butter
2 teaspoons good curry pow-der

salt, pepper
2–3 bunches of water cress
lemon juice
olive oil

SERVES 6–8

Hard boil 8 eggs; plunge into cold water until cooled; remove shells and cut in two lengthwise. Place the yolks in a small bowl, add to them ¼ pound well-creamed sweet butter, and continue creaming together until well mixed. Season to taste with salt and pepper and about 2 teaspoons good curry powder. Fill the 2 white sides of each egg level full with this mixture and place them together, reforming the whole eggs. Wipe clean with damp cloth.

Have ready 2–3 bunches of water cress, well washed and carefully picked over, with the toughest part of stems discarded. When ready to assemble the salad, chop the water cress slightly and season to taste with lemon juice, salt, and olive oil. Arrange water cress in a level layer in shallow salad bowl and then stand the eggs, big end down, on this bed. Serve at once.

## ENDIVES AND AVOCADO SALAD
## HERBS SALAD DRESSING

| | |
|---|---|
| 12–16 endives | 2 tablespoons of water |
| 4 ripe avocados | ⅔ cup of good olive oil |
| 1 package dried mixed exotic herbs for seasoning | 1 tablespoon of chopped parsley |
| ¼ cup of tarragon vinegar | |

SERVES 6–8

Remove outer leaves of 12–16 endives, and cut off their bottoms. Split in four lengthwise, wash carefully, shake dry, and cut crosswise in 1-inch-length pieces. Follow directions on the package of seasoning for making salad dressing. Pour over the endives to which you have added the meat from 4 perfect avocados, scooping it out with a silver soup spoon. Sprinkle with chopped parsley and serve.

## GRANDMOTHER SCHAFFNER'S POTATO SALAD

| | |
|---|---|
| 12 medium-size old potatoes | 1 tablespoon powdered sugar |
| ⅔ cup finely chopped celery | ½ teaspoon salt |
| ⅓ cup finely chopped onion | ½ teaspoon pepper |
| 6 egg yolks | 1 cup heavy cream |
| 6 tablespoons vinegar | 1 cup mayonnaise |
| 4 tablespoons butter | |

SERVES 6–8

Prepare ⅓ cup finely chopped onion and ⅔ cup cut fine celery. Put the yolks of 6 raw eggs in an enamel pan. In a separate enamel pan heat 6 tablespoons vinegar until steaming hot but not boiling. Beat the yolks slightly and then stir them in the hot vinegar slowly. Place pan over very low flame, or over boiling water, and stir vigorously and constantly until the mixture is thick, or for about 1½ minutes in all. Remove from fire.

In a separate bowl cream 4 tablespoons butter with 1 tablespoon powdered sugar, ½ teaspoon salt, and ½ teaspoon coarsely ground pepper. Add the prepared chopped onion and celery and mix well. Then stir in gradually the egg-and-vinegar mixture. Mix well with spoon and cool. Now beat 1 cup heavy cream until stiff and fold it into the cooled mixture. Last of all fold in 1 cup of mayonnaise. Place in refrigerator until ready to make the salad.

Meanwhile scrub about 12 medium-size old potatoes and boil them in their skins in plenty of salted water until done, about 30 minutes. Drain thoroughly and place in *pre-heated oven* to dry off a bit. Remove from oven and cool. Peel and slice crosswise. Place in bowl and pour over them the dressing in alternate layers. Mix ever so gently just before serving.

## LILA'S EGGS TARRAGON

| | |
|---|---|
| 12 eggs | 2 cups sour cream |
| 2 cups boiled dressing | juice of 6 limes |
| juice of 2 small onions | 2 teaspoons granulated sugar |
| 2 tablespoons fresh tarragon | 2 teaspoons dry mustard |
| salt, pepper | 2–3 bunches fresh water cress |

SERVES 6–8

Hard boil 12 eggs in the usual way; plunge into cold water to cool for 15 minutes. Crack the shells gently all over and peel; rinse off in cold water. Wash 2–3 bunches of fresh water cress, remove tough stems, wrap in wet towel, and refrigerate until ready to arrange and serve the salad. Squeeze and strain the juice from 6 small limes. Add about ¼ teaspoon coarsely ground pepper, ¼ teaspoon salt, 2 teaspoons granulated sugar, 2 teaspoons dry mustard, and the grated juice of 2 small white onions. Mix with wooden spoon. Now add, in alternate lots, 2 cups boiled dressing and 2 cups sour cream, beating the whole with rotary-beater. When ready to serve the salad, spread the water cress on a large serving-platter and arrange on this bed the 12 eggs, neatly sliced. Pour the dressing over all and serve cold, accompanied by toasted and buttered pilot crackers.

## ROMAINE SALAD WITH CHOPPED WATER CRESS

| | |
|---|---|
| 2 heads fresh romaine | French dressing |
| 1 bunch water cress | |

SERVES 6–8

Wash carefully 2 heads fresh romaine. Cut or break into small pieces. Shake dry and place in wet cloth in refrigerator until crisp. In the meantime make a good French dressing (page 318). Put in the refrigerator to chill. Also chill the salad bowl and the salad plates. Wash and remove the big stems from 1 bunch water cress. Shake dry and chop the cress until as fine as chopped parsley. When ready to serve the salad, put the romaine in the cold bowl and pour over it some French dressing. Then sprinkle the whole with all of the chopped water cress. Send to the table—to be tossed there before serving.

## SALAD WITH EGG DRESSING

| | |
|---|---|
| 2 heads Boston lettuce | ¼ cup lemon juice, or cider |
| 6 hard-boiled eggs | vinegar |
| ¾ cup heavy cream | freshly ground black pepper |
| 1 teaspoon prepared mustard | salt |

SERVES 6–8

Prepare 2 heads Boston lettuce in the usual way and dry carefully. Hard boil 6 eggs, plunge into cold water, and cool. Have ready a well-chilled salad bowl. Put the yolks of the 6 eggs into a potato-ricer and push them through, letting them fall into the bottom of the bowl. Add a little prepared mustard (about 1 teaspoon), and, stirring with a wooden spoon, add gradually about ¾ cup heavy cream, or enough to make the mixture the consistency of a light cream sauce. Season to taste with salt and freshly ground black pepper, and add about ¼ cup strained lemon juice, or cider vinegar. Add the salad, toss lightly, and sprinkle over all the chopped whites of the 6 eggs. Serve on cold plates. Romaine, chicory, or escarole may be prepared in the same manner.

## STRING BEAN SALAD WITH SAUCE VINAIGRETTE

3–4 pounds string beans                 chervil, or parsley
sauce vinaigrette

SERVES 6–8

Using a sharp knife, cut off both sides of 3–4 pounds of tender string beans, leaving them whole. Wash and tie them in 8–10 bundles. Put them into an enamel pan; sprinkle with salt and a tiny pinch of soda; and pour boiling water over them, enough to cover. Stand by, and when the water comes to a boil again, skim very carefully and cook until the beans are tender, but not floppy, 10–15 minutes. Drain well. Let the cold water run over them a second.

Place them on a serving-platter, all neatly in a row. Remove the strings, sprinkle with salt, and, when cool, place in refrigerator until ready to serve—at which time be sure there is no water in bottom of serving-platter. Pour over them a sauce vinaigrette (page 321), sprinkle with chervil (or parsley), and serve. Be sure the salad plates are ice cold.

## TOMATO SALAD, FINES HERBES

8–10 small ripe tomatoes                 2 tablespoons chopped tarra-
red-wine French dressing                      gon and chervil, mixed

SERVES 6–8

Pour boiling water over 8–10 small ripe red tomatoes. Plunge into cold water and pull off the skins. Place in refrigerator to chill thoroughly. Prepare 2 tablespoons finely chopped tarragon and chervil, mixed. Make a good tart French dressing using red-wine vinegar (page 318). When ready to serve the tomatoes slice them, or quarter them if you prefer; place in chilled salad bowl; pour over them the well-seasoned French dressing; and sprinkle with the chopped herbs. Mix lightly and serve at once.

## SURPRISE VEGETABLE SALAD
## (FOR A BUFFET PARTY)

**An equal quantity of:**

| | |
|---|---|
| 1 cup sliced boiled beets | French dressing |
| 1 cup sliced boiled string beans | chopped chervil, tarragon, and chives |
| 1 cup sliced boiled carrots | 2–3 pounds new boiled pota- |
| 1 cup boiled green peas | toes |
| 1 cup boiled green lima beans | |

SERVES 6–8

Prepare and cook separately, in the usual manner, an equal quantity of the following vegetables, allowing in all 1 cup of vegetables for each person: Sliced boiled beets, sliced string beans, sliced carrots, green lima beans, and green peas, plus 2–3 pounds of new potatoes boiled with their skins on, peeled, sliced, and dressed with French dressing while still warm.

When ready to serve, arrange the vegetables (which must be very cold) in layers in a large salad bowl, starting with beets, then lima beans, then string beans, then carrots, and finally peas. When this is accomplished, pour over all a tart, well-seasoned French salad dressing. Now cover the whole with a layer of potatoes, previously dressed but not chilled—and be sure that the peas are completely hidden. Sprinkle the top with chopped mixed fresh herbs and serve.

# Salad Dressings

Before giving basic recipes for salad dressings, may I remind you that there are many varieties of vinegar on the market, and—variety being the spice of life—it might be fun to try out a few of them. For instance, try basil, garlic, mint, tarragon, sage, or mixed-herb vinegars for a change; also try white-wine vinegar, as well as my favorite, red-wine vinegar. Raspberry, French burgundy, elder, eschalot, and fines-herbes vinegars were on the market the last time I investigated the matter.

I suggest you keep on hand: 2 pepper mills with a supply of good white and black whole peppercorns; curry powder; fresh Hungarian paprika; Worcestershire sauce; olive oil, or peanut oil; lemons; imported prepared mustard and dry mustard; and fresh cayenne. Fortified with the above, plus the all-important salad greens and a source of supply for fresh tarragon, dill, chives, chervil, or parsley, it would seem reasonable to suppose that you could mix a salad to please anyone's fastidious desire. Never forget one basic rule: the better the oil and the vinegar, the better the salad dressing—this is no place to economize.

## BOILED DRESSING FOR POTATO SALAD

| | |
|---|---|
| 1 teaspoon salt | ¼ cup water |
| 2 tablespoons sugar | ⅛ pound butter |
| 1 tablespoon flour | 4 egg yolks |
| dash of pepper | ½–1 cup heavy cream, or |
| ½ cup vinegar | 1 cup sour cream |

Put in small bowl 1 teaspoon salt, 2 tablespoons sugar, 1 tablespoon flour, and a dash of pepper. Add to it, stirring until smooth,
½ cup mixed-herb vinegar and ¼ cup water. Beat the yolks of
4 eggs well and add them to the mixture. Then strain the whole
into top of small double boiler. Add ⅛ pound butter, place over
boiling water, and cook, stirring furiously, until well thickened
—but be careful to remove immediately from the fire the second
it is done, so that it won't curdle. It should be quite thick as it is
to be thinned when cold with about ½ cup of heavy cream, or
1 cup sour cream. Makes 2 generous cups.

## CHICKEN-LIVER DRESSING

| | |
|---|---|
| 2 chicken livers | 1 heaping teaspoon prepared |
| 1 carrot | mustard, preferably tarra- |
| 1 onion | gon-flavored |
| 1 stalk celery | salt, pepper |
| parsley | 4 tablespoons olive oil |
| 2 egg yolks | 1 dessert spoon red-wine vine- |
| | gar |
| | 4 tablespoons red wine |

Wash 2 chicken livers and boil until tender with 1 carrot, 1 onion,
1 stalk celery, and a bit of parsley. Pass the livers only through a
fine sieve. Do the same with the yolks of 2 hard-boiled eggs. Place
liver and egg yolks together in a bowl with 1 heaping teaspoon
prepared mustard. Mix to a paste, add freshly ground pepper and
some salt, and pour in, drop by drop, 4 tablespoons olive oil,

stirring always in the same direction. Now thin this by adding 1 dessert spoon red-wine vinegar and about 4 tablespoons red wine—and it is ready to serve. This dressing is very good on a salad of chicory.

## BASIC FRENCH SALAD DRESSING FOR PLAIN GREEN SALAD
### [made with red-wine vinegar]

1 teaspoon salt
dash of freshly ground pepper
6 tablespoons olive oil

2 tablespoons wine vinegar, or
lemon juice

Put the salt and pepper in a bowl. Add the olive oil, stir well, then add the vinegar, or lemon juice, bit by bit. This amount is sufficient for 1 head of lettuce.

## CHOPPED WATER-CRESS DRESSING

2 bunches fresh water cress
Juice of 1 lemon
1 tablespoon tarragon vinegar

8 tablespoons olive oil
salt, pepper

SERVES 6–8

Wash and remove big stems from 2 bunches of water cress. Shake dry and chop the cress until as fine as chopped parsley. Add this just before serving to the juice of 1 lemon mixed with 1 tablespoon tarragon vinegar and 8 tablespoons olive oil. Season to taste with 1 scant teaspoon salt and a dash of pepper.

## MUSTARD DRESSING

1 tablespoon imported pre-
    pared mustard
salt, freshly ground pepper

juice of 1 lemon
¾ cup heavy cream

Place 1 tablespoon prepared mustard in a bowl, add some freshly ground pepper and a little salt, and the juice of 1 lemon. Stir well; add gradually ¾ cup heavy cream. Serve on hard-boiled eggs and on green salads.

## HERB DRESSING

1 teaspoon dry mustard
½ teaspoon salt
coarsely ground black pepper
   to taste
¼ cup tarragon vinegar

½ cup chopped parsley
1 tablespoon cut chives
chervil
½ cup olive oil

SERVES 6–8

Place 1 teaspoon dry mustard in a bowl. Add some coarsely ground black pepper and about ½ teaspoon salt. Then, if you have any, add 1 tablespoon chervil and crush all together. Add ¼ cup good tarragon vinegar; mix well; and add ½ cup olive oil. Then add ½ cup chopped parsley and 1 tablespoon cut chives. Mix well and place in refrigerator for half an hour before using.

## HARD-BOILED-EGG DRESSING

3 egg yolks
1 teaspoon prepared mustard
freshly ground black pepper
big pinch of salt

3 tablespoons olive oil
1 tablespoon tarragon vinegar
2 tablespoons heavy cream

Place the yolks of 3 hard-boiled eggs in a bowl, add 1 teaspoon prepared mustard, some freshly ground black pepper, a big pinch of salt, and mix well. Stir in gradually 3 tablespoons olive oil, and then add gradually 1 tablespoon of tarragon vinegar. By now it may look slightly curdled. At this point stir in gradually, until smooth again, about 2 tablespoons of heavy cream.

## MAYONNAISE: HOW TO MAKE IT

2 egg yolks
1 teaspoon salt
white pepper
pinch of cayenne
½ teaspoon dry mustard

1–2 tablespoons lemon juice,
    or vinegar
1⅓ cups olive oil
1 tablespoon boiling water

There is nothing difficult about making mayonnaise, except the eggs and the olive oil must be of the same temperature, and the oil must be added very, very slowly in the beginning. Either vinegar or lemon juice may be used to give it a tart taste. In either case, start by putting the yolks of 2 eggs in a small bowl, adding to them 1 teaspoon salt, a little white pepper, a pinch of cayenne, and ½ teaspoon of dry mustard, if you like.

Stir well, preferably with a small wooden spoon, and add 1 tablespoon lemon juice, or vinegar. Then add gradually, drop by drop at first, stirring constantly, 1⅓ cups olive oil. Whenever it gets too thick, add a few additional drops lemon or vinegar. At the very last add, gradually, 1 tablespoon boiling water. This improves the consistency and helps to keep it from separating. Heavy cream may or may not be added to thin it to the right consistency, depending on what it is to be served with.

## ELECTRIC-BLENDER MAYONNAISE

2 whole eggs
2 tablespoons cider vinegar
½ teaspoon dried mustard
1 teaspoon salt
¼ teaspoon white pepper

¼ teaspoon cayenne
2 cups olive oil
1 tablespoon strained lemon
    juice

SERVES 6–8

Place in glass container of electric-blender 2 whole eggs, 2 tablespoons cider vinegar, ½ teaspoon dry mustard, 1 teaspoon salt, ¼ teaspoon white pepper, and ¼ teaspoon cayenne. Cover container, turn on motor, set at low speed, and run motor while you count five. Remove cover and continue mixing at low speed while you add gradually 2 cups olive oil. Continue mixing while you count five. Turn off motor and transfer the mayonnaise to a small bowl. Stir in gradually 1 tablespoon strained lemon juice, and it is ready to serve.

## MUSTARD, CREAM AND HERB DRESSING

1 cup heavy cream
¼ teaspoon pepper
½ teaspoon salt
2 heaping teaspoons prepared
    mustard

1 tablespoon chopped fresh
    herbs (dill, tarragon, or
    parsley)

SERVES 6–8

Partially whip 1 cup heavy cream, stir in ½ teaspoon salt, ¼ teaspoon coarsely ground pepper, and 2 heaping teaspoons prepared mustard. Mix well and add 1 tablespoon cut fresh dill, tarragon, or parsley. Serve on endive salad.

## SAUCE VINAIGRETTE

1 teaspoon salt
½ teaspoon coarsley ground
    black pepper
1 tablespoon cider vinegar
⅓ cup red-wine vinegar
chopped chervil

1 heaping tablespoon of onion,
    chopped fine
1 tablespoon of capers,
    chopped fine
⅔ cup olive oil
chopped tarragon leaves

Put 1 teaspoon salt into a glass jar that has a cover. Add ½ teaspoon coarsely ground black pepper, 1 tablespoon cider vinegar, ⅓ cup red-wine vinegar, and 1 heaping tablespoon onion, chopped very fine. Also add 1 tablespoon capers, chopped fine, and last of all ⅔ cup olive oil. Cover. Chill thoroughly. Just before serving, add a few chopped tarragon leaves and a little chopped chervil, if obtainable, although these are not essential.

## SPICED-VINEGAR DRESSING FOR PICKLED-BEET SALAD

¾ cup cider vinegar
½ cup sugar
1 scant teaspoon powdered
   cinnamon
pinch of powdered allspice

1 teaspoon whole mustard
   seed
pinch of powdered cloves
¼ teaspoon of salt

Place ingredients in enamel pan, bring to a boil, and simmer 5 minutes. Pour hot over sliced beets and chill before serving.

# 10

# *Desserts*

*George H. Ellwanger in his* Pleasures of the Table *quotes from Grimod de la Reynière's* Almanach des gourmands: *"True gourmands have always finished their dinner before the dessert; that which is eaten after the roast is done only out of pure politeness." All I can say, Monsieur Grimod de la Reynière, is that there are an extraordinary number of terribly polite people in this world. Perhaps it is just the reverse with me. I am very polite about the rest of the meal, but secretly what I am interested in is: "What's for dessert?"*

# Creams and Custards

Creams and custards are my favorite form of dessert, and so the first section is quite naturally devoted to them. To reach a pinacle of perfection, quite a bit of care, yet fortunately no great culinary skill is required in their making. Follow directions carefully, never allow a custard to boil, and use fresh ingredients, and I promise successful results. Sooner or later you will find me calling for caramelized molds, caramelized syrup, or praline powder: in order to avoid bewilderment, let us start with directions for them.

## HOW TO CARAMELIZE A MOLD

Put 1 cup or more granulated sugar (amount depending on how large a mold is to be caramelized), into a heavy aluminum pan; moisten with half as much cold water. Let stand a few minutes, then place on fire, and cook without stirring until it turns to strup and becomes a beautiful golden brown (about 10 minutes). Watch carefully, for if it cooks too long, it will be bitter, and if it doesn't cook long enough, it will be tasteless.

Remove from fire the second it has reached the desired shade of brown and pour out immediately into the mold or molds to be caramelized. Tilt the molds back and forth and around to coat sides and bottom of the dish all over, being careful not to burn yourself. If you wish to caramelize a glass ovenproof dish, it is safer to heat the dish slightly by washing it in hot water and drying it well before adding the carmel.

## HOW TO MAKE CARAMELIZED SYRUP

Proceed exactly as with caramelizing a mold, using at least 1 cup sugar. Use a deep pan. When the sugar is a golden brown, remove from fire and pour into the syrup the same amount of hot water as you used of sugar. This will cause the caramel to bubble way up, so be careful not to burn yourself. When the bubbling has subsided, stir, place back on fire, and let it boil again until the caramel has melted and the whole is a thick syrupy consistency (about 8–9 minutes). Remove from fire and cool before using. This syrup may be kept for several days in a tightly covered glass jar.

## HOW TO MAKE PRALINE POWDER

Wipe clean on a cloth 1 cup shelled almonds and 1 cup shelled filberts or hazelnuts. Place them in a medium-size aluminum frying-pan and sprinkle over them 2 generous cups granulated sugar. Place on moderate flame and cook gently until the sugar melts and caramelizes to a golden brown and until the skins on the nuts begin to crack open. Tilt the pan gently back and forth during the cooking process and poke the nuts occasionally with a wooden spoon—but avoid stirring. When every bit of sugar has melted and become the desired golden brown, remove from fire immediately and pour out onto a lightly buttered cookie sheet, spreading it out thin with a wooden spoon. Let it become quite cold and brittle.

The next step is to reduce the nuts and caramel to a fine powder. Break the caramel into fairly small pieces, place in a heavy canvas bag, and pound with a heavy mallet until the nuts are slightly crushed. Then run the whole through the meat-grinder, using the medium blade. Next sift this powder through the flour-sifter; run the part that won't sift through the meat grinder once more, and sift again—repeating the process until the whole is a fine powder. Place immediately in a clean dry glass fruit jar and add to it a piece of vanilla bean. Close tightly and keep in a cool dry place until ready to use.

## CHOCOLATE BAVARIAN CREAM

2 envelopes plain gelatin
½ cup cold water
2 cups milk
4 eggs
½ cup sugar

1 teaspoon vanilla
2 cups heavy cream
12 sections triple-vanilla chocolate

Melt 12 sections triple-vanilla chocolate in 4 tablespoons cold water over hot water. Soak 2 envelopes plain gelatin in ½ cup cold water. Scald 2 cups milk. Beat the yolks of 4 eggs with ½ cup of sugar. To this add the hot milk and cook in a double boiler until thickened, at which time add the gelatin and stir until dissolved. Add the whole gradually to the chocolate. Stir until well mixed. Cool over cold water about 10 minutes, stirring occasionally, and then place in refrigerator for about 1 hour, or until it begins to jell, at which time fold in 2 cups whipped heavy cream, and last of all, fold in the stiffly beaten whites of 4 eggs. Pour into 2 1½-quart-size molds that have been dipped in cold water and place in refrigerator to chill. When ready to serve, turn out onto 2 serving-plates and serve with slightly whipped cream.

## COFFEE BAVARIAN CREAM

2 envelopes plain gelatin
4 tablespoons cold water
1 cup very strong black coffee
4 eggs

1 cup of milk
2 cups heavy cream
½ cup sugar

SERVES 6–8

Soak 2 envelopes gelatin in 4 tablespoons cold water. Have ready 1 cup strong boiling-hot coffee. Add the gelatin to the coffee and stir until dissolved. In the meantime, scald 1 cup of milk with ½ cup sugar and pour it into the beaten yolks of 4 eggs. Cook a minute or two over boiling water until thickened, then stir this into the coffee gelatin. Next add 2 cups heavy cream. Cool, then place in refrigerator until it is about to become stiff, at which time beat with a rotary-beater for 5 minutes. Then fold in the stiffly beaten whites of 4 eggs. Pour the mixture into a 2-quart-size mold that has been rinsed in cold water and place in refrigerator until well chilled. When ready to serve, turn out onto a platter and accompany with a chocolate custard sauce (page 402) or a vanilla custard sauce (page 404).

## BAKED CUSTARD WITH CINNAMON-FLAVORED CARAMEL GLAZE

*[Pre-heat oven to 325°]*

| Custard: | Glaze: |
|---|---|
| 1 quart milk | 1 cup granulated sugar |
| 5 tablespoons granulated sugar | ¼ cup cold water |
| 6 eggs | 1 teaspoon powdered cinnamon |
| 2 teaspoons vanilla | ¼ cup hot water |

SERVES 6–8

Scald together 1 quart milk and 5 tablespoons granulated sugar. Break 6 eggs into a bowl and beat slightly with rotary-beater. Add to the scalded milk, stir well, flavor with 2 teaspoons vanilla, and strain into a 1½-quart-size baking-dish. Place dish in shallow pan of hot water in slow pre-heated oven and bake until set through, about 1¼ hours. Remove from oven and make the glaze.

Place 1 cup granulated sugar in small heavy aluminum pan. Stir in 1 teaspoon powdered cinnamon. Moisten with ¼ cup cold water. Place on fire and bring to a boil. Cook 2 minutes. Remove from fire, cool 1 minute, and add ½ cup of boiling water. Stir well and place back on fire just long enough to bring it to a lively boil. Pour over surface of hot custard. Cool and chill until ready to serve.

## GINGER BAVARIAN CREAM

| | |
|---|---|
| 2 cups preserved ginger, cut fine | 4 egg whites |
| 2 envelopes (2 tablespoons) of plain gelatin | 8 egg yolks |
| | 1 cup sugar |
| 4 tablespoons cold water | 2 cups heavy cream |
| 2 cups milk | 6–8 tablespoons ginger syrup |

SERVES 6–8

Prepare 2 cups finely cut preserved ginger. Soak 2 envelopes gelatin in 4 tablespoons cold water. Make a custard of 2 cups milk, 8 egg yolks, and 1 cup sugar; add gelatin, stir until dissolved and well mixed. Cool and then chill in refrigerator until it begins to jell, at which time beat well with rotary-beater. Then fold in 2 cups well-beaten heavy cream and the whites of 4 eggs beaten until stiff. Last of all fold in 1 cup prepared ginger. Pour mixture into 2 1½-quart-size molds, and chill for several hours. When ready to serve, turn out onto a pretty platter and surround with the remaining ginger, to which you have added 6–8 tablespoons ginger syrup.

## ORANGE BAVARIAN CREAM

| | |
|---|---|
| 2 envelopes plain gelatin | 10 tablespoons granulated sugar |
| 4 tablespoons cold water | |
| ⅔ cup orange juice | 2 eggs |
| ⅔ cup orange marmalade | 2 cups heavy cream |
| 1 cup milk | 8 navel oranges |
| | ¼ teaspoon lemon extract |

SERVES 6–8

Dissolve 2 envelopes of gelatin in 4 tablespoons cold water and add ⅔ cup orange juice. Place in top of double boiler over hot water and add ⅔ cup orange marmalade (chopped fine). Heat 1 cup milk to boiling point, sweeten with 4 tablespoons of sugar, and add it to the well-beaten yolks of 2 eggs. Cook in top of another double boiler over boiling water until thickened. Add to the marmalade-and-gelatin mixture; stir well; and cool. Then add ¼ teaspoon lemon extract and 2 cups heavy cream. Place in refrigerator for about ¾ hour, or until it begins to jell, at which time beat it with a rotary-beater for 5 minutes. Fold in 2 egg whites beaten stiff, and when well mixed, place in 2 1-quart-size ring molds which have been rinsed in cold water. Place in refrigerator to chill and set for at least 1 hour.

In the meantime, using a sharp knife, cut off the rind from 8 navel oranges, leaving none of the white part. Cut out the wedge-shaped pieces and sweeten to taste with about 6 tablespoons sugar. When ready to serve, dip the bottom of the molds in hot water, loosen the sides, and turn out onto shallow dessert plates. Fill centers with sliced oranges and serve.

## PRALINE BAVARIAN CREAM

2 cups milk
2 envelopes plain gelatin
½ cup water
8 egg yolks

3 tablespoons of granulated sugar
2 cups heavy cream
10–12 tablespoons praline powder

SERVES 6–8

To make praline Bavarian cream for 6–8 people, you will need 2 molds that hold about 4 cups of liquid each. In the top of a double boiler heat 2 cups milk over boiling water. Soak 2 envelopes plain gelatin in ½ cup water for 10 minutes. Beat the yolks of 8 eggs and add to them 3 tablespoons sugar. Stir the hot milk into the yolks and then pour the mixture back into the top of the double boiler. Add the gelatin, and stir and cook until the custard thickens and coats the spoon. Let the mixture cool, beating it from time to time with a wire whisk.

When cold and just beginning to jell, add 2 cups stiffly beaten heavy cream and beat mixture well. Then add 9–10 tablespoons of praline powder (page 326). Pour into molds which have been rinsed in cold water and place in refrigerator to chill and set. When ready to serve, dip the bottom of the molds into hot water and turn out onto round platters. Sprinkle lightly over the top of each more praline powder and send to the table accompanied by a bowl of coffee custard sauce (page 403).

## BLANC-MANGE

½ pound shelled almonds and 24 more
3 cups cold water
1½ cups light cream
2 envelopes plain gelatin

4 tablespoons cold water
⅔ cup powdered sugar
1 teaspoon almond extract
1 box frozen strawberries

SERVES 6–8

Blanch ½ pound shelled almonds and 24 more. Wash them and put them to soak about 1 hour in a bowl containing 3 cups clear cold water. Save the water. Dry the almonds on a towel, reserve 24 of them, and then grate the rest in a nut-grater. Put them in a bowl and pour the 3 cups cold water back over the grated almonds. Cover them with wax paper and place in refrigerator for about 2 hours. Line a sieve with a clean strong white napkin that has been carefully washed in cold water and wrung dry. Place the soaked nuts in the napkin over the sieve. Gather up the corners of the cloth and tie securely. The next process is to squeeze out every bit of almond water, letting it run into the bowl. This takes time, but is worth the trouble. When you can't squeeze out any more, you should have 2 cups or more of the almond milk. Untie the bag, place the remaining almond powder in a bowl, and add to it 1 cup light cream. Repeat the squeezing process, using the same cloth, and add the resultant almond cream to the almond milk. You should now have 3 cups of milky liquid.

Soak 2 envelopes plain gelatin in 4 tablespoons cold water in the top part of a small enamel double boiler for 5 minutes. Add to it ½ cup light cream, place pan over boiling water and stir until the gelatin has completely melted. In the meantime, add a scant ⅔ cup of powdered sugar to the almond milk and stir until dissolved, at which time stir it into the hot gelatin cream. Remove from fire immediately and flavor with 1 scant teaspoon almond extract. Stir well and pour into a 1-quart-size ring mold that you have rinsed in cold water. Cover with wax paper and place in refrigerator to set stiff for 1 hour or more. Turn out onto a pretty plate and fill center with defrosted frozen strawberries garnished with the 24 additional blanched almonds which you have slivered with a sharp knife. Serve at once.

## STRAWBERRY BAVARIAN CREAM

4 boxes frozen strawberries
2 envelopes plain gelatin
2 cups heavy cream

4 tablespoons cold water
4 tablespoons sugar

SERVES 6–8

Defrost 2 boxes frozen strawberries, following the directions on the box, and strain off all the juice. Soak 2 envelopes plain gelatin in 4 tablespoons cold water. Heat 2 cups heavy cream to scalding point over direct low flame in the top of a double boiler with 4 tablespoons of granulated sugar. Add the gelatin and stir until dissolved. Remove from fire and add gradually the strawberry juice. Cool, and place in refrigerator to chill until it begins to set, at which time beat with rotary-beater for 5 minutes. Then fold in the strawberries from which the juice was removed. Pour into a 2-quart-size ring mold rinsed in cold water and place in refrigerator for at least 2 hours to chill and set.

Then, 2 hours before you will be ready to serve the dessert, defrost another 2 boxes frozen strawberries. When ready to serve, dip the mold into hot water, loosen edges, and turn out in the center of a shallow dessert dish. Fill the center with the defrosted strawberries and serve at once, accompanied by macaroons.

## BRIAN CONNELLY'S MARQUISE AU CHOCOLAT

½ pound triple-vanilla sweet
   chocolate
1 cup confectioner's sugar
¾ pound sweet butter

4 eggs
2 tablespoons very strong black
   coffee

Butter lightly a 1-quart-size melon mold. Melt ½ pound triple-vanilla sweet chocolate over hot water in top of double boiler with 2 tablespoons very strong black coffee, stirring constantly. Cool. Beat yolks of 4 eggs until light and stir them into the chocolate. Add 22 tablespoons (2¾ bars) very soft sweet butter and stir until well mixed, then add gradually 1 cup confectioner's sugar. Beat with rotary- or electric-beater for at least 10 minutes. Fold in the stiffly beaten whites of 4 eggs, using about 50 folds to incorporate the whites until they completely dissappear. Place in buttered mold and refrigerate for 3 hours. Half an hour before serving, dip mold up to its cover in boiling hot water for just a second and then turn out on serving-platter. Leave at room temperature until ready to serve, accompanied by lady-fingers.

## COEUR A LA CREME

2 8-ounce packages of cream
   cheese
2 8-ounce boxes of creamed
   cottage cheese
1 cup light cream

½ cup heavy cream
½ pint sour cream
2 heart-shaped baskets
1 pint jam

SERVES 6–8

Mix together, using large silver fork, 2 8-ounce packages cream cheese and two 8-ounce boxes creamed cottage cheese, adding gradually 1 cup light cream. Line two heart-shaped baskets, or molds with holes in bottom, with cheesecloth wrung out in cold water. Fill the molds level full with the well-mixed cheeses. Fold edges of cheesecloth over the top to cover cheese. Place on plates in refrigerator to chill for several hours.

Fold back the cheesecloth and turn the hearts out onto 2 serving-plates. Carefully remove cheesecloth. Mix together ½ pint sour cream and ½ cup heavy cream; when smooth pour half of it over each heart. Serve at once with 2 cups of your favorite jam and heated French bread or rolls.

## COFFEE JELLY WITH RUM SAUCE

| | |
|---|---|
| 4 tablespoons gelatin | 5 cups strong black coffee |
| 2 cups cold water | 1⅓ cups granulated sugar |

SERVES 6–8

First make 5 cups very strong clear black coffee. Soak 4 envelopes plain gelatin in 2 cups of cold water for 5 minutes. Add 1⅓ cups granulated sugar to the very hot coffee; stir in the soaked gelatin. Stir well. Pour into a 1½-quart-size mold, cool, and refrigerate until set firm, 2–3 hours. Run knife around the edge, dip mold quickly into boiling water and out again and turn out on serving-plate. Serve with rum sauce.

## CREME BRULEE
*[Pre-heat oven to 275°]*

| | |
|---|---|
| 1 quart heavy cream | 2 teaspoons vanilla |
| 2 tablespoons granulated sugar | light-brown sugar |
| 8 egg yolks | |

SERVES 6–8

Heat 1 quart heavy cream in a double boiler until hot, but not scalding. Add 2 tablespoons granulated sugar, stir until dissolved, then add 8 well-beaten egg yolks and 2 teaspoons vanilla. Mix well and pour into a shallow glass baking-dish, 12″ by 7½″ by 1½″, so as to have the custard about 1½ inches deep. Place the dish in hot water and bake in a slow oven until set. Cool, and place the dish in the refrigerator for several hours to chill thoroughly.

Remove from the refrigerator and cover the surface of the custard with ¼ inch of soft light-brown sugar, free from lumps —dark brown sugar will not do! Place the dish under a blazing red-hot broiler and watch very carefully. The top of the sugar should melt and run together, leaving a shiny caramel top. As I have said before, watch very carefully, or it will catch fire and burn. When the entire surface is glazed, remove and cool. Place back in refrigerator to chill thoroughly. It must be ice cold to be good. A light tap of the spoon breaks through the glaze.

## FLOATING GATEAU PRALINE

| Custard sauce: | Gâteau: |
|---|---|
| 6 egg yolks | ¼ pound burnt sugared al- |
| 3 cups milk | monds |
| 6 tablespoons sugar | 6 egg whites |
| 1 teaspoon vanilla | 12 tablespoons powdered sugar |
| | 1 teaspoon vanilla |
| | carmelized baking-dish |

SERVES 6–8

First make the custard in the usual way, using 6 egg yolks, 3 cups milk, and 6 tablespoons sugar, and cooking it in a double boiler until it coats the spoon. Cool and flavor with 1 teaspoon vanilla. Place in refrigerator and chill thoroughly.

Next caramelize an angel-cake tin, using 1 cup sugar (page 325). Next pound ¼ pound burnt sugared almonds (the brownish-red ones procurable in certain candy stores) in a canvas bag until reduced to a powder. Beat the whites of 6 eggs in a big bowl until stiff, then beat in 12 tablespoons powdered sugar, adding it gradually. Flavor with 1 teaspoon of vanilla and fold in the powdered almonds. Place in caramelized angel-cake tin, place tin in a pan of hot water in a *pre-heated* 350° *oven* and bake slowly for 1 hour, or until well risen. Cool and place in refrigerator until ready to serve. Turn out carefully into a round deep bowl, pour the custard around but not over the gâteau, and serve at once.

## GATEAU MALAKOFF

1 pound glacéed mixed nuts    ¾ pound sweet butter
7 egg yolks                   ½ cup powdered sugar
5 tablespoons sugar           1 teaspoon vanilla
1 quart milk                  ladyfingers
vanilla

SERVES 6–8

This is the ultimate in fancy desserts—and it's very easy to make. It must be made a day ahead, and therefore it is ideal for a big party menu, leaving more time free to cook the rest of the meal the day of the party. It is very rich, but extremely good. You will need 1 pound of the very best glacéed mixed nuts, the variety that has plenty of caramelized sugar on them, preferably hazelnuts and almonds; walnuts and pecans and a few cashews are permissible—but definitely no peanuts, please! Put these nuts through the meat-grinder, using a medium blade. Sift the resultant nut-and-caramel powder through the flour-sifter and regrind that part which won't sift through. Repeat the process until the whole is reduced to a uniform fine-powdered mixture.

Now make 1 quart of thick liquid custard in the usual way, using the yolks of 7 eggs, 5 tablespoons sugar and 1 quart milk. When it has cooled, flavor it with vanilla and proceed to cream ¾ pound sweet butter until nice and creamy, add gradually ½ cup of powdered sugar, and then, little by little, incorporate the powdered nuts. Stir in 1 teaspoon vanilla and 6 tablespoons of the cold custard. This will soften the mixture to just the right consistency. Now line a round 3-pint-size mold with ladyfingers, placing 2 cut in halves to form a cross on the bottom of the dish. Add the nut-and-butter mixture carefully, so as not to disturb the ladyfingers. If you use the size of dish mentioned above, the ladyfingers will stick up a little too far; cut them off with a sharp knife to the level of the dish. Place a piece of heavy wax paper over the whole and cover the dish with a plate. Place in refrigerator overnight.

Just before serving, remove from refrigerator and turn out onto a round, rather deep serving-platter (if it doesn't slip out easily, lay a hot cloth on it for a second). Pour some of the custard around it and serve, accompanied by a bowl containing the rest of the custard.

## FLOATING HEART
*[Pre-heat oven to 300°]*

| | |
|---|---|
| 1 cup granulated sugar | 10-ounce package frozen red |
| 8 egg whites | raspberries |
| 1 teaspoon vanilla | 1 cup heavy cream |
| | 2 tablespoons powdered sugar |

SERVES 6–8

Beat the whites of 8 eggs until stiff enough to hold a peak; then beat in gradually 1 cup of granulated sugar; flavor with 1 teaspoon vanilla. Spread part of this meringue carefully over bottom of large heart-shaped cake pan (one that will hold 5 cups of liquid). Add the rest of the meringue to fill the pan level full. Place pan in shallow pan of hot water and bake 15 minutes. Remove from oven and let it stay undisturbed for about 1½ hours. It will shrink away from the sides of the pan, but if it sticks in spots, run a small knife carefully between the meringue and side of pan. Turn out carefully onto extra-large round serving-platter.

In the meantime defrost 1 package frozen red raspberries, following directions on box. Rub through a fine sieve. Discard seeds. Sweeten with 2 tablespoons powdered sugar. Beat 1 cup heavy cream about 2 minutes until thick, but not stiff. Carefully fold in the raspberry purée. Pour around the meringue heart, but not over it, and serve at once. If a less rich dessert is desired, omit the cream and substitute the plain raspberry purée, using 2 packages in this case.

## FLOATING ISLAND

1 quart milk, plus 1 cup
12 level tablespoons granulated
    sugar

6 eggs
3 teaspoons vanilla
nutmeg

SERVES 6–8

Heat in top of double boiler over boiling water 1 quart milk sweetened with 6 level tablespoons granulated sugar. Beat the yolks of 6 eggs with a rotary-beater, but not very long. When the milk is scalding hot, add a little of it to the egg yolks and stir, then add the yolks gradually to the rest of the hot milk, stirring constantly. Cook, stirring continuously, until the custard thickens enough to coat the spoon, 5–6 minutes. Be careful not to overcook. Remove from fire and cool, stirring occasionally.

When cool, flavor with 2 teaspoons of vanilla and pour into a large, not too deep dessert dish. Now beat the whites of 6 eggs until stiff, and beat in gradually 6 tablespoons granulated sugar. Put 1 cup cold milk into a large clean frying-pan. Fold into the whites 1 teaspoon vanilla and then, using a large serving-spoon, drop the meringue in mounds into the milk. Place the pan on a low flame and let the milk come to a boil. Remove from fire, and carefully lift the meringue islands out of the milk with a sieve spoon and place them side by side on the custard. Cool and place in refrigerator to chill before serving. If you like, a little grated nutmeg may be sprinkled over the whites, or a bowl of grated sweet chocolate may be passed separately with the custard.

## PAUL'S HAZELNUT CREAM

½ cup shelled hazelnuts
⅓ cup and ¼ cup granulated
    sugar
5 sections of triple vanilla
    chocolate

3 eggs
2 cups heavy cream
1 teaspoon vanilla

SERVES 6–8

First place ½ cup shelled hazelnuts in a small heavy frying-pan. Sprinkle with ⅓ cup granulated sugar. Place over low flame and watch carefully, tilting the pan occasionally, until the sugar has melted and turned a golden brown and the nuts are lightly toasted and glazed with the resultant caramelized sugar. Poke with a wooden spoon if necessary to coat the nuts evenly with the caramel. Pour out into lightly buttered tin and cool until completely hard. Break into several pieces and put through rotating nut- or cheese-grater to reduce to a powdery consistency. Next place 5 sections of triple vanilla chocolate in the same grater and reduce to a powdery consistency.

Separate the yolks from the whites of 3 eggs. Beat 2 cups heavy cream until stiff, and using the same beater, beat the yolks until light and creamy, gradually adding ¼ cup granulated sugar. Using another beater, beat the whites until stiff. Add the grated nuts to the yolks, mix well with a spoon, then stir in the grated chocolate. Fold this into the whites and flavor with 1 teaspoon of vanilla. Last of all, fold this mixture into the stiffly beaten cream. Transfer to a glass serving-dish and chill for several hours. Serve, accompanied by ladyfingers.

## CHOCOLATE POTS DE CREME

| | |
|---|---|
| 2 cups heavy cream | 1⅓ cups semi-sweet chocolate |
| 6 egg yolks | morsels |
| ¼ cup granulated sugar | 1 teaspoon vanilla |

SERVES 6–8

Put 2 cups heavy cream in top of double boiler. Add ¼ cup granulated sugar. Place over boiling water and scald. Remove from fire and add 1⅓ cups of semi-sweet chocolate morsels and stir until completely melted. Beat yolks of 6 eggs and gradually beat into them the hot chocolate cream. Place top of double boiler over boiling water again and cook, stirring constantly, until well thickened, about 3 minutes. Remove from fire, stir in 1 teaspoon vanilla, and then pour into 8 small custard cups (½-cup size). When cool, place in refrigerator to chill, before serving.

## CARAMEL POTS DE CREME
*[Pre-heat oven to 325°]*

3 cups heavy cream                 ½ cup caramelized syrup
6 egg yolks

SERVES 6–8

Scald 3 cups heavy cream in top of enamel double boiler over boiling water. Sweeten to taste with about ½ cup caramelized syrup (page 326) and mix well. Then pour mixture into the beaten yolks of 6 eggs. Stir. Pour into 8 small custard cups, place them in a pan of hot water, and cook slowly in pre-heated oven 25–30 minutes, or until an inserted knife comes out clean. Cool and serve well chilled.

## COFFEE POTS DE CREME
*[Pre-heat oven to 325°]*

7 egg yolks                        3 cups heavy cream
¾ cup very strong black            3–4 tablespoons granulated
   coffee                             sugar

SERVES 6–8

Add ¾ cup very strong clear black coffee to 3 cups scalded heavy cream. Sweeten to taste with 3–4 tablespoons granulated sugar. Pour over the beaten yolks of 7 eggs and stir well. Pour into 8 small custard cups, place them in pan of hot water, and bake in pre-heated slow oven until an inserted knife comes out clean, 25–30 minutes. Cool. Chill thoroughly before serving.

## VANILLA POTS DE CREME
*[Pre-heat oven to 325°]*

3 cups heavy cream                 1 teaspoon vanilla
3 tablespoons granulated sugar     6 egg yolks

SERVES 6–8

Heat 3 cups heavy cream with 3 tablespoons granulated sugar in top of enamel double boiler over boiling water. Beat the yolks of 6 eggs with rotary-beater, but not too long. Add the hot cream gradually to the eggs, stirring well; then flavor with 1 teaspoon vanilla. Strain into 8 small custard cups. If you happen to be the proud possessor of a set of real little cream pots with covers, so much the better.

Put the cups or pots in a pan of hot water and place in pre-heated moderate (325° to 350° F.) oven to bake slowly until an inserted knife comes out clean, about 25 to 30 minutes. Be careful not to overcook. Cool, and then place in refrigerator. Serve well chilled in the cups in which they were baked.

## DICK'S SYLLABUB

3 cups Cassonade sugar
1¾ cups good Madeira
1 quart heavy cream
2 quarts light cream
1 teaspoon rosewater
grated rind 3 lemons

1 teaspoon of rosemary needles (tied securely in little bag with a foot of string attached)
2–3 packages of frozen raspberries, or, better still, 1½ quarts of ripe raspberries
1 pound cake

SERVES 18–24

Dissolve 3 cups of Cassonade sugar (a moist brown sugar from France) in ¾ cups good Madeira. If Cassonade is not procurable, substitute granulated or light-brown sugar.

Pour 1 quart heavy cream and 2 quarts light cream into a deep 1-gallon-size crock. Add the grated rind of 3 lemons and 1 teaspoon rosewater. Beat for a second or two, then add gradually the sugared Madeira. Place 1 teaspoon rosemary needles in center of small piece of linen and tie securely, with a foot of string attached. Tie the other end to the lid of the crock and drop the bag into the cream; poke it down so that it will become saturated and sink into the cream. Cover and place crock in refrigerator for at least 36 hours.

When ready to serve, place 1–2 spoonfuls fresh or frozen sugared raspberries in goblet-shape glasses. Fill the glasses half full with the cream mixture, ladled out from the crock. In a separate bowl beat part of the remaining mixture with rotary-beater just long enough to make froth and as it forms fill the glasses with the froth. Place a spoon in each and serve at once, accompanied by pound cake, which may be dunked into the syllabub, or eaten with the syllabub.

## RATAFIA CREAM

6–8 blanched, split apricot kernels

1 quart heavy cream

4 tablespoons powdered sugar

6 egg yolks

¼ teaspoon almond extract

SERVES 6–8

Ratafia cream is a first cousin to our beloved crème brulée. Put 6–8 blanched, split dried apricot kernels in top of a double boiler with 1 quart thick cream. Add 4 tablespoons powdered sugar and bring the cream slowly to the scalding point. Beat the yolks of 6 eggs well, pour a little of the hot cream gradually into the eggs, then add the eggs gradually to the rest of the hot cream. Continue cooking, stirring constantly, until the cream thickens. Remove from the fire and stir occasionally until cool enough to be poured into sherbet glasses. Taste, and if it needs more flavor, add ¼ teaspoon almond extract. Place in refrigerator for at least 8 hours. Serve very cold, accompanied by ladyfingers.

## SUPER-SUPERLATIVE CHOCOLATE MOUSSE

1 pound of triple-vanilla chocolate

½ cup granulated sugar

½ cup water

10 egg yolks

2 teaspoons vanilla

10 egg whites

Melt together in top of double boiler 1 pound triple-vanilla chocolate and ½ cup granulated sugar moistened with ½ cup water. Stir while melting until smooth and free from lumps. Remove from fire and cool, stirring from time to time. When cool, add the well-beaten yolks of 10 eggs. Stir in 2 teaspoons vanilla. Beat the whites of 10 eggs until stiff enough to hold a peak. Add the chocolate to the whites and beat with the rotary-beater just long enough to incorporate all the whites. Pour into a deep earthenware crock or wide-mouthed glass jar, preferably one with a cover. Cover and place in refrigerator overnight, or for at least 12 hours. Place a white or pink napkin around the crock and serve, accompanied by ladyfingers.

## UPSIDE-DOWN CARAMEL CUSTARD
### [Pre-heat oven to 325°]

| | |
|---|---|
| 5 tablespoons granulated sugar | 2 teaspoons vanilla |
| 6 eggs | caramelized baking-dish |
| 1 quart milk | |

SERVES 6–8

First caramelize a 1½-quart-sized round baking-dish with 1 cup sugar (page 325). Break 6 eggs into a bowl. Beat with a rotary-beater, but not too long. Add to them 5 tablespoons granulated sugar, 1 quart scalded milk, and 2 teaspoons vanilla. Stir until sugar dissolves, then strain into the carmelized baking-dish. Place dish in pan of hot water in slow *pre-heated 325° oven* and bake until set, about 1¼ hours. Cool and chill thoroughly before turning out on round shallow dessert dish. If you want to serve 8 people, make separately 2 cups of custard sauce (page 404) and pour it, well chilled, around but not over the caramel custard. Serve accompanied by cake or cookies.

## ZABAGLIONE

| | |
|---|---|
| 8 egg yolks | 1 cup Marsala wine |
| ½ cup sugar | pinch of cinnamon |

SERVES 6–8

Beat the yolks of 8 eggs well, adding gradually ½ cup sugar. When light and creamy in color, add 1 cup Marsala wine. Place in top of large double boiler over boiling water and beat with rotary-beater continuously until the mixture foams way up, is heated through, and begins to thicken well, about 5 minutes. Be careful not to overcook it. Pour immediately into 8 champagne glasses and serve at once. A pinch of cinnamon is sometimes added. This is equally good served very cold; pour into glasses and place in refrigerator for several hours before serving.

# Puddings

### BREAD PUDDING
*[Pre-heat oven to 350°]*

16 slices white bread
½ pound butter
1 cup seedless raisins
4 teaspoons cinnamon
8 whole eggs

6 cups hot milk
2 teaspoons vanilla, or lemon
    extract
2 cups heavy cream
1⅓ cups granulated sugar

SERVES 6–8

Wash 1 cup seedless raisins and soak in warm water until plump, about 10 minutes. Drain and pat dry. Remove crusts from 16 ½-inch-thick slices white bread. Butter copiously and cut in four, making 4 squares of each. Butter lightly 2 rectangular glass baking-dishes, 10″ by 6″ by 1½″. Place 15 squares of bread in each. Sprinkle each dish with about 1 teaspoon cinnamon, and ½ cup raisins. Cover with another layer of bread, and sprinkle again with cinnamon. Beat 8 whole eggs. Heat 6 cups milk, sweeten with 1⅓ cups granulated sugar, and mix with the eggs. Flavor with 2 teaspoons vanilla, or lemon extract. Pour over the bread in the 2 dishes, dividing it equally. Place dishes in pans of hot water and bake until set through like custard and brown on top, 30–40 minutes. Serve hot with pitcher of heavy cream.

## GRAHAM-CRACKER PUDDING
*[Pre-heat oven to 325°]*

3 egg yolks
3 egg whites
1½ cups granulated sugar
2 cups rolled graham-cracker
  crumbs

1 teaspoon baking powder
1 cup finely chopped walnuts
2 teaspoons vanilla
4 tablespoons cold water
2 cups heavy cream

SERVES 6–8

Beat yolks of 3 eggs with 4 tablespoons cold water until light. Mix together in separate bowl 2 cups graham-cracker crumbs, 1½ cups granulated sugar, and 1 teaspoon baking powder. Add to yolks and flavor with 2 teaspoons vanilla. Mix well. Beat whites of 3 eggs until stiff but not dry, and fold into the first mixture. Place in well-buttered 1½-quart-size baking-dish and bake 40–45 minutes. Serve hot with plenty of whipped, but not sweetened cream.

## CARAMEL RICE PUDDING

⅔ cup long-grain rice
1 quart milk
2 tablespoons butter
8 egg yolks

1½ cups granulated sugar
2–3 thin pieces of lemon rind
1 teaspoon vanilla

Caramelize a 1½-quart-size glass baking-dish, using 1 cup granulated sugar (page 325). Wash ⅔ cup rice thoroughly and put it in the top of an enamel double boiler with 2–3 thin pieces of lemon rind. Add 1 quart milk. Cook with cover on over boiling water, stirring occasionally, until creamy, about 1½ hours. Add 2 tablespoons butter and ½ cup granulated sugar. Remove from fire and add the well-beaten yolks of 8 eggs. Place in caramelized mold. *Pre-heat oven to moderate 350°.* Place mold in dish of hot water and bake about 15 minutes, or until the caramel begins to melt. Be careful not to overcook. Remove from oven and cool

—but do not put it in the refrigerator. When ready to serve, turn out onto a round shallow dessert dish, pour around it some thick custard sauce (page 404) and serve, accompanied by more sauce in a pitcher or sauce boat. (This pudding is also delicious served hot with cold custard sauce. To serve it hot, allow it to cool first and then reheat it in a dish of hot water in the oven before turning it out of the mold.)

## CHOCOLATE ALMOND PUDDING

9 sections triple-vanilla chocolate
4 tablespoons cold water
⅔ cup granulated sugar
⅔ cup all-purpose flour
6 tablespoons butter
36 blanched almonds
1 teaspoon vanilla
3 eggs

**Frosting:**
¼ cup granulated sugar
2 pieces triple-vanilla chocolate
1 tablespoon water
1 tablespoon butter
16 additional blanched almonds

SERVES 6–8

Butter and flour a 1½-quart-size ring mold. Put 36 blanched almonds through the nut-grater. Sift through coarse sieve to remove larger pieces and run these through the grater once more. Place 9 sections triple-vanilla chocolate in top of enamel double boiler. Add 4 tablespoons cold water, place over boiling water, and stir until the chocolate has melted and is a smooth thick consistency, about 5 minutes. Remove from fire and add 6 tablespoons soft butter. Stir until the butter has melted, then add the unbeaten yolks of 3 eggs one at a time, stirring well after each addition. Now gradually stir in ⅔ cup granulated sugar and flavor with 1 teaspoon vanilla. Fold in the sifted grated almonds, and, next, sift and fold in gently ⅔ cup all-purpose flour. Beat the whites of the 3 eggs until stiff, but not dry, and fold them gently into the chocolate mixture. Place in buttered and floured ring mold and bake in *pre-heated moderate 350° oven* for about ½ hour, or until an inserted cake-tester comes out clean. Remove from oven and cool. Run a knife around the edges and turn out gently onto a not too shallow, round serving-dish. Ice with the following chocolate frosting.

Put 2 pieces of triple-vanilla chocolate in top of small enamel double boiler. Add ¼ cup granulated sugar and 1 tablespoon butter, and moisten with 1 tablespoon cold water. Place over boiling water and cook for 5 minutes, stirring just long enough to mix. Remove from fire, cool slightly, and spread over the top and sides of pudding. Garnish with additional almonds, blanched or not as you prefer. This cake may be served as it is, or the center may be filled with thick liquid custard sauce (page 404) just before serving.

## FIG PUDDING

½ pound sun-dried figs
1 cup bread crumbs and 1 extra crust
4 ounces beef suet
1 cup flour
1 tablespoon baking powder
½ cup granulated sugar

5 tablespoons brandy
½ teaspoon lemon extract
grated rind of 1 lemon
2 whole eggs
½ cup milk
1-quart-size steamed-pudding mold

SERVES 6–8

Butter a 1-quart-size steamed-pudding mold, and butter and flour a small piece of white cloth. Put 4 ounces fresh beef suet through the meat-grinder, using the medium blade. Repeat the process 3 times. Place a few peices of dry crust of bread in grinder and turn until it goes through, which will prepare the way for the ½ pound of stemmed sun-dried figs that must now be put through. Sprinkle resultant mixture with 1 cup bread crumbs, ½ cup granulated sugar, and the grated rind of 1 lemon. Toss with large fork until well mixed. Sift together 1 cup of flour and 1 tablespoon baking powder. Beat 2 eggs well and add to them ½ cup milk. Add this to the bread mixture, stir well, and sift in gradually the flour and baking powder. Season with 1 tablespoon of brandy and ½ teaspoon of lemon extract.

Fill the buttered mold, packing the mixture well down. Cover with buttered floured cloth and lid, and clamp on the rim of the mold. Place on rack in large pot, and pour sufficient boiling water around it to immerse the mold about three quarters of its height. Cover and boil gently for 2¾ hours, replacing water as it evaporates with more boiling water. When done, lift mold carefully out of the water, remove clamp, cover, and cloth. Run knife around the edge and turn out carefully onto deep hot round platter. Heat ¼ cup brandy and pour over the pudding, light it, and send it blazing merrily to the table. Cut and serve with beaten cream-and-egg sauce.

## PLUM PUDDING

½ pound fresh beef kidney suet
1 stale loaf white bread
1½ cups light-brown sugar
2 cups currants
1 cup seedless raisins
1 cup black seeded raisins
½ cup mixed candied dried fruits
1 cup flour
¾ teaspoon salt

2 tablespoons cinnamon
1 teaspoon nutmeg
2 teaspoons ginger
1 teaspoon cloves
pinch of ground allspice
grated rinds of 1 lemon and 1 orange
2 cups chopped apples
6 eggs
½ cup brandy, and more
1 teaspoon vanilla

SERVES 12

For a great big enormous pudding prepare ½ pound of fresh beef kidney suet, pulling it apart and removing all the bits of stringy substance, thin membrane. Then chop it fine in a big wooden bowl. There should be 2 cups of it. Next grate the inside of a loaf of dry, stale white bread until you have 6 cups of it. Put the suet in a great big bowl. Sprinkle it with 1½ well-packed cups light-brown sugar. Add the bread crumbs.

Next, wash and dry 2 cups currants. Wash and dry 1 cup

seedless raisins. Cut in halves 1 well-packed cup black seeded raisins. Prepare ½ cup of mixed candied dry fruits by cutting them into tiny thin pieces. Put all these fruits in a bowl and sprinkle them with 1 cup of flour into which you have sifted ¾ teaspoon of salt, 2 tablespoons cinnamon, 1 teaspoon nutmeg, 2 teaspoons ginger, 1 teaspoon cloves, and a pinch of ground allspice. Toss the fruits around so that they will be well floured all over and then add them to the other ingredients. Now add the grated rinds of 1 lemon and 1 orange. Next, peel and chop fine enough tart apples to make 2 cupfuls. Put them with the rest of the ingredients. In a separate bowl, beat 6 whole eggs well and stir them into the pudding. Last of all, stir in ½ cup good brandy and 1 teaspoon of vanilla.

Butter copiously a 3-quart-size pudding mold, or 2 1½-quart-size molds if you prefer to make two puddings and keep one for a future party. If you have no real pudding mold, use earthenware mixing bowls. Next flour the mold or molds, as the case may be, and fill them with the pudding mixture, leaving, however, a little room for the pudding to swell. If you have used a pudding mold, lay a small square of buttered, floured cloth over the pudding and put on the cover. If you have used mixing bowls, wring out in cold water a square of heavy white cloth for each bowl, butter these cloths and flour them, and lay them over the bowls, floured side next to the pudding. Stretch smoothly and tie down securely with white cord, wrapping the cord around under the rim several times. Cut off the corners of the cloth, leaving a deep neat ruffle.

Now put an inverted plate in the bottom of a large kettle big enough to hold the pudding bowl. Set the bowl on the plate and pour boiling water around it up to the level of the bowl. If you made two puddings, arrange the second one in the same manner in a separate pan. Cover and boil—not too violently— 6–7 hours, adding more boiling water as necessary. When cooked, if to be eaten immediately, drain, remove the cloth, turn out carefully onto a big plate with a deep rim, and put a sprig of holly in the top. Pour over it some heated brandy, light it, and send pudding blazing to the table, accompanied by hard sauce (page 366) or by lemon and vanilla sauce (page 405).

## PUMPKIN PUDDING
*[Pre-heat oven to 325°]*

| | |
|---|---|
| 4 cups fresh, or canned, pumpkin | dash of nutmeg |
| 1 cup light-brown sugar | 2 scant teaspoons salt |
| 2 tablespoons molasses | 2 tablespoons melted butter |
| 1 cup granulated sugar | 2 tablespoons brandy |
| 3 teaspoons cinnamon | 6 well-beaten eggs |
| 3 teaspoons ginger | 4 cups heavy cream |

SERVES 6–8

Add 4 cups fresh or canned mashed pumpkin to 1 cup light-brown sugar, 2 tablespoons molasses, and 1 cup white sugar. Mix well and add 3 level teaspoons ground cinnamon, 3 level teaspoons ground ginger, a dash of nutmeg, 2 very scant teaspoons salt, 2 tablespoons melted butter, 2 tablespoons good brandy, 6 well-beaten eggs, and, last of all, 4 cups heavy cream.

Caramelize 2 1½-quart-size ovenproof glass dishes (page 325) and pour the mixture into them. Place the molds in pans of warm water and bake in a pre-heated moderate oven until set, about 50 minutes. Remove from oven, cool, and place in refrigerator until ready for use. Turn out on 2 glass plates and serve with a small bottle of kirsch and a pitcher of cream; each person can sprinkle a few drops on the pudding to his taste.

## RICH CHOCOLATE PUDDING WITH COFFEE CUSTARD SAUCE

| | |
|---|---|
| ½ pound triple-vanilla sweet chocolate | 4 egg yolks |
| ½ pound sweet butter | 2 tablespoons cold water |

SERVES 6–8

Melt ½ pound of triple-vanilla chocolate in the top of an enamel double boiler with 2 tablespoons of cold water over hot, not boiling water, stirring constantly. Remove from fire and add little by little ½ pound very fresh sweet butter, stirring it well with a silver tablespoon. Beat the yolks of 4 eggs and add them to the mixture. When well mixed, put in a buttered mold and place in refrigerator overnight. To turn out, dip mold in boiling water a second, cover with dessert plate, and turn upside down. (Serve with coffee custard sauce page 403).

## SCANDINAVIAN PUDDING

| | |
|---|---|
| 1 envelope plain gelatin | grated rind of 2 lemons |
| ½ cup cold water | pinch of salt |
| 5 eggs | ¾ cup toasted, blanched, and |
| ¾ cup granulated sugar | slivered almonds |
| juice of 1 lemon | 1 cup heavy cream |

SERVES 6–8

To prepare the almonds, first blanch ¾ cup almonds by pouring boiling water over them and allowing them to soak 5 minutes. Drain and pinch off the skins. Wash and dry thoroughly. Cut in paper-thin slices, using a sharp knife. Spread out on cloth and allow to dry out for several hours before toasting. To toast, spread out on shallow pan, place in *pre-heated 450° oven* and cook until toasted a light golden brown, about 5 minutes.

To make the pudding, place in top of small enamel double boiler 1 envelope of gelatin. Add ½ cup cold water, stir, and soak 5 minutes. Place pan over boiling water and stir until gelatin has dissolved. Remove from fire and cool until luke-warm. In the meantime, separate the yolks from the whites of 5 eggs. Beat the yolks until light and creamy adding gradually ¾ cup granulated sugar. Prepare the grated rind of 2 lemons, over which strain immediately the juice of 1 lemon. Add this to the egg yolks; then add the cooled gelatin; and beat well. Add a pinch of salt to the 5 egg whites, and beat until stiff. Fold into egg yolks until no more whites may be seen. Then pour immediately into a 1½-quart-size bowl, or mold, which you have rinsed in cold water. Cover and chill until firm. When ready to serve, dip bowl or mold into boiling water for just a second, run a knife around the edge, and turn out carefully onto pretty serving-dish. Garnish with ¾ cup toasted slivered almonds and serve, accompanied by a bowl of slightly whipped cream.

## SUSIE'S PRESIDENT'S LEMON PUDDING PIE
*[Pre-heat oven to 350°]*

| Crust: | Filling: |
|---|---|
| 1¼ cups pastry flour | 2 cups soft bread crumbs |
| 3 tablespoons butter | 1½ cups sugar |
| 3 tablespoons vegetable short- | 2 lemons, juice and rind |
| ening | 4 egg yolks |
| 2–3 tablespoons ice water | ½ cup melted butter |

Meringue:
4 egg whites
8 tablespoons granulated sugar
¾ teaspoon cream of tartar
1 teaspoon vanilla

SERVES 6–8

Place 1¼ cups sifted pastry flour in a bowl. Work in with finger tips 3 tablespoons butter and 3 tablespoons vegetable shortening. Moisten with 2–3 tablespoons ice water. Form into ball. Roll out on floured pastry cloth. Line an 8½-inch pie plate with the pastry.

In the meantime, pluck the soft crumb from a loaf of white bread until you have 2 cups. Pour over it ½ cup of melted butter. Grate the rind of 2 lemons. Beat the yolks of 4 eggs until light, and beat in 1½ cups granulated sugar. Add the juice and rind, and stir lightly with fork into the bread. Place in raw crust and bake slowly in pre-heated 350° F. oven 45 minutes or until set and very lightly browned.

Beat the whites of 4 eggs to which you have added ¾ tea-spoon of cream of tartar, until stiff enough to hold a peak, then gradually beat in 8 tablespoons granulated sugar. Flavor with 1 teaspoon of vanilla and continue beating a second or two. Pile lightly on the lemon pie, being sure the meringue touches the crust all around. Return to oven and bake until a golden brown, 10–15 minutes. Serve luke-warm.

## SUSIE'S POTATO PUDDING
*[Pre-heat oven to 350°]*

| | |
|---|---|
| 4 large potatoes | 4 eggs |
| 4 tablespoons butter | juice and grated rind of 4 lemons |
| 1 cup milk | ons |
| 2 cups granulated sugar | confectioner's sugar |

SERVES 6–8

Peel 4 large potatoes. Quarter and cook until tender in boiling salted water. Drain well, add 4 tablespoons butter, and mash, adding gradually 1 cup hot milk. Remove from fire and stir in 2 cups granulated sugar. Add the strained juice and grated rind of 4 lemons. Beat the yolks of 4 eggs until light and add to the potato mixture. Mix well. Beat the whites of 4 eggs until stiff and fold into the other ingredients. Place in buttered 2-quart-size baking-dish. Place dish in shallow pan of hot water and bake in moderate 350°–375° oven until well risen and browned, about 45 minutes. Sprinkle with confectioner's sugar. Serve hot with lemon sauce flavored with vanilla (page 405).

# Soufflés

## GENERAL DIRECTIONS FOR MAKING SOUFFLES

The idea of achieving a soufflé seems rather terrifying to most cooks, but actually there is nothing to it. General directions for making a sweet soufflé should read: "First throw away your panic. Then take out the egg-beater, butter, sugar, and a baking-dish. Light your oven, set it at 350°–375°, and proceed with confidence and a light heart, as well as a light hand."

Most soufflés require a cream-sauce base. If required, start by making it, measuring the given ingredients carefully and accurately. When cooked, remove from fire, add your sugar, melted chocolate, jam, or other sweetening and flavoring ingredients, then add the required number of well-beaten egg yolks, and beat well. The mixture may then stand a reasonable time until you are ready to bake the soufflé, at which time beat the number of egg whites indicated until stiff enough to hold a peak and fold them carefully into the cream-sauce mixture. Place in buttered and sugared baking-dish; place dish in another dish or pan of hot water; and bake in pre-heated oven undisturbed 40–45 minutes (depending on eccentricity and accuracy of your oven), or until well risen and brown on top, and almost firm to a light touch. When done, remove from oven, dust copiously with confectioner's sugar in which you have kept a vanilla bean, and serve immediately accompanied by the required sauce.

## ALMOND AND APRICOT JAM SOUFFLES
*[Pre-heat oven to 350°]*

| | |
|---|---|
| 4 dozen shelled almonds | 8 eggs |
| 4 tablespoons butter | 2 cups apricot jam (page 356) |
| 6 tablespoons flour | 4 tablespoons kirsch |
| 2 cups hot milk | confectioner's sugar. |
| ½ cup granulated sugar | |

First blanch 4 dozen almonds by allowing them to soak a few minutes in boiling water, then pinch off their skins. Put them in a bowl of cold water in the refrigerator until ready to make the soufflés, at which time sliver the drained almonds using a sharp knife. Next make a thick cream sauce using 4 tablespoons butter, 6 tablespoons flour, and 2 cups hot milk. When thick and smooth stir in ½ cup granulated sugar, the well-beaten yolks of 8 eggs, and 2 cups apricot jam flavored with 4 tablespoons kirsch and the slivered almonds.

Butter 2 2-quart-size glass baking-dishes and sprinkle each with 1 tablespoon granulated sugar. Beat the whites of 8 eggs until stiff, but not dry, and fold them into the apricot mixture. Pour into the 2 dishes, dividing it equally. Place dishes in shallow pan of hot water and bake 40–45 minutes. Sprinkle with confectioner's sugar in which you have kept a vanilla bean, and serve at once with hot apricot-jam sauce (page 400).

NOTE  Any jam may be substituted for the apricot jam, both in the soufflés and in the sauce.

## APRICOT JAM

| | |
|---|---|
| 6 pounds fresh apricots | 2 cups water |
| 9 cups granulated sugar | |

Wash 6 pounds fine fresh ripe apricots. Split them in two, and remove the pits, placing the apricots in cold water as you go along. Next crack open the pits, take out the kernels, put them in a bowl, pour boiling water over them, cover and allow them to steep 5 minutes. Next, pinch off their brown skins and place them in a little bowl covered with cold water. Now put 9 cups granulated sugar in a large pan and moisten it with 2 cups water. Bring to a boil, skim well, and boil 5 minutes without stirring. Then add the well-drained apricots and continue boiling, skimming carefully, stirring frequently to avoid sticking.

When the juice sheets from the side of the spoon, and the jam is thick and transparent, add the well-drained blanched kernels and pour or ladle the jam into hot sterilized pint-sized fruit jars. Adjust the rubbers which you have previously scalded, put on the tops (preferably glass), and seal tight. It should take about 50 minutes for the jam to cook to the right consistency, but be careful not to overcook it, as jam thickens when it cools. This quantity should make about 5 pints.

## CHOCOLATE SOUFFLES

*[Pre-heat oven to 350°]*

| | |
|---|---|
| ½ pound semi-sweet chocolate | ⅔ cup granulated sugar |
| 4 tablespoons butter and more | 2 teaspoons vanilla |
| ½ cup cold water | 8 eggs |
| 6 tablespoons flour | confectioner's sugar |
| 2 cups milk | |

SERVES 6–8

Melt ½ pound semi-sweet chocolate in ½ cup cold water in top of small double boiler over hot, not boiling water. Stir until the chocolate is free from lumps. Remove from fire. Now make a cream sauce using 4 tablespoons butter, 6 tablespoons flour, and 2 cups hot milk. Cook until smooth and thick. Remove from fire and stir in ⅔ cup granulated sugar, the melted chocolate, 2 teaspoons vanilla, and the well-beaten yolks of 8 eggs. Beat the whites of 8 eggs until stiff but not dry, and fold into the chocolate mixture. Pour carefully into 2 well-buttered and sugared 2-quart-size glass baking-dishes, dividing it equally. Place dishes in shallow pans of hot water and bake 40–45 minutes. Sprinkle with confectioner's sugar in which you have kept a vanilla bean, and serve at once with coffee custard sauce (page 403).

## CHOCOLATE PRALINE SOUFFLES

Make exactly as above, but add to the chocolate mixture just before adding the whites 6 tablespoons praline powder (page 326).

## COCONUT AND MARMALADE SOUFFLES

| Soufflés: | Sauce: |
|---|---|
| 1 cup orange marmalade | 2 cups heavy cream |
| 8 egg whites | 4 egg yolks |
| 1½ cups moist coconut | ½ cup granulated sugar |
| 10 tablespoons granulated sugar | 2 teaspoons vanilla |
| 2 teaspoons vanilla | |
| 2 teaspoons butter | |

SERVES 6–8

Butter the top parts of 2 2-quart-size enamel double boilers (preferably with rounded bottoms). Sprinkle each with 1 tablespoon of granulated sugar. Beat the whites of 8 eggs until stiff, then beat in gradually ½ cup of granulated sugar. When very stiff, fold in 2 teaspoons vanilla and 1 cup orange marmalade, and 1½ cups canned moist coconut, cut into smaller shreds with scissors. Pour in sugared pans, place over boiling water, cover tightly with lids, and cook for about 30 minutes. In the meantime make the sauce.

For the sauce, first beat the yolks of 4 eggs until very light. Beat into them gradually ½ cup granulated sugar. Flavor with 2 teaspoons vanilla. In a separate bowl beat 2 cups heavy cream until stiff. Fold the cream into the egg mixture.

When the soufflés are cooked they should have risen almost

to the tops of the pans. Remove lids and place pans directly over low heat for about ½ minute. This is to brown the soufflés lightly on the bottoms so that when they are turned out onto hot platters they will be a beautiful light golden-caramel color. To turn out, run a knife around the edge of each, place serving-plates on the pans and turn upside down. The soufflés should slip out easily. Serve at once accompanied by the sauce.

## COLD CHOCOLATE SOUFFLE

2 envelopes plain gelatin
    (2 tablespoons)
2 cups milk
4 eggs
½ cup powdered sugar

1 teaspoon vanilla
3 cups heavy cream
½ pound triple-vanilla choco-
    late

SERVES 6–8

Fold a piece of heavy wax paper in two lengthwise and wrap around a 1½-quart-size soufflé dish (one with straight sides), so that it will reach well above the top rim, and secure with fine string. (Into this you will pour a chocolate Bavarian cream and gelatin mixture that will be more than the dish can hold; the paper will hold in the rest. Once the gelatin has set firmly, the string should be cut and the paper carefully pulled away giving the effect of a soufflé that has risen well above the level of the dish. A bit of nonsense, but fun to make. To add realism to the effect sift confectioner's sugar copiously over the top—just before serving since it melts if done ahead of time.)

To make the chocolate mixture, first separate the yolks from the whites of 4 eggs. Put 2 cups heavy cream in a deep bowl. Break apart ½ pound triple-vanilla sweet chocolate and place in top of enamel double boiler; add 6 tablespoons cold water; place over hot water and stir until completely melted. Soak 2 envelopes of plain gelatin in ½ cup cold water. Scald 2 cups milk in top of large enamel double boiler. Beat the yolks of 4 eggs until light and beat in ½ cup powdered sugar. Stir this grad-ually into hot milk and cook 4–5 minutes, stirring constantly, until it coats the spoon. Add the gelatin and stir until completely melted, then stir the hot custard into the chocolate gradually. When well mixed, cool over cold water for 10 minutes, stirring occasionally. Then place in refrigerator for about 1 hour, or until it begins to jell, at which time, beat the whites of 4 eggs until stiff, and with the same beater beat 2 cups heavy cream until stiff. Flavor the chocolate mixture with 1 teaspoon vanilla, fold in the whipped cream and, last of all, the beaten whites. When no more whites show, pour carefully into the prepared soufflé dish. The mixture should be sufficient to come at least 1 inch above the level of the dish. Chill until very firm, at least 2 hours. Carefully cut the string and remove the paper. Sprinkle with confectioner's sugar and serve at once with a separate bowl of slightly whipped cream.

## ORANGE SOUFFLES
*[Pre-heat oven to 350°]*

| | |
|---|---|
| 4 navel oranges | 2 cups powdered sugar |
| 8 eggs | confectioner's sugar |

SERVES 6–8

Grate the rind of 2 navel oranges. Then using a sharp knife, pare the 2 oranges and another 2, cutting well in so that none of the white part is left. Do this over a plate so as not to lose the juice. Then slice down into and between the membranes and remove the sections of orange pulp in as perfect pieces as possible. Butter 2 1½-quart-size glass baking-dishes and sprinkle each with 1 tablespoon powdered sugar. Place the remaining membrane of the oranges in a sieve and press on them over a little bowl to extract whatever memaining juice there may be. Add to this juice the grated orange rind.

Place the orange sections in the 2 buttered and sugared baking-dishes, dividing equally. Separate the yolks from the whites of 8 eggs. Beat the yolks until light with a rotary-beater, then slowly beat in 2 cups powdered sugar. Follow with the rind and juice. Beat the whites of 8 eggs until stiff but not dry and fold them carefully into the yolks. Pour over the oranges in the baking-dishes, dividing equally. Place dishes in shallow pans of hot water and bake 40–45 minutes. Sprinkle the top of each with confectioner's sugar and serve at once with hot Zabaglione sauce (page 406).

## VANILLA SOUFFLE
*[Pre-heat oven to 350°]*

| | |
|---|---|
| 4 level tablespoons butter | 8 eggs |
| 6 level tablespoons flour | 2 teaspoons vanilla |
| 2 cups hot milk | 2 cups heavy cream |
| ½ cup granulated sugar | confectioner's sugar |

SERVES 6–8

Butter and sprinkle with granulated sugar 2 2-quart-size glass baking-dishes. Heat 2 cups milk. Melt 4 tablespoons butter in top of small double boiler over boiling water. Stir into butter 6 tablespoons flour and add the hot milk gradually to make a thick smooth cream sauce. Continue cooking 1 minute, then remove from fire, and stir in ½ cup granulated sugar. Then add the well-beaten yolks of 8 eggs and beat well. Flavor with 2 teaspoons vanilla.

Three quarters of an hour before you will be ready to serve the soufflés, beat the whites of 8 eggs until stiff and fold them carefully into the cream-sauce and egg-yolk mixture. Pour carefully into the 2 baking-dishes, place in shallow pan of hot water, and bake 45–50 minutes, at which time they should have risen to top of dishes, be a golden brown on top, and just barely set through. Sprinkle with confectioner's sugar in which you have kept a vanilla bean, and serve at once, accompanied by a pitcher of slightly beaten heavy cream and a small bottle of kirsch.

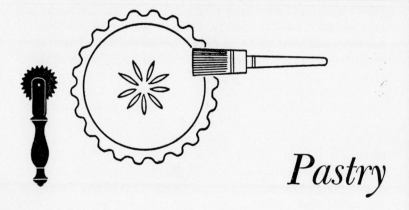

*Pastry*

## RECIPE AND GENERAL DIRECTIONS FOR MAKING PLAIN PIE CRUST

2½ cups pastry flour, or all-purpose flour
1 teaspoon salt
3–6 tablespoons ice water

6 tablespoons vegetable shortening
6 tablespoons sweet butter

Please buy a canvas cover for your bread board and rolling-pin. These may be purchased in large department or hardware stores and are a great boon to pastry-making. They must be treated with flour before using. Follow directions on the package carefully, and you will bless the inventor forever. You will be delighted to find that the pastry just never sticks to either the rolling-pin or the board—and you can imagine what a help that would be—and, besides, consider the added joy of having no sticky floury bread board to wash.

For 2 single large pie shells, or 1 large 2-crust pie, use 2½ cups pastry flour, or all-purpose flour. Sift it with 1 level teaspoon salt. Work into it 6 level tablespoons vegetable shortening and 6 level tablespoons sweet butter, using 2 knives, a pastry-cutter, or you cold finger tips (if you have a light touch). When mealy in consistency, moisten with 3–6 tablespoons ice water (no more), adding a small amount at a time. To make a 2-crust pie, form the pastry into 2 flat balls, wrap in wax paper, and refrigerate for about 15 minutes before using. Place 1 ball of pastry on your floured pastry board or canvas, press out into a flat cake, using the rolling-pin, then roll out to ⅛-inch thickness, keeping the dough in a circular form and using as light a pressure as possible. To lift into the pie pan, place rolling-pin crosswise at top of circle, lift the top of the pastry, and hold it against the pin. Then roll the pin toward you, rolling the pastry up onto the pin as you go. Unroll onto the pie pan so as completely to cover the pan. Let it settle well down into the pan before you trim off the excess pastry with floured scissors, leaving, however, about ½ inch hanging over the edge. This edge is rolled up over the top pastry to form a secure edge. Fill the pie with filling, then roll the second half of the pastry in the same manner. Cover the pie and with scissors cut off excess at the same point as the bottom crust. Roll the overhanging pastry together to form a thick edge, then crimp or flute the edge using your floured fingers, a fork, or a gadget sold especially for the purpose (I use my fingers). Prick the entire surface of the pie with a floured fork before placing it on the bottom rack of your oven, which has been *pre-heated to 450°*. Leave the pie there for about 10 minutes, or until the edges are slightly browned, then place it on the rack in the center of your oven, reduce the heat to 350°, and bake until the filling is cooked and the pie is well browned all over. The time required will depend on the filling.

To bake unfilled pastry shells, divide the pastry in half, roll out, line, and trim 2 tins as per directions above. Roll the overhanging edges under to form a double edge, but be sure the crust still comes slightly beyond the edge of the pan. Press the dough against the edge as you crimp it to keep it from shrinking away while baking. Prick the bottom surface of the crusts all over to prevent them from humping up while baking. Chill thoroughly in refrigerator before baking if time permits. Place in a *pre-heated 450° oven*, and bake about 15 minutes, or until crisp and delicately browned.

## "MY CRUST"—A VERY TENDER CRUST FOR TARTS AND TARTLETS

2⅔ cups of pastry flour
2 teaspoons of granulated
   sugar

1 teaspoon of salt
1 cup of sweet butter
2 eggs

This crust is very good, but very tender and breaks easily. It should be mixed and well refrigerated before using. Sift together 2⅔ cups pastry flour, 1 teaspoon salt, and 2 teaspoons granulated sugar. Work into this with finger tips 1 cup sweet butter. Bind together with 2 whole eggs beaten slightly. Form into 2 balls of equal size. Wrap in wax paper and flatten out into cake shapes. Refrigerate for several hours. This amount is sufficient for 2 9-inch tarts, or 12 large individual tarts.

## RICH WARM-WATER PIE CRUST

1½ cups butter
3 cups pastry flour

1 teaspoon salt

This is enough for 2 small, 9-inch, double-crust pies.

Wash 1½ cups butter in cold water, kneading it until it is of the consistency of putty. Put it into a clean cloth and squeeze it to extract any water. Sift together 3 cups pastry flour with 1 teaspoon salt. Mix the butter into the flour with cold finger tips. Moisten with as little warm water as possible. Form into 2 balls, place in heavy wax paper, and refrigerate 2–3 hours before using.

## ANOTHER PASTRY FOR TARTS

2 cups pastry flour
¼ teaspoon salt

½ cup granulated sugar
1 egg

Sift together 2 cups pastry flour and ¼ teaspoon salt. Sift again into a bowl and make a well in it. In a separate bowl beat 1 egg and then beat into the egg ½ cup granulated sugar until light and creamy. Pour the mixture into the well and add 6 tablespoons soft butter. Now gradually work the whole into a smooth paste, using a fork at first and ending with your fingers. Form into a ball and roll out onto a lightly floured pastry cloth or board.

## APPLE PIE
### [Pre-heat oven to 450°]

| Filling: | Pastry: |
|---|---|
| 8–9 large green cooking-apples | 2½ cups all-purpose flour |
| 2 cups granulated sugar | 1 teaspoon salt |
| 1 tablespoon cinnamon | 6 tablespoons vegetable short- |
| 2 tablespoons butter | ening |
| | 6 tablespoons butter |
| | 3–6 tablespoons ice-water |

SERVES 6–8

First mix and chill plain pie crust (page 362). Peel and core 8–9 big green cooking-apples. Slice them fine into a big bowl, sprinkling them as you go along with 2 cups granulated sugar sifted with 1 tablespoon ground cinnamon. Roll out 1 ball of pastry and line a 10½-inch ovenproof glass pie plate, allowing for an edge that hangs over the rim a bit. Fill with half of the sliced apples and dot with 2 tablespoons butter. Add remainder of apples, distributing them so that they do not heap in the center —but the dish must be well packed and quite full. Roll out second ball of pastry and cover the apples. Trim and roll bottom and top crust so as to form a thick edge, then crimp or flute prettily.

Prick the entire surface and place in hot oven to bake quickly for about 10 minutes. Then reduce heat to 350° and bake until the juice begins to flow, 45–50 minutes longer, by which time it should be a lovely golden brown all over. Eat while warm (not hot), if possible. Sprinkle the top with confectioner's sugar just before serving. Serve a pitcher of heavy cream with it. For a gala occasion cover the surface of pie quickly just before serving with *soft* hard sauce.

## SOFT HARD SAUCE

8 tablespoons butter                    ¼ cup brandy
1½ cups confectioner's sugar

Cream ¼ pound sweet butter with electric-beater and add gradually 1½ cups sifted confectioner's sugar. Add ¼ cup brandy and continue beating until very light and fluffy. Contrary to the general procedure, do not chill. Spread quickly over the warm (not hot) pie just before serving.

## TARTE AUTRICHIENNE

| Pastry: | Filling: |
|---|---|
| 2⅔ cups pastry flour | 16 large apples |
| 6 tablespoons granulated sugar | 1 cup water |
| ½ pound sweet butter | juice of 2 lemons |
| 2 tablespoons vinegar | 2½ cups granulated sugar |
| | ½ teaspoon powdered cinnamon |
| | ½ pound butter |
| | ½ cup seedless raisins |
| | 1 cup blanched almonds, cut fine |

SERVES 6–8

Make a paste by sifting together 2⅔ cups pastry flour with 6 tablespoons sugar. Work into this ½ pound sweet butter. Moisten with 2 tablespoons vinegar. Form into a flat ball and place in refrigerator for 1 hour.

In the meantime make some applesauce, using 16 large apples. Peel, quarter, and core; cook until tender in 1 cup water sweetened with 2½ cups granulated sugar; crush with potato-masher; add 1 cup seedless raisins, juice of 2 lemons, 1 teaspoon powdered cinnamon, and ½ pound butter, and continue simmering until well cooked down. Remove from fire and cool.

Roll out the pastry, line 2 9-inch pie tins, and crimp the edges. Fill with the apple mixture, place in *pre-heated 425°–450° oven*, and bake 30–40 minutes. Fifteen minutes before they will be done, sprinkle each with ½ cup blanched almonds, cut in little slivers. Serve hot, accompanied by slightly whipped heavy cream.

## COCONUT CUSTARD PIE

| Pastry: | Filling: |
|---|---|
| 2½ cups pastry flour | 2 4-ounce cans moist coconut |
| pinch of salt | 6 whole eggs |
| 6 tablespoons vegetable shortening | 6 tablespoons granulated sugar |
| 6 tablespoons butter | 3 cups milk |
| 6 tablespoons ice water | 2 teaspoons vanilla |
| 1 egg white | 1 scant teaspoon nutmeg |
| | ¼ cup light-brown sugar |

First make the pastry. Sift together 2½ cups pastry flour with a pinch of salt. Work into this with the finger tips 6 tablespoons vegetable shortening and 6 tablespoons butter. Moisten with not more than 6 tablespoons ice water. Form into a flat ball, wrap in wax paper, and chill for at least ½ hour.

Now open 2 4-ounce cans moist coconut. Reserve ¾ cup. Spread the rest out on a tin and place in *pre-heated 450° oven* to bake. Watch it carefully and stir occasionally until a light golden brown. Remove from the oven and cool.

Now roll out the crust and line a large 10½-inch ovenproof glass pie plate with it. Trim, roll under the edges, and crimp prettily. Brush the bottom of the pastry with a little raw white of the egg. Place temporarily in refrigerator while you mix the custard.

Break 6 whole eggs into a big bowl and beat them slightly.

Add 6 tablespoons granulated sugar, stir well, then add 3 cups rich milk. Flavor with 2 teaspoons vanilla and 1 scant teaspoon grated nutmeg. Now spread the untoasted ¾ cup coconut evenly over the surface of the pie, and strain over it the custard mixture. Place in *pre-heated 475° oven* and bake 10 minutes, at which time the crust of the pie should have browned lightly. Reduce the heat to 350° and continue baking until it tests done in the center, about ½ hour longer (to test, stick a small knife down into the center of the custard and if it comes out clean, the custard is done).

Sprinkle over the entire surface of the pie a thin coating of light-brown sugar, about ¼ cup; then spread over it evenly the toasted coconut.

Light your grill, and when it is very hot place the pie under it for just a second or two to toast lightly. Remove from grill and cool. Serve cold.

## TWO BUTTERSCOTCH PECAN PIES
*[Pre-heat oven to 375°]*

| Crust: | Filling: |
|---|---|
| 2½ cups pastry flour | 6 eggs |
| 6 tablespoons butter | 2 cups white corn syrup |
| 6 tablespoons vegetable shortening | 2 cups light-brown sugar |
| | 4 tablespoons flour |
| 4–6 tablespoons ice water | 2 cups pecans, chopped fine |
| | 2 teaspoons vanilla |
| | 4 tablespoons butter |

SERVES 6–8

Line 2 9-inch pie tins with the pastry (page 362) but do not prick it or bake it before filling. Fill with the following mixture: Beat 6 whole eggs; add 2 cups white corn syrup, 2 cups light-brown sugar, 2 cups pecans, chopped fine, and 2 teaspoons vanilla; sift in 4 tablespoons flour; and stir in 4 tablespoons melted butter. Bake 50–60 minutes, or until firm in the center. Serve luke-warm with cream.

## CRANBERRY PIE
*[Pre-heat oven to 425°]*

2½ cups flour
1 teaspoon salt
6 tablespoons vegetable short-
    ening

6 tablespoons sweet butter
1¼ cups light-brown sugar
4 tablespoons molasses
4 cups of cranberries

SERVES 6–8

First mix the crust by sifting together 2½ cups flour with 1 tea-spoon salt. Cut into it 6 level tablespoons vegetable shortening and 6 tablespoons sweet butter. Work the fat into the flour lightly, using your finger tips. When well mixed and mealy in consistency, moisten with ⅓ cup cold water, form into a ball, roll in wax paper, and place in refrigerator for a few minutes while you prepare the cranberries.

Wash and pick over carefully 4 cups cranberries. Cut them in half, one by one. Now take half of the pastry, roll it out, and line a 9-inch pie tin with it; then fill the shell with the cranberries and 1 tightly packed cup light-brown sugar. Trickle over all 2 generous tablespoons molasses. Cover with top crust, having first moistened the rim of the under-crust with water. Trim and crimp the edge. Now make a 1½-inch crosslike incision in the center of the pie and roll back the flour flaps, forming a fairly large square hole in the center. Prick the rest of the surface of the pie all over with a fork.

Place in 425° oven for about 10 minutes, then reduce the heat to 325° F. Continue cooking slowly for about 1 hour longer. Every so often during the cooking process, replenish the liquid in the pie as it boils down, by pouring into the hole in the center a little hot thick syrup made by boiling together a minute or two 2 tablespoons molasses, ¼ tightly packed cup light-brown sugar, and ¼ cup water. The pie, when done, should be moist and syrupy inside and the bottom crust should be almost cara-melized on the bottom. Serve warm, accompanied by rat-trap cheese.

## TWO LEMON MERINGUE PIES

### Pastry
2½ cups pastry flour
1 teaspoon salt
6 tablespoons vegetable short-
    ening
6 tablespoons butter
3–6 tablespoons ice water

### Filling:
14 tablespoons (⅞ cup) corn-
    starch
3 cups granulated sugar
3 cups boiling water
2 tablespoons grated lemon
    rind
6 egg yolks
6 tablespoons butter
½ cup strained lemon juice

### Meringue:
6 egg whites
¾ cup granulated sugar
1½ teaspoons cream of tartar
1 teaspoon vanilla

SERVES 6–8

Mix and chill pastry as directed for plain pie crust (page 362).
Now make the filling. Mix together in top of large enamel double
boiler ⅞ cup cornstarch with 3 cups granulated sugar. Prepare 2
tablespoons grated lemon rind and pour over it ½ cup strained
lemon juice. Add to cornstarch and sugar gradually, stirring constantly, 3 cups boiling water. Cook over low direct heat, stirring
constantly, until thick and boiling. Then, still stirring, place over
boiling water and cook 10 minutes longer. Beat the yolks of 6
eggs well, then add a little of the cornstarch to the eggs before
adding them gradually to the remainder of the cornstarch. When
well mixed, add 6 tablespoons butter and stir until melted. Then
add lemon juice and rind. Remove pan from double boiler and
cool while you bake the crust.

   *Pre-heat oven to hot 450°.* Roll out pastry and line 2 small
9-inch ovenproof glass pie plates. Crimp the rolled under edges
prettily. Prick the entire surface of each with a fork and bake for
about 15 minutes, or until lightly browned all over. Cool and
fill with cooled filling, distributing the filling equally. Reduce heat

of oven to 350° and proceed with the mixing of the meringue.

Add 1½ teaspoons cream of tartar to 6 egg whites in a big bowl and beat until stiff enough to hold a peak, then gradually beat in ¾ cup granulated sugar, flavor with 1 teaspoon vanilla, and continue beating a second or two. Pile lightly on the filling in the 2 pies, being sure the meringue touches the crust all around to prevent its shrinking away from the edges while browning—be sure that all the filling is covered too. Bake until a golden brown, 10–15 minutes. Serve cold.

## TWO PUMPKIN PIES WITH CARAMEL GLAZE
*[Pre-heat oven to 450°]*

| | |
|---|---|
| 1 1-pound, 13-ounce can pumpkin, or 3 cups home-cooked pumpkin | 3 teaspoons ground cinnamon |
| | 3 teaspoons ground ginger |
| | ¼ teaspoon powdered cloves |
| 1 cup light-brown sugar | 4 eggs |
| 1 cup granulated sugar | 1 cup heavy cream |
| 1 teaspoon salt | 1 cup scalded milk |
| 2 tablespoons molasses | 1 cup pecan halves |

SERVES 6–8

Personally I think this is the best pumpkin pie I ever ate. Line 2 9-inch ovenproof glass pie plates with plain pie crust (page 362), and crimp the edges, but do not prick the bottoms. Refrigerate while you prepare the filling. Open a 1-pound, 13-ounce can pumpkin, or use 3 cups of home cooked pumpkin; put through a sieve. Place it in a large bowl, add 1 cup light-brown sugar, 1 cup granulated sugar, 1 scant teaspoon salt, 2 tablespoons molasses, ¼ teaspoon powdered cloves, 3 level teaspoons ground cinnamon, and 3 level teaspoons of ground ginger. Mix well. Beat 4 whole eggs slightly and stir them into the pumpkin mixture. Last of all add 1 cup heavy cream and 1 cup milk that you have scalded together. Mix well. Fill the 2 crusts. Place in a hot oven for 10 minutes, then reduce heat to 350°, and continue cooking slowly 30 minutes longer, or until set. Watch carefully, and turn the heat even lower if custard is cooking too fast, which would cause it to become watery. Remove from oven and cool partially while you make the caramel glaze.

For the caramel glaze, place 1 cup granulated sugar in a small heavy aluminum pan with deep sides. Moisten with ½ cup cold water. Have ready ½ cup boiling water, in a separate pan. Place the moistened sugar on the fire and cook slowly, without stirring, until it caramelizes to a golden brown. Remove from fire and add immediately the hot water, being careful not to burn yourself as the water will cause the burned sugar to bubble way up. When it calms down, place pan back on fire and stir until the caramel and water have become a syrup. Cook a minute or two, or until quite thick. Remove from fire and cool while you decorate the top of the pies with 1 cup pecan halves, divided equally. Trickle the caramel over the nuts, endeavoring to cover all the surface of the pies with a thin glaze. The caramel should be cooked enough to be thick, but not long enough to harden.

## A FLAMING RAISIN AND NUT PIE

| Filling: | Crust: |
|---|---|
| 2½ cups seeded muscat raisins | 2½ cups flour |
| 1 cup granulated sugar | 1 teaspoon salt |
| 1 cup water | 6 tablespoons butter |
| grated rind of 2 lemons | 6 tablespoons vegetable short- |
| 2 cups chopped walnut meats | ening |
| 3–4 tablespoons heated brandy | 3–6 tablespoons ice water |

SERVES 6–8

Follow directions for mixing plain pastry (page 362). Refrigerate while you prepare the filling. Cook together for 10 minutes, or until thick and syrupy, 2½ cups seeded muscat raisins, 1 cup granulated sugar, 1 cup water, and the grated rind of 2 lemons. Remove from fire and add 1 teaspoon vanilla and 2 cups chopped walnut meats. Cool.

Roll out half of the pastry and line a 10-inch ovenproof glass pie plate with it. Fill with raisin-nut mixture, cover with rest of pastry, trim edges, and save the trimming. Roll the 2 edges of pastry under to form a secure rim, then flute the edges prettily. Make a hole in the center by making a crosslike incision. Lay around this to form a design 7 small diamond-shaped pieces of pastry cut from the trimmings, rolled out thin. Also cut a narrow strip of pastry, roll it around your finger, and insert your finger and the pastry down into the hole in the pie. Remove your finger and leave the pastry behind, thus forming a rose in the center. Now insert where your finger was a cone-shaped metal pastry-tube end, to keep the rose from closing up while baking. Make 5 small incisions around the rest of the pie, and place in *pre-heated 475° oven* to bake until lightly browned, about 15 minutes. Then reduce heat to 350° and continue baking for 10 minutes longer, or until the juice begins to bubble up through the incisions. Remove from oven and when cool, carefully remove the tube from the center of the rose.

Reheat the pie before serving, but just before sending to the table, pour into the center of the rose, 3–4 tablespoons heated brandy. Turn out the lights in the dining-room, light the brandy in the rose, and watch it burn out before cutting and serving.

## ANGEL PIE
*[Pre-heat oven to 225°]*

| Meringue: | Filling: |
|---|---|
| 4 egg whites | ½ cup granulated sugar |
| ¼ teaspoon cream of tartar | juice and grated rind of 1 |
| 1 cup granulated sugar | lemon |
| 1 teaspoon vinegar | 4 egg yolks |
| ½ teaspoon vanilla | 1 cup heavy cream |

SERVES 6–8

Butter an oblong cake pan, 7″ by 11″ by 1½″. Beat the whites of 4 eggs with rotary-beater until they stand in peaks. Add ¼ teaspoon cream of tartar and beat in gradually 1 cup granulated sugar. Sprinkle with 1 teaspoon vinegar and ½ teaspoon vanilla and beat a second or two longer. Place in buttered pan as smooth as possible and bake slowly for about 1 hour.

While it is baking, make the lemon filling. Place in the top of an enamel double boiler ½ cup granulated sugar, the juice of 1 lemon, the grated rind of 1 lemon, and 3 tablespoons hot water. Mix and add the beaten yolks of 4 eggs. Cook over boiling water, stirring constantly until well thickened. Remove from fire and cool.

When the cake is done, remove from fire, cool slightly, and turn out gently onto large oblong platter. When cold, spread the filling evenly over the top. Then cover the filling with 1 cup heavy cream whipped until stiff, but not sweetened. Just before serving, decorate with tiny forget-me-not or geranium blossoms. Cut at table in 6 or 8 pieces.

## APRICOT PASTRIES

**Pastry:**
2½ cups flour
6 tablespoons vegetable shortening
6 tablespoons butter
3–6 tablespoons ice water

**Filling:**
1 11-ounce box dried apricots
2 cups cold water
1¼ cups granulated sugar
confectioner's sugar

**Sauce:**
2 eggs
⅔ cups confectioner's sugar
3 tablespoons kirsch, or
2 teaspoons vanilla

SERVES 6–8

First mix the pastry. Sift together 2½ cups all-purpose flour and 1 scant teaspoon salt. Work into the flour 6 generous tablespoons vegetable shortening and 6 generous tablespoons sweet butter, using a pastry-cutter or your cold finger tips. When mealy in consistency, moisten with 3–6 tablespoons ice water (no more), adding a small amount at a time. Form into 2 flat balls, wrap in wax paper, and chill while you prepare the apricots.

Wash carefully, one by one, a 11-ounce box dried apricots. Place the apricots in an enamel saucepan, cover with 2 cups cold water, place on moderate heat, and cook gently for about 15 minutes. Add 1¼ cups granulated sugar and continue cooking until the syrup is very thick, about 10 minutes longer. Watch carefully, as they burn easily. Remove from fire and cool.

When ready to complete the dessert, roll out the pastry balls one at a time, forming 2 rectangles approximately 8″ by 10″. Distribute half of the apricots lengthwise in overlapping rows on half of each pastry. Trickle over them whatever syrup there is, moisten the edges, fold the plain halves over covering the apricots, press the edges together to seal securely, and mark edges prettily with the prongs of a silver fork dipped in flour. Transfer carefully to a buttered tin and cut several small slits in each to allow steam to escape while baking. Place in *pre-heated 475° oven* and bake until lightly browned, about 15 minutes. At this time slip a spatula carefully under each pastry to loosen from the pan, in case they stick. Reduce heat to 300° and continue cooking until you are sure that the pastry is done through, about 10 minutes longer. Transfer carefully to a lightly buttered serving-platter. When ready to serve, warm in moderate oven, sprinkle copiously with confectioner's sugar in which you have kept a vanilla bean, and send to table to be cut and served with the following yellow sauce.

Beat 2 egg whites until stiff and then beat in gradually ⅓ cup confectioner's sugar. In a separate bowl, using the same beater, beat until light and creamy 2 egg yolks, adding gradually ⅓ cup confectioner's sugar. Flavor the yolks with 2–3 tablespoons good kirsch. Fold in the whites and serve at once.

## GALETTE FOURE DE CREME PATISSERIE

|  | Cream Filling: |
|---|---|
| 1 galette split in two (page 377) | 4 egg yolks |
| confectioner's sugar | ¾ cup granulated sugar |
|  | 1 cup hot milk |
|  | 1 cup butter |
|  | ¼ vanilla bean |

SERVES 6–8

Scald 1 cup milk with ¼ of a vanilla bean, split in two. Beat 4 egg yolks until light with ¾ cup of granulated sugar; add gradually to hot milk. Cook in top of double boiler over boiling water until mixture coats the spoon. Remove from fire and cool.

In the meantime cream 1 cup butter. When the custard is cold, beat it gradually into the butter. Chill and spread between the 2 layers of galette. Sprinkle with confectioner's sugar and serve cut in pie-shaped pieces.

## CHESS TARTLETS

| Pastry: | Filling: |
|---|---|
| 1⅓ cups pastry flour | 1 cup pecans, or walnuts |
| 3 tablespoons granulated sugar | 1 cup seedless raisins |
| ¼ pound butter | 1 cup butter |
| 1 tablespoon vinegar | 2½ cups granulated sugar |
| | 6 egg yolks |
| | 1 teaspoon vinegar |
| | 2 egg whites |

SERVES 10–12

Line 12 large muffin or tartlets tins with a paste made in the following manner: Sift together 1⅓ cups pastry flour with 3 tablespoons granulated sugar. Work into this ¼ pound butter. Moisten with 1 tablespoon vinegar. Form into a ball and roll thin. When the tins are lined, place in refrigerator while you prepare the filling.

Chop together in a wooden bowl 1 cup pecans, or walnuts, with 1 cup seedless raisins. Cream together 1 cup butter with 2 cups granulated sugar. Add the beaten yolks of 6 eggs. Flavor with 1 teaspoon vanilla and 1 teaspoon vinegar. Add the chopped nuts and raisins, then fold in the stiffly beaten whites of 2 eggs. Fill the raw tartlets with this, place in *pre-heated 400° oven* and bake until well risen and beginning to brown. Then reduce heat to 350° and continue baking until set, about ½ hour in all. Turn off heat, open oven door, and allow tartlets to cool. They will sink a little in the center, which is as it should be. When cool,

beat the whites of 4 eggs until stiff, beat in 8 tablespoons granulated sugar, flavor with vanilla, and pile on tartlets. Bake in
350° oven 10–15 minutes, or until brown. Serve cool, but not
chilled.

## GALETTE WITH BLAZING MINCEMEAT

| | |
|---|---|
| 2 cups sifted pastry flour | 1 egg yolk |
| ½ teaspoon salt | 1 whole egg beaten with 1 |
| 1 teaspoon sugar | tablespoon of cold water |
| ½ teaspoon baking powder | confectioner's sugar |
| ⅜ pound sweet butter | 3–4 cups mincemeat |
| ⅓ cup cream | kirsch |

SERVES 6–8

Sift some pastry flour and measure out 2 cups of it. Sift it again
with ½ teaspoon salt, 1 teaspoon sugar, and ½ teaspoon baking
powder. Work into this with finger tips ⅜ pound sweet butter (or
1½ bars). Moisten with ⅓ cup cream, beaten slightly with the
yolk of 1 egg. Mix with a big fork until it may be formed into a
ball. Flatten the ball a bit, then wrap it in waxed paper and place
in refrigerator for several hours.

When ready to bake, *pre-heat oven to 500°*, and then proceed to roll out the dough on a lightly floured board, forming a
perfect circle ½-inch thick. Place carefully on lightly buttered tin.
With a knife score the surface of the cake, forming a pattern of
diamonds all over. Now beat together 1 whole egg and 1 tablespoon cold water, using a fork, just long enough to mix well.
Then paint the surface of the galette with the egg. Be sure your
oven is hot, put the galette into the oven, and bake 15 minutes,
or until lightly browned all over. Then decrease the heat to 400°
and cook about 25 minutes longer. Watch carefully and don't let it
burn. Serve hot. If you must cook it ahead of time, reheat before
serving, and just before serving sprinkle it lightly with confectioner's sugar. Accompany it with 3–4 cups mincemeat that you
have cooked for 1 hour over boiling water in a double boiler.
Pour over the mincemeat at table 2–3 tablespoons kirsch that has

been heated separately over a low flame in the kitchen and sent to table in a little pitcher. Light the kirsch and let it burn out while you cut the galette in pie-shaped pieces to be eaten with the hot mincemeat.

## CUSTARD TART

*[Pre-heat oven to 350°]*

| | |
|---|---|
| 30 graham crackers | ½ teaspoon salt |
| 1¾ cups granulated sugar | 2½ cups scalded milk |
| 1 teaspoon cinnamon | grated rind of 2 lemons |
| ⅜ pound butter | 5 egg yolks |
| 5½ tablespoons cornstarch | 1 teaspoon vanilla |
| ½ cup cold milk | |

SERVES 6–8

Roll 30 graham crackers very, very fine. Add to them ¾ cup granulated sugar and 1 heaping teaspoon cinnamon. Mix well together, then work them into ⅜ pound butter that has been well creamed. Reserve half of this mixture. With the other half line a straight-edged 9-inch pie tin, pressing the mixture evenly over the bottom and around the sides. This takes a little patience, but is possible. When ready, put it into a moderate pre-heated oven and bake 10 minutes. Remove from the oven and cool.

In the meantime make the cream. Mix together 1 cup granulated sugar with 5½ tablespoons cornstarch and a scant ½ teaspoon salt. Add ½ cup cold milk gradually to form a smooth mixture. Scald 2½ cups milk and add them gradually to the mixture, stirring constantly until smooth. Add the grated rinds of 2 lemons. Cook over boiling water 10 minutes until thick and smooth. Beat the yolks of 5 eggs and add a little of the thickened custard to them. Stir well, then add this to the rest of the custard, and cook 2–3 minutes longer. Flavor with 1 teaspoon vanilla. Cool slightly.

Then pour custard into the cracker shell and spread evenly. Cover the entire surface of the custard with an even coat of the remaining crackers. Bake 20 minutes in a moderate 350° oven.

Remove, cool, and refrigerate for several hours. Turn out onto a large round serving-plate and before serving cut as you would cut a pie.

## FRUIT TARTLETS

| Pastry: | Filling: |
|---|---|
| 2⅔ cups all-purpose flour | 1 12-ounce glass raspberry or |
| 6 tablespoons granulated sugar | currant jelly |
| ½ pound sweet butter | 1 quart strawberries, or |
| 2 tablespoons cider vinegar | 1 quart raspberries, or |
| | 1 pound black or red cherries, or |
| | 16 canned apricots and 1 cup apricot jam |

MAKES 16 TARTLETS

Sift together 2⅔ cups all-purpose flour and 6 tablespoons granulated sugar. Work into this with finger tips ½ pound sweet butter at room temperature—in other words, not too hard or too soft. Moisten with 2 tablespoons cider vinegar, using at this point a large silver fork for mixing. Gather it all together and place on wax paper. Wrap loosely and press into a 1-inch-thick slab. Refrigerate 1 hour.

Remove from refrigerator and allow to stand at room temperature until you can dent it slightly with your finger, then remove wax paper and roll out on lightly floured pastry board or cloth to about ¼-inch thickness. Using a 4- or 5-inch fluted cookie-cutter, stamp out as many circles as possible. Gather the scraps together and roll out again until you have cut 16 circles. Invert muffin tins and lay the circles on the backs of the pans and press them lightly so that they take the form of the pans. Place temporarily in refrigerator while you *pre-heat oven to hot 425°*. Prick the pastry with a fork in several places and bake for 12–15 minutes, or until lightly browned. Watch carefully the last 3 minutes of cooking. Remove pans from oven and cool.

The tartlets may be filled with fresh strawberries, or fresh raspberries, or pitted red or black sweet cherries, or canned apricot halves. With all except apricots, first place a scant tablespoon of red raspberry or currant jelly in each as you lift them carefully one by one from the pan. Fill them with as many of the fresh berries or cherries as they will hold comfortably. When this is accomplished heat the remainder of the jelly over a low heat just a second or two to soften it partially, stirring while you do so. Trickle the jelly over the fruit to glaze it prettily and to fill the tartlets. With the apricots, substitute a little apricot jam for the glaze. I recommend serving these as soon as possible after assembling. Sour cream or slightly whipped heavy cream may be served with these but is not essential.

# Frozen Desserts

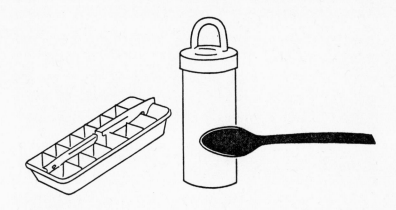

When the mercury is going steadily up and your spirits are going steadily down, a frozen refreshment is sure to revive you. In 1798 a M. Velloni of Paris was so convinced of this that he established a magnificent ice-cream parlor at 10 boulevard des Italiens and outfitted it in the most luxurious fashion with comfortable lounges and marble-topped tables so that his patrons might partake of frozen refreshments in ease and comfort. He wasn't a good manager, however, and he eventually failed and later committed suicide, after turning over his business to an employee Tortoni, who made a great success of the business and retired in 1825 with a nice fat income—leaving to posterity his world-famous Biscuits Tortonis.

Much earlier, in 1660, Procope Cultelli, an Italian, established a coffeehouse in the rue de l'Ancienne-Comédie of Paris and brought to the attention of the French public his "frigid niceties" flavored with coffee, vanilla, and so forth. Soon they were the height of fashion, but they were indeed frigid and solid in their texture, for they were nothing more nor less than frozen blocks of ice. Vatel, the famous chef who committed suicide over a cod that didn't arrive is accredited with being one of the first to perfect the art of making ices. He made a great hit by serving colored eggs as a sweetmeat when Louis the Magnificent paid a visit to Chantilly, the eggs being frozen ice, compact as marble.

It wasn't until 1734 that a M. Reaumure tried to remedy the texture of these ices. It bothered him terribly that they were so hard. It was then discovered that if the ingredients were stirred and scraped from the sides of the container while freezing, much better results were obtained.

Carlo Gatti, an Italian, is said to have introduced the trade in ices in England in 1842. In America (to quote from the Wisconsin Academy of Sciences, Arts and Letters) Dolly Madison is credited with having officially introduced frozen confections to Washington society; and shortly after Nancy Johnson, the wife of a young naval officer, is supposed to have invented the present-day cream-freezer. Whether this is true or not, one thing is certain—ice cream is probably more popular here than anywhere in the world, and, in my humble opinion, we excel in its making.

## GENERAL DIRECTIONS FOR FREEZING AND PACKING FROZEN DESSERTS IN A CRANK FREEZER

First, do not forget that cream and other liquids expand when frozen, so do not fill the freezing-cylinder more than two thirds full. The mixture should be well chilled before being placed in the freezing-container. Be sure the dasher is properly adjusted before covering. Place the container where it should be in the tub, perched on its little pivot. Next, clamp down the top and fasten securely at the side. Try the handle to be sure that all is in running order. The usual proportion of ice to salt for freezing creams or sherbets in a crank freezer is 8 parts of ice to 1 part of ice-cream salt. The good old mallet plus a strong canvas bag are still requisites for cracking the ice to the desired fine state.

It is perfectly possible, however, in many localities to order from your local ice-dealer ice that is all chopped and ready to use. When the space between the container and the tub has been well packed with salt and ice, turn the crank slowly at first, faster later, until it becomes very difficult to turn any more—which indicates that the mixture is frozen. At this point loosen clamp at side, drain off excess brine, wipe top of cylinder clean, and remove cover. Next, remove the dasher, scooping off as much of the frozen mixture as possible; also scrape down the inside of the container, packing the mixture down firmly. Cover top of container with several thicknesses of heavy wax paper and replace cover. Seal tight by winding a piece of adhesive tape around the edge of the cover and plugging the hole in the top with a little cork kept for the purpose. Again pour off all excess brine and repack the space between the cylinder and the tub with more ice and salt, using this time 4 parts of ice to 1 part of salt. Pile plain ice on top of cover with an old bath mat. Ice cream should be packed and allowed to ripen 3–4 hours before being served. When sherbets are made, they should be allowed to ripen for 2 hours.

If the frozen mixture is to be repacked into a fancy mold or molds, have the molds well chilled; and when the mixture is frozen and the dasher has been removed, pack the molds firmly to overflowing with the frozen mixture. Cover with heavy wax paper, cover tightly, and seal with adhesive tape, or by spreading butter around the edge, before burying mold in a big tub of ice and salt, using 4 parts of ice to 1 part of salt.

To unmold a frozen dessert, take the mold from the ice mixture, rinse off in cold water, remove cover and paper, and run a knife around the edge, inserting it not more than 1 inch from the top. Invert the mold in the center of a serving-dish and place a cloth wrung out in warm water over the mold for just a second to hasten the coming-out process. Garnish and serve at once.

## FOUNDATION RECIPES FOR ALL ICE CREAMS

The two foundation recipes for all ice creams are: Philadelphia ice cream (no eggs), or frozen custard or French ice cream. Fruit may be added to either when the cream is partially frozen. Personally I prefer adding fruit to Philadelphia ice cream. The fruit to be added should be mashed and sweetened to taste with a 28° syrup that has been allowed to cool before using. Berries should be mashed through a seive to remove the seeds.

## HOW TO MAKE (APPROXIMATELY) A 28° SYRUP

2 cups granulated sugar                1½ cups cold water

Moisten 2 cups granulated sugar with 1½ cups cold water. Stir until dissolved. Wipe down the inside edges of the pan with a damp cloth. Place on the fire and boil 5 minutes without stirring, counting from the time the syrup is actually boiling.

# Ice Creams

## PHILADELPHIA VANILLA ICE CREAM
### [for crank freezer]

1½ quarts light cream          2 teaspoons vanilla
1⅛ cups granulated sugar

SERVES 6–8

Scald 1½ quarts light cream in a double boiler (it is scalded when tiny bubbles appear around the edge of the cream close to the pan). Add 1⅛ cups granulated sugar and stir until dissolved. Then add 2 teaspoons vanilla. When cold, freeze, turning slowly at first, increasing the speed as it freezes. When stiff remove dasher and pack.

## BLACKBERRY ICE CREAM

1 quart blackberries          1½ cups water
1 teaspoon lemon juice        1 quart heavy cream
2¾ cups sugar

Wash 1 quart blackberries, drain, and crush them well. Add 1 teaspoon lemon juice, sweeten to taste with a 28° syrup made by boiling 2 cups granulated sugar moistened with 1½ cups water for 5 minutes, counting from the time it actually boils. Don't stir while it boils. Use just enough of the syrup to make the berries taste nice and sweet. (The rest of the syrup may be kept in a covered jar in the refrigerator for several days for further sweetening of sliced fruits and so forth.)

Let the blackberries stand 1 hour, then mash through a fine sieve. Throw away the seeds. Scald 1 quart heavy cream in a double boiler and add ¾ cup sugar. Stir until melted, then cool and chill. Freeze to a mush, then add the blackberry pulp, and continue freezing until stiff. Remove dasher, pack for 3 hours, turn out, and serve.

## FRENCH ICE CREAM WITH POWDERED CINNAMON OR KIRSCH

| | |
|---|---|
| 5 cups light cream | 6 egg yolks |
| 1 split vanilla bean | powdered cinnamon, or kirsch |
| ¾ cup granulated sugar | |

SERVES 6–8

Scald 5 cups light cream with a split vanilla bean. Add ¾ cup granulated sugar and stir until dissolved. Beat the yolks of 6 eggs well and add the hot cream gradually. Cook in double boiler until it coats the spoon. Don't overcook. Cool, chill, freeze, and pack.

Serve with this powdered cinnamon in a salt shaker, or kirsch in a little pitcher or glass bottle, to be sprinkled or poured over the ice cream, according to taste of each individual.

## BANANA ICE CREAM

| | |
|---|---|
| 1 pint rich milk | ¾ cup granulated sugar |
| 1 split vanilla bean | 2 large bananas |
| 6 egg yolks | 2 cups heavy cream |

SERVES 6–8

Put a split vanilla bean in 1 pint rich milk and scald it. Beat the yolks of 6 eggs well, then add gradually ¾ cup of granulated sugar, and continue beating until thick and light. Remove the vanilla bean from the hot milk and add the milk gradually to the eggs. Cook in a double boiler until it coats the spoon. Remove from fire and cool, stirring occasionally.

Just before freezing, add the pulp of 2 large bananas, mashed smooth with a silver fork, and 2 cups scalded and cooled heavy cream. Freeze in the usual manner, remove dasher, scrape down sides, and pack to ripen for 3–4 hours. Follow general directions for packing ice cream (page 383).

## FRENCH VANILLA ICE CREAM
### [for crank freezer]

| | |
|---|---|
| 5 cups light cream | ¾ cup granulated sugar |
| 1 split vanilla bean | 6 egg yolks |

SERVES 6–8

Scald 5 cups light cream with a split vanilla bean. Add ¾ cup granulated sugar and stir until dissolved. Beat the yolks of 6 eggs well and add the hot cream gradually. Cook in double boiler until it coats the spoon. Don't overcook. Cool, chill, freeze, and pack.

## COFFEE ICE CREAM WITH GRATED CHOCOLATE

| | |
|---|---|
| ¾ cup freshly roasted ground coffee | 1½ cups milk |
| 1½ cups 28° syrup | 6 egg yolks |
| 1½ cups heavy cream | 1 cup grated triple-vanilla chocolate |

SERVES 6–8

Make some coffee extract by placing in a glasss jar ¾ cup good coffee, freshly roasted and ground to a powder, and pouring over it enough cold water to moisten it well; cover tightly and place in refrigerator overnight. When ready to use, strain through several thicknesses of cheesecloth. If made this way, the coffee flavor is much more pronounced than when made with boiling water. This should give you about ½ cup strong coffee.

When ready to make the ice cream, make some 28° syrup (page 384). Mix 1½ cups heavy cream with 1½ cups milk, add 1½ cups syrup, and scald in double boiler. Beat the yolks of 6 eggs, add them gradually to the cream, and continue cooking until it coats the spoon. Remove from fire and when it is cold, add the coffee extract.

Freeze in the usual way (page 383). Remove the dasher and pack in a melon mold, coating the sides well; in the center put 1 cup grated triple-vanilla chocolate and cover well with more cream. Pack away for 3 hours, turn out, and serve at once. The grated chocolate may be served in a separate bowl, if preferred.

## CHOCOLATE ICE CREAM

½ pound unsweetened choco-       2 cups milk
    late                         1½ cups sugar
4 cups heavy cream               ½ vanilla bean

SERVES 6–8

Melt slowly in a double boiler ½ pound unsweetened chocolate. Scald in a double boiler 4 cups heavy cream and 2 cups milk with 1½ cups sugar and ½ vanilla bean, cut in two lengthwise. When scalded, add a little of this to the chocolate to make a smooth mixture, then add the chocolate gradually to the cream. Cool (not in the refrigerator), stirring from time to time. Freeze and pack in the usual way, removing, of course, the vanilla bean. Serve with Ray's coffee sauce (page 403).

## CARAMEL ICE CREAM

½ cup caramel syrup            5 cups light cream
1 teaspoon vanilla             6 egg yolks
½ cup granulated sugar

SERVES 6–8

Scald 5 cups light cream in a double boiler. Add ½ cup sugar and stir until dissolved. Beat the yolks of 6 eggs well and add the hot cream gradually. Place back in the top of a double boiler and cook a minute or two until slightly thickened, stirring constantly.

Remove from fire and cool. Add ½ cup caramel syrup (page 326) and 1 teaspoon vanilla. Chill, freeze, and pack.

## COCONUT ICE CREAM

3 coconuts (*save* the coconut milk)    5–6 tablespoons sweetened condensed milk

limes

SERVES 6–8

Make 3 holes with an ice pick in a coconut, piercing it where the 3 soft spots are located. Drain and save carefully all the milk therein. Next, break open the coconut by wrapping it in a cloth, resting it on the floor or on some other hard surface, and then giving it a few sharp blows with a hammer. If by any chance the nut has black spots inside, it is not good. Discard it and its juice and start all over again. You will need 3 coconuts and their milk to make enough ice cream for 6–8 people. When the nuts are all open, separate the meat from the shell in as large pieces as possible.

When all the meat has been extracted, the next step is to cut off all the thin brown outer skin with a sharp knife. Drop the pieces as you prepare them into a bowl of cold water. Next, grate all the pieces on a coarse grater. This takes forever, but it's worth it. Put the grated meat in a big bowl, saving out, however, about ½ cup of it, which is to be sprinkled over the ice cream before serving. To the grated coconut in the big bowl add 4 cups boiling water. Beat thoroughly and work it together with a wooden spoon. Let it stand for 10 minutes to cool.

Now place a sieve over a bowl, line it with a large clean piece of heavy cheesecloth, place about one third of the moistened coconut in it, gather up the ends of the cloth, and proceed to squeeze the cloth tight to extract every drop of juice. Repeat the process until all the coconut has been squeezed dry of its own juice and the water that was poured over it. You should now have about 4½ cups of milky water. Cover the bowl with wax paper and a plate and place in the refrigerator to cool thoroughly. The cream in the coconut will float to the top, just as it does in real milk. When this happens, skim off carefully with a spoon. It should give you about 1½ cups of smooth delicious cream.

Measure out 5–6 tablespoons sweetened condensed milk and thin it by adding 1 cup of the left-over, now very watery-looking milky water. Add to this the coconut milk that you drained from the 3 coconuts, and last of all stir in the coconut cream. Altogether you should have now about 5 cups of liquid, ready to be frozen in the usual manner. If you like, add about ½ cup more from the top of the watery milk to stretch the amount a bit.

Pour it all into the freezing-cylinder of your freezer (2 quart size, pack it, using 1 cup ice-cream salt to every 8 cups cracked ice. Turn until so stiff you can't turn any more. Now remove the lid carefully and the dasher—well scraped—pack the ice cream down well, put wax paper over the top, and replace the lid, carefully plugged with a cork. Drain the freezer and repack, using 1 cup salt to 4 cups ice.

When ready to serve, remove from the ice, wipe the top clean before opening, and turn out into a chilled bowl. Sprinkle the grated coconut that you held in reserve over the whole and garnish the dish with limes cut in quarters. A little lime juice is squeezed by each person over the cream before eating.


## REFRIGERATOR COFFEE-CARAMEL PARFAIT

| | |
|---|---|
| 1½ cups milk | 2 egg yolks |
| 2 tablespoons ground coffee | ½ cup granulated sugar (for |
| ½ cup granulated sugar (for | custard) |
| caramel) | 1 teaspoon vanilla |
| ½ cup hot water | 1½ cups heavy cream |

SERVES 6–8

Set your refrigerator control at coldest. Put 1½ cups milk in top of double boiler and add 2 tablespoons of ground coffee. Place over boiling water, cover, and let it cook until the milk is scalding hot; then strain it immediately through a cheesecloth that has been dampened and stretched over a sieve.

In the meantime put ½ cup granulated sugar in a deep aluminum saucepan, place it on the fire, and let it melt, tilting the pan back and forth gently to avoid burning; let it remain until it turns a golden brown, then remove from fire, and pour into it immediately ½ cup boiling water. Be careful not to burn yourself, for the hot water will cause the syrup to boil way up. When it calms down, stir with a spoon, place back on fire, and bring to a boil again, stirring constantly, until a thick syrup is formed. If necessary, a little more water may be added to help it melt. The syrup must be thick, but not thick enough to harden when it cools.

When it has cooled, add the scalded milk, place back on fire, and stir until the syrup has combined with the milk. Then place the whole over boiling water and stir into it gradually the yolks of 2 eggs, beaten until light and creamy with ½ cup granulated sugar. Continue cooking, stirring all the while, until thickened. Remove from fire and cool, stirring occasionally. When quite cold, add 1 teaspoon vanilla and fold into it 1½ cups heavy cream, whipped until stiff. Pour into deep freezing-tray of refrigerator and place in freezing-compartment to freeze. Allow about 4 hours. Turn out on chilled platter and serve at once.

## GINGER ICE CREAM
*[for crank freezer]*

| | |
|---|---|
| 5 cups heavy cream | ¼ teaspoon powdered ginger |
| 1 cup milk | 1 teaspoon vanilla |
| ½ cup granulated sugar | ¼ cup ginger syrup (from the |
| ¾ cup chopped preserved ginger | preserved ginger) |

SERVES 6–8

Scald together in top of enamel double boiler 5 cups heavy cream and 1 cup milk. Add ½ cup granulated sugar and stir until dissolved. Flavor with 1 teaspoon vanilla, ¼ teaspoon powdered ginger, and ¼ cup syrup from the preserved ginger. Freeze to a mush, add ¾ cup finely chopped preserved ginger, freeze until stiff. Remove dasher, and pack for several hours.

## PEACH ICE CREAM

4 cups light cream          ¾ cup granulated sugar
4–5 ripe peaches            1 teaspoon vanilla (optional)
28° syrup

SERVES 6–8

Peel 4–5 ripe peaches, slice fine, and sweeten to taste with 28°
syrup (page 384). Crush well or rub through a coarse sieve. This
should make about 2 cups of pulp. Scald 4 cups light cream in a
double boiler. Add ¾ cup granulated sugar and stir until dissolved. Add 1 teaspoon vanilla (optional), cool, and chill before
freezing. When half-frozen, add the sweetened peach pulp and
continue freezing until very stiff. Remove dasher, scrape down
sides and pack to ripen 3–4 hours. Follow general directions for
packing ice cream (page 383).

## REFRIGERATOR-FROZEN MERINGUED
## WHIPPED CREAM

5–6 meringues              3 egg yolks
¾ cup granulated sugar     3 cups heavy cream
⅓ cup water                1 teaspoon vanilla

SERVES 6–8

Set the control of the refrigerator at the coldest degree. Next,
make a syrup by boiling ¾ cup granulated sugar moistened with
⅓ cup of water until it reaches the soft-ball-in-water stage. Then
beat it gradually into the well-beaten yolks of 3 eggs. Stir in 1
cup cream and cook over hot water, stirring constantly, until well
thickened. Remove from fire and cool, stirring frequently.

Flavor with 1 teaspoon vanilla. Beat 2 cups heavy cream
until almost, but not quite stiff, and fold it carefully into the
custard mixture. Add 5–6 small dry meringues (page 471) broken
into several pieces, place in a large freezing-tray of the refrigerator, and set in freezing-compartment to freeze until stiff. The
mixture must not be stirred during the freezing-process. Turn

back the temperature control to a less cold degree and let the cream ripen a little while before serving. Turn out onto a platter garnished with raspberries.

## STRAWBERRY ICE CREAM

4 cups light cream
1 pint ripe strawberries
28° syrup

¾ cup granulated sugar
1 teaspoon vanilla (optional)

SERVES 6–8

Wash and hull 1 pint ripe strawberries and sweeten to taste with 28° syrup (page 384). Crush well and rub through a sieve. Scald 4 cups light cream, sweeten with ¾ cup granulated sugar, cool, and chill before freezing. When partially frozen, add the sweetened strawberry pulp and continue freezing until stiff. Remove dasher, scrape down the sides, and pack to ripen for 3–4 hours. Follow general directions given for packing ice cream (page 383).

## BLAZING BAKED ALASKA
*[Pre-heat oven to 450°]*

1 thin sheet of sponge cake
2-quart mold of ice cream
8 tablespoons granulated sugar

1 vanilla bean
8 egg whites
kirsch

SERVES 6–8

Lay on a large baking-dish a thin sheet of sponge cake, that you have cut in an oval shape, 1-inch larger all around than a 2-quart melon mold of ice cream. If you have a good caterer, order your favorite ice cream packed in a 2-quart mold—and ask to have it packed well, so that it will be very stiff. *Pre-heat oven well ahead of time to 450°–500°*, so that it will be very hot when you are ready to assemble the baked Alaska. Measure out 8 tablespoons granulated sugar that has been kept in a tight container with a vanilla bean cut in several pieces. Separate the whites from the yolks of 8 fresh eggs and place in the refrigerator. Save 2 halves of the eggshells, choosing those that have no cracks in the bottom. Put a little good kirsch in a small enamel pan.

Now remove the whites from the refrigerator and put them in a bowl. Beat until stiff, then gradually add the sugar, beating continually, until very light. Unpack the mold and place ice cream in center of the sponge cake. Cover immediately with the meringue so that every bit of cream and cake is well covered. Now place the eggshells, open side up, on top of the meringue. Push them down out of sight and pop the dish into a very hot oven, for about 2 minutes, shutting the door. It will brown quickly, so watch carefully, but don't open the oven door too wide. When brown, remove from the oven and pour a little of the kirsch, which has been previously slightly heated, into each eggshell. Light the kirsch and send blazing to the table.

## TINY CHOCOLATE CUPS WITH FROZEN FILLING

| | |
|---|---|
| 1 cup heavy cream | ¼ pound sweet butter |
| ½ cup powdered toasted hazelnuts | ½ teaspoon vanilla |
| | ½ teaspoon almond extract |
| ½ pound triple-vanilla chocolate | ¼ cup powdered sugar |

SERVES 6–8

Place ½ pound triple-vanilla chocolate, broken in sections, in top of small enamel double boiler with ¼ pound sweet butter. Stir over hot water until melted and well blended. Now pour 1 tablespoon of it into 2 small fluted paper cupcake-liners (one inside the other for reinforcement), and tilt it around in your hand until the entire inner surface is coated with a thin layer of chocolate. Place in empty ice-cube container in freezing-compartment of refrigerator and continue. the process until you have prepared 8 cups. Now starting with the first, repeat the process to reinforce each with a second coating of chocolate. Allow to remain in freezing-compartment until set firm. Then, taking each in turn, remove outer cup and set aside while you carefully pull away and discard the inner cup, freeing the chocolate cup. When free, place it back in the outer cup and return to freezing compartment until all are prepared.

Now make the filling. Beat 1 cup heavy cream until almost stiff, then add gradually ¼ cup powdered sugar. Flavor with ½ teaspoon vanilla and ½ teaspoon almond extract. Do not beat too long as the mixture should not be too stiff. Fold in 2 tablespoons hazelnut powder. Now fill the little chocolate cups level full with the cream and sprinkle the top of each with lightly toasted hazelnut powder. Return to freezing-compartment, set at freezing-point, and allow to remain undisturbed until frozen stiff, about 1 hour. Slip them out of their paper cups and serve at once on individual dessert plates.

A different filling may be made by omitting the nuts and adding instead to the cream (flavored in this case only with vanilla), 1 heaping teaspoon powdered instant Sanka. Sanka, believe it or not, has a better flavor in this instance than powdered coffee.

NOTE   To make powdered toasted hazelnuts, place ½ cup shelled nuts in shallow pan in 400° oven until the brown skins begin to crack open and nuts are lightly browned. Rub in tea cloth to take off the skins. Pick out the nuts and when cold put through the nut-grater. Sift through coarse sieve to remove any stray larger pieces of nuts.

# *Sherbets*

## APRICOT GRANITE

| | |
|---|---|
| 18 whole peeled canned apricots, or 18 fresh apricots | ½ cup Madeira |
| 1½ cups 28° syrup | ¼ teaspoon almond extract |
| juice of 5 lemons | 1½ cups water |

SERVES 6–8

Remove the pits from 18 large peeled canned, or fresh, apricots and press the pulp through a sieve. Add 1½ cups 28° syrup (page 384) to the pulp. Add strained juice of 5 lemons, ½ cup of Madeira, ¼ teaspoon almond extract, and 1½ cups cold water. Cool and chill, then freeze to a mush in crank freezer or refrigerator tray. Serve at once in tall sherbet glasses, accompanied by macaroons.

## BLACK RASPBERRY ICE

2 quarts black raspberries
2 scant cups granulated sugar
4 cups water

2 tablespoons strained lemon
juice

SERVES 6–8

Wash and crush well 2 quarts black raspberries. Push through a fine sieve with a wooden spoon to extract all the pulp and juice. Discard the seeds. This should give you 2 generous cups of pulp. Boil together for 5 minutes, skimming carefully, 2 scant cups granulated sugar moistened with 4 cups water. Add this to the pulp and strain through cheesecloth. Measure and add just enough cold water to make 7 cups in all. Then stir in 2 tablespoons lemon juice. Cool and freeze.

## COFFEE GRANITE

1½ cups drip-grind Italian
    roast coffee
2 quarts boiling water

1½ cups granulated sugar
2 cups cold water
2 cups heavy cream, or more

SERVES 6–8

This is delicious served on a very hot day after lunch or dinner instead of dessert—especially when eaten out of doors.

Make 6 cups very strong, clear, drip coffee, using 1½ cups drip-grind Italian roast coffee and 2 quarts boiling water. Strain through cheesecloth. Moisten 1½ cups granulated sugar with 2 cups cold water. Stir and place on fire. Boil for 3 minutes without stirring, counting from time it first comes to a boil. Add to this the 6 cups strong black coffee. Cool. Freeze until mushy in crank freezer. If you have no freezer, place in 2 deep or 4 shallow freezing-trays of your refrigerator, turn control to coldest, and freeze, stirring frequently, until mushy, about 1 hour, depending on refrigerator.

Have ready 6–8 chilled parfait glasses and a pitcher heavy cream. Scrape the coffee granité with sturdy spoon, and when ready to serve, fill glasses ¾ full. Rush to table accompanied by the cream, which is poured over the coffee as desired, the whole to be eaten leisurely with a spoon. Ladyfingers, especially if home-made, are good with this.

## PINEAPPLE ICE MERINGUED

| | |
|---|---|
| 1½ cups granulated sugar | strained juice of 2 lemons |
| 2½ cups water | 4 egg whites |
| 1 large ripe pineapple | 1 teaspoon vanilla |

SERVES 6–8

First make a syrup by boiling together for 5 minutes 1 cup granu-lated sugar and 2½ cups water. While the syrup is cooling, slice a large ripe pineapple in two lengthwise, cutting through the leaves and all; with the aid of a sharp knife, a fork, and a spoon, scoop or cut out the pulp of the fruit, leaving the 2 pineapple shells intact. Now chop or shred the pulp very fine, being care-ful not to include any of the core and not to lose any of the juice. When it is ready, add it to the syrup and also add the strained juice of 2 lemons. If you have an electric-blender, put the mixture into the glass container and run at medium speed for 30 seconds; if not, don't worry, as it is not essential, only making the pineapple ice a little finer in texture.

This may be frozen in the usual way in a crank freezer, or it may be frozen in a 1½-quart-size electric-refrigerator freezer. If you have neither, proceed as follows. Turn freezing-control of your refrigerator to coldest degree. Place pineapple mixture in

2 shallow or 1 deep ice tray and freeze as you would ice cubes. Watch carefully and when almost firm, turn into chilled bowl and beat with rotary- or electric-beater until smooth. Return to freezing-tray and continue freezing until firm. The entire freezing-time in my refrigerator takes about 1 hour, but only experience will tell with yours.

In the meantime place the pineapple shells in refrigerator to chill until ready to serve the dessert. *Pre-heat oven to 500°.* Place shells side by side on a large ovenproof glass pie plate, and, working quickly, fill both halves heaping full with the pineapple ice. Return to refrigerator while you beat the whites of 4 eggs until stiff. Beat in gradually ½ cup granulated sugar and flavor with 1 teaspoon vanilla. Quickly spread this over the pineapple ice in the shells, being sure to cover all the ice. Place dish in oven and allow to stay until the meringue is lightly browned all over, about 3 minutes. Serve at once.

## ORANGE-WATER ICE AMBROSIA

| | |
|---|---|
| 3 navel oranges | ¼ cup lemon juice |
| powdered sugar | grated rind of 2 oranges |
| 1 quart water | freshly grated coconut, or |
| 2 cups granulated sugar | canned moist coconut |
| 3 cups strained orange juice | |

SERVES 6–8

Peel 3 navel oranges and remove the sections with a sharp knife. Sprinkle lightly with powdered sugar and place in the refrigerator to chill. Make some orange-water ice in the following manner: Boil 1 quart water with 2 cups granulated sugar for 5 minutes. Add 3 cups strained orange juice, ¼ cup lemon juice, and the grated rind of 2 oranges. Cool, strain, and then freeze, using 8 parts of ice to 1 part of salt. Pack for 2 hours, using 4 parts of ice to 1 part of salt.

When ready to serve, turn out into a deep bowl, garnish with the sliced orange sections, sprinkle the whole copiously with coconut, and serve at once.

## REFRIGERATOR GRAPEFRUIT SHERBET

6 grapefruit
2 tablespoons gelatin (1 enve-
    lope)
½ cup cold water

1½ cups granulated sugar
1 cup boiling water
4 egg whites

SERVES 6–8

Soften 2 tablespoons gelatin in ½ cup cold water. Moisten 1½ cups granulated sugar with 1 cup boiling water and boil for 2 minutes. Stir in the gelatin. Squeeze and strain the juice from 6 grapefruit (this should give you about 5 cups of juice). Add juice to the gelatin, stir well, cool, pour into 2 refrigerator freezing-trays, turn control to coldest, and freeze until mushy, ½–1 hour, depending on your refrigerator. Scrape into large bowl. Beat the whites of 4 eggs until stiff and fold into the partially frozen sherbet. Continue freezing until firm, about 2 hours, and serve.

## REFRIGERATOR FROZEN STRAWBERRY ICE

2 quarts strawberries
2 cups granulated sugar

1 cup water
juice of 1 lemon

SERVES 6–8

Wash and hull 2 quarts strawberries. Add 2 cups granulated sugar, 1 cup cold water, and the strained juice of 1 lemon. Rub through a fine sieve. Mix well and place in 2 shallow or 1 deep freezing-tray of refrigerator, setting control to coldest degree. Freeze until almost firm. Remove to mixing-bowl and beat until very light. Place back in freezing-compartment and continue freezing until firm. Turn back the control slightly to warmer and allow to remain undisturbed until ready to serve, accompanied by cake or cookies.

# Dessert Sauces

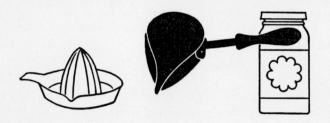

## APRICOT JAM SAUCE

1 cup apricot jam                    ½ cup of water
6 tablespoons kirsch

SERVES 6–8

Heat together to boiling point in a small enamel pan 1 cup apricot jam, 6 tablespoons kirsch, and ½ cup water. Pour into serving-bowl and serve at once.

## AUDREY'S BUTTERSCOTCH SAUCE

1 teaspoon vanilla                   ½ teaspoon salt
1½ cups granulated sugar             ½ cup butter
1 cup light corn syrup               2 cups heavy cream

SERVES 6–8

Mix together in a saucepan 1½ cups granulated sugar, 1 cup light corn syrup, ½ teaspoon salt, ½ cup butter, and 1 cup heavy cream. Place over low heat and cook to soft-ball stage (234° by the candy thermometer), stirring occasionally. Remove from fire and stir in gradually another cup of heavy cream. Place back on fire and cook again for 1–2 minutes, or until thick and smooth. Remove from fire and stir in 1 teaspoon vanilla. Serve hot or cold on ice cream.

## AUDREY'S AMBER SAUCE

2 cups light-brown sugar      ½ cup butter
1 cup light corn syrup      1 teaspoon vanilla
1 cup heavy cream

SERVES 6–8

Mix together in saucepan 2 cups light-brown sugar, 1 cup corn syrup, and 1 cup heavy cream. Add ½ cup butter. Cook over low heat, stirring constantly, for 5 minutes. Remove from fire and add 1 teaspoon vanilla. Serve hot or cold on vanilla ice cream.

## COCONUT CREAM

2 fresh coconuts      boiling water

SERVES 6–8

Break open 2 coconuts, saving the coconut milk. Cut off brown outer thin skin, placing the meat in a bowl of cold water, as you go along. Next grate all the meat, place it in a bowl, and pour over it just enough boiling water to moisten it well. Let it stand 1 hour, mashing it now and then with a wooden or silver spoon.

Put all this into a strainer which you have lined with a piece of strong clean linen and placed over a bowl to catch the juice. Squeeze the cloth, gathering it up on all sides; continue squeezing to extract as much of the milk as possible. Put the coconut back into a bowl and make a second extraction in the same way, using less water this time. Add the first milk to the second and place in a bowl in the refrigerator, covering it carefully with wax paper and a plate; don't disturb it for several hours.

When ready to serve, you will find that the fat in the milk

will have come to the surface, forming a solid cake. Place this carefully in a cold pitcher, and then add to it gradually just enough coconut milk to soften it to the consistency of heavy cream. Serve at once.

## CHOCOLATE CUSTARD SAUCE

2 cups milk
½ cup semi-sweet chocolate
    morsels

4 egg yolks
½ cup granulated sugar
1 teaspoon vanilla

SERVES 6–8

Place ½ cup semi-sweet chocolate morsels in top of enamel double boiler. Add 2 cups cold milk and place over boiling water Stir until the chocolate has completely melted into the milk. Add ½ cup granulated sugar and stir. Beat the yolks of 4 eggs until light. Add a little of the chocolate milk to the eggs and stir well, then add the yolks gradually to remainder of the chocolate milk, stirring constantly. Cook over boiling water until well thickened, 4–5 minutes. Remove from fire. Flavor when cold with 1 teaspoon vanilla. Chill before serving.

## HOT CHOCOLATE SAUCE

3 squares unsweetened choco-
    late
1¾ tablespoons butter

¾ cup boiling water
1¼ cup granulated sugar
1 teaspoon vanilla

SERVES 6–8

Put 3 squares unsweetened chocolate in top of an enamel double boiler and melt it over hot water, stirring constantly. When melted, add 1¾ tablespoons sweet butter and stir in gradually ¾ cup boiling water. Place directly on fire and bring to a boil, stirring constantly. Then add, little by little, 1¼ cups granulated sugar. Boil for 5 minutes, remove from fire, cool, and add 1 teaspoon vanilla. This sauce can stand until you are ready to serve it, and it will not turn to sugar or do strange things. Reheat before serving.

## RAY'S COFFEE SAUCE FOR ICE CREAM

2 cups sugar
1 cup heavy cream
2 tablespoons butter

2 heaping tablespoons instant coffee
2 tablespoons boiling water
2 teaspoons vanilla

SERVES 6–8

Put 2 cups granulated sugar in an enamel saucepan, add 1 cup heavy cream and 2 tablespoons butter, and stir. Bring to a boil and cook until thickened, about 4–5 minutes, stirring occasionally. Dissolve 2 heaping tablespoons instant coffee in 2 tablespoons boiling water and add to sauce. Continue cooking, stirring occasionally, until a little dropped on a plate is gooey in consistency, or about 5 minutes longer. Remove from fire, and flavor with 2 teaspoons vanilla. Serve hot on coffee, vanilla, chocolate, caramel, praline, macaroon, or coffee-macaroon ice cream.

NOTE   Powdered Sanka may be substituted for the powdered coffee.

## COFFEE CUSTARD SAUCE

3 cups milk
6 tablespoons granulated sugar
6 egg yolks

1 cup extra strong coffee
1 teaspoon vanilla

SERVES 6–8

Make 1 cup extra strong coffee. Heat 3 cups milk in top of double boiler and sweeten with 6 tablespoons granulated sugar. Add the strong coffee, and stir. Then beat the yolks of 6 eggs with a rotary-beater, but not too long; add a little of the hot coffee and milk to the eggs, then add the eggs gradually to the hot coffee and milk, stirring constantly. Continue cooking, stirring constantly, until the custard coats the spoon, but be careful not to overcook. Remove from fire and cool, then add 1 teaspoon vanilla. Chill until ready to use.

## BEATEN CREAM-AND-EGG SAUCE

| | |
|---|---|
| 2 eggs | 4 tablespoons powdered sugar |
| 1 cup heavy cream | ¼ cup brandy |

SERVES 6–8

Have ready 2 egg yolks in a little bowl, 2 egg whites in another bowl, and 1 cup heavy cream in a third bowl. When ready to serve the sauce, first beat the egg whites until stiff; next, using the same beater without washing it, beat the cream until stiff; then last of all beat the egg yolks until nice and light, adding gradually 4 tablespoons powdered sugar.

Add ¼ cup brandy to the yolks, fold yolks into the cream, and then fold all into the whites. Serve at once.

## CUSTARD SAUCE

| | |
|---|---|
| 6 egg yolks | 6 tablespoons granulated sugar |
| 3 cups milk | 1 teaspoon vanilla |

SERVES 6–8

Heat in top of enamel double boiler over boiling water 3 cups milk sweetened with 6 tablespoons granulated sugar. Beat the yolks of 6 eggs with a rotary-beater. When the milk is scalding hot, add a little of it to the egg yolks and stir, then add the yolks gradually to the rest of the milk, stirring constantly. Cook, stirring continuously, until the custard thickens enough to coat the spoon, 5–6 minutes. Be careful not to overcook. When cool, flavor with 1 teaspoon vanilla.

## FROZEN CREAM

**2 cups heavy cream**
SERVES 6–8

Place 2 cups heavy unbeaten cream in one of the freezing-trays of your refrigerator. Allow it to freeze, without stirring, until almost but not quite stiff. This will take ½–1½ hours, depending on your refrigerator. Scrape out into a little bowl, preferably silver, and serve at once with hot fruit.

## LEMON AND VANILLA SAUCE

**1 cup sugar**
**2 tablespoons cornstarch**
**2 cups boiling water**
**¼ pound butter**

**juice and grated rind of 1 lemon**
**1 teaspoon vanilla**

SERVES 6–8

Mix together 1 cup sugar with 2 tablespoons cornstarch. Add 2 cups boiling water gradually, stirring constantly. Cook 5 minutes. Remove from fire. Add ¼ pound butter. Stir until melted. Add the juice and grated rind of 1 lemon and 1 teaspoon vanilla. Serve hot on plain hot cake, with plum pudding, or with fig pudding.

## ORIENTAL SAUCE

**1 quart ripe strawberries**
**powdered sugar**
**grated rind of 1 orange**

**1 teaspoon lime juice**
**1 cup currant jelly**
**2 cups whipped cream**

SERVES 6–8

Stem and wash 1 quart ripe strawberries. Slice them and sweeten them to taste with powdered sugar. Grate the rind of 1 large orange and sprinkle over the strawberries. Squeeze 1 teaspoon lime juice over all and stir in lightly 1 cup currant jelly beaten soft with a fork. Prepare 2 cups whipped cream, fold it carefully into

the other ingredients, and send to the table with vanilla ice
cream.

## RAISIN AND RUM SAUCE FOR VANILLA
## ICE CREAM

½ cup seeded muscat raisins     ¼ cup water
½ cup dark rum     1 inch stick cinnamon bark
thin peels from ½ lemon and     1 vanilla bean
    ½ orange     ¼ pound jumbo walnut meats
½ cup granulated sugar

Soak ½ cup seeded muscat raisins in ½ cup dark rum for about
1 hour. Remove thin peel from ½ lemon and ½ orange, being
careful not to include any of the white bitter part. Cut into thin
shreds, then cover with water, and simmer for a minute or two;
then drain.

Boil together for 2 minutes ½ cup granulated sugar, ¼
cup water, a stick of whole cinnamon, and a 1-inch piece of
vanilla bean. Remove the cinnamon and vanilla, and add the
raisins and the rum. Boil 2–3 minutes longer. Remove from fire
and add the lemon and orange rind. Add another 2–3 spoonfuls
of rum and heat before serving as a sauce for vanilla ice cream. As
an accompaniment, serve jumbo-size shelled walnut halves with
the ice cream instead of cookies.

## ZABAGLIONE SAUCE

12 egg yolks            ⅔ cup kirsch
1 cup of sugar

Beat the yolks of 12 eggs in top of large double boiler until very
light, adding gradually 1 cup sugar. When light and creamy in
color, add ⅔ cup kirsch. Place over boiling water and beat continuously with rotary-beater until the mixture foams way up and is
heated through—but be careful not to overcook it. Pour into a
serving-bowl and serve at once.

# Fruit Desserts

*W*hen the Creator placed the first man in the Garden of Eden he commanded him to nourish himself with the fruit it contained. (Genesis 2:16.) Could anything be pleasanter?

## APPLE CHARLOTTE
### [Pre-heat oven to 500°]

8 slices white bread
¼ pound butter
4 tablespoons granulated sugar

2½ cups applesauce (fresh or canned)
powdered cinnamon

SERVES 6–8

Cut and trim 8 slices white bread. Cut again in quarters. Melt ¼ pound butter in a small frying-pan. Dip one side of each piece of bread lightly in the butter and line a glass baking-dish, 10″ by 6″ by 1½″, with the bread, buttered side next to the dish. Sprinkle the bread with 2 tablespoons granulated sugar and plenty of powdered cinnamon. Fill the dish almost level full with about

2½ cups applesauce. Sprinkle with 2 tablespoons sugar, more cinnamon, and pour the remaining butter over all.

Last of all cover the surface of the applesauce with more squares of buttered bread, buttered side up. Bake about 20 minutes, or until a beautiful golden brown. Remove from oven, turn out carefully on large platter, and serve at once with pitcher of cream.

## BOILED APPLE DUMPLINGS

| | |
|---|---|
| 6–8 small juicy apples | ¾ cup milk |
| 2 cups flour | quince preserves, or jelly |
| 1 teaspoon salt | granulated sugar |
| 4 teaspoons baking powder | confectioner's sugar |
| 4 tablespoons butter | light cream |

SERVES 6–8

Peel and core 6–8 small juicy apples. Make a biscuit dough by sifting 2 cups flour with 1 teaspoon salt and 4 teaspoons baking powder. Work into this with the finger tips 4 generous tablespoons butter. Then moisten until of the right consistency to roll out with about ¾ cup milk. Prepare 6–8 pieces of old linen: dip in boiling water and flour well.

Roll out the dough on a floured board to ⅛ inch or so in thickness. Cut squares large enough to cover the apples. Place an apple in the center of each square. Fill the center of the apple with some quince preserves and sprinkle the apple with sugar. Wet the edges of the dough with milk and fold together with the points meeting on the top. Push the edges slightly together. Place each dumpling in a cloth and tie securely, but leave plenty of room for the dumpling to swell.

Boil plenty of water in a big pot and put the dumplings in when boiling. Cover at once and continue to boil for 45 minutes without once removing the cover. Remove the cloths and place dumplings on a hot platter. Serve with confectioner's sugar and light cream, or a bowl of preserved quinces or jelly and a pitcher of light cream.

## APRICOTS DIABLE
*[Pre-heat oven to 450°]*

1 12-ounce glass apricot jam
1½ dozen small almond mac-
    aroon halves
1 1-pound, 14-ounce can whole
    peeled apricots

¼ cup of praline powder (page
    326)
¾ cup of kirsch
¼ cup powdered sugar

If you are looking for an easy and delicious party dessert, this is it. The only difficult part is the required praline powder, but if you keep it on hand, as I do, in a tightly sealed fruit jar, the putting together of this dessert is just a matter of 1–2 minutes of preparation and 5–10 minutes of cooking.

Place 18 small almond macaroon halves, flat side up, side by side in a rectangular shallow glass baking-dish, 7″ by 11½″ by 2″. Soften 1 cup apricot jam with ¾ cup kirsch. Spread a small quantity of this on each macaroon and cover with ½ peeled canned apricot, round side up. Sprinkle with ¼ cup praline powder, followed by ¼ cup powdered sugar. Add ¾ cup apricot juice to the remainder of the jam and kirsch and heat over boiling water. Place the baking-dish in hot oven for 5 minutes to heat, then place under broiling unit to brown lightly. Serve at once accompanied by the sauce in a separate little bowl with a ladle.


## CANNED APRICOTS WITH APRICOT JAM
## AND KIRSCH

2 1-pound, 14-ounce cans
    peeled whole apricots
½ cup apricot jam

½ cup kirsch
3 dozen shelled and blanched
    almonds

Cover 3 dozen blanched almonds with cold water and soak in refrigerator for several hours. Open 2 1-pound, 14-ounce cans peeled whole apricots, and drain, but save the juice. Remove the pits. Place ½ cup apricot jam in top of enamel double boiler and mix with ½ cup apricot juice and ½ cup kirsch. Add the apricots. Place over boiling water until heated through. Serve hot or cold, garnished with the crisp blanched almonds.

## BAKED BANANAS WITH COCONUT CREAM
[Pre-heat oven to 450°]

8 bananas                          1 cup honey
⅛ pound butter                     coconut cream

SERVES 6-8

First make the coconut cream (page 401). Half an hour before you will be ready to serve the dessert, peel 8 bananas and lay them side by side in a buttered baking-dish. Dot with about ⅛ pound butter and pour over them 1 cup clear honey. Place in a hot 450°–475° oven and bake until brown and well puffed. Serve immediately accompanied by the coconut cream.

## APRICOT GELATIN

2 1-pound, 14-ounce cans          1 cup boiling water
    whole peeled apricots          2 dozen blanched almonds
4 oranges                          ½ teaspoon almond extract
2 lemons                           1 cup slightly whipped heavy
1 cup granulated sugar                 cream, or
4 envelopes plain gelatin          1 cup Apricot brandy
1 cup cold water

SERVES 6-8

Drain 2 large 1-pound, 14-ounce cans peeled apricots and save the juice. Remove pits and rub the apricots through a sieve, using a wooden spoon or potato-masher. Discard the pulp that will not go through. Squeeze the juice of 4 oranges and 2 lemons and strain into the apricot juice. Sweeten with 1 cup granulated sugar. Add the apricot pulp and ½ teaspoon almond extract. Soak the contents of 4 envelopes plain gelatin in 1 cup cold water for 5 minutes. Add to the soaked gelatin 1 cup actively boiling water and stir until well dissolved. Then stir it into the apricot mixture. Mix well and pour into 2 1½-quart-size molds. Refrigerate until well set, at least 3 hours.

In the meantime blanch 2 dozen almonds and soak them in cold water in the refrigerator, so that they become nice and white and crisp. When ready to serve the dessert, run a sharp knife around the edge of each mold. Dip the bottoms quickly in and out of a shallow pan of hot water, and turn out onto 2 round serving-plates. Garnish with the well-drained almonds and serve accompanied by 1 cup slightly whipped heavy cream, or, even better, Apricot brandy in a little decorative bottle instead, to be poured over the dessert before eating.

## HOW TO SERVE CHERRIES OR STRAWBERRIES IN PERFECT MOUNDS

This takes a little time, but is very easy. Choose a bowl that has a round bottom, the size depending on the number of cherries or strawberries to be used. The fruit should be washed, but not stemmed. The most perfect ones are placed closely side by side, tails or stems inside, so as to line the bowl completely with a perfect layer; then the rest of the bowl is packed tightly and carefully, stems always up. The top layer is made as even as possible, the stems being down this time. A flat plate is then put on the bowl and it is put into the refrigerator to chill before being turned out carefully, like a child's mud-pie, onto a large serving plate covered with green leaves which have been washed and dried.

## RIPE FIGS WITH HONEY AND CREAM

| | |
|---|---|
| **2 dozen ripe green figs** | **2 cups heavy cream** |
| **¾ cup clear honey** | |

SERVES 6–8

Peel 2 dozen ripe green figs carefully and cut them in quarters. Pour over them ¾ cup clear honey thinned with ¾ cup boiling

water. Cool and refrigerate for several hours before serving. When
ready to serve, accompany by a pitcher of heavy cream.


## SUGARED GRAPES

Pink Emperor or Green Mal-       crystallized sugar
   aga grapes       2 egg whites

Wash firm Pink Emperor or Malaga grapes and dry them well.
Beat the whites of 2 eggs very slightly. Dip the grapes in bunches
in and out of the beaten egg, shake off all the excess egg, then
lay the grapes on a big piece of paper and sprinkle copiously
with crystallized sugar (the kind used by bakers on sugar buns).
Then turn the bunches over and sprinkle again copiously with
sugar and do not disturb until the white of egg has dried and
the crystals have become firmly attached. Place on a pretty
serving-plate covered with green galax leaves that have been
washed and dried well. If the crystallized sugar is not procurable,
granulated sugar may be used instead.


## SLICED ORANGES WITH CARAMEL
## AND CHOPPED PECANS

1 cup granulated sugar       6–8 big navel oranges
½ cup cold water       ¾ cup coarsely chopped
1 cup hot water          pecans

SERVES 6–8

First make some caramel. Put 1 cup granulated sugar in deep
aluminum pan and moisten with ½ cup cold water. Place pan on
fire and cook, without stirring, until a light golden brown, about
8 minutes. Remove from fire and, being careful not to burn yourself, when it bubbles way up, add 1 cup boiling water. Place back
on fire and stir until caramel is melted. Then continue cooking,
without stirring, until thick and syrupy 6–7 minutes.

Cool caramel while you peel with a sharp knife 6–8 big navel oranges (one for each person), cutting well into the fruit so that you slice off every bit of the white membrane. Then put the oranges in the refrigerator to chill a while. Later, slice them crosswise in even ¼-inch slices—on a plate so as not to lose any of the juice—taking care not to disarrange the pieces, in order that the oranges may be reshaped to look like whole ones. Secure with toothpicks temporarily. Arrange in shallow serving-dish just large enough to hold them. Pour over them half of the caramel. Cover with wax paper and place in refrigerator to chill until ready to serve.

In the meantime prepare ¾ cup coarsely cut or chopped pecans. Just before serving remove toothpicks, trickle the rest of the caramel over the oranges, and sprinkle with the pecans.

## MARTY'S SLICED ORANGES WITH ORANGE CREAM

| | |
|---|---|
| 6 navel oranges | 1 cup granulated sugar |
| 1¼ cups strained fresh orange juice | 5 egg yolks |
| | ½ pint heavy cream |
| grated rind of 2 navel oranges | |

SERVES 6–8

First prepare 1¼ cups freshly squeezed, strained orange juice. Grate the rind of 2 navel oranges and add immediately to the juice. Peel 6 navel oranges. With a sharp knife cut off all the white part; then carefully remove the pulp sections in moon-shaped pieces by slicing between the skins. Place in serving-dish and refrigerate until ready to serve.

Now make the sauce. Beat the yolks of 5 eggs until light with rotary-beater. Then beat in gradually 1 cup granulated sugar. Stir in the strained orange juice. Place mixture in top of large 2-quart enamel double boiler over boiling water and cook, beating constantly with rotary-beater (preferably electric), until it foams way up and is well thickened, or about 4 minutes. Remove from fire and cool.

When cold, refrigerate until ready to serve, at which time beat ½ pint heavy cream until stiff and fold it carefully into the orange sauce. Pour over the sliced oranges and serve at once—with or without angel or sponge cake, or lady fingers.

## FRESH ORANGE JELLY WITH ORANGE AND GRAPEFRUIT SECTIONS

2 cups strained fresh orange juice
strained juice of ½ lemon
grated rind of 1 navel orange
2 envelopes plain gelatin

1½ cups boiling water
½ cup granulated sugar
½ cup powdered sugar
2 seedless white grapefruit
4 navel oranges

SERVES 6–8

Prepare 2 cups strained fresh orange juice. Add to it the strained juice of ½ lemon and the grated rind of 1 navel orange. Soak 2 envelopes plain gelatin in ½ cup of this juice for 5 minutes, then stir it into 1½ cups boiling water. Add ½ cup granulated sugar and stir until dissolved. At this point, add the remainder of the orange juice. Transfer to a pretty serving-bowl. When cool, cover and place in refrigerator for several hours, or until set firm.

In the meantime, using a sharp knife, cut away all the peel and white part of 2 fine seedless white grapefruit and 4 large navel oranges. Cut down into the pulp between the sections and remove the fruit in whole perfect pieces. Sprinkle with about ½ cup powdered sugar and chill. Serve both the jelly and the fruit at the table to be eaten together. A spoonful of Cointreau or curaçao on each helping adds to the delicious flavor of this simple and very refreshing dessert.

## FRESH ORANGE AND RICE GELATIN DELIGHT

1 cup rice
2 quarts boiling water
1 cup granulated sugar
juice of 3 oranges (1 cup)
1 envelope unflavored gelatin

grated rind of 1 navel orange
½ cup heavy cream
1 tablespoon powdered sugar
1 teaspoon vanilla
4 navel oranges

SERVES 6–8

Wash 1 cup rice and cook 18 minutes in 2 quarts boiling water. Empty into sieve and allow cold water to run over it. Drain thoroughly. Soak 1 envelope unflavored gelatin in ⅓ cup water 5 minutes. In the meantime, moisten 1 cup of granulated sugar with ½ cup water and boil 5 minutes; cool 1 minute, add the soaked gelatin, and stir until thoroughly dissolved. Add grated rind of 1 navel orange and the strained juice of 3 oranges (1 cup). Next add the well-drained rice.

When mixture is cool, place in refrigerator until it is about to set firm, about 2 hours. At this point fold in ½ cup heavy cream, beaten until stiff and flavored with 1 teaspoon vanilla and 1 tablespoon powdered sugar. Transfer to round 1-quart-size baking-dish —it should be level full. Cover and chill until set firm.

In the meantime, with a sharp knife remove all peel and white part from 4 navel oranges and cut them crosswise in thin slices. When ready to serve the dessert run a knife dipped in hot water around the edge and turn it out on large round serving-platter. Garnish with the orange slices around the edge. Sprinkle the oranges with powdered sugar and serve.

## ALICE'S PEACH SCHAUM TORTE
*[Pre-heat oven to 250°]*

| | |
|---|---|
| 8 large ripe peaches | 2 teaspoons vanilla |
| ½ pint heavy cream | 1 teaspoon white vinegar |
| 6 egg whites | 1 teaspoon water |
| 2 cups granulated sugar | confectioner's sugar |
| ¼ teaspoon salt | |

SERVES 6–8

Place 6 egg whites in the large bowl of an electric-beater. Add ¼ teaspoon salt, 2 teaspoons vanilla, 1 teaspoon white vinegar, and 2 teaspoons water. Beat at high speed until whites are stiff, then add very gradually 2 cups granulated sugar. Place ⅔ of mixture in a lightly buttered and floured spring mold, spreading it evenly. Using a teaspoon, make small kisses of the rest of the meringue, dropping them so that they touch each other in the form of a circle on a buttered and floured cookie sheet (form the circle the same size as the spring mold).

Bake 1 hour or longer in a very slow oven (250°). Remove the circle of kisses about ½ hour sooner than the big torte, as they will be done sooner. Run a sharp knife carefully around the torte, then loosen the clamps of the spring mold, and remove the rim carefully. Slip a sharp knife between the torte and the bottom of the tin and slip the torte carefully onto a large round serving-plate. Also run a sharp knife under the circle of kisses and place it carefully on top of the large meringue.

Fill the center with freshly sliced peaches, lightly sprinkled with confectioner's sugar, and top with whipped cream.

## HOT PEACHES WITH KIRSCH AND ALMONDS

| | |
|---|---|
| 12 peaches | 2 cups sugar |
| 2 dozen shelled almonds | kirsch |

Heat some water to boiling point, pour over 2 dozen shelled almonds, and let them soak 3 minutes. Then pinch off skins, cover the almonds with cold water, and put in refrigerator to chill. Moisten 2 cups sugar with 1½ cups cold water in a saucepan; stir until sugar dissolves. Have ready a small pan of boiling water. Put the sugar on the fire to boil.

In the meantime plunge 12 peaches, one at a time, into the boiling water for a second or two; let the cold water run over them, then peel. The skins should come off easily. Cut the peaches in half as you go along, remove the pits, and put the halves and the pits into the boiling syrup. If the peaches are ripe, a minute or two will be sufficient to cook them. As they are done, remove them from the syrup and place them in an oval baking-dish.

When they are all done, pour the syrup over them, straining out the pits. The juice should be a pretty pale pink. When ready to serve, place the dish in a moderate oven just long enough to heat the peaches. When hot remove from oven and place in each half a blanched almond or two. Serve, accompanied by a pitcher or little bottle of kirsch.

## HOT CANNED PEACHES WITH
## RASPBERRY PRESERVE SAUCE

2 1-pound, 13-ounce cans freestone elberta peaches
½ cup seedless black raspberry
preserves

24 blanched almonds
¼ cup white framboise liqueur

Have ready 24 blanched almonds that have been soaked in cold
water in refrigerator until crisp. Open 2 large cans of freestone
elberta peaches, drain off all but 1½ cups juice, and heat them
over boiling water in top of enamel double boiler.

In top of smaller double boiler over boiling water heat ½
cup seedless black raspberry preserves, softened to desired consistency with about ¼ cup white framboise. Place fruit and juice
in serving-bowl, pour the sauce over the peaches, garnish with
drained almonds, and serve at once.

## PEARS WITH CHEESE

One of the best desserts in the world is a ripe juicy pear eaten
with any good cheese.

## PEARS A LA CUILLERE

6–8 perfect ripe pears
black-currant jam

kirsch

SERVES 6–8

Wash 6–8 perfect pears that have been well chilled. Cut a little
slice off the bottom of each and, with a sharp knife or apple-corer,
remove the cores, but save the pieces you cut off. Fill the pears
with black-currant jam mixed with kirsch, and replace the bottoms. Place the pears, stem side down, in glasses of the right
dimension. The pears are to be eaten with a teaspoon—more
kirsch being added, if desired, while eating them.

## PEARS IN COINTREAU WITH FROZEN CREAM

| | |
|---|---|
| 8–9 large, perfect pears | 2 cups heavy cream |
| 3 cups light-brown sugar | 1 cup Cointreau |
| 4 cups water | 1 lemon |

SERVES 6–8

Peel 8–9 large firm, perfect pears, leaving them whole with their stems. Put immediately into cold water containing the strained juice of 1 lemon to prevent them from turning black.

In the meantime, make a syrup of 3 cups light-brown sugar and 4 cups water. Boil syrup a few minutes, then drain the pears, and add them to the syrup and cook until they are tender and transparent—but avoid overcooking as they must not be mushy and must stand alone. Partially fill a teacup with Cointreau. When the pears are done, lift each one separately and dip it in the Cointreau until well saturated. Put pears in a big glass dish, piling them in a pyramid if possible. Continue to boil the syrup until moderately thick, then add the Cointreau in which the pears were dipped, and cool before pouring over the pears. Refrigerate until ready to serve.

About 30 minutes before dinner empty 2 cups heavy cream into an ice tray in your freezing-compartment, turning the control to highest. By the time you are ready to serve the pears this cream should be crystallized and not quite stiff. Scrape into a well-chilled silver bowl and pass with the pears, over which you have poured at the last minute another ¼ cup Cointreau.


## SLICED RAW PEARS IN ORANGE JUICE
## AND CURACAO

| | |
|---|---|
| 2 cups orange juice | 5–6 tablespoons powdered |
| 6–8 juicy pears | sugar |
| | 6–8 tablespoons curaçao |

SERVES 8

Squeeze and strain 2 cups orange juice. Sweeten with 2 table-spoons powdered sugar and chill well. Fifteen minutes before serving, peel, core, and slice very thin 6–8 large juicy ripe pears and sprinkle with 3–4 tablespoons powdered sugar. Add 6–8 table-spoons curaçao to the orange juice and pour over the pears. Serve in a glass bowl.

## PINEAPPLE WITH PEELED GREEN GRAPES AND KIRSCH

1 large ripe pineapple      1 pound green muscat grapes
½ cup powdered sugar      kirsch

Peel, core, and slice in fairly small pieces a large ripe pineapple. Sprinkle with ½ cup powdered sugar and chill. In the meantime, peel 1 pound of green grapes, slit them halfway through, length-wise, and remove pits. Add them to the pineapple and continue chilling for several hours. An hour before serving, sprinkle with kirsch, or, if you prefer, serve the kirsch separately in a tiny bottle at table, to be sprinkled over the fruit by each person to taste. Serve pineapple and grapes in a glass bowl packed in an-other bowl of crushed ice.

## SLICED ACE PLUMS

18 ripe Ace plums      ¼–½ cup powdered sugar
SERVES 6–8

Ace plums are the sweetest, most delicious plums in the world. They look like nothing at all on the outside, having sort of a mot-tled brown color, but inside they are a luscious red—and they come and go in the markets before you know it. So, keep your eyes open toward the end of summer, and pounce upon them greedily when you do see them. To serve, peel with a sharp knife and slice in thin moon-shaped pieces as you would peaches. Sprinkle them lightly as you go along with ¼–½ cup powdered sugar. Cover and refrigerate for 1–2 hours before serving.

## FRESH PINEAPPLE IN KIRSCH

2 large juicy pineapples     1 cup water
1½ cups granulated sugar     ½ cup kirsch

Once peeled and cored, slice 2 large juicy pineapples in small pieces, using a silver knife. Saturate with a syrup made by boiling the cores in 1½ cups granulated sugar moistened with 1 cup water for 5 minutes. When cool, pour over all ½ cup kirsch. Chill thoroughly before serving.

## POMEGRANATE ICE WITH FRESH FRUIT

4 large ripe pomegranates     1 teaspoon vanilla
juice of 4 lemons     fresh fruit in season
2 cups granulated sugar

SERVES 6–8

In my desire to include a recipe for every fruit, I was hard put to think of one for pomegranates. Then I was inspired to make a frozen ice. I tried it out on Joe, and you could hear the applause from afar. Soon thereafter, with Sophie Kerr coming to dinner, I tried it again, glorifying it with fresh fruit: the last raspberries of the season, a few strawberries, a few seedless grapes, and 2 navel oranges. It must be good, for Sophie called the next day to say it was the most delicious dessert she had ever eaten—and what greater praise could there be!

Moisten 2 cups granulated sugar with 2½ cups boiling water, and boil for 5 minutes. Squeeze and strain the juice of 4 lemons. Cut 4 large pomegranates in half—on a plate so as not to lose the juice—and squeeze on large glass lemon-squeezer. Place seeds and juice in a large enamel pan and add the lemon juice and hot sugar syrup. Strain through fine sieve, pressing hard on the seeds to extract all the juice. This should give you about 6 cups of ruby red juice. Allow to cool completely; then flavor it with 1 teaspoon vanilla.

Freeze in usual way in crank freezer (page 383) or place in 2 freezing-trays of refrigerator and freeze until almost firm, remembering to turn your control to highest point. In about 1 hour it should be frozen to mushy stage. Transfer the contents of both trays to a deep tray, mix well together, and continue freezing until stiff, 1–2 hours longer. Serve in chilled champagne glasses, covered or not with fresh fruit in season.

## RASPBERRIES IN RASPBERRY SAUCE

8 pints fresh raspberries            powdered sugar

SERVES 6–8

Pick over carefully 8 pints fresh raspberries. Wash and drain well. Place two thirds of them in a glass serving-bowl and put it in refrigerator until ready to serve. Rub the rest of the raspberries through a fine sieve placed over a bowl to catch all the juice and pulp. Sweeten to taste with plenty of powdered sugar. Stir until sugar has dissolved, then set in refrigerator to chill. When ready to serve the berries, pour the juice over them and serve, accompanied by ladyfingers or angel cake.

## RED RASPBERRY GELATIN WITH RASPBERRY SAUCE

6 10-ounce packages frozen red      3 envelopes plain gelatin
    raspberries                      1 cup granulated sugar

SERVES 6–8

Defrost 6 packages frozen raspberries, following directions on package. This will take 3½ hours at room temperature. Place fine sieve over a bowl. Empty raspberries and juice into sieve and rub pulp of raspberries through mesh into juice. Save the seeds. This should give you about 3¾ cups thick juice. Save out 1¼ cups, sweeten with ½ cup granulated sugar, and place in covered jar in refrigerator until ready to serve as a sauce for the gelatin.

Soak 3 packages plain gelatin in 1¼ cups cold water for 5 minutes. Place seeds in enamel pan, add 1¾ cups cold water. Place on fire, bring to boil, remove from fire, and strain off the juice. Add ½ cup granulated sugar to hot juice and stir. Place on fire, bring to boiling point, add the soaked gelatin, and stir until gelatin has melted. Add the remaining 2½ cups of the first extraction of cold juice and pulp. Stir well, pour into 1½-quart-size mold. Chill until set firm, about 4 hours. When ready to serve, turn out onto deep serving-platter and pour chilled sauce around it.

## STRAWBERRIES WITH STRAWBERRY JAM

2 quarts strawberries
½ pint strawberry jam
¼ cup kirsch

blanched, unsalted pistachio nuts

SERVES 6–8

Wash and stem 2 quarts fine big strawberries. Place them in a bowl and pour over them just before serving 1½-pint jar strawberry jam softened with ¼ cup Kirsch. Sprinkle a few shelled, blanched pistachio nuts over all, and serve.

## JOE'S DELICES DU PRINTEMPS

3 quarts strawberries
½ cup powdered sugar
3 tablespoons brandy

3 tablespoons curaçao
1 quart vanilla ice cream
1 cup heavy cream

SERVES 6–8

Wash and hull 3 quarts ripe strawberries. Crush one third of them with a silver fork and sweeten them with ½ cup powdered sugar.

Add 3 tablespoons of brandy and the same of curaçao. About 15 minutes before you will be ready to serve the dessert, allow 1 quart vanilla ice cream to soften slightly at room temperature. Beat 1 cup heavy cream until stiff. Add the crushed strawberries to the softened ice cream and mix together. Fold in the whipped cream. Pour this over the uncrushed strawberries. Place in refrigerator until ready to serve.

## HEAVENLY STRAWBERRIES

| | |
|---|---|
| 2 quarts strawberries | 1 cup milk |
| 1 cup powdered sugar | 2 egg yolks |
| 2 oranges | 2 tablespoons granulated sugar |
| grated rind of 2 oranges | 1 teaspoon vanilla |
| ⅓ cup of curaçao | 1 cup heavy cream |

SERVES 6–8

Stem, wash, and drain well 2 quarts ripe strawberries. Place them in a pretty bowl. Sprinkle with 1 cup powdered sugar, the grated rind of 2 oranges; and pour over them the strained juice of 2 oranges and ⅓ cup curaçao. Refrigerate for several hours.

In the meantime, make 1 cup liquid custard in the usual way, using 2 egg yolks, 1 cup of milk, 2 tablespoons granulated sugar, and 1 teaspoon vanilla. Cool and chill.

When ready to serve the strawberries, beat 2 cups heavy cream until stiff and fold stiff cream into the cup of custard. Pour cream-and-custard mixture over the strawberries so as to completely hide them. Serve at once with meringues or ladyfingers.

## PLUMP STRAWBERRIES

2 quarts strawberries              ¼ cup water
1 cup granulated sugar

SERVES 6–8

Wash, pick over, and stem 2 quarts strawberries. Make a syrup of
1 cup sugar and ¼ cup water. When thick, pour over the berries,
and let it cool completely. Place berries on fire again and let them
just come to a boil. Remove from fire and cool. Place in a glass
dish on ice. Serve very cold.

## KAY'S STRAWBERRY COTTAGE PUDDING
*[Pre-heat oven to 350°]*

**Cake batter:**

4 egg whites                       2 boxes of frozen strawberries
½ cup butter                       ⅔ cup of butter (1⅓ bars)
1⅓ cups granulated sugar           2 cups confectioner's sugar
2¼ cups sifted pastry flour
3 level teaspoons baking pow-
    der
1 cup milk
1 teaspoon vanilla
⅓ teaspoon salt

SERVES 6–8

Measure out 2¼ cups sifted flour. Put back in sifter and add to it
3 teaspoons baking powder and ⅓ teaspoon salt; sift again. Cream
well ½ cup butter and add to it gradually 1⅓ cups granulated
sugar; beat until fluffy. Add to this the sifted flour alternately
with 1 cup milk, and flavor with 1 teaspoon vanilla. Beat the
whites of 4 eggs until stiff, but not dry, and fold them into the
batter carefully. Put the batter into 2 well-buttered and floured
loaf-shaped bread pans approximately 9″ by 5″ by 2½″. Bake
35–40 minutes, or until an inserted straw comes out clean.

Meanwhile prepare a bowl of strawberry and hard sauce. Cream ⅔ cup sweet butter until very soft and then add to it gradually 2 cups sifted confectioner's sugar. (Use an electric-beater if you have one.) When very fluffy, add the strained juice from 2 boxes defrosted frozen strawberries. Continue beating a second or two, then fold in the strawberries. Serve at once with the warm cake which you have turned out onto 2 serving-platters and cooled slightly. The butter will separate and look a bit odd, but that is as it should be.

## WATERMELON FILLED WITH FRESH FRUIT AND WATER ICE AND CHAMPAGNE

| | |
|---|---|
| 1 large oval watermelon | 6 apricots |
| 2 cups granulated sugar | 6 ripe red plums |
| 1 quart orange ice | 4 ripe peaches |
| 3 dozen blanched almonds | confectioner's sugar |
| 1 quart fine strawberries | 1 split of champagne |
| 1 pint raspberries | 2 tablespoons curaçao (op- |
| 1 pint blackberries | tional) |

SERVES 6–8

Cut a large watermelon in half. With a large potato-scooper, cut from the center of half of the watermelon 2–3 cupfuls of watermelon balls. Put them immediately in the refrigerator, and then with a big spoon remove the rest of the pulp from the same half, leaving a shell about 1¼ inches thick. Place the shell on ice while you prepare the rest of the ingredients.

First make a pitcher of syrup by boiling 2 cups sugar with 1 cup water for 5 minutes. Cool. When cold, pour a little over the watermelon balls. Now make 1 quart of orange ice (page 398). Freeze and pack. Wash and stem 1 quart fine strawberries. Dry them on a cloth and place in a bowl. Pour a little of the syrup over them and place in refrigerator. Do the same with 1 pint raspberries and 1 pint blackberries. Wash and quarter 6 apricots and add a little syrup; do the same with 6 red plums.

When ready to serve the watermelon, remove from the icebox

and empty the water ice into the center, squashing it to make an even bed over the bottom. On this bed arrange the different prepared fruits in stripes, alternating a light-colored fruit with a dark-colored one. The middle section is reserved for some sliced peaches, which must be peeled, sliced, and sweetened at the last moment. The edge of the watermelon is sprinkled copiously with confectioner's sugar to make it look frosted. Sprinkle top with blanched almonds.

A small bottle of well-chilled champagne in which 2 tablespoons curaçao have been mixed may be poured on just before serving, but is not essential. Because of the nature of this dish, it must be placed on the table and served from there, as it is naturally too heavy to pass. This is a perfect dish for a hot-summer-night party in the garden by moonlight.

## COMPOTE OF FRUIT

| | |
|---|---|
| 8 pink-cheeked peaches | 8 pears |
| 8 blue plums | 8 red plums |
| 8 apricots | 2 cups granulated sugar |

SERVES 6–8

Wash 8 perfect pink-cheeked peaches, 8 blue plums, 8 apricots, 8 pears, and 8 red plums. Make a syrup by boiling 2 cups granulated sugar with 1 cup water for 5 minutes. Then put the whole peaches into this. Let them boil a minute, then fish them out, and let cold water run over them. The skin will pinch off, leaving the pink cheek. Put the peaches back in the syrup until they are tender but not mushy. Put them on a platter to drain, and in the same syrup place the pears, which you have peeled and left whole. Cook until tender, then put them on a platter to drain. In the same juice put the whole apricots, also the red and blue plums. Cook until they pop open. Then drain and put them on a plate. Continue to simmer the juice while you arrange the fruits on a large glass dish. When the juice has boiled down and is quite thick, cool, and then pour it over the fruits. Place in refrigerator and serve very cold.

## MIXED FRUIT

| | |
|---|---|
| 4 oranges | 2 cups of green seedless grapes |
| 2 grapefruit | or 1-pound can in heavy |
| 1 quart fresh strawberries | syrup |
| 1½ cups granulated sugar | 2 12-ounce cans sliced man- |
| 2 bananas | goes in light syrup |

SERVES 6–8

With a sharp knife remove peel from 4 navel oranges, cutting deep enough to cut off all the white part. Cut down into and between the sections to loosen the pulp in as perfect pieces as possible. Place in large bowl. Cut 2 large seedless grapefruit in half and with spoon scoop out the pulp and add it to the oranges. Squeeze the remaining juice in grapefruit over both. Sprinkle with 1 cup granulated sugar, and mix lightly. Wash 1 quart fresh strawberries, one by one, and remove stems. Drain on paper towel, cut in half, and place in separate bowl. Sprinkle with ½ cup sugar. Wash a bunch of seedless green grapes and pick them from the stem until you have 2 cups. Add these to the oranges and grapefruit. Place both bowls in refrigerator to chill until ready to serve. At this time combine the contents of both bowls, and add 1 can sliced mangoes and their juice and 2 ripe bananas, sliced at the last moment. The mangoes give a new flavor to this refreshing and delightful dessert.

# Cakes and Special Cake Desserts

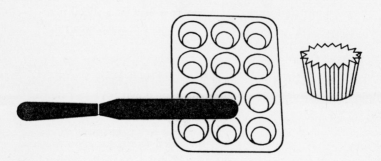

## ALICE'S GOLD AND WHITE ANGEL CAKE

*[Pre-heat oven to 325°]*

| Gold batter: | White batter: |
|---|---|
| 6 egg yolks | 6 egg whites |
| ¾ cup granulated sugar | ½ teaspoon cream of tartar |
| pinch of salt | pinch of salt |
| 1 teaspoon baking powder | ¾ cup granulated sugar |
| ¾ cup pastry flour | ½ cup pastry flour |
| ¼ cup boiling water | ½ teaspoon almond extract |
| ½ teaspoon vanilla | |

Mix white batter first. Sift together 4 times ¾ cup granulated sugar, ½ cup pastry flour, a pinch of salt, and ½ teaspoon cream of tartar. Beat whites of 6 eggs well and fold in gradually the dry ingredients. Flavor by folding in ½ teaspoon almond extract. Place in angel-cake tin.

Now mix gold batter. Sift together 4 times ¾ cup granulated sugar, a pinch of salt, ¾ cup pastry flour, and 1 teaspoon baking powder. Beat yolks of 6 eggs until light and fold in gradually dry ingredients, alternating with ¼ cup boiling water. Fold in ½ teaspoon vanilla. Place by spoonfuls on top of white batter in pan.

Bake 1 hour. Don't peek for 30 minutes. Invert pan on cake rack and allow cake to cool completely before trying to remove it. Run a sharp knife around the edge and center to loosen it, and the cake should fall out easily.

## APRICOT UPSIDEDOWN CAKE
### [Pre-heat oven to 375°]

**Batter:**

¼ pound butter

1 cup light-brown sugar

1 large can halved pitted apricots

1 cup slightly beaten heavy cream

1 cup sifted flour

1 teaspoon baking powder

3 eggs

1 cup granulated sugar

5 tablespoons apricot juice

Put ¼ pound butter in an oblong baking-tin or cake tin, 11″ by 7″ by 1½″. Place in oven just long enough to melt the butter, then remove from oven and add 1 tightly packed cup light-brown sugar, spreading it evenly over the bottom of the pan. Open 1 large can halved pitted apricots and drain well, but save the juice. Lay the apricot halves, cut side up, on top of the sugar.

Now sift some cake flour and measure out 1 cup. Place in sifter and add 1 teaspoon baking powder. Separate the yolks from the whites of 3 eggs. Beat the yolks until very light, then add gradually 1 cup granulated sugar. When very light and creamy, add 5 tablespoons of apricot juice; mix well; then sift and fold in gradually the flour and baking powder. Now beat the whites until stiff and fold them carefully into the mixture. Pour over the apricots and spread evenly, being careful not to fill the pan too full: it should not go quite to the top. If there is too much batter, put the remainder in 2–3 small individual cake tins, to be baked at the same time as the big one. Bake about 35 minutes, or until an inserted cake-tester comes out clean. Keep in warm place until ready to serve. Turn out upsidedown onto a large platter. Serve with 1 cup slightly beaten heavy cream.

## BLACK-WALNUT CAKE
*[Pre-heat oven to 375°]*

½ cup butter
1¼ cups powdered sugar
½ cup milk
1 teaspoon vanilla
almond extract
2 cups flour

2½ teaspoons baking powder
pinch of salt
5 egg whites
½ cup well-floured broken
  black walnuts

Cream ½ cup butter, add gradually 1¼ cups powdered sugar, and beat until very light. Add ½ cup milk, 1 teaspoon vanilla, and a few drops of almond extract. Now add 2 cups flour that you have sifted three times with 2½ level teaspoons baking powder. Add a pinch of salt to 5 egg whites and beat until stiff, but not dry. Fold egg whites into the mixture carefully; then fold in very lightly ½ cup well-floured broken black-walnut meats. Pour into a well-buttered oblong cake tin, 11″ by 7″ by 1½″, and bake about 25 minutes. When cool, frost with twice-cooked frosting (page 457).

## CHOCOLATE ANGEL CAKE
*[Pre-heat oven to 325°]*

¾ cup cake flour
1¼ cups powdered sugar
1 teaspoon cream of tartar
1 teaspoon vanilla

¼ teaspoon almond extract
10 egg whites
¼ cup cocoa

Sift some cake flour, and measure out ¾ cup of it. Add to the flour ¼ cup cocoa and ¼ cup powdered sugar, and sift 3 times. Now beat the whites of 10 eggs until foamy, then add 1 level teaspoon cream of tartar, and continue beating until stiff enough to form and hold a peak when the beater is withdrawn—but be careful not to beat too long. Now fold into this gradually 1 cup powdered sugar. Sprinkle 1 teaspoon vanilla and ¼ teaspoon almond extract over all, and fold into the mixture gradually the flour and cocoa. Pour or sheet it into an angel-cake tin and bake slowly 55 minutes, or until an inserted straw comes out clean. Invert the pan on a cake rack and cool for at least 1 hour before attempting to remove it from the pan. Frost with mocha cocoa frosting (page 456), if desired.

## CHOCOLATE LAYER CAKE WITH EXTRA-SPECIAL CHOCOLATE FROSTING
### [Pre-heat oven to 350°]

| | |
|---|---|
| 2 cups pastry flour | 2 eggs |
| 1 teaspoon soda | 3 squares unsweetened choco- |
| ¼ teaspoon salt | late |
| ½ cup butter | 1 cup milk |
| 1¼ cups granulated sugar | 1 teaspoon vanilla |

Sift some pastry flour and measure out 2 cups of it. Place in sifter with 1 teaspoon baking soda and ¼ teaspoon salt, and sift 3 times. Cream ½ cup butter thoroughly and add gradually 1¼ cups granulated sugar. When light and fluffy, add 2 whole eggs, one at a time, beating well after each. Melt 3 squares unsweetened chocolate in top of small double boiler over hot water, stirring constantly. Add the chocolate to the egg-and-butter mixture and beat well. Then add the sifted flour, a little at a time, alternately with 1 cup milk, beating after each addition until smooth. Flavor with 1 teaspoon vanilla. Butter 2 9-inch layer-cake pans and divide the batter between the two of them. Place in oven and bake 25–30 minutes, or until it tests done in the center with a cake-tester. Turn out on racks to cool. When cold, frost with extra-special chocolate frosting (page 455). Spread between the layers and over the sides and top.

## CHOCOLATE COATED PAVE DE MARRONS

| Pavé: | Chocolate coating: |
|---|---|
| 1 pound imported French chestnut purée (canned) | ½ pound triple-vanilla chocolate |
| ½ pound sweet butter | ½ cup granulated sugar |
| 1 cup granulated sugar | ½ cup water |
| ½ pound triple-vanilla chocolate | |
| 3 tablespoons water | Custard: |
| 2 egg yolks | 1 teaspoon vanilla |
| 1 teaspoon vanilla | 5 egg yolks |
| | 4 tablespoons granulated sugar |
| | 3 cups milk |

The day before—using an electric-beater, if you have one—cream ½ pound sweet butter; add gradually 1 cup granulated sugar, 2 egg yolks, one at a time, 1 can French chestnut purée (adding it, also, little by little). Flavor with 1 teaspoon vanilla. In a separate pan over boiling water, melt ½ pound triple-vanilla chocolate, broken into sections, along with ½ cup granulated sugar moistened with ½ cup water. When smooth and free from lumps, add this to the chestnut purée and continue beating until thoroughly mixed. Place in a brick-shaped buttered rectangular mold, 8″ by 4″ by 3″, making sure it is well packed with no air pockets. Cover and chill overnight.

Also make a liquid custard. Heat 3 cups milk with 4 tablespoons granulated sugar in top of enamel double boiler. Separate the yolks from the whites of 5 eggs. Beat the yolks until light and creamy and add a little of the scalded milk to the eggs, then add the eggs gradually to the remainder of the milk, stirring constantly. Cook until thick enough to coat the spoon. Remove from fire and cool, stirring occasionally. Flavor with 1 teaspoon vanilla. Chill thoroughly until ready to serve.

The afternoon of the party, turn the chestnut pavé out onto a pretty oval serving-platter. This takes a bit of care and patience. Dip a silver knife into boiling water and run it carefully around the edge of the pavé. Place the dish for a minute or two into hot water to soften slightly. Ease it out gently. Place back in refrigerator while you make the chocolate coating.

Place ½ pound triple-vanilla chocolate, broken into sections, in top of double boiler. Add ½ cup water and ½ cup sugar. Place over boiling water and stir until chocolate has melted. Place over low direct heat and stir constantly until it comes to boiling point; continue cooking slowly for 1 minute. Remove from fire and cool, stirring occasionally. When cool, pour gradually over the pavé, smoothing it down and around the sides, as you would frost a cake. When all the chocolate has been used, wipe the edge of platter clean, if necessary, with a cloth dipped in hot water. Place in refrigerator to chill until the chocolate has set. When ready to serve, pour liquid custard into separate bowl to be passed with a ladle when the pavé has been cut in ½-inch-thick slices at the table. Ladyfingers are good with this superlatively rich French dessert.

## COCONUT TEA CAKE
*[Pre-heat oven to 350°]*

½ cup butter
1⅓ cups granulated sugar
1 cup milk
2¼ cups pastry flour
3 teaspoons baking powder
1 teaspoon vanilla
1 scant teaspoon lemon extract
½ cup egg whites
2 cups light-brown sugar
1 can moist coconut

Cream ½ cup butter and add to it gradually 1⅓ cups granulated sugar. When light and fluffy, add alternately 1 cup milk and 2¼ cups pastry flour that you have sifted with 3 teaspoons baking powder. Add 1 teaspoon vanilla and 1 scant teaspoon lemon extract. Last of all fold in carefully ½ cup whites of eggs (about 4) beaten until stiff, but not too dry. Place in 2 well-buttered oblong cake tins, 7″ by 11″.

Sift over each pan, to make a smooth layer, 1 cup light-brown sugar. Sprinkle over the sugar 1 can moist coconut, dividing it equally between the 2 pans. Place in oven and bake until it tests done, 25–30 minutes. Cut in squares when partially cooled and serve while still warm with tea. The coconut should be a lovely golden brown. Watch carefully while baking, and turn the light down slightly if the coconut begins to brown too fast.

## CHEF KINA'S ROYAL HAWAIIAN FRESH COCONUT CAKE
*[Pre-heat oven to 350°]*

Cake:
2 tablespoons butter
1 cup milk
2 cups flour
3 teaspoons baking powder
4 eggs
1 teaspoon lemon extract
2 teaspoons vanilla
2 cups granulated sugar

Filling:
1 fresh coconut
2 cups milk
4 tablespoons cornstarch
½ cup granulated sugar
4 eggs
syrup (⅔ cup sugar moistened with ½ cup water)
3 tablespoons curaçao light cream

Frosting:
1 cup egg whites
1 cup granulated sugar
vanilla

First make 2 layers of sponge cake. Put 2 tablespoons sweet butter and 1 cup milk in saucepan. Butter well 2 round 9-inch cake tins and dust them with flour. Sift together 3 times 2 cups flour with 3 teaspoons baking powder. Heat the milk and butter to boiling point and remove from fire. Break 4 whole eggs into a large bowl. Beat very well with rotary-beater and then beat in gradually 2 cups granulated sugar. When very light, flavor with 1 teaspoon lemon extract and 2 teaspoons vanilla. Then fold in lightly the sifted flour. Last of all add the hot milk gradually. It will seem very thin, but that is as it should be.

When well mixed, pour into the 2 pans, and if there seems to be too much batter, make a little sample cake besides. Bake until a beautiful golden brown, about 30 minutes, or until an inserted straw comes out clean. Turn upside down on a cake rack to cool. Place a wet towel on the pans for a minute or two to help the cakes fall out of the pans. You may have to tease them a bit to loosen them.

Next, break open a medium-size coconut, remove the shell, and peel off the thin brown skin; then grate it. Reserve 1 cup grated meat and place the rest in the refrigerator until ready to use it. Put the cup of reserved coconut into an enamel pan and add 2 cups milk. Mix together in a bowl 4 level tablespoons cornstarch with ½ cup granulated sugar. Beat the yolks of 4 eggs and then beat into the yolks the cornstarch and sugar.

In the meantime, bring the milk and coconut to a boil, remove from fire, and stir gradually into the egg mixture. Place the whole back into the enamel pan, place on low flame, and cook, stirring vigorously, until it comes to a boil and has thickened. Remove from fire and cool.

When ready to finish the cake, split the 2 layers in half horizontally, making four layers. Moisten ⅔ cup sugar with ½ cup water and boil 4 minutes, or until thick and syrupy. Remove from fire and stir into it 3 tablespoons curaçao. Stir into the custard a little of this syrup and a very little light cream, just enough to make the custard of the right consistency to spread easily. Now put one of the split layers, brown side down, on a large round serving-plate. Sprinkle it with some of the syrup and spread the layer with one third of the custard filling. Add another layer of cake, brown side down, and repeat the process, ending up with the top layer of cake, brown side up. You are now ready to ice the cake with coconut meringue frosting.

For the coconut meringue frosting, put 1 cup egg whites in a large bowl and beat with rotary-beater until stiff, then gradually beat in 1 cup granulated sugar, and flavor with vanilla. Continue beating until very stiff, at which time spread the sides of the cake copiously with part of the meringue and pat or sprinkle lightly with some of the grated coconut. Then pile the rest of the meringue on the top of the cake and spread evenly; sprinkle the rest of the coconut over all. The sooner this cake is eaten, the better. It is a tremendous cake, but extremely good—if chef Kina and I do say so.

## DATE TORTE
*[Pre-heat oven to 375°]*

4 eggs
2 cups honey
2 cups chopped pitted dates
2 cups heavy cream
2 teaspoons vanilla
1 cup chopped walnuts

pinch of salt
1 teaspoon baking powder
2 cups sifted toasted bread
    crumbs
½ cup flour

SERVES 6–8

Beat the yolks of 4 eggs, add 2 cups honey, and continue beating until well mixed. Add 2 cups chopped pitted dates, 2 teaspoons vanilla, 1 cup chopped walnuts, and 2 cups sifted toasted bread crumbs mixed with ½ cup flour, a pinch of salt, and 1 teaspoon of baking powder. Last of all fold in the stiffly beaten whites of 4 eggs.

Place the mixture in a well-buttered oblong cake tin, 7″ by 11″ by 1½″, and bake 25–30 minutes. Take out of oven, cut in 8 pieces, and serve immediately with slightly whipped cream.

## DOBOSCH CAKE
*[Pre-heat oven to 475°]*

**Cake:**
confectioner's sugar
9 egg yolks
7 egg whites
⅞ cup granulated sugar
1¼ cups sifted cake flour
1 teaspoon vanilla
butter or vegetable shortening

**Filling:**
5 squares of unsweetened
    chocolate
7 egg yolks
1⅛ cups powdered sugar
2 tablespoons heavy cream
1 teaspoon vanilla
¼ pound butter

**Glaze:**
2 cups granulated sugar
1 cup cold water

First spread wax paper over a large table and sift a little confectioner's sugar over it. Next turn 3 9-inch cake tins upside down and butter the bottoms lightly (vegetable shortening may be substituted). The paper-thin layers for this cake will be baked on the outside, not the inside of the tins. Now break the yolks of 9 eggs into a big bowl and put 7 of the whites into another bowl. Stir the yolks with a big spoon and add 7⁄8 cup granulated sugar gradually. Keep stirring and beating with a spoon until very thick and creamy, about 20 minutes. Next sift 3 times 1¼ cups sifted cake flour; fold into mixture. Flavor with 1 teaspoon vanilla, and last of all fold in carefully the whites of the 7 eggs, beaten until stiff.

Now spread 2 serving-spoons of batter evenly over the bottom buttered surface of one of the cake tins. The batter should be about ⅛ inch thick and even all over. Place in oven and bake until a light brown, or 2–3 minutes. In the meantime, cover the bottom of another of the pans with batter so that it will be ready to be put into the oven when you remove the first one. When you do remove the first one, remove the thin cake from the pan by running under it a large spatula and then turning it, brown side down, onto the sugared wax paper. Keep calm and loosen the edges first, and endeavor to get the cake off without breaking it. If you do break it, don't worry—the next one will seem easier and practice will prove perfect. Proceed until all the batter has been baked, at which time you should have 12–14 of these ⅛-inch-thick layers of sponge cake.

Put layers together with a thin coating of chocolate filling, one layer piled on top of the other. Start by sprinkling a large cake plate lightly with powdered sugar and lay on it one of the most perfect layers. Keep the most perfect one for the top layer, which should not be covered with the filling. The tablespoon of filling which you would have used for it should, however, be reserved for future use, at which time it will be stirred into a caramel glaze that will be the final touch to the completed cake.

Now proceed with the chocolate filling in the following manner. Put 5 squares of unsweetened chocolate in the top of a small enamel double boiler. Place over hot water on low flame, cover, and let it melt slowly, stirring from time to time. When completely melted, remove from fire until ready to use. In the meantime, break the yolks of 7 eggs into the top of a large enamel double boiler. Stir and add gradually 1⅛ cups confectioner's sugar. When well mixed, place over boiling water and beat with rotary-beater constantly (an electric-beater may be used), until the eggs and sugar are very thick and creamy and feel quite warm (not hot), to the touch—about 7 minutes. Remove from fire and cool, stirring constantly, at which time add gradually the melted chocolate into which you have stirred 2 tablespoons heavy cream. If the cream does strange things to the chocolate, don't worry about it; just add it gradually to the egg yolks and beat well. It will all be smooth and thick when you have added all the chocolate. Flavor with 1 teaspoon vanilla, then into the whole stir ¼ pound butter that you have previously creamed. The filling is now ready to spread. Don't be too generous with the chocolate as you spread it, for it must cover the 12–14 layers—and don't forget to keep out 1 tablespoon for the final glazing.

To make the glaze, put 2 cups granulated sugar in an aluminum saucepan. Moisten it with 1 cup cold water, stir until melted, then wipe down the insides of the pan with a damp cloth or wet pastry brush so that no granules of sugar remain on the sides. Place pan on fire and cook, without stirring, until mixture becomes a light golden brown (320° on the candy thermometer). If crystals form on the inside of the pan as it cooks, wipe them down into the syrup with a wet pastry brush. When done, remove pan from the fire and plunge it immediately into a basin of cold water (this prevents the syrup from continuing to cook, which would cause it to become too dark and overdone). In about 3 minutes it should have cooled sufficiently. Add the reserved tablespoon of chocolate filling and stir with a wooden spoon until well mixed. Pour over the cake covering it with a thin caramel glaze that will harden to the crack stage, which is as it should be. If you work quickly, you will be able to cover the sides of the cake as well as the top, smoothing the glaze on with a spatula knife dipped in boiling water. This is difficult to accomplish perfectly. The cake may be eaten the day it is cooked, but it is even better the day after. When the time comes to cut the cake, be prepared to have the glaze crack unevenly as you cut the slices; it can't be helped, but it will still taste divine.

## HAZELNUT TORTE
[*Pre-heat oven to 500°*]

| | |
|---|---|
| 1 heaping cup hazelnuts | 1⅓ cups granulated sugar |
| 4 egg whites | ½ teaspoon vinegar |
| 1 cup cream | 2 tablespoons powdered sugar |
| 2 teaspoons vanilla | confectioner's sugar |

SERVES 6–8

Put 1 heaping cup hazelnuts in a pan in a hot 500° oven for about 10 minutes, or until the skins crack open and the nuts are lightly browned. Remove from oven, place in tea cloth, and rub them together to loosen the skins. Pick out the nuts and cool. When cold, put them through a nut-grater to powder them. Sift through coarse sieve to remove any large pieces that may have slipped through the grater. Measure out 1½ cups of the resultant powdered nuts. Line 2 layer-cake tins neatly with heavy wax paper. Beat the whites of 4 eggs until stiff, then beat in gradually 1⅓ cups granulated sugar. Continue beating for a few minutes; add 1 teaspoon of vanilla and ½ teaspoon cider vinegar; and beat at least 5 minutes longer. Fold in 1½ cupfuls hazelnut powder, and spread mixture evenly in the 2 paper-lined pans.

Place in *pre-heated slow 350°–375° oven* and bake until firm to the touch and lightly browned, 30–40 minutes, depending on your oven. Remove from oven one at a time; turn out carefully; upside down, on a cake rack; and immediately attempt to pull off the wax paper, working very cautiously. If you find this is difficult, place the rack back in the oven for a few minutes longer to dry out the top surface. In the meantime try removing the paper from the other torte. When both are paper free, place aside until ready to serve, at which time beat 1 cup heavy cream until just barely stiff, sweeten to taste with about 2 tablespoons powdered sugar, and flavor with 1 teaspoon of vanilla. Fold in the remainder of the hazelnut powder and spread between the 2 tortes, placing the first one, bottom side up, on a large round serving-plate and the second, top side up. Sprinkle with confectioner's sugar (in which you have kept a vanilla bean), and serve immediately, cut in pie-shaped pieces.

## LAMB CAKE FOR EASTER

### Equipment and materials:

1 cast-aluminum lamb mold
1 yard pale blue ½-inch-wide
   satin ribbon
1 miniature bell
2 toothpicks
1 7-inch skewer
a few pins

2 sheets typewriter paper
green vegetable coloring
red vegetable coloring
blue vegetable coloring
real or artificial baby roses and
   forget-me-nots

### Batter:

1 pound butter
1 pound granulated sugar
1 pound flour
1 teaspoon vanilla
½ teaspoon lemon extract
½ teaspoon salt
10 eggs

### Twice-cooked frosting:

1½ cups granulated sugar
½ cup water
2 egg whites
⅛ teaspoon cream of tartar
1 teaspoon vanilla
2 cans moist coconut

### Ornamental frosting:

1 cup sifted confectioner's
   sugar
1 egg white
pinch cream of tartar

In order to make this divinely beautiful culinary creation, you must first procure a cast aluminum mold in the shape of a lamb, lying down. These molds come in 2 sections; the bigger half representing the front view of the reclining lamb; the other half, a lid, representing the back view of the lamb. These molds are obtainable at kitchen specialty shops.

When the great day arrives and you are about to make the cake, make sure that you have on hand all the ingredients and all the trimmings listed above. The finished lamb will consist of a pound cake baked in the cast-aluminum mold. The lamb when baked will be frosted with white twice-cooked frosting, on which you sprinkle a goodly amount of shredded coconut to represent the wool. You will trace on the lamb's face 2 pink eyebrows, 2 nostrils, and a mouth, using pink ornamental frosting, and 2 bright blue eyes, made of the same frosting colored blue. Around the base of the lamb will be a bed of green grass made by rubbing a little green coloring into more of the coconut. In the grass you will plant baby pink roses or blue forget-me-nots, or both, and around the neck of the lamb you will tie a yard of ½-inch-wide pale blue satin ribbon to which you have attached a lovely little tinkling bell.

And now for the actual making of the cake. First butter the insides of the mold copiously (both halves), being sure to get down well into all the crevices with plenty of butter. *Pre-heat your oven to 300°.* In the buttered mold you are going to bake a pound cake. The recipe given will be too much batter for the mold, but as long as you are going to the effort of making the cake, you might as well make the whole recipe and bake the rest of the batter in a separate pan. The cake itself is delectable and keeps beautifully (and, besides, once you have made the lamb you will probably be in such a state of rapture over it that the idea of cutting him will be more than you can bear). Once the lamb mold has been well buttered, also butter a loaf-cake pan, 9″ by 5″ by 2½″, before proceeding with the task of mixing the batter for the pound cake (page 446).

When the batter is mixed and ready, fill the larger half of the lamb mold (the face and front half) level full of batter. Place toothpicks horizontal with each ear on top of the batter, and a 7-inch skewer perpendicularly on top of the batter, running from top of the head down to the front feet—these are to reinforce the head and ears to keep them from breaking when the baked cake is removed from the mold. Now place the empty half of the mold carefully on top of the filled mold, so that it is well closed. The batter will rise just sufficiently to fill out the top mold. Place the mold on a flat tin and it is ready to be baked. Put the left-over batter in the buttered loaf-cake pan, and place both cakes in the pre-heated oven to bake slowly about 1 hour and 15 minutes. When they have baked 1 hour and 5 minutes, test the loaf cake with a cake-tester or in the usual manner, and if it is done, remove it from the oven. This will give you some clue to whether the lamb cake is also done. If you think it is, attempt very carefully to lift off the lid. If it comes off easily, the cake is about done. Otherwise, let it remain about 5 minutes longer and try again. By this time, the lid should lift off easily. If necessary remove from the oven and help the process a bit by prying the lid off cautiously with a knife, but the chances are it will come off beautifully.

When the lid has been removed, however, place the cake back in the oven, minus the lid, for 5 minutes to brown it and dry it out a bit. Then remove cake from the oven and let cool completely in the mold before attempting to remove it. In the meantime make a batch of ornamental frosting (page 456), making, however, only one third the recipe, using 1 cup confectioner's sugar and the white of 1 egg, with a tiny pinch of cream of tartar. When it is nice and stiff, cover the bowl with a wet cloth and place in refrigerator until ready to color part of it pink and part of it blue. Also make 2 paper cornucopias, using typewriter paper, and secure them with pins. Snip off the end of each, leaving a very small opening on one and a slightly larger one on the other.

When the lamb has cooled, lift it very carefully out of the mold and get ready for the fun. Take one third of the white ornamental frosting you have made and spread it over the center of a large oval serving-platter, then plant the lamb on this bed and let it set while you proceed with the making of the twice-cooked frosting. Be sure, however, to cover the remaining white ornamental frosting with a wet cloth so that it will not set until you are ready to color and use it.

Make the full amount of twice-cooked frosting (page 457). Then, without getting into a panic, start with the head of the lamb and frost the entire surface with a nice even coat of white frosting. Some of it may drop down onto the platter, but don't worry about it, because this will be covered with green grass. As soon as the lamb is completely frosted, sprinkle the entire body with a heavy coat of coconut, representing the lamb's wool— refraining, however, from putting any over the lamb's face, except a bit between the two ears. In other words, make the lamb look as real as possible.

You are now ready to color some coconut a bright green by rubbing into it a few drops of green vegetable coloring. Sprinkle this carefully around the base of the lamb, covering as much of the platter as possible. By now the twice-cooked frosting should have set sufficiently to allow you to trace the eyes, nose, and mouth onto the lamb's face. To do this, divide the remaining ornamental frosting into 2 parts. Color half of it a bright blue and the other a pretty pink. Put the pink in the cornucopia having the smallest opening, the blue in the other. Now with the pink trace on the face of the lamb a nose, a mouth, and eyebrows where they should be; and, using the blue, make 2 large dots for the eyes. When these have set, put the silver bell on the satin ribbon and tie it around the lamb's neck, making a bow with 2 streamers.

You may now plant the forget-me-nots and baby pink roses here and there in the green grass; or you may use up the remaining pink and blue frosting to imitate flowers in the grass, or to write an Easter message around the rim of the platter. If by now you are not in a state of rapture, I give up!

## EIGHT MERINGUE SWANS

| | |
|---|---|
| 8 egg whites | 1 teaspoon vanilla |
| 2 cups granulated sugar | pinch of salt |

Trace out on heavy tracing-paper (cut to fit 2 15"-by-12" cookie sheets) the five parts, as illustrated, of 8 swans four on each sheet.

Add a pinch of salt to 8 egg whites and beat with rotary-beater until stiff enough to hold a peak; then beat in gradually 1¼ cups granulated sugar, still using rotary-beater. Flavor with

1 teaspoon vanilla and then fold in carefully another ¾ cup sugar. The mixture must be very stiff.

Trace out the heads and necks and wings and tails of the birds with the meringue mixture, using part of the meringue at a time, placed in pastry bag fitted with small no. 27, open-star tip. Squeeze hard with a steady hand so that the meringue shapes will be about ½ inch deep. Change tip on bag to large-star tip and first fashion the 8 ovals about the same depth. Once this is accomplished, build up the sides with at least 2 additional layers making hollow-shape ovals. These represent the bodies of the swans.

When completed, place the pans in *pre-heated oven, set at the very lowest temperature possible.* The meringues should dry out rather than actually cook. Watch carefully and bake until they feel firm to the touch, about 65 minutes. If necessary, turn off the heat temporarily while baking to keep oven at lowest possible temperature, as the swans are prettier if white in color when done. Remove from oven and, with the help of a spatula, loosen from paper as soon as possible.

When ready to assemble, have ready vanilla ice cream with which to fill the bodies. Then insert the neck and head of swan at one end of each, pushing it gently down into the ice cream. Next insert the 2 wings, smooth side in, and last of all insert the tails. Serve at once.

## MILDRED'S CHEESE CAKE

| | |
|---|---|
| 6 egg yolks | ¼ pound butter |
| ¾ cup granulated sugar | pinch of salt |
| juice of 1 lemon | ⅓ cup granulated sugar |
| 2 tablespoons flour | 2 tablespoons cinnamon |
| 2 pounds cream cheese | 6 egg whites |
| 1 cup heavy cream | confectioner's sugar |
| grated rind of 1 lemon | 24 zwieback (1 box) |

For years I had tried to make cheese cake, with no success. I watched, with my own eyes, this recipe being made by Mildred Knopf, and the result was a cheese cake divine.

Put the yolks of 6 eggs in a big bowl. Sit down and put the bowl in your lap and beat the eggs with a big, big spoon; add ¾ cup granulated sugar and stir it well into the yolks. Squeeze the juice of 1 lemon and strain it into the egg and sugar; grate the rind and add it, too. Sift 2 level tablespoons sifted flour into the mixture and stir it in. Put 2 pounds cream cheese into a wooden bowl and mash it with a fork. Add it to the egg-and-sugar mixture, stir with the spoon until blended; and then add 1 cup heavy cream and stir until as smooth as possible. Add a tiny pinch of salt.

Now melt ¼ pound butter. Measure out ⅓ cup granulated sugar and stir into it 2 tablespoons cinnamon. Then roll out on a board 24 zwieback; when fine, place in a bowl and add the sugar and cinnamon. Mix, add the melted butter, and stir well. Now cover first the bottom, then the sides of a spring-form cake tin (2½ inches deep and 10 inches wide) with a thin coating of the crumb mixture, patting it gently on with the fingers and being careful not to have the crumbs too thickly spread.

When this is accomplished—and it does take patience—beat the whites of 6 eggs until stiff, fold them into the cheese mixture, and pour the whole carefully into the mold. Sprinkle the top very lightly with a few more crumbs. Place on rack in center of cold oven. Shut the door, set the regulator to 375°, and bake 1 hour, testing with a straw. When done, turn off the heat, but leave the cake in the oven with the door open to cool off. When almost cold, loosen the edges by running a knife carefully around. When completely cold, remove from oven, unfasten the spring at the side of the pan carefully. Sprinkle the top with confectioner's sugar—and it is ready to serve.


## POUND CAKE

*[Pre-heat oven to 300°]*

| | |
|---|---|
| 2 cups butter (1 pound) | 10 eggs (1 pound) |
| 2 cups granulated sugar (1 pound) | 1 teaspoon vanilla |
| | ½ teaspoon lemon extract |
| 4½ cups sifted flour (1 pound) | ½ teaspoon salt |

Line 2 buttered loaf-cake tins, 9" by 5" by 2½", with buttered white typewriter paper. Sift some cake flour and measure out 4½ cups. Sift twice more with ½ teaspoon salt. Place in sifter ready to sift into the cake batter. Cream until very soft 1 pound butter. Then cream into it gradually 2 cups granulated sugar. When very fluffy and light, add the well-beaten yolks of 10 eggs and beat again until very light. Add gradually 4½ cups sifted flour. When well mixed, flavor with 1 teaspoon vanilla and ½ teaspoon lemon extract. Last of all fold in the whites of 10 eggs, beaten until very stiff. Divide the batter into 2 parts and put it into the loaf-cake tins. Bake slowly for about 70–85 minutes, or until it tests done.

## SOPHIE KERR'S GIGANTIC LADY BALTIMORE CAKE

Having read Sophie's article in a recent Vogue, "Lady Baltimore —book and cake," I couldn't wait to try my hand; and I made it, following her directions. The result was a cake to end all cakes in size and deliciousness. Here is how to make it:

Prepare 1 cup finely cut pecans and put aside another 2 dozen for decorative purposes later on. (Sophie gave us a choice between pecans or walnuts. I chose pecans; you may prefer walnuts.)

Soak 2 cups seeded raisins plus 24 more in ½ cup first-rate brandy for 1 hour. Blanch 12 almonds.

Mix and bake in 3 layers the white cake (page 449). Mix and bake in 2 layers the yellow cake (page 449), adding ¾ cup pecans to the batter.

Make double the recipe for raisin-nut filling (page 452), substituting ¼ cup cut pecans for the walnuts and using 4 times as many raisins, or 2 cups.

When the cakes have cooled, spread the filling between the 5 layers—alternating white with yellow, starting with a white layer and ending up with a white layer. Put 3 long skewers down into the cake to keep the layers from slipping until the cake has been frosted.

Make double the recipe for twice-cooked frosting (page 457), flavoring it with almond extract. Frost sides of cake first and then cover the top, using up the remainder of the frosting and piling it on thick and smoothly. Wait until the frosting is just about to harden on the surface and then add the all-important decorations as follows (removing the skewers first). Place in the center a perfect pecan-half, or a big round ruddy raisin. Put on a ring of blanched almonds and beyond that a ring of brandy-soaked raisins that have been patted dry on paper toweling. The outer ring should be pecans again, and—Sophie goes on to say—as a final fling, you may add a row of silver *dragées*. If you are as pleased as I was to achieve this work of culinary art, you will be very pleased indeed.

## SPICY PUMPKIN CAKE
### [*Pre-heat oven to 350°*]

| | |
|---|---|
| ½ cup butter | 4 teaspoons baking powder |
| 1 cup granulated sugar | 1 teaspoon salt |
| 2 eggs | 2 teaspoons cinnamon |
| ¼ cup milk | ½ teaspoon nutmeg |
| 1 cup cooked pumpkin | ½ teaspoon cloves |
| ½ cup bran | 1 teaspoon vanilla |
| 1¾ cups flour | |

Butter 2 10-inch cake tins. Cream ½ cup butter with 1 cup granulated sugar. When light, add 2 unbeaten eggs and mix well. Combine ¼ cup milk with 1 cup cooked pumpkin and stir into egg-and-sugar mixture. Then add ½ cup bran and mix well. Place 1¾ cups flour in a sifter; add 4 teaspoons baking powder, 1 teaspoon salt, 2 teaspoons cinnamon, and ½ teaspoon cloves; and sift it gradually into the first mixture, beating well after each addition. Flavor with 1 teaspoon vanilla.

Pour mixture into buttered tins and bake until it tests done, about 25–30 minutes. Turn out onto cake plates, sprinkle with confectioner's sugar, and serve while still hot, accompanied by plenty of whipped cream; or turn out onto cake rack and, when cool, ice with twice-cooked vanilla frosting, see (page 457).

## YELLOW LAYER CAKE
*[Pre-heat oven to 375°]*

½ cup butter
1¼ cups granulated sugar
3 egg yolks
3 cups flour
4 teaspoons baking powder

¾ cup of milk
1 teaspoon vanilla
3 egg whites
pinch of salt

Butter 2 layer-cake pans well. Cream ½ cup butter and add to it gradually 1¼ cups granulated sugar. Then add 3 well-beaten egg yolks. Sift 2 cups flour with 4 level teaspoons baking powder. Add flour alternately to the batter with ¾ cup milk. Add 1 teaspoon vanilla. Beat the whites of 3 eggs with a pinch of salt until stiff, not dry, and fold them into the batter. Put batter into 2 tins, dividing it equally. Spread evenly, place pans in moderate oven, and bake until a cake-tester comes out clean, about 20 minutes. Turn out immediately onto cake grills. When cold, frost between layers and on top and sides with chocolate frosting (page 454).

NOTE   Add cut pecans to batter before folding in whites if to be used for Lady Baltimore Cake (page 447).

## WHITE LAYER CAKE
*[Pre-heat oven to 375°]*

½ cup sweet butter
1¼ cups powdered sugar
2 cups sifted flour
2½ teaspoons baking powder

pinch of salt
5 egg whites
1 teaspoon vanilla
½ cup milk

Butter 2 large round layer-cake tins. Prepare 2 cups sifted flour. Sift flour with 2½ teaspoons baking powder. Cream ½ cup sweet butter with 1¼ cups powdered sugar until light and fluffy. Add 1 teaspoon vanilla. Now add a pinch of salt to the whites of 5 eggs

and beat them until stiff, but not dry. Add to the sugar and butter the sifted flour alternately with ½ cup milk. Lastly fold in
the whites. Put into the 2 cake tins and bake about 25 minutes, or
until an inserted straw comes out clean. Turn out immediately
onto cake racks to cool before putting together with chosen filling
and frosting; or frost each separately with caramel frosting (page
454) and out in small pieces as needed to serve with dessert.

## WHITE PLUM CAKE
### [Pre-heat oven to 350°]

| | |
|---|---|
| ½ pound almonds | ½ teaspoon nutmeg |
| ½ pound white raisins | ¼ teaspoon salt |
| ¾ cup butter | 1 teaspoon vanilla |
| 1 cup granulated sugar | ½ teaspoon lemon extract |
| 4 eggs | ¼ cup cold water |
| 2 cups flour | 1 cup shredded coconut |
| 1 teaspoon baking powder | |

Blanch ½ pound almonds, reserve 12 of them for decoration of
the cake, and shred the rest with a sharp knife. Scald ½ pound
white raisins, soak until plump, and then dry well. Cream ¾
cup butter with 1 cup granulated sugar; add the beaten yolks of
4 eggs; and beat well. Sift 2 cups flour with 1 teaspoon baking
powder, ½ teaspoon grated nutmeg, and ¼ teaspoon salt. Put 1
teaspoon vanilla and ½ teaspoon lemon extract in ¼ cup water.
Add it alternately with the flour to the butter-and-egg mixture.

When well mixed, add the raisins and the almonds, which
have been lightly floured, and 1 cup shredded coconut. Now fold
in the stiffly beaten egg whites and pour into a large well-greased
bread tin that has been carefully lined with buttered typewriter
paper. Bake for about 1 hour, or until an inserted straw comes out
clean.

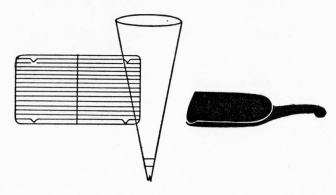

# *Fillings and Frostings*

Not all cakes require a frosting. Angel cake and sponge cake are almost better without frosting. Frosting, however, helps to retain moisture and, when used with fillings, adds to the richness and goodness of many cakes. In many cases, the frosting may also be used as a filling, but in some instances a different filling is desirable. To frost a cake, first brush off the excess crumbs, and be sure the cake is cold. If the cake is a layer cake, spread the bottom layer first with frosting or filling and lay the second layer on top. If more layers are to be used, continue in the same manner. Next, frost the top and sides of the cake with the desired frosting. Heap frosting around the edge of the top of cake, then with spatula spread the frosting over the edge and around the sides of the cake. Put the remaining frosting in the center of the top of the cake and spread with spatula lightly to the edge of the cake. If coconut is to be added, sprinkle it over all while the frosting is still moist.

# *Fillings*

## CHOCOLATE FILLING FOR LAYER CAKE

2 egg yolks
¾ cup granulated sugar
¼ cup milk
½ tablespoon butter

pinch of salt
2 squares unsweetened chocolate
1 teaspoon vanilla

Beat the yolks of 2 eggs until very light. Add ¾ cup granulated sugar and beat until light. Add ¼ cup milk, ½ tablespoon butter, and a pinch of salt. Melt 2 squares unsweetened chocolate in a double boiler. Put the egg-and-sugar mixture in a deep enamel pan and cook, stirring furiously, until it boils up hard. Cook a minute or two, then remove from fire, and stir in the melted chocolate and 1 teaspoon vanilla. Beat until thick and smooth, then spread between layers of cake.

## RAISIN-AND-NUT FILLING FOR LAYER CAKE

¾ cup granulated sugar
3 tablespoons cold water
1 egg white
½ teaspoon vanilla

½ cup chopped seeded or seedless raisins
2 tablespoons chopped walnuts
½ teaspoon lemon extract

Place in the top of an enamel double boiler ¾ cup granulated sugar, the unbeaten white of 1 egg, and 3 tablespoons cold water. Place over boiling water, beat with rotary-beater 7 minutes; remove from fire; and continue beating until very thick and cooled. Then fold in 2 tablespoons chopped walnuts, ½ cup chopped seeded or seedless raisins, and flavor with ½ teaspoon vanilla and ½ teaspoon lemon extract. Spread between layers of cake.

## VANILLA FILLING

4 tablespoons granulated sugar  ½ cup cold milk
4 tablespoons cornstarch  3 egg yolks
1¾ cups hot milk  1 teaspoon vanilla

Mix together in a little bowl 4 tablespoons granulated sugar and 4 tablespoons cornstarch. Add gradually ½ cup cold milk to form a smooth mixture. Heat to boiling point in top of enamel double boiler 1¾ cups milk. Add a little of the hot milk to the sugar-and-cornstarch mixture, then add the cornstarch mixture slowly to the remainder of the hot milk, stirring constantly. Cook over boiling water stirring all the while until well thickened and perfectly smooth. Then cover and cook, stirring occasionally, for 20 minutes. Remove from fire and add a part of the hot cornstarch to the well-beaten yolks of 3 eggs, then add the eggs to the cornstarch and mix well. Cook 1 minute longer, remove from fire, and cool; then flavor with 1 teaspoon vanilla. When completely cold, spread between three layers of cake.

# *Frostings*

## BUTTER CREAM FROSTING

⅛ pound sweet butter  2 cups sifted confectioner's
3–4 tablespoons heavy cream  sugar
 1 teaspoon vanilla

Sift 2 cups confectioner's sugar into a bowl. Heat to scalding point about 4 tablespoons heavy cream and melt in it ⅛ pound sweet butter. Stir the hot cream into the sugar gradually until smooth and of the right consistency to spread. Flavor with 1 teaspoon vanilla and spread on cake. This is especially good for angel cake.

## CARAMEL FROSTING

1 pound light-brown sugar          pinch of salt
¼ pound sweet butter               2 teaspoons vanilla
1 cup heavy cream

Put 1 pound light-brown sugar in an enamel pan and moisten it
with 1 cup heavy cream. Add a tiny pinch of salt and ¼ pound
sweet butter. Place on fire and boil until it forms a soft ball when
dropped into cold water. Remove from fire and add 2 teaspoons
vanilla and cool. Beat with silver spoon until creamy and thick
enough to spread.

## CHOCOLATE FROSTING

4 egg yolks                        pinch of salt
3 cups granulated sugar            8 squares unsweetened choco-
1 cup milk                           late
2 tablespoons butter               2 teaspoons vanilla

Beat the yolks of 4 eggs until light, add 3 cups granulated sugar
gradually, and beat well. Add 1 cup milk, 2 tablespoons butter,
and a tiny pinch of salt. Melt 8 squares unsweetened chocolate
in a double boiler. Cook the first mixture in a deep enamel pan,
stirring hard, until it boils up hard; then cook 2 minutes. Remove
from fire, add the melted chocolate and 2 teaspoons vanilla. Beat
until well mixed and thick enough to spread.

## EASY CHOCOLATE FROSTING

4 squares unsweetened choco-       ⅛ teaspoon salt
   late                            7 tablespoons milk
3 tablespoons butter              1 teaspoon vanilla
3 cups confectioner's sugar

Melt 4 squares unsweetened chocolate and 3 tablespoons butter over hot water. Measure 3 cups sifted confectioner's sugar and add ⅛ teaspoon salt, 7 tablespoons milk, and 1 teaspoon vanilla; blend. Add hot chocolate mixture and mix well. Let stand, stirring occasionally, until of right consistency to spread on cake.

## EXTRA-SPECIAL CHOCOLATE FROSTING

2 eggs
2 cups confectioner's sugar
pinch of salt
1 teaspoon vanilla

¼ cup milk
5 squares unsweetened chocolate
2 tablespoons butter

Break 2 whole eggs into a bowl containing 2 cups confectioner's sugar and a pinch of salt. Add 1 teaspoon vanilla and ¼ cup milk. Beat well, then pack the bowl in another bowl, and surround with ice cubes. Melt 5 squares unsweetened chocolate with 2 tablespoons butter in a little pan over hot water, stirring constantly. Add this gradually to the sugar-and-egg mixture and continue beating with rotary-beater until very thick, about 10 minutes. Spread frosting between and over the top and sides of 2 layers of cake.

## LEMON BUTTER FROSTING

½ cup butter
3 cups sifted confectioner's sugar
1 teaspoon grated lemon peel

2 tablespoons strained lemon juice
½ teaspoon lemon extract
2 tablespoons heavy cream

Cream ½ cup butter with 3 cups sifted confectioner's sugar. Add 1 teaspoon grated lemon peel, 2 tablespoons heavy cream, 2 tablespoons strained lemon juice, and ½ teaspoon lemon extract. When well mixed and smooth, spread between and on top of two-layer cake.

## MOCHA COCOA FROSTING

⅓ cup strong black coffee          4 cups confectioner's sugar
⅓ cup sweet butter                 ½ teaspoon salt
4 tablespoons cocoa                1 teaspoon vanilla

Make ⅓ cup strong black coffee extract or infusion. Cream ⅓ cup sweet butter until very smooth and soft. Sift together 4 tablespoons unsweetened cocoa, 4 cups of confectioner's sugar, and ½ teaspoon salt; add gradually to the butter. Add coffee until of the right consistency to spread. Stir in 1 teaspoon vanilla and spread.

## ORNAMENTAL OR ROYAL ICING

3 egg whites                       ½ teaspoon cream of tartar
1 pound confectioner's sugar       1 drop ultramarine blue vege-
1 dessertspoon strained lemon          table coloring
    juice, or

The following recipe will make enough ornamental icing to decorate a big cake. It is best to separate the whites of eggs 12 hours before using them, keeping them in the refrigerator until ready to use. All utensils must be perfectly clean and free from grease or oil. Use a china, glass, or procelain round-bottomed bowl and a wooden spoon to beat the icing. Sift 1 pound of confectioner's sugar through a fine sieve or sifter kept especially for the purpose—don't use the flour-sifter.

Put 3 unbeaten egg whites in a big bowl, add one third of the sugar, and beat until smooth and creamy. Then add about 1 dessertspoon strained lemon juice, or ½ teaspoon cream of tartar. Add more sugar and beat. Keep on beating, adding the rest of the sugar gradually. Continue beating until the mixture is so thick and firm that, when the spoon is drawn up and out of the mixture, it will leave a peak in the center of the icing which doesn't settle back or topple over. The more you beat it, the lighter and firmer and fluffier it gets, so don't be afraid of beating it too much. When made, cover at once with damp cloth until ready to use.

## TWICE-COOKED FROSTING

½ cup water
1½ cups granulated sugar
2 egg whites

⅛ teaspoon cream of tartar
1 teaspoon vanilla

Boil 1½ cups granulated sugar, moistened with ½ cup of water, until it forms a soft ball in cold water. In the meantime, beat the whites of 2 eggs until stiff, but not dry. Add the cooked syrup slowly to the whites, beating with a rotary-beater, then add ⅛ teaspoon cream of tartar and 1 teaspoon vanilla, and continue beating with a spoon until smooth and thick. Put over boiling water and stir until you feel the spoon grating slightly over the bottom of the bowl, at which time remove from fire and spread immediately over the cake.

## QUALITY FROSTING

1½ cups granulated sugar
1¼ cups light-brown sugar
½ cup boiling water

3 egg whites
1 teaspoon vanilla

Place 1½ cups granulated sugar in a pan; add 1¼ cups light-brown sugar, and moisten with ½ cup boiling water. Cook without stirring until it registers 220° by a candy thermometer. Remove from fire and pour it gradually into the stiffly beaten whites of 3 eggs. Continue beating until cooled. Place over boiling water and cook, stirring constantly, with a silver spoon until spoon makes a gritty sound. Remove from fire and add 1 teaspoon vanilla. Continue beating until cooled and very stiff. Spread between and over 3 layers of white or yellow cake.

# Crêpes and Pancakes

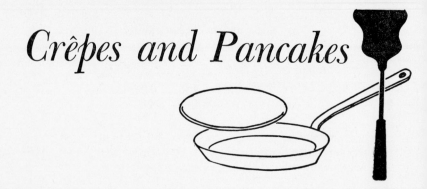

## FRENCH CREPES

2 cups flour
3 eggs
½ teaspoon salt
2 teaspoons granulated sugar

2¼ cups milk
1 teaspoon kirsch, or brandy
1 teaspoon vanilla
⅛ pound butter

SERVES 6–8

Make the batter several hours before you will be ready to cook the crêpes. Sift 2 cups flour into a bowl. Make a hole in the center and break 3 eggs into it; also add ½ teaspoon salt and 2 teaspoons sugar. Add gradually 2¼ cups milk to form a smooth batter. Flavor with 1 teaspoon brandy, or kirsch, and 1 teaspoon vanilla. Place in refrigerator until ready to use.

To make the crêpes, heat a small 5-inch frying-pan and sprinkle it with salt. Scour it out with a paper and wipe clean. Heat the pan, add a small piece of butter, and tilt the pan so that the butter runs all over the bottom. Pour a small quantity of the batter in and tilt immediately, so as barely to cover the bottom of the pan. Don't put in too much batter at a time, for the crêpes must be paper thin. When brown on one side, toss over on the other and cook until brown on that side. Keep warm while you make all the crêpes.

## RAY'S CREPES SOUFFLES

Crêpes:
French crêpe batter (page 458)

Sauce:
6 tablespoons kirsch
4 tablespoons powdered sugar
4 tablespoons butter

Filling:
3 tablespoons butter
3 egg yolks
3 egg whites
1 cup hot milk
2 tablespoons granulated sugar
1 tablespoon heavy cream
½ vanilla bean
3 teaspoons cornstarch
3 teaspoons rice flour
3 teaspoons white flour

SERVES 6–8

Mix the batter following directions for French crêpes (page 458), and when it has stood for several hours, bake the crêpes, piling them one on top of the other until you have used all the batter. When they are all cooked, lift them one by one and pile them on another plate—so that they will not stick together and will be easier to handle in the next process.

In the meantime make the following cream filling. Melt 1 tablespoon butter and add to it 3 teaspoons cornstarch, 3 teaspoons rice flour, and 3 teaspoons white flour. Add to this gradually 1 cup hot milk to make a smooth sauce. Add 2 tablespoons granulated sugar, ½ vanilla bean, and 1 tablespoon heavy cream. Cook in double boiler slowly for 15 minutes, stirring with care so that it will be very smooth. Remove from the fire; add the well-beaten yolks of 3 eggs and 2 tablespoons butter; and last of all fold in the well-beaten whites of 3 eggs.

*Pre-heat the oven to moderate 375°.* Lay the crêpes out on a big board, and put 1 heaping teaspoon of the cream filling in the center of each. Then fold over edges making little cushions. Place them one next to the other on a slightly buttered ovenproof-glass pie plate. Bake in oven 8–10 minutes. Just before serving cover with a little sauce made by heating 6 tablespoons kirsch with 4 tablespoons powdered sugar. Light it, and when it burns out, add little by little 4 tablespoons butter.

## CREPE KENNE SUCRE
### [Pre-heat oven to 450°]

| | |
|---|---|
| 1 box gingerbread mix | ¾ cup confectioner's sugar |
| 1 cup cold water | 1 tablespoon powdered cinna- |
| 4 tablespoons soft sweet butter | mon |
| ¾ cup ginger marmalade | |

Sophie Kerr showed me a fan letter describing some gingerbread-mix pancakes that were concocted some 50 years ago by a fine old colored chef—who would make 200 of them for a high-school party, sometimes sprinkling them with confectioner's sugar and spices. Part of the directions read as follows:

"A gingerbread mix, thin baked crisp, spread with butter and jam, roll in packets 1″ in diameter, for a party can be made ahead and crisped in a hot oven in 8 minutes."

I struggled with 3 different versions (none of which would roll) before I decided that I would be justified in putting the recipe under pancake desserts. It is a strange recipe to say the least, but delicious in the final version—the ginger marmalade touch was Joe's brilliant suggestion.

Butter and flour 3 large cookie sheets. Mix 1 box gingerbread mix, using 1 cup cold water and following directions on box for hand-beaten method. Distribute 6 cakes on each pan, making 18 cakes. Bake until firm to the touch, about 15 minutes, watching carefully as they burn easily. Remove pans from the oven, cover with a tea cloth wrung out in cold water, and allow to steam until cold.

Remove cakes from tins with pancake-turner and spread bottom side up, on wax paper that you have sprinkled with a mixture of confectioner's sugar and 1 tablespoon powdered cinnamon. Spread all of them with soft butter, using 4 tablespoons. Now spread 9 of them with ginger marmalade, using ¾ cup.

Top these with remaining 9 and sprinkle again with cinnamon sugar. Serve at once.

NOTE  These are also very good warmed up in moderate 400° oven—watch carefully as they burn easily.

## APPLE PANCAKE WITH BLUEBERRY SAUCE
*[Pre-heat oven to 450°]*

| Pancakes: | Sauce: |
|---|---|
| 3–4 Mc Intosh or Roman | 2 cups blueberries |
| Beauty apples | ¼ cup granulated sugar |
| juice of 2 lemons | |
| ½ cup all-purpose flour | |
| ¼ teaspoon salt | |
| 2 whole eggs | |
| 1⅓ cups milk | |
| 10 tablespoons butter | |
| ½ cup granulated sugar | |
| ¼ cup powdered cinnamon | |

SERVES 6–8

Peel and core 3–4 apples, preferably Mc Intosh or Roman Beauties, and slice thin. Squeeze over them the juice of 2 lemons. Make a smooth batter by sifting ½ cup all-purpose flour with ¼ teaspoon salt into a small bowl; make a well in the center and break into it 2 whole eggs. Stir with a spoon until smooth and then thin gradually with 1⅓ cups milk.

Heat a very large iron frying-pan on top of the stove. Add 3 tablespoons butter and when melted, cover the surface of the pan with half of the apples. Cook over a moderate flame for 2–3 minutes until apples are slightly transparent; then pour over them half of the batter, being sure that it runs evenly over the apples. Cook over a moderate flame for about 3 minutes, turning the pan so that the pancake cooks evenly all over. Sprinkle generously with a mixture of ½ cup granulated sugar and ¼ cup powdered cinnamon.

Place in pre-heated oven and bake about 6–7 minutes. Have ready a large round hot serving-platter, and with the help of a spatula transfer the pancake onto the platter. Sprinkle again with sugar and cinnamon and a few drops of lemon juice drained from the apples. Dot with 2 tablespoons butter and roll up neatly. Keep warm while you repeat the process. When both pancakes are done, pour over them a hot blueberry sauce, made by cooking 2 cups crushed blueberries with ¼ cup granulated sugar for 10 minutes. Serve at once.

## GERMAN APPLE PANCAKE

### [Pre-heat oven to 450°]

| | |
|---|---|
| 6 eggs | 2 tart apples |
| 1 cup all-purpose flour | 2 lemons |
| 1 teaspoon salt | 1 cup powdered sugar |
| 1 cup milk | 1 tablespoon powdered cinna- |
| ¼ pound butter | mon |

SERVES 6–8

Spread bottom and sides of 2 large 11-inch iron frying-pans with 4 tablespoons butter, dividing it equally. Core and peel 2 large tart apples. Slice them fine and squeeze the juice of 1 lemon over them to prevent them from turning brown while you mix the batter. Break 6 eggs into a bowl and beat until very light with rotary-beater. Add 1 cup all-purpose flour sifted with 1 teaspoon salt. Then add 1 cup milk and beat until smooth and free from lumps.

Pour into the 2 pans, dividing it equally. Cover with the thin slices of apple. Place in hot oven and bake 20–25 minutes, decreasing the heat gradually to 350°. When done they should be well puffed around the sides and nice and brown, but be careful not to allow them to brown too much. Slip out onto 2 large platters, spread with 4 tablespoons soft butter, sprinkle copiously with cinnamon sugar (made of 1 cup confectioner's sugar mixed with 1 tablespoon powdered cinnamon). Squeeze 2 lemons over all and serve at once, cut in pie-shaped pieces.

## AUNT MINNIE'S YANKEE PANCAKES

¾ cup yellow cornmeal
½ cup flour
1½ cups graham (whole
    wheat) flour
½ cup molasses
½ teaspoon salt

2 teaspoons baking powder
2 eggs
¾ cup milk
3 pounds vegetable shortening
    (for frying)

MAKES 3 DOZEN

Mix and sift together ¾ cup yellow cornmeal, ½ cup all-purpose white flour, 1½ cups graham (whole wheat) flour, ½ teaspoon salt, and 2 generous teaspoons baking powder. Beat 2 eggs and stir in ¾ cup milk and ½ cup molasses. Add to dry mixture and stir to make stiff batter. Melt at least 3 pounds fresh vegetable shortening in deep-fat fryer and heat to 370° by the fat thermometer. Drop by teaspoonfuls into the fat, without crowding, and cook until a golden brown. Remove from fat as cooked and drain on paper towels. Cool and sprinkle with confectioner's sugar before eating.

NOTE   In spite of the name, Yankee pancakes are a variety of cruller.

## MY VERSION OF BLINTZES WITH SOUR CREAM AND JAM
*[Pre-heat oven to 400°]*

French crêpes batter
⅛ pound butter
½ cup seedless black raisins
2 8-ounce cartons creamed cot-
    tage cheese
2 tablespoons granulated sugar
½ teaspoon freshly grated
    lemon rind

1 teaspoon vanilla
pinch of salt
1 well-beaten egg
shaker of confectioner's sugar
2 cups sour cream
1½ cups of any preferred jam

SERVES 6–8

Prepare in advance French crêpes batter (page 458); chill until ready to use. Wash ½ cup seedless black raisins, cover with cold water, bring to a boil, drain, and pat dry on paper towel. Put 2 8-ounce cartons creamed cottage cheese through a sieve, add ½ teaspoon freshly grated lemon rind, 2 tablespoons granulated sugar, 1 teaspoon vanilla, a pinch of salt, and stir in 1 well-beaten egg. Fold in the raisins. Have ready a buttered rectangular baking-dish, 12″ by 7½″ by 1½″.

Heat a 7-inch frying-pan, add 1 teaspoon butter, and tilt the pan so that it is buttered all over the inside. Pour about ¼ cup of the batter in the pan when the butter is sizzling hot and tilt the pan so that the batter covers the entire bottom surface of the pan with a thin coating. Cook over moderately hot flame until nice and brown on the bottom, then with the aid of a pancake-turner, or a palette knife, flop the pancake over onto the other side and cook for about ½ minute longer. Transfer this to a large plate, browner side down, and place in the center about 1 heaping tablespoon of the cheese mixture. Fold 2 sides over and then fold ends over making a neat little package of the whole. Place the pancake, smooth side up, in the baking-dish. Repeat the process until you have made 8 or more little packages. Pour over them ⅛ pound sweet butter that has been melted, but not allowed to brown. Place the dish in the pre-heated oven and bake for about 15 minutes, or until well heated through. Send to table accompanied by a sifter of confectioner's sugar—in which you have kept a vanilla bean—to be sifted over the blintzes, and a bowl of your favorite jam and 2 cups sour cream to be eaten with the blintzes.

# Cookies

## CHRISTMAS COOKIES
*[Pre-heat oven to 400°]*

### Cookies:
2 eggs
1½ well-packed cups light-
brown sugar
2 cups flour
½ teaspoon baking soda
1 heaping teaspoon cinnamon
½ teaspoon cloves
1 teaspoon vanilla
1 generous tablespoon molasses
1 tablespoon melted butter
2–3 tablespoons boiling water
½ cup seedless raisins, cut in
two
½ cup almonds, sliced fine

### Icing:
1½ cups sifted confectioner's
sugar
3 tablespoons hot milk
1 teaspoon butter
1 teaspoon vanilla
½ teaspoon or more almond
extract

Prepare ½ cup sliced almonds and ½ cup seedless raisins, cut in two, and flour lightly. Butter 2 large cookie sheets. Break 2 eggs into a bowl, and beat slightly. Add 1½ cups of light-brown sugar and stir. Add 2 cups of flour sifted with 1 heaping teaspoon cinnamon, ½ teaspoon baking soda, and ½ teaspoon cloves. Stir well. Add 1 teaspoon vanilla, 1 generous tablespoon molasses, and 1 tablespoon melted butter. Now add enough boiling water to make the dough on the runny side, 2–3 tablespoons. Last of all add the prepared raisins and nuts. Stir and spread very thin over the 2 cookies sheets. Do not worry if there does not seem to be enough dough to cover; it puffs up and fills in the holes when it bakes. Bake about 10 minutes.

In the meantime prepare the icing. Stir into 1½ cups sifted confectioner's sugar about 3 tablespoons hot milk in which you have melted 1 teaspoon butter. Flavor with 1 teaspoon vanilla and about ½–1 teaspoon almond extract. Spread this over the hot cookies. Cut cookies in squares or diamonds but do not remove from pan until they are cold and the icing has set.


## CHRISTMAS CINNAMON STARS

| | |
|---|---|
| 9 egg whites | grated rind and juice of ½ |
| 1 pound powdered sugar | lemon |
| 2 rounded teaspoons ground | 1 pound shelled almonds |
| cinnamon | ¼ pound granulated sugar |

Beat the whites of 9 eggs until stiff, then add gradually 1 pound powdered sugar, and continue beating for ½ hour with an electric beater. Take out 6 tablespoons of the mixture to ice the cookies with later. Then add to the rest 2 rounded teaspoons of ground cinnamon and the grated rind and juice of ½ lemon. Fold in 1 pound shelled, but not blanched almonds, that have been wiped clean on a cloth and ground fine and powdery with a nut-grinder. Then at the last moment add ¼ pound granulated sugar. Place the mixture in the refrigerator for about 1 hour.

When ready to make the cookies, take out a little of the mixture at a time and put it on a board sprinkled with granulated sugar. Pat or roll out lightly to ⅜-inch thickness, sprinkling the top of the dough lightly with sugar, too. Cut out with a star-cutter and place on lightly buttered and floured cookie sheets. (Dipping the cutter each time in sugar will help to keep the cutter from sticking to the dough.)

Place the cookies in a *pre-heated moderate 325° oven* for 1 hour, or until the cookies lift off easily from the pan. Remove from oven, cool slightly, and then ice them with the whites you have reserved. Place them back in the oven for a few minutes, just long enough to dry out the icing, but not long enough to let them brown at all.

## COCONUT BALLS
### [Pre-heat oven to 300°]

2 egg whites
2 cups granulated sugar

1 teaspoon vanilla
2 boxes dry coconut

Beat the whites of 2 eggs until stiff and beat in gradually ⅔ cup granulated sugar. Flavor with 1 teaspoon vanilla. Add 2 boxes fresh dry coconut and form into 18 balls of uniform size. Place on buttered cookie sheets and bake in pre-heated oven until lightly browned and firm to the touch, or about 30 minutes. Remove from tin with help of a spatula.

## DATE BARS
### [Pre-heat oven to 375°]

¾ cup butter
¾ cup light-brown sugar
1¼ cups rolled oats
1¼ cups cake flour
½ teaspoon baking soda

1 tablespoon cold water
1 pound pitted dates
1 cup water
½ cup granulated sugar
1 teaspoon vanilla

Cream ¾ cup butter with ¾ cup light-brown sugar and work into this 1¼ cups rolled oats and 1¼ cups cake flour that you have sifted with ½ teaspoon baking soda. Moisten with 1 tablespoon cold water. Chill while you prepare the following filling.

Cook together for 5 minutes 1 pound pitted chopped dates, 1 cup water, and ½ cup granulated sugar. Add 1 teaspoon vanilla.

Butter a square cake tin, 8″ by 8″ by 1″. Line the bottom with half of the chilled paste, rolled out. Spread with filling and cover with the rest of the paste. Bake about 25 minutes. Let stand in pan until cool, then cut in squares and turn out.

## FUSS COOKIES
### [Pre-heat oven to 325°]

| | |
|---|---|
| 1 cup butter | 3½ cups sifted cake flour |
| 7 tablespoons granulated sugar | confectioner's sugar |
| pinch of salt | 4 dozen pecans |
| 1 tablespoon vanilla | |

MAKES 4 DOZEN

Cream 1 cup butter with 7 tablespoons granulated sugar. Add a pinch of salt and 1 tablespoon vanilla. Work into this gradually 3½ cups sifted cake flour. This makes a very stiff dough. Make little balls of the dough and place on buttered cookie sheets. Place a pecan in the center of each, or a dab of jelly. Bake in oven until a light brown. Sprinkle with confectioner's sugar.

## LADYFINGERS
### [Preheat oven to 450°]

| | |
|---|---|
| 2 eggs | 1 teaspoon vanilla |
| 5 extra egg yolks | few drops lemon extract |
| 1 cup flour | powdered sugar |
| 1 teaspoon baking powder | confectioner's sugar |
| ½ cup granulated sugar | |

Put 2 whole eggs and 5 extra yolks into the top of a large enamel double boiler. Have ready 1 cup flour sifted with 1 level teaspoon baking powder. Add ½ cup granulated sugar to the eggs and beat with rotary-beater just long enough to mix. Place pan over hot water and continue beating until the mixture feels luke-warm. Remove from fire and continue beating until mixture will stick to finger without dripping off when finger is inserted and withdrawn. Now add 1 teaspoon vanilla and a few drops of lemon extract. Fold in the sifted flour, using a large spoon or a wire whisk.

Put all but ½ cup of batter in a pastry bag that has a large plain round tube. Squeeze out in 3-inch strips (not too close together) onto cookie sheets covered with typewriter paper. Work quickly. Sift powdered sugar over all and place in a pre-heated oven. Bake for about 5 minutes, or until a very delicate brown. They should still feel soft to the touch when ready to be taken out of the oven. Cool slightly, then turn the sheets of paper upside down and wet the backs. Turn sheets right side up and with the aid of a knife remove the ladyfingers, sticking them together two by two with the reserved batter as you remove them. When all baked and stuck together, sprinkle lightly with confectioner's sugar. The recipe makes about 3 dozen whole ladyfingers.

## MATRIMONY COOKIES

| Filling: | Pastry: |
|---|---|
| 1 cup water | 1½ cups uncooked oatmeal |
| ¾ cup light-brown sugar | 1 cup granulated sugar |
| 1 6½-ounce package pitted dates | 1 teaspoon soda |
| | 1 pinch salt |
| ½ cup chopped pecans (optional) | ½ cup butter |
| | 1 teaspoon vanilla |
| | 1½ cups sifted flour |

First make the filling. Cut the dates with scissors that you dip occasionally in hot water. Pour over dates ¾ cup light-brown sugar and 1 cup water. Place on moderate flame and cook, stirring frequently, until thick, 15–20 minutes. Remove from flame and cool. Add ½ cup chopped pecans, if a richer filling is desired.

Now mix the pastry. Reduce 1½ cups uncooked oatmeal to a flour consistency by putting it through a meat-grinder, using

a medium blade. Add 1½ cups white sifted flour,—sifted again
with 1 teaspoon baking soda—1 cup granulated sugar, and a
pinch of salt. Mix well with a fork, then work in with your finger
tips ½ cup soft butter. Sprinkle with 1 teaspoon vanilla. This
should make a rather dry mixture. Put half of it into a square
8-inch cake pan and pat it evenly over the bottom. Spread the
cooled date mixture evenly over the entire surface. Cover with
the remaining pastry mixture and pat it firmly until evenly dis-
tributed. Place in *pre-heated 350° oven* and bake until done,
25–35 minutes. Cut into 16 squares while still warm, but do not
remove from pan until cold.

## PECAN FINGERS
*[Pre-heat oven to 350°]*

### Cake:
1 cup flour
¾ cup sugar
1½ teaspoons double-acting
    baking powder
½ teaspoon salt
¼ cup vegetable oil
3 egg yolks
½ cup cold water
1 teaspoon vanilla
1 teaspoon grated lemon rind
½ cup egg whites
¼ teaspoon cream of tartar

### Frosting:
2 cups finely chopped pecans
½ cup butter
3 cups sifted confectioner's
    sugar
⅓ cup heavy cream
2 teaspoons vanilla

Sift together into a mixing bowl 1 cup flour, ¾ cup granulated
sugar, 1½ teaspoons double-acting baking powder, and ½ teaspoon salt. Make a well in center and add in order ¼ cup vegetable oil, 3 egg yolks, and ⅜ cup cold water. Beat with spoon
until smooth. Place ½ cup egg whites in a big bowl, add ¼ teaspoon cream of tartar, and whip until it forms very stiff peaks.
Pour egg-yolk mixture gradually over egg whites, gently folding
with rubber-scraper until just blended. Do not stir. Pour into

ungreased deep square pan, 8″ by 8″ by 2″. Bake 30 minutes. Immediately turn pan upside down, resting edges of pan on 2 other pans. Let hang until cold. Loosen from edge of pan and turn out on wax paper. Cut cake in 1-inch slices, then in two, making 16 pieces. Frost on all sides and ends with the frosting and roll in finely chopped pecans.

To make the browned-butter frosting, melt ½ cup butter over low heat until a light golden brown. Remove from heat, blend in 3 cups sifted confectioner's sugar, and moisten with 2 teaspoons vanilla and about ⅓ cup heavy cream.

## RAISIN SQUARES
### [Pre-heat oven to 375°]

| | |
|---|---|
| 1½ cups seedless raisins | Pastry: |
| ¼ cup granulated sugar | ¾ cup butter |
| ½ cup water | ¾ cup light-brown sugar |
| rind of ½ lemon | 1¼ cups rolled oats |
| ¼ cup chopped pecans, or walnuts | 1¼ cups cake flour |
| | ½ teaspoon baking soda |
| | 1 tablespoon water |

Make the same pastry as for date bars (page 467). Prepare the following filling. Cook together for a few minutes 1½ cups seedless raisins, ¼ cup granulated sugar, ½ cup water, and the thin rind from ½ lemon. Cool and run through grinder, using medium blade. At this point, mix in ¼ cup chopped pecans, or walnuts. Spread between 2 layers of paste, and bake about 25 minutes. Cool, then cut in squares, and turn out.

## VANILLA KISSES OR MERINGUES
### [Pre-heat oven to 250°]

| | |
|---|---|
| 3 egg whites | 1 teaspoon vanilla |
| ¾ cup powdered sugar | |

Put the whites of 3 eggs into a bowl and beat with rotary-beater until stiff; then add gradually ½ cup powdered sugar, beating constantly. Sprinkle with 1 teaspoon vanilla and beat again; then add another ¼ cup of powdered sugar and beat still longer, or until very stiff. Drop in oval-shaped mounds onto typewriter paper covering 2 long cookie sheets. Make about 12 large ovals if you are going to use the meringues for meringue glacés, or make about 24 if you are to use them as little cakes to serve with dessert or tea. Sift a very little extra powdered sugar over all and blow off the excess sugar.

Place tins in pre-heated very slow 250° oven to bake until they may be easily lifted from the paper and are a delicate brown, or 1–1¼ hours in all. If you have any difficulty removing them from the paper, lay the papers for a second on a wet cloth to dampen the paper a bit. Then, using a spatula, try again; they should come off with no difficulty. If you like a moist meringue, cook them slightly less.

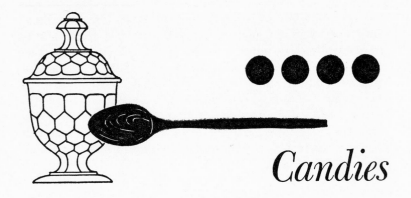

# Candies

## CHOCOLATE BOUCHEES

| | |
|---|---|
| 3 6-ounce packages semi-sweet chocolate morsels | ½ cup shelled almonds |
| 1¼ cups granulated sugar | ½ cup shelled hazelnuts |
| | 1 teaspoon vanilla |

Wipe clean on a cloth ½ cup shelled almonds and ½ cup shelled hazelnuts. Put into a heavy aluminum frying-pan and sprinkle over them 1¼ cups granulated sugar.

Place pan on a moderate flame and let the sugar melt and caramelize. Poke the nuts occasionally with a wooden spoon and tilt the pan constantly back and forth as the sugar melts. Avoid stirring, and don't allow the sugar to get too brown. When every bit of sugar has melted, the skins on the nuts have begun to crack open, and the sugar has become a golden brown syrup, remove from fire. Pour out immediately onto a lightly buttered cookie sheet, spreading it out with a wooden spoon. Let it become quite cold and brittle.

The next step is to reduce the nuts and caramel to a paste. Break the caramel into small pieces, and put it through the meat-grinder, using the coarsest blade. Replace this blade with the medium blade and put the whole through the grinder again. Replace the medium blade with the finest blade and repeat the grinding process. Now add to this mixture ⅓ cup semi-sweet chocolate morsels, distributing them evenly through the mixture; then put it through the grinder for the fourth time, still using the finest blade. And now that that is done, I hate to tell you but it all has to be gone through again for the fifth and last time. When accomplished, sprinkle the now slightly oily mixture with 1 teaspoon vanilla and form the mixture into 13 big balls (about the size of golf balls). Why 13? So that you can sample one of bouchées when they are done and still have a dozen.

Place them on a buttered tin in a cool place (but not in the refrigerator) for a couple of hours to harden up a bit, at which time place 2 packages semi-sweet chocolate morsels in the top of a double boiler over warm water, registering not more than 120° by the candy thermometer. Stir constantly until the chocolate has completely melted. This will take a long time, half an hour or so. Do not place the double boiler over a flame but if the water cools too much, add a little more hot water to the cooled water. When the chocolate has completely melted stir it for a few seconds longer.

Then, working in a cool room free from drafts, dip the chocolate-nut balls into the melted chocolate one at a time, rolling them around with the fingers or a fork until coated all over. Drop them onto a cooky sheet covered with wax paper, endeavoring to make a little curl on top of each. When the chocolate coating has set, wrap each bouchée in aluminum foil and place in cool place until ready to eat, which should be as soon as possible.

## NOUGAT DE MONTELIMAR

1 1-pound, 1-ounce jar pure
   light honey
2 cups granulated sugar
½ cup cold water
½ pound shelled blanched
   almonds (about 1½ cups)

1 teaspoon vanilla
½ cup unsalted pistacho nuts
½ cup toasted hazelnuts
5 large sheet wafers
3 egg whites

Have ready 2 shallow square tins, 7½" by 7½" by 1", lined on the bottom and sides with sheet wafers. Also have ready 2 extra sheet wafers, cut 7½" by 7½", which will be used as top coatings to the nougat. Next, put ½ pound (about 1½ cups) previously blanched and dried almonds in a shallow pan and place in 375° oven for about 10 minutes or until crisp and ever so lightly toasted. Be careful not to brown them too much. Remove from the oven and cut each in three pieces. Keep warm. Also have ready ¼ cup blanched unsalted pistacho nuts and ½ cup lightly toasted hazelnuts from which you have rubbed off as much of the husks as possible.

Now put the contents of a 1-pound, 1-ounce jar pure light honey in a heavy aluminum pan and place on low flame, and cook, stirring frequently with a wooden spoon until it reaches the hard crack stage, or registers 290° by the candy thermometer. Remove from fire and pour it slowly onto the well-beaten whites of 3 eggs, beating constantly—preferably with an electric-beater. When all the honey has been incorporated, and well mixed, stop beating long enough to place in a small heavy aluminum pan 2 cups granulated sugar moistened with ½ cup cold water on the fire to cook until it in turn registers 290° by the thermometer. While it is cooking, continue beating the honey-and-egg mixture. When the sugar syrup has reached the right stage, pour it gradually into the honey-and-egg mixture, beating constantly. Continue beating until cooled and very stiff. Add 1 teaspoon vanilla, the warm crisp almonds, the pistachos, and the hazelnuts. Continue beating with a silver spoon until you can't beat any more; then pour carefully into the 2 pans lined with wafer sheets. Cover the top of each with a large square of wafer sheet and let it settle awhile. Place a piece of heavy wax paper over each and a square pan of the same dimensions on top of each and weight them lightly with a small book or two.

Place in cold room for 24 hours before attempting to cut the nougat, at which time turn out carefully onto a wooden board and, using a heavy knife, cut each square of nougat into 16 smaller squares. Have ready 8 dozen pieces of sheet wafers, cut ¾″ wide by 2″ long. Place these on all the exposed sticky sides of the squares of nougat. Then wrap each piece neatly and amply in pieces of heavy wax paper, cut approximately 6″ by 7″. Pack the squares in a box lined with heavy wax paper and keep in cold place until ready to eat.

# Index

Alaska, Blazing, Baked, 393–4
Albondigas, 27
Alice's:
Gold and White Angel Cake,
428–9
Peach Schaum Torte, 415–16
Almond:
and Apricot Jam Soufflé, 356
Curried, 6–7
Amber Sauce, Audrey's, 401
Angel Cake:
Alice's Gold and White, 428–9
Chocolate, 430–1
Angel Pie, 373–4
Antipasto, Italian, 4
Apple:
Boiled Dumplings, 408
Charlotte, 407–8
German Pancakes, 462
Pancakes with Blueberry
Sauce, 461–2
Pie, 365–6
Apricots:
Canned, with Apricot Jam and
Kirsch, 409–10
Diable, 409
Gelatin, 410–11
Granite, 395–6
Jam and Almond Soufflé, 356
Jam Sauce, 400
Jam Soufflé, 356–7
Pastries, 374–5
Upsidedown Cake, 429–30

Asparagus:
Asperges en Petits Pois, 258–9
Hot Boiled, 258
Salad, 309–10
Soup, 28
Asperges en Petits Pois, 258–9
Aspic:
Crystal-clear, 60
Quick, 309–10
and Veal Chops, 160–1
Audrey's:
Amber Sauce, 401
Butterscotch Sauce, 400–1
Aunt Minnie's Yankee Pancakes,
463
Autre Pâté "Vieu-Logi," 189–90
Avocado:
and Endive Salad, 311
à la Tahiti, 9–10

Bacon, with Cheese Scramble, 54
Bananas:
Baked with Coconut Cream,
410
Caramelized, 214–15
Ice Cream, 386–7
Bangkok Curried Lobster, 93
Bass, Striped:
Baked, 79–80
Boiled, 78–9
Bavarian Cream:
Chocolate, 327

Bavarian Cream (continued)
Coffee, 327–8
Ginger, 329
Orange, 329–30
Praline, 330–1
Strawberry, 332
Bay Scallops Almondine, 100–1
Beans:
Boiled, with Potato Salad,
11–12
Flageolets, 269–70
Lima, Purée, 261
Red Kidney, Marion's Mexi-
can Bean Loaf, 262–3
Red Kidney, Marion's Spiced
Spanish, 261–2
Red Kidney, in Red Wine,
260–1
String, Almondine, 263–4
String, Chopped and
Creamed, 265
String, Salad, 314
White, Boiled, with Truffles,
259
White, Purée, 260
Béarnaise Sauce, 298
in Electric Blender, 299
with Lamb, 149–50
Beef:
Boiled Corned-Beef Dinner,
136–7
à la Bourguignonne, 127–9
Broth, 29
en Daube, 130–1
Fillet en Croute, 125–7
Filletini Arrosto, 133–4
Marinated Fried Steak, 138–9
à la Mode, 132–3
Moist Corned-Beef Hash, 138
Paul's Stew, 134–5
Pot au Feu, 124–5

Beef (continued)
Pot Roast, 135–6
Roast, 123–4
Sirloin in Wine Sauce, 141
Steak au Poivre, Le, 141–2
Stroganoff, 129–30
Tamale Pie, 139–40
Beets, Harvard:
Chopped and Creamed, 265
Divine, 265
Bill Chan's Chicken in Foil, 22
Black Raspberry Ice, 396
Black-walnut:
Cake, 430
Sauce, on Sardines, 4–5
Blackberry Ice Cream, 385
Blanc-mange, 331–2
Blanquette of Veal, 162–3
Blender (Electric) Recipes:
Hollandaise Sauce, 301–2
Mayonnaise, 320–1
Sauce Béarnaise, 299
Blini with Caviar and Sour
Cream, 14–15
Blintzes, 463–4
Blue Fish, Baked, 81–2
Bonita, Baked, 82
Borsch:
Brian Connelly's, 30–1
Salmon Natasha, 97–8
Bread:
French, Buttered, 20
Pudding, 345
Pudding, Erma's, 64–5
Brian Connelly's:
Bangkok Siamese Chicken
Curry, 217–18
Borsch, 30–1
Marquise au Chocolate, 333
Rice and Shrimp, 106–7
Brulée, Crème, 334–5

Brussels Sprouts with Caraway Seeds, 266
Butter Cream Frosting, 453
Butterscotch:
Pecan Pie, 368
Sauce, Audrey's, 400–1

Cabbage:
Cole Slaw, 310
Mother's Moonlight, 264
Cakes:
Alice's Gold and White Angel, 428–9
Apricot Upsidedown, 429–30
Black-walnut, 430
Chocolate Angel, 430–1
Chocolate Coated Pavé de Marrons, 432–3
Chocolate Layer with Chocolate Frosting, 431
Coconut, Chef Kina's Royal Hawaiian Fresh, 434–5
Coconut Tea, 433–4
Date Torte, 436
Dobosch, 436–9
Hazelnut Torte, 439–40
Lady Baltimore, Sophie Kerr's, 447–8
Lamb, for Easter, 440–3
Meringue Swans, 443–5
Mildred's Cheese Cake, 445–6
Pound, 446–7
Pumpkin, Spicy, 448
White Layer, 449–50
White Plum, 450
Yellow Layer, 449
Caldillo de Pescado, 82–3
Calf's Liver, 186–7
Canapés, see Hors d'œuvres

Canards:
aux Navets, Braised, 238–9
aux Olives, 239–40
Candies:
Chocolate Bouchées, 473–4
Nougat de Montelimar, 474–5
Caneton aux Petits Pois, 240–1
Cannelloni, 62–3
Capons, Boned Roast Stuffed, 226–7
Caramel:
Frosting, 454
Ice Cream, 388–9
Pots de Crème, 340
Rice Pudding, 346–7
Upsidedown Custard, 343
Caramelized:
Bananas, 214–15
Mold, How to Make, 325–6
Syrup, How to Make, 326
Caraway-seed Soufflé, 54–5
Carrots:
Mashed, 267
Spanish, 267
Vichy, 266–7
Cassoulet, 182–4
Catherine's Soup, 29–30
Cauliflower with Cream Sauce, 268
Caviar:
with Blini and Sour Cream, 14–15
Fresh, on Toast, 15
Celery Root in Mustard, 10
Charles Hazard Durfee's Johnny Cake, 64
Cheddar-Cheese Soup, 31–2
Cheese:
Bread Pudding, 64–5
Cake, Mildred's, 445–6
and Rice Soufflé 71–2

Cheese (continued)
  Sauce, 56
  Scramble with Bacon, 54
  Soufflé, 56
  Soufflés, Petite, 55
  Soup, 31-2
Cherries in Mounds, 411
Chess Tartlets, 376-7
Chicken:
  Boiled, 197-8
  Boned, Stuffed, 226-7
  Boned, Stuffed Breasts,
    Olivette, 205-6
  Breasts with Corn and Cream,
    204-5
  Brian Connelly's Bangkok
    Siamese Curry, 217-18
  en Cocotte, 203-4
  Cold Boiled, Yorkshire Style,
    198-9
  Curry, 213-14
  Curry, Cold, 212-13
  Custard, Baked, 208-9
  in Foil, 22
  Fried, with Cream Gravy,
    209-10
  Gogi's, with Walnuts, 252-3
  Gumbo, 206-8
  Liver Dressing, 317-18
  Liver Pâté, 21
  Persian, 224-6
  Poulet à l'Estragon, 215-16
  Poulet Fondue à la Crème,
    210-11
  Poulet à l'Oseille, 219-20
  Poulet Parton, 216
  Revised Poulet Fondue à la
    Crème, 211-12
  Roast, with Gravy, 200-1
  Roast, with Sauce Piani, 201-2

Chicken (continued)
  Roast, Stuffed with Noodles,
    202-3
  Sauté Archiduc, 220-1
  Tart, Fancy, 221-4
Chive-and-butter Sauce, 199-200
Chocolate:
  Almond Pudding, 347-8
  Angel Cake, 430-1
  Bavarian Cream, 327
  Bouchées, 473-4
  Brian Connelly's Marquise au
    Chocolat, 333
  Cups with Frozen Filling,
    394-5
  Custard Sauce, 402
  Filling for Layer Cake, 452
  Frosting, 454
  Frosting, Easy, 454-5
  Frosting, Extra-special, 455
  Ice Cream, 388
  Layer Cake with Chocolate
    Frosting, 431
  Mousse, Super-superlative,
    342-3
  Pavé de Marrons, Coated,
    432-3
  Pots de Crème, 339
  Praline Soufflé, 358
  Pudding, Rich, 351-2
  Sauce, Hot, 402-3
  Soufflé, 357-8
  Soufflé, Cold, 359-60
Chowder, 41-2
  see also Soup
Christmas:
  Cinnamon Stars, 466-7
  Cookies, 465-6
Coconut:
  Balls, 467

Coconut (continued)
  Cake, Chef Kina's Royal
    Hawaiian, 434–5
  Cream Sauce, 401–2
  Custard Pie, 367–8
  Ice Cream, 389–90
  and Marmalade Soufflé, 358–9
  Tea Cake, 433
Codfish, Cold Boiled, 83–4
Cœur à la Crème, 333–4
Coffee:
  Barvarian Cream, 327–8
  Caramel Parfait, in Refrigera-
    tor, 390–1
  Custard Sauce, 403–4
  Granite, 396–7
  Ice Cream with Grated Choc-
    olate, 387–8
  Jelly with Rum Sauce, 334
  Pots de Crème, 340
  Ray's Sauce for Ice Cream,
    403
Colache, 285
Cole Slaw, 310
Compote of Fruit, 426
Cookies:
  Christmas, 465
  Christmas Cinnamon, 466–7
  Coconut Balls, 467
  Date Bars, 467–8
  Fuss, 468
  Ladyfingers, 468–9
  Matrimony, 469–70
  Pecan Fingers, 470–1
  Raisin Squares, 471
  Vanilla Kisses or Meringues,
    471–2
Corn:
  Baked, 268
  Bread, Thin, 268

Corn (continued)
  Pudding with Buttered
    Crumbs, 269
Corned Beef:
  Dinner, Boiled, 136–7
  Hash, Moist, 138
Corn-meal Crisps, 40–1
Crabmeat:
  Baked, 84–5
  Cold Sauce for, 291–2
Crabs:
  Creole Crêpes, 85–6
  Soft-shelled, Sautéed, 86–7
Cranberry:
  Pie, 369
  Sauce de Luxe, 292
Cream-cheese and Caper
    Spread, 5
Cream-of-tapioca Veal Broth, 33
Cream Sauce, 291–2
  with Egg, Beaten, 404
  with Hard-boiled Egg, 297–8
Creams and Custards:
  Baked Custard with Caramel
    Glaze, 328–9
  Blanc-mange, 331–2
  Brian Connelly's Marquise au
    Chocolat, 333
  Caramel Pots de Crème, 340
  Chocolate Bavarian, 327
  Chocolate Mousse, Super-
    superlative, 342–3
  Chocolate Pots de Crème, 339
  Cœur à la Crème, 333–4
  Coffee Bavarian, 327–8
  Coffee Jelly with Rum Sauce,
    334
  Coffee Pots de Crème, 340
  Crème Brulée, 334–5
  Dick's Syllabub, 341–2
  Floating Gateau Praline, 335–6

Creams and Custards (continued)
Floating Heart, 337
Floating Island, 338
Gateau Malakoff, 336–7
Ginger Bavarian, 329
How to Caramelize and Mold,
325–6
How to Make Caramelized
Syrup, 326
How to Make Praline Powder,
326–7
Orange Bavarian, 329–30
Paul's Hazelnut Cream, 338–9
Praline Bavarian, 330–1
Ratafia Cream, 342
Strawberry Bavarian, 332
Upsidedown Caramel Custard,
343
Vanilla Pots de Crème, 340–1
Zabaglione, 343–4
Crème Brulée, 334–5
Creole Crab Crêpes, 85–6
Crêpes:
Creole Crab, 85–6
French, 458
Kenne Sucre, 460
Soufflés, Ray's, 459–60
Crisps, Corn-meal, 40–1
Cucumber:
Jelly with Shrimp, 105–6
in Sour Cream, 8
and Tomatoes, 8–9
Curry:
Almonds, 6–7
Chicken, 213–14
Chicken, Bangkok, 217–18
Chicken, Cold, 212–13
Eggs, Hard-boiled, 11, 57–9
Eggs and Water-cress Salad,
310–11
Gnocchi, 66–7

Curry (continued)
Guinea Hens, 247–8
Lamb, 151
Lamb, Noisettes of, 152–3
Lobster, Bangkok, 93
Sauce, with Hard-boiled Egg,
294
Shrimp, 3
Veal Chops, 164–5
Custard:
Baked with Caramel Glaze,
328–9
Sauce, 404–5
Tart, 378–9
see also Creams and Custards

Date:
Bars, 467–8
Torte, 436
Délices du Printemps, Joe's,
422–3
Desserts, Fruit:
Apple Charlotte, 407–8
Apple Dumplings, Boiled, 408
Apricot Gelatin, 410–11
Apricots Canned, with Apricot
Jam and Kirsch, 409–10
Apricots Diable, 409
Bananas, Baked, with Coconut
Cream, 410
Cherries in Mounds, 411
Compote, 426
Délices du Printemps, Joe's,
422–3
Figs, Ripe, with Honey and
Cream, 411–12
Grapes, Sugared, 412
Mixed, 427

Desserts, Fruit (continued)
Orange Jelly, Fresh, with Orange and Grapefruit Sections, 414
Orange and Rice Gelatin Delight, 414–15
Oranges with Caramel and Pecans, 412–13
Oranges with Orange Cream, Marty's, 413–14
Peach Schaum Torte, Alice's, 415–16
Peaches, Canned, with Raspberry Preserve Sauce, 417
Peaches, Hot, with Kirsch and Almonds, 416
Pears with Cheese, 417
Pears in Cointreau with Frozen Cream, 418
Pears à la Cuillere, 417
Pears, Sliced Raw, in Orange Juice and Curaçao, 418–19
Pineapple, Fresh, in Kirsch, 420
Pineapple with Peeled Green Grapes and Kirsch, 419
Plums, Sliced Ace, 419–20
Raspberries in Raspberry Sauce, 421
Raspberry Gelatin with Raspberry Sauce, 421–2
Strawberries, Heavenly, 423
Strawberries in Mounds, 411
Strawberries, Plump, 424
Strawberries with Strawberry Jam, 422
Strawberry Cottage Pudding, Kay's, 424–5
Watermelon Filled with Fruit and Champagne, 425–6
Deviled Pecans, 6

Dick's Syllabub, 341–2
Dijonnaise Sauce, 300
Dobosch Cake, 436–9
Duck:
Braised Canards aux Navets, 238–9
Canards aux Olives, 239–40
Caneton aux Petits Pois, 240–1
Jellied, à l'Orange, 242–3
Dusty's Mississippi Seafood Gumbo, 115

Eggs:
Baked in Custard, 53–4
Curried, Hard-boiled, 11, 57–9
Dressing, 319
Jellied, 59–60
Lila's, Tarragon, 312–13
Sautéed, Hard-boiled, 63–4
and Water-cress Salad, Curried, 310–11
Eleanor's Fried Swordfish Steaks, 108–9
Electric Blender Recipes, see Blender, Electric
Endives:
and Avocado Salad, 311
Braised, on a Bed of Mushrooms, 270–2
Erma's Cheese Bread Pudding, 64–5
Escalopes de Veau à l'Estragon, 165–6

Figs:
Pudding, 348–9
Ripe, with Honey and Cream, 411–12
Ripe, with Prosciutto, 13
Fillet de Bœuf en Croute, 125–7
Filletini Arrosto, 133–4

Fillings, Cake:
  Chocolate, 452
  Raisin and Nut, 452
  Vanilla, 453
Fish:
  in Aspic with Water-cress
    Sauce, 110–12
  Boiled, 77–8
  Chowder, 41–2
  and Dill Soufflé, 90
  and Mushroom Custard, 89–90
Flageolets, Dried, 269–70
Floating:
  Gateau Praline, 335–6
  Heart, 337
  Island, 338
Flounder:
  Baked Fillets, 88
  Goujonettes, 87–8
Foie Gras, 22–3
French:
  Bread, Buttered, 20
  Crêpes, 458
  Ice Cream with Cinnamon or
    Kirsch, 386
  Vanilla Ice Cream, 387
  Salad Dressing, Basic, 318
Fresno Ham Steaks, 181
Frostings:
  Butter Cream, 453
  Caramel, 454
  Chocolate, 454
  Chocolate, Easy, 454–5
  Chocolate, Extra-special, 455
  Lemon Butter, 455
  Mocha Cocoa, 456
  Ornamental or Royal, 456–7
  Quality, 457
  Twice-cooked, 457
Frozen Cream Sauce, 405

Frozen Desserts, 381–2
  Chocolate Cups with Fro-
    zen Filling, 394–5
  Foundation Recipes, 384
  General Directions, 383–4
  How to Make 28° Syrup, 384
Fruit Desserts, see Desserts,
  Fruit
Fruit Tartlets, 379–80
Fuss Cookies, 468

Gabrielle's Cabbage, Potato,
  and Sausage Dish, 185–6
Galette:
  with Blazing Mincemeat,
    377–8
  Foure de Crème Patisserie,
    375–6
Galotsie Polonaise, 184
Game, Bread Sauce for, 290
Gateau:
  Malakoff, 336–7
  Praline, Floating, 335
Gazpacho, 34–5
Gigot de Sept Heures (Gigot à
  la Cuillere), 148–9
Ginger:
  Bavarian Cream, 329
  Ice Cream, 391
  Sauce, 295
Gnocchi, 65
  Curried, 66–7
  Tartlets, 18–19
Gogi's Pheasants or Chickens
  with Walnuts, 252–3
Goose:
  Liver, Hot, 22–3
  Roast with Sage and Onion
    Stuffing, 244–5
Goujonettes of Flounder, 87–8

Graham-cracker Pudding, 346
Grandmother Schaffner's Potato
    Salad, 311–12
Grapefruit Sherbet, in Refrigera-
    tor, 399
Grapes, Sugared, 412
Greek Rice Soup, 35–6
Green Peppers, Marinated, 13–
    14
Guacamole, Tomatoes, 9
Guinea Hen:
    with Black-walnut-and-bread
        Stuffing, 246–7
    Curried, 247–8
Gumbo:
    Chicken, 206–8
    Mississippi Seafood, 115–16


Ham:
    Baked, in Crust of Dough,
        177–8
    Boiled, with Greens, 178–9
    Cassoulet, 183–4
    Galotsie Polonaise, 184
    Sauce for, 299–300
    Sauce, on Rice Pancakes, 72–3
    Steaks, Fresno, 181
    Steaks and Hominy in Cream,
        180–1
    and Veal Roast Rolled, 170–1
Haricot d'Agneau, 154–5
Hazelnut:
    Cream, Paul's, 338–9
    Torte, 439–40
Herb:
    Dressing, 319
    Sauce, Creamed, 292–3
Hollandaise, 300–1
    in Electric Blender, 301–2

Hominy:
    Grits, Boiled, 272
    and Ham Steaks in Cream,
        180–1
Honeydew Melon à la Venise,
    12
Hors d'œuvres:
    Almonds, Curried, 6–7
    Avocados à la Tahiti, 9–10
    Beans and Potato Salad, 11–
        12
    Blini, 14–15
    Caviar, Fresh, 15
    Celery Root in Mustard, 10
    Chicken in Foil, 22
    Chicken Liver Pâté, 21
    Cream-cheese and Caper
        Spread, 5
    Cucumbers in Sour Cream, 8
    Cucumbers and Tomatoes,
        8–9
    Figs and Prosciutto, 13
    Foie Gras, 22–3
    French Bread, 20
    Gnocchi Tartlets, 18–19
    Goose Liver, 22–3
    Green Peppers, Marinated,
        13–14
    Italian Antipasto, 4
    Leeks Vinaigrette, 16
    Marion's Pâté, 23
    Melon, Honeydew à la Venise,
        12
    Melons, Polka-dot, 12–13
    Mushrooms, Marinated, 7
    Mushrooms, Raw, 7–8
    Pecans, Deviled, 6
    Pineapple and Water-cress
        Juice, 13
    Quiche Lorraine Tartlets, 19–
        20

Hors d'œuvres (continued)
Salmon, Smoked, 15–16
Sardines with Black-walnut
Sauce, 4–5
Sardines in Sliced Lemon, 10
Sesame-seeded Wafer, 5
Shrimp, Curried, 3
Tomato and Zucchini, 20–1
Tomatoes Guacamole, 9
Trout, Smoked, 16
Tuna Fish in Chili Sauce,
10–11
Hungarian Goose Liver, 22–3

Ice Cream:
Banana, 386–7
Blackberry, 385
Blazing Baked Alaska, 393–4
Caramel, 388–9
Chocolate, 388
Coconut, 389–90
Coffee-caramel Parfait, 390–1
Coffee with Grated Chocolate,
387–8
French with Cinnamon, 386
French Vanilla, 387
Ginger, 391
Meringued Whipped Cream,
392–3
Peach, 392
Philadelphia Vanilla, 385
Strawberry, 393
see also Frozen Desserts
Italian Antipasto, 4

Jellied Duck à l'Orange, 242–3
Joe's Délices du Printemps,
422–3
Johnny Cake, Durfee's, 64

Jon Stroup's:
Pork Tenderloin, 174–5
Veal and Ham, 170–1

Kay's Strawberry Cottage Pud-
ding, 424–5
Kidney Beans, Red:
Marion's Mexican Bean Loaf,
262–3
Marion's Spiced Spanish
Beans, 261–2
in Red Wine, 260–1
Kidneys:
Lamb, 186
Veal, in Mustard, 193–4
Veal, Rognoni alla Venesiana,
190

Lady Baltimore Cake, Sophie
Kerr's, 447–8
Ladyfingers, 468–9
Lamb:
Boiled Leg of, with Caper
Sauce, 146–7
Braised Leg of, with Olives,
147–8
Cassoulet, 182–4
Curried Noisettes, 152–3
Curry, 151–2
with Garland of Vegetables,
145–6
Gigot de Sept Heures, 148–9
Haricot d'Agneau, 154–5
Kidneys, 186
Poached Leg of, with Sauce
Béarnaise, 149–51
Roast Leg of, à la Française,
144
Roast Rack of, Persille, 144

Lamb (continued)
Shish Kebab, 155-6
Stew, 153-4
Lamb Cake for Easter, 440-3
Lee Erickson's Fish and Dill
Soufflé, 90
Leeks Vinaigrette, 16
Lemon:
Butter Frosting, 455
Meringue Pie, 370-1
Pudding Pie, Susie's President's, 353-4
and Vanilla Sauce, 405
Lila's:
Eggs Tarragon, 312-13
Iced Shrimp Bisque, 36
Lima Beans:
and Pea Soup, 36-7
Purée, 261
Liver:
Calf's, 186-7
Pâté, Chicken, 21
Lobster:
Bangkok Curried, 93
Mayonnaise, 91
Mousse Surprise, 91-3
and Salmon Pie, 112-14
Sauce for, 291-2
and Shrimp, 93-4
Stew, 45
Thermidor, 94-5
Lois's Wild-rice and Shellfish
Casserole, 118

Macaroni Pie, 67-8
Madeira Sauce, 293-4
Madelin's Sesame-seeded Wafers, 5
Maître d'Hôtel Butter, 296

Malakoff, Gateau, 336-7
Marchand de Vin Sauce for
Steak, 295
Marinated:
Green Peppers, 13-14
Mushrooms, 7
Marion's:
Mexican Bean Loaf, 262-3
Pâté, 23
Spiced Spanish Beans, 261
Marty's Sliced Oranges with
Orange Cream, 413
Matrimony Cookies, 469-70
Mayonnaise:
in Blender, 320
How to Make It, 320
Meat Loaf, 187-8
Melon:
Honeydew à la Venise, 12
Polka-dot, 12-13
Watermelon Filled with Fruit
and Champagne, 425-6
Meringue Swans, 443-5
Mexican Pozole, 38-40
Mildred's Cheese Cake, 445-6
Milk Onion Soup, 41
Mincemeat Galette, 377-8
Mint Sauce, 296
Mississippi Seafood Gumbo,
115-16
Mixed Fruit, 427
Mocha Cocoa Frosting, 456
Mornay Sauce, 302-3
Mother's Moonlight Cabbage,
264
Mousse:
Chocolate, Super-superlative,
342-3
Lobster Surprise, 91-3
Shad Roe, 102-3
Mousseline Sauce, 303

Mushrooms:
  and Braised Endives, 270–2
  and Fish Custard, 89–90
  Marinated, 7
  Raw, in Cream Dressing, 7–8
  Sauce with Veal and Ham
    Roast, 170–1
  Tartlets, 17–18
Mustard:
  Cream and Herb Dressing,
    321
  Dressing, 318–19
  Sauce for Flounder, 296–7

Nassau Fish Chowder, 41–2
Newburg Sauce, 303–4
Noodles, 68–9

Okra Daube, 272
Omelette, 50
  Tuna Fish, 52–3
  Variations, 51
Onion:
  Soup with Milk, 41
  Spiced and Creamed, 273
  Tart, 274
Orange:
  Bavarian Cream, 329–30
  Jelly, Fresh, with Orange and
    Grapefruit Sections, 414
  and Rice Gelatin Delight,
    414–15
  Sliced with Caramel and Pe-
    cans, 412–13
  Sliced with Orange Cream,
    Marty's, 413–14
  Soufflé, 360
  Water-ice Ambrosia, 398
Oriental Sauce, 405–6
Ornamental Icing, 456–7
Osso Bucco, 169–70

Oysters:
  Scalloped, 95–6
  Stew, 42–3

Pancakes:
  Apple, with Blueberry Sauce,
    461
  Aunt Minnie's Yankee, 463
  Blintzes, 463–4
  German Apple, 462
  with Rice and Ham Sauce,
    72
Parsley, Fried, for Fish, 77
Parsnips, Mashed, 273–4
Pastry:
  Apricot, 374–5
  Chess Tartlets, 376–7
  Custard Tart, 378–9
  Fruit Tartlets, 379–80
  Galette Foure de Crème Pa-
    tisserie, 375–6
  Galette with Blazing Mince-
    meat, 377–8
  see also Pie Crust
Pâté:
  Chicken Liver, 21
  Marion's, 23
  "Vieu-logi," 188–9
Paul's:
  Beef Stew, 134–5
  Hazelnut Cream, 338–9
Peaches:
  Hot, Canned, with Raspberry
    Preserve, 417
  Hot, with Kirsch and Al-
    monds, 416
  Ice Cream, 392
  Schaum Torte, Alice's, 415–
    16

Pears:
with Cheese, 417
in Cointreau with Frozen
    Cream, 418
à la Cuillere, 417
Raw, Sliced, in Orange Juice
    and Curaçao, 418–19
Peas:
Green, Deep-dish Tart, 276–7
Green, à la Française, 275–6
and Lima-bean Soup, 36–7
Soup with Whipped Cream,
    43–4
Pecans:
Deviled, 6
Fingers, 470–1
Peppers, Green, Marinated, 13–
    14
Persian Chicken, 224–6
Petits Pois à la Française, 275–6
Petits Pots de Crème au Fro-
    mage, 60–1
Pheasant:
in Cream, 251
Gogi's, with Walnuts, 252–3
Roast, 249–50
Roast, with Gin and Juniper
    Berries, 250–1
Philadelphia Vanilla Ice Cream,
    385
Pie:
Angel, 373–4
Apple, 365–6
Butterscotch Pecan, 368
Coconut Custard, 367–8
Cranberry, 369
Lemon Meringue, 370–1
Pumpkin, 371
Raisin and Nut, Flaming,
    372–3
Tarte Autrichienne, 366–7

Pie (continued)
see also Pastry and Pie
    Crust
Pie Crust:
Directions for Plain Crust,
    362–3
for Tarts, 364–5
Tender, for Tarts, 364
Warm-water, Rich, 364
Pineapple:
Fresh, in Kirsch, 420
Ice, Meringued, 397–8
with Peeled Green Grapes
    and Kirsch, 419
and Water-cress Juice, 13
Plum:
Cake, White, 450
Pudding, 349–50
Sliced Ace, 419–20
Poisson à la Mexicaine, 80–1
Polka-dot Melons, 12–13
Pomegranate Ice with Fresh
    Fruit, 420–1
Pork:
Cassoulet, 182–4
Chops in the Auvergne, 175–6
Chops in Casserole, 176
Galotsie, Polonaise, 184
Pâté "Vieu-logi," 188–9
Roast Loin, 173–4
Tenderloin with Apricots,
    174–5
Pot au Feu, 124–5
Pot Roast, 135–6
Potage du Curé, 44–5
Potatoes:
Anna, 278
Boiled, 279
Boiled, Dressing for, 317
Boiled New Potatoes with
    Dill, 279–80

Potatoes (continued)
  à la Crème, 278–9
  Mashed, Lemon-flavored, 280
  New, Cooked in Consommé, 280
  Provincial, 281
  Pudding, Susie's, 354
  Salad, 311–12
  Salad, with Beans, 11–12
  Shalmaar, 281–2
  Soup, 28–9
  Sweet, for Stuffing, 231–2
  Sweet, with Marrons Glacés, 283–4
  and Water-cress Soup, 47
Pots de Crème:
  Caramel, 340
  Chocolate, 339
  Coffee, 340
  Vanilla, 340–1
Poulet:
  à l'Estragon, 215–16
  à l'Oseille, 219–20
  Parton, 216–17
Poulet Fondue:
  à la Crème, 210–11
  à la Crème, Revised, 211–12
Pound Cake, 446–7
Pozole, Mexican, 38–40
Praline:
  Bavarian Cream, 330–1
  Chocolate Soufflé, 358
  Floating Gateau, 335–6
  Powder, How to Make, 326
Prosciutto, with Ripe Figs, 13
Provincial Potatoes, 281
Pudding:
  Bread, 64–5, 345
  Caramel Rice, 346–7
  Chocolate, Rich, 351–2
  Chocolate Almond, 347–8

Pudding (continued)
  Fig, 348–9
  Graham-cracker, 346
  Lemon, Susie's President's, 353
  Plum, 349–50
  Potato, Susie's, 354
  Pumpkin, 351
  Scandinavian, 352–3
  Strawberry Cottage, Kay's, 424–5
Pumpkin:
  Cake, Spicy, 448
  Pie with Caramel Glaze, 371–2
  Pudding, 351

Quality Frosting, 457
Quasi de Veau, 161–2
Quiche Lorraine, 19–20, 61–2

Radishes with Coquilles de Beurre, 5–6
Raisin:
  and Nut Filling for Layer Cake, 452–3
  and Nut Pie, Flaming, 372–3
  and Rum Sauce for Ice Cream, 406
  Squares, 471
Raspberries:
  in Raspberry Sauce, 421
  Red, Gelatin with Raspberry Sauce, 421–2
Ratafia Cream, 342
Ravioli with Tomato Sauce, 69–71
Ray's:
  Crêpes Soufflés, 459–60

Ray's (continued)
Coffee Sauce for Ice Cream, 403
Stuffing, 229–30
Refrigerator Ices:
Coffee-caramel Parfait, 390–1
Grapefruit Sherbet, 399
Meringued Whipped Cream, 392–3
Strawberry Ice, 399
Remoulade Sauce, 304–5
Rice:
and Cheese Soufflé, 71–2
Pancakes with Ham Sauce, 72–3
and Shrimp, 106–7
Soup, Greek, 35–6
Wild, with Shellfish, 118–20
Wild, in Stuffing, 230–1
Risotto, Tomato, 73–4
Roast:
Beef, 123–4
Capons, Boned Stuffed, 226–7
Chicken, Sauce Piani, 201–2
Chicken with Gravy, 200–1
Chicken stuffed with Noodles, 202–3
Duck, 239–41
Goose with Sage-and-onion Stuffing, 244–5
Guinea Hen, 246–7
Lamb, Leg of, 143
Lamb, Rack of, 144
Pheasant, 249–50
Pheasant with Gin and Juniper Berries, 250–1
Pork Loin, 173–4
Turkey, Directions for, 228–9
Turkey, Boned Stuffed, 232–5
Turkey with Cream Gravy, 235–6

Roast (continued)
Turkey with Ray's Stuffing, 229–30
Turkey with Sweet-potato Stuffing, 231–2
Veal with Carrots and Onions, 157–8
Veal and Ham, Rolled, 170–1
Robert's Boiled Ham and Greens, 178–9
Rockingham Lobster Stew, 45
Rognoni alla Venesiana, 190
Romaine Salad with Chopped Water Cress, 313
Rose Visinho's:
Tuna, Marinated, 114–15
Tuna Steaks, Fresh, 109
Royal Icing, 456–7
Rum and Raisin Sauce for Ice Cream, 406
Rutabagas, Mashed, 282


Saffron Sauce for Fish, 290
Salad Dressing:
Boiled, for Potato Salad, 317
Chicken-liver, 317
Chopped Water-cress, 318
Egg, 313–14
Egg, Hard-boiled, 319
French, Basic, 318
Herb, 319
Mayonnaise, How to Make, 320
Mayonnaise, in Blender, 320–1
Mustard, 318–19
Mustard, Cream, and Herb, 321
Sauce Vinaigrette, 321–2
Spiced-vinegar, for Beets, 322

Salads:
  Asparagus, 209
  Aspic, Quick, 209–10
  Cole Slaw, 310
  Curried Egg and Water-cress, 310–11
  with Egg Dressing, 313–14
  Endives and Avocado, 311
  Lila's Eggs Tarragon, 312–13
  Potato Salad, Grandmother Schaffner's, 311–12
  Romaine, with Chopped Water Cress, 313
  String Bean, 314
  Surprise Vegetable, 315–16
  Tomato, 314–15
Salmon:
  Borsch, 97
  Coulibiac, 99–100
  with Horseradish Cream, 96–7
  and Lobster Pie, 112–14
  Smoked, on Toast, 15–16
Sardines:
  Canapés in Black-walnut Sauce, 4–5
  in Sliced Lemon, 10
Sauces:
  Béarnaise, 298
  Béarnaise, in Blender, 299
  Black-currant, for Pheasant, 289
  Bread, for Game, 289
  Browned Butter, 289–90
  Chive and Butter, 199–200, 236–7
  Clarified Butter, 290
  Cranberry de Luxe, 292
  Cream, 291–2
  Cream, with Hard-boiled Egg, 297–8

Sauces (continued)
  Curried Cream, with Hard-boiled Egg, 294
  Dijonnaise, 300
  Ginger, 295
  for Ham or Venison, 299–300
  Herb, Creamed, 292–3
  Hollandaise, 300–1
  Hollandaise, in Blender, 201–2
  Madeira, 293–4
  Maître d'Hôtel Butter, 296
  Marchand de Vin, 295
  Mint, 296
  Mornay, 302–3
  Mousseline, 303
  Mustard, for Flounder, 296–7
  Newburg, 303–4
  Remoulade, 304–5
  Saffron, for Fish, 290–1
  for Shrimp, Lobster, or Crab Meat, 291
  Tartar, 304
  Tomato, 305
Sauces, Dessert:
  Apricot Jam, 400
  Audrey's Amber, 401
  Audrey's Butterscotch, 400–1
  Chocolate, Hot, 402
  Chocolate Custard, 402
  Coconut Cream, 401–2
  Coffee, Ray's, 403
  Coffee Custard, 404
  Cream-and-egg, Beaten, 404
  Custard, 404
  Frozen Cream, 405
  Lemon and Vanilla, 405
  Oriental, 405–6
  Raisin and Rum for Ice Cream, 406

Sauces, Dessert (continued)
 Soft Hard, 366
 Zabaglione, 406
Sausage, Cabbage, and Potatoes,
 185–6
Scalloped Oysters, 95–6
Scallops Almondine, 100–1
Scandinavian Pudding, 352–3
Senegalese Soup, 32–3
Sesame Seeds, on Wafers, 5
Seviche, 116–17
Shad, Baked Boneless, 117–18
Shellfish and Wild-rice Casse-
 role, 118–20
Sherbets:
 Apricot Granite, 395–6
 Black Raspberry Ice, 396
 Coffee Granite, 396–7
 Grapefruit, in Refrigerator,
 399
 Orange-water Ice Ambrosia,
 398
 Pineapple Ice Meringued,
 397–8
 Strawberry Ice, in Refrigera-
 tor, 399
Shish Kebab, 155–6
Shrimp:
 in Beer with Dill, 104–5
 Bisque, Lila's, 36
 Boiled, 101–2
 Broiled, 103–4
 in Cream with Hominy, 105
 with Cucumber Jelly, 105–6
 Curried, 3
 and Lobster, 93–4
 and Rice with Dill, 106–7
 Sauce for, 291–2
 Soup, 45–6
Sophie Kerr's Gigantic Lady
 Baltimore Cake, 447–8

Sorrel Soup, Fresh, 33–4
Soufflés:
 Almond and Apricot Jam, 356
 Apricot Jam, 356–7
 Caraway-seed, 54–5
 Cheese, 56
 Chocolate, 357–8
 Chocolate, Cold, 359–60
 Chocolate Praline, 358
 Coconut and Marmalade,
 358–9
 Directions, 355
 Fish and Dill, 90
 Orange, 360–1
 Petite Cheese, 55
 Rice and Cheese, 71–2
 Vanilla, 361
Soups:
 Albondigas, 27
 Asparagus, 28
 Beef Broth, 29
 Borsch, Brian Connelly's, 30–1
 Catherine's, 29–30
 Cheddar-cheese, 31–2
 Cream-of-tapioca Veal Broth,
 33
 Fish Chowder, Nassau, 41–2
 Lima-bean and Pea, 36–7
 Lobster Stew, Rockingham, 45
 Onion, Milk, 41
 Oyster Stew, 42–3
 Pea, with Whipped Cream,
 43–4
 Potage du Curé, 44–5
 Potato, Baked Idaho, 28–9
 Pozole, Mexican, Rice, Greek,
 35–6
 Shrimp, 45
 Sorrel, Fresh, 33–4
 Veal Broth, 33, 46

Soups (continued)
  Water-cress and Potato, 47
  *see also* Soups, Cold
Soups, Cold:
  Asparagus, 28
  Gazpacho, 34–5
  Senegalese, 32–3
  Shrimp Bisque, 36
  Vichyssoise Meadowbrook,
    46–7
Spanish Carrots, 267
Spiced-vinegar Dressing, 322
Squash, Summer:
  Colache, 285
  in Cream, 282–3
  Custard à la Viola, 283
Steak:
  Marinated, Fried, 138–9
  au Poivre, Le, 141–2
  Sirloin in Wine Sauce, 141
Stew:
  Lamb, 153–4
  Lobster, 45
  Oyster, 42–3
Strawberries:
  in Mounds, 411
  Plump, 414
  with Strawberry Jam, 422
Strawberry:
  Bavarian Cream, 332
  Cottage Pudding, Kay's, 424–5
  Heavenly, 423
  Ice, in Refrigerator, 399
  Ice Cream, 393
  Joe's Délices du Printemps,
    422–3
String Beans:
  Almondine, 263–4
  Chopped and Creamed, 265
  Salad, 314

Stuffing:
  Black-walnut-and-bread, 246–7
  Orange-flavored Sweet-potato,
    231–2
  Ray's, 229–30
  Sage-and-onion, 244–5
  Wild-rice, 230–1
Super-superlative Chocolate
    Mousse, 342–3
Surprise Vegetable Salad, 315
Susie's:
  Potato Pudding, 354
  President's Lemon Pudding
    Pie, 353–4
Sweet Potatoes with Marrons
    Glacés, 283–4
Sweetbreads Hollywood, 192–3
Swordfish:
  Broiled, 107–8
  Fried, 108–9
Syllabub, Dick's, 341–2


Tamale Pie, 139–40
Tapioca Veal Broth, 33
Tart:
  Chicken, 221–4
  *see also* Pastry, Tartlets
Tarter Sauce, 304
Tarte Autrichienne, 366–7
Tartlets:
  Gnocchi, 18–19
  Mushroom, 17–18
  Quiche Lorraine, 19–20
Tendrons de Veau à l'Estragon,
    166–7
Tomatoes:
  and Cucumbers, 8–9
  Guacamole, 9
  Risotto, 73–4
  Salad, Fines Herbes, 314–15

Tomatoes (continued)
Sauce, 305
Sauce with Ravioli, 69–70
and Zucchini, 20–1
Tongue with Sauce, 191
Trout, Smoked, with Horseradish Cream, 16
Truffles and White Beans, 259
Truites aux Amandes, 115
Tuna Fish:
in Chili Sauce, 10–11
Marinated Fresh, 114–15
Omelette, 52–3
Steaks, 109
Turkey:
Boiled, with Chive and Butter Sauce, 236–7
Boned Stuffed, 232–5
Roast, with Cream Gravy, 235–6
Roast, with Orange-flavored Sweet-potato Stuffing, 231–2
Roast, with Ray's Stuffing, 229–30
Roast, with Wild-rice Stuffing, 230–1
Turnips, Glazed, 284
Twice-cooked Frosting, 457

Upsidedown Caramel Custard, 343

Vanilla:
Filling, 453
Ice Cream, French, 387
Ice Cream, Philadelphia, 385
Kisses or Meringues, 471–2

Vanilla (continued)
Pots de Crème, 340–1
Soufflé, 361
Veal:
Autre Pâté "Vieu-logi," 189–90
Birds, 167–8
Blanquette, 162–3
Braised Quasi de Veau, 161–2
Broth, 33, 46
Chops, Braised, en Gelée, 160–1
Chops, Curried, 164–5
Chops with Mustard Sauce, 159–60
in Cream, 158–9
Escalopes à l'Estragon, 166–7
and Ham Roast, Stroup's, 170–1
Osso Bucco, 169–70
Pâté "Vieu-logi," 188–9
Roast, with Onions and Carrots, 157–8
Tendrons à l'Estragon, 166–7
Vitello Tonato, 171–2
Vegetables, 256–7
Surprise Salad, 315
Venison, Sauce for, 299–300
Vichyssoise Meadowbrook, 46–7
Vinaigrette Sauce, 321–2
Vitello Tonato, 171–2

Walnut Cake, Black, 430
Water Cress:
Dressing, 318
Juice with Pineapple, 13
and Potato Soup, 47
Watermelon with Fruit, Water Ice, and Champagne, 425–6
White Layer Cake, 449–50

White Plum Cake, 450
White Sauce, 291–2
Wild-rice and Shellfish Casserole, 118–20


Yams and Oranges, 284–5
Yankee Pancakes, Aunt Minnie's, 463

Yellow Layer Cake, 449
Yorkshire Pudding, 123–4


Zabaglione, 343–4
    Sauce, 406
Zucchini:
    Colache, 285
    and Tomato, 20–1

# A NOTE ON THE AUTHOR

JUNE PLATT (*Mrs. Joseph B. Platt*) *was born in Springfield, Illinois, and educated in twenty-six schools in England, France, and the United States. Mrs. Platt, who lives in New York City, is the mother of two sons. She attended cooking school and art school, beginning her professional career as an artist. In the early thirties she began writing monthly food articles for* House and Garden, *and since 1942 has been writing intermittently, devoting her major efforts to her full-time occupation as a designer of wallpaper, rugs, and other home decorations. Mrs. Platt's books include* June Platt's Party Cook Book, June Platt's Plain and Fancy Cook Book, June Platt's Dessert Cook Book, Serve It and Sing, *and* The Best I Ever Ate, *the last of which was co-authored with Sophie Kerr.*

## A NOTE ON THE TYPE

*This book is set in* ELECTRA, *a Linotype face designed by* W. A. DWIGGINS (1880–1956), *who was responsible for so much that is good in contemporary book design. Although much of his early work was in advertising and he was the author of the standard volume* Layout in Advertising, *Mr. Dwiggins later devoted his prolific talents to book typography and type design, and worked with great distinction in both fields. In addition to his designs for Electra, he created the Metro, Caledonia, and Eldorado series of type faces, as well as a number of experimental cuttings that have never been issued commercially.*

*Electra cannot be classified as either modern or old-style. It is not based on any historical model, nor does it echo a particular period or style. It avoids the extreme contrast between thick and thin elements which marks most modern faces, and attempts to give a feeling of fluidity, power, and speed.*